OpenStack
Cloud
Computing

OpenStack Cloud Computing

by John Rhoton

with contributions from:

Jan De Clercq and Franz Novak

Recursive Press

OpenStack Cloud Computing

By John Rhoton

Copyright © 2014 Recursive Limited. All rights reserved.

Recursive Press is an imprint of Recursive Limited.

The RP logo is a trademark of Recursive Limited.

Published simultaneously in the United States and the United Kingdom.

ISBN-10: 0-9563556-8-4

ISBN-13: 978-0-9563556-8-3

British Library Cataloguing-in-Publication Data

Application submitted.

Revision: 20140304162946

Contents

Preface

This book examines the deployment of cloud-based architectures using OpenStack technologies. Our overriding objective is to provide a comprehensive picture of the primary design considerations and implementation options. Our focus is not a high-level overview of cloud computing, so we do not elaborate on the business benefits of the technology. There are numerous books on the market that cover these topics, including Cloud Computing Explained and others listed in the bibliography.

This is also not a book about OpenStack technologies. Rather it is about implementing a cloud architecture based on OpenStack. The distinction may seem subtle, but it does have a significant impact on the scope of the material. There are some areas of cloud computing that OpenStack does not directly address. And there may be functions that it does cover but not as well as complementary products and services.

We have tried to put as much substance to the concepts as possible by including a number of references to vendors and service providers that are active in cloud computing today. This is not an endorsement of any particular solutions nor do we attempt to weigh strengths and weaknesses in the products. We may omit important information or characterize the services in different terms than the vendors. Therefore, we would encourage you to perform your own research before deciding on a particular service or eliminating it from your list of options.

Obviously, this text is not an exhaustive survey of all the available tools that might be used to supplement OpenStack. Given the volatile nature of the cloud landscape, we cannot even imply a guarantee that companies mentioned in this book will still be in business when you read about them or that they will offer the same functionality.

Nonetheless, we believe that you will get a better picture of what is happening in cloud computing with some actual examples and rough descriptions of the services currently on offer in the market place – if for no other reason than to give you a starting point for your own analysis.

Audience

You can look at the deployment of any IT system from many different perspectives, which depend on the operational role of the reader and the technical charter of the organization implementing the technology.

This material caters primarily to consultants, architects, technologists and strategists who are involved with the planning and implementation of information technology in large enterprises. Our background is heavily biased toward international corporations and the challenges they face in implementing new technologies.

However, most of the contents of this book will apply to the full spectrum from service providers to small and medium businesses. Indeed, one of the effects of cloud computing is to remove some of the artificial segmentation barriers that differentiate larger and smaller organizations.

There are many stakeholders who are involved in implementing new projects and who might be affected by a completely overhauled service delivery model. The chief executive officers, and others on the executive board, may be concerned about the strategic impact of cloud computing. The IT managers must plan the portfolio. The architects need some background to design the end-to-end system. The technologists require a starting point for a deep technical analysis that will support them as they implement and support the actual infrastructure.

In addition to the organizational role of the reader, it is vital to recognize that each topic will take on its own flavor depending on the vantage point of the practitioner, whether it is the cloud consumer, cloud provider, application developer or regulator. In each case, it is worthwhile for the stakeholders to appreciate the challenges of the others. We have written this book primarily from the standpoint of the business customer, but have endeavored to include the most important elements of the other viewpoints too.

Each perspective is unique but, nonetheless, critical to the success of the overall objectives. We provide as much insight as we can for each viewpoint. This may mean that some sections will be less interesting for some readers. But we hope there is some value for everyone. To keep the discussion simple, we have placed the enterprise at the center of all our explanations. This means that when we mention customers and suppliers without any further qualifications, we mean enterprise customers and suppliers.

Organization and Structure

This book is structured as twenty-five chapters divided into ten parts:

Analyze - Any analysis begins with a systematic assessment. This section examines the notion of cloud computing and its delivery layers (SaaS, PaaS, IaaS) as well as common delivery models (private, public). We then proceed to look at how cloud is typically adopted in the enterprise starting with virtualization and automation to flexibility in sourcing its services.

Assess – Before implementing OpenStack, it is worthwhile to look at the alternatives. There are many commercial offerings for each type of cloud from IaaS to SaaS. The choice of OpenStack depends to a large extent on the value proposition of an open-source infrastructure service that caters to both private and public service providers. But there are also other open-source frameworks that are almost directly comparable, so the selection process should also consider them.

Initiate – The first step in getting started is to construct a clear picture of how the system should work. This means getting the system working in a pilot scenario with a minimum set of standard components. But you also need to make sure that you will eventually be able to address your requirements and integrate with your legacy environment. You might need more complex topologies or you may need to create linkages to additional components or ecosystems.

Assemble – The design of an OpenStack-based solution begins with the OpenStack services themselves. While it is possible to replace the individual modules, it is generally a good idea to start with the base solution and see to what extent it meets the business requirements. In particular, the core components of an infrastructure service include compute, storage and networking.

Deploy – After the initial design and implementation work is complete, you may have demonstrated the feasibility of the technology but that is a far cry from ensuring it will work in production, particularly for highly scalable workloads. The first task is to roll out the OpenStack software itself onto the bare machines in the data center. The second is to design the orchestration of the workloads so that they are able to launch easily and automatically.

Operate – Once deployed, the administration chores begin. On the one hand, there are proactive tasks to set policies, re-allocate resources and tailor the configuration of standard services based on user needs. On the other hand, it is also important to detect any unforeseen events. We must also keep an eye on trends in order to detect and resolve issues as they occur and to project where future problems may arise in order to prevent them.

Account – Financial governance is a top concern of almost every business. It relies on ensuring visibility of what activities generate expenses and what trends these cost drivers are projecting. Whether the charges are invoiced to external parties, cross-charged to internal departments or merely reported to show value to the business, the numbers are critical in sustaining a compelling business case.

Secure – OpenStack itself is neither particularly secure nor insecure. Security is a discipline that requires systematic application. This means the first task of a risk analysis is simply to make sure all the components are implemented securely. After verifying that the configuration adheres to best practices, it is important to be vigilant of any newly found exploits and supplement the bare infrastructure with further layers of security. Other than the base infrastructure, a key component of the overall security model is identity and access management and the enforcement of consistent policies governing user activity.

Empower – One intent of cloud computing is to create an environment that maximizes the benefits of economy of scale. At some point, it may reach a size where failures are inevitable. The most effective solutions will not attempt to prevent them at any cost but rather ensure that the infrastructure and applications are able to withstand these through their high level of redundancy and automated self-healing. A parallelized architecture also enables autoscaling which reduces the human effort required when load changes. Finally, autonomous operation requires the reduction of dependencies on other vendors or technologies and products.

Extend – Getting the software deployed and working efficiently in production is not the end of the journey. Technology and markets are in constant evolution making it necessary to perpetually adapt. But beyond these externally imposed changes, it is always possible to improve business value by building and extending the infrastructure. Moving up the cloud stack into platforms will drive increased efficiencies for new workloads. Analytics allows IT to generate more business value. And any improvements in the underlying software will help to support new business initiatives and give additional impetus to the community that is building it.

Most chapters begin with a general overview of the challenges that any cloud deployment faces. Some readers with a strong background in cloud computing will find the topics familiar and may want to skim these sections. Nonetheless, we found it useful to include them because many readers will not previously have looked at the topics in a systematic fashion.

Using this baseline, we then show which functions OpenStack fulfills and how a typical deployment may implement them. In some cases, we complete the picture by elaborating on how to supplement the technology with other tools and processes.

Feedback

A direct consequence of the print-on-demand model we have used for this book, and actually one of its primary benefits, is the flexibility it gives the author and publisher to incorporate incremental changes throughout the publication lifecycle. We would like to leverage that advantage by drawing on the collective experience and insights of our readers.

You may find errors and omissions. Or you may actually find some parts of the book very useful and interesting. Regardless of your feedback, if you have something to say then we'd love to hear from you. Please feel free to send us a message at:

john.rhoton@gmail.com, jan.declercq@hp.com or franz.novak@hp.com.

We can't guarantee that we will reply to every message but we will do our best to acknowledge your input!

Acknowledgements

You can find a large part of the information contained in this book on the public Internet. The OpenStack documentation covers many details of OpenStack and there are numerous blogs and other valuable resources that supplement it with practical advice. We have filled some of the gaps and tied all the pieces together, but we have tried to recognize the original sources where possible, both to give them credit and to make it easier for you to dig deeper should you wish.

We have received considerable help from Gill Shaw, who provided excellent proofreading and copy editing assistance. We would also like to acknowledge Elisabeth Rinaldin, who contributed to the design of the cover and layout.

A number of subject-matter experts and reviewers have provided valuable technical input, including: Patrick Joubert, David Fishman, Nicholas Chase, Kirill Ishanov, Jay Chaudhury, Sanjay Mishra, and Nick van der Zweep. We applaud the many sources listed at the end of the book, which have helped us immensely as we have dived into the details of the topics we have presented. Last but not least, we would like to point out that there would be no content to describe without the vision and creative talent of engineers at Rackspace, Red Hat, IBM, HP, Mirantis and other contributors to OpenStack.

We would also like to point out that some of the sections in this book were first published by IBM developer Works[1].

---

[1] http://www.ibm.com/developerWorks/

Analyze

Any analysis begins with a systematic assessment. This section examines the notion of cloud computing and its delivery layers (SaaS, PaaS, IaaS) as well as common delivery models (private, public). We then proceed to look at how cloud is typically adopted in the enterprise starting with virtualization and automation to flexibility in sourcing its services.

Chapter 1

Study the Cloud

OpenStack is currently the most popular consortium-led Infrastructure as a Service (IaaS) software stack. It was initiated by Rackspace Cloud and NASA. Since its founding, it has seen wide industry endorsement and now numbers over one hundred supporters, including many of the industry's largest organizations, such as IBM, AT&T, Canonical, HP, Rackspace, Red Hat and SUSE.

This book is centered on OpenStack. But before we dig into what OpenStack is, why it is important and how it works, let's take a step back and spend a couple of chapters making sure we are on the same page in our understanding of how it fits into the IT landscape.

There has been a lot of buzz about cloud computing the last few years. IT vendors have embraced the newest hype, which now dominates the computing landscape. Customers have found the concept fascinating and devoted significant resources to assessing its benefits and challenges.

Unfortunately, many have been deterred by what they have found. Even though its potential is largely undisputed, there are many obstacles that complicate an immediate deployment. According to most surveys, security concerns rank top of these lists.

By now, you probably have a good idea what the term "cloud computing" means – and perhaps even how it works. But, if you are responsible for protecting systems or applications, then a theoretical analysis of a new trend is only of limited use. Instead, you will want to understand the technical options and their potential impact on your business.

We have deliberately avoided spending much space on a foundational overview of cloud computing. If you are interested in a business-oriented perspective of the advantages and challenges to an enterprise implementation, then you may want to start with *Cloud Computing Explained* or one of the other introductory books listed in the bibliography. We will assume that you already have a good grasp of the basics and are ready to proceed to the next level.

ANALYZE

That said, we did want to make sure that we are working from the same conceptual foundation. Your notion of cloud computing may be perfectly valid and yet significantly different from ours. To minimize any confusion and ensure a common framework and terminology, we will indulge in a brief characterization of what cloud computing means to us and describe the main services and delivery models.

Core Attributes

In the simplest sense, a cloud represents a network and, more specifically, the global Internet. Cloud computing, by inference, is the use of computational resources that are hosted remotely and delivered through the Internet. That is the basic idea underlying the term. It may be sufficient for your non-technical friends and colleagues, but shouldn't be adequate for anyone reading this book.

If you have ever tried to isolate the core meaning of "Cloud Computing" by looking for an authoritative definition, you will have quickly discovered that the term entails many different notions. There is some disagreement among the experts as to what constitutes the essence of this fundamental shift in technology. Some are able to articulate their perspectives more elegantly than others, but that doesn't mean they are accepted any more universally.

The most commonly recognized definition in use today was articulated by the National Institute of Standards and Technology (NIST) (2011):

> Cloud computing is a model for enabling convenient, on-demand network access to a shared pool of configurable computing resources (e.g., networks, servers, storage, applications, and services) that can be rapidly provisioned and released with minimal management effort or service provider interaction.

Unfortunately, neither the NIST formulation, nor any interpretation of what it means, is universally accepted. A pragmatic approach to distilling the essence of the term is to examine the assortment of attributes of typical cloud solutions. This doesn't imply that every cloud attribute is essential to cloud computing, or that any combination qualifies a given approach as fitting the cloud paradigm. On their own, they are neither necessary nor sufficient prerequisites to the notion of cloud computing. However, the more of these attributes apply to a given implementation, the more likely others will accept it as a cloud solution.

If there is one element of cloud computing that can be considered a core concept, it is that of resource pooling. Generally, resources are shared across customers in a public environment and across departments or cost centers in a private implementation. The increased scale allows for better allocation and utilization, which contribute to additional benefits.

An informal survey of blogs and tweets, as well as published literature, on the subject reveals some other key components, including:

Off-premise: The service is hosted and delivered from a location that belongs to a service provider. This usually has two implications: The service is delivered over the public Internet, and the processing occurs outside the company firewall. In other words, the service must cross both physical and security boundaries.

Elasticity: One main benefit of cloud computing is the inherent scalability of the service provider, which is made available to the end-user. The model goes much further in providing an elastic provisioning mechanism so that resources can be scaled both up and down very rapidly as they are required. Since utility billing is also common, elasticity can equate to direct cost savings.

Flexible billing: Fine-grained metering of resource usage, combined with on-demand service provisioning, facilitate a number of options for charging customers. Fees can be levied on a subscription basis, or can be tied to actual consumption, or reservation, of resources. Monetization can take the form of placed advertising or can rely on simple credit card charges, in addition to elaborate contracts and central billing.

Virtualization: Cloud services are usually offered through an abstracted infrastructure. They leverage various virtualization mechanisms and achieve cost optimization through multi-tenancy.

Service delivery: Cloud functionality is often available as a service of some form. While there is great variance in the nature of these services, typically the services offer programmatic interfaces in addition to user interfaces.

Universal access: Resource democratization means that pooled resources are available to anyone authorized to utilize them. At the same time, location independence and high levels of resilience allow for an always-connected user experience.

Simplified management: Administration is simplified through automatic provisioning to meet scalability requirements, user self-service to expedite business processes, and programmatically accessible resources that facilitate integration into enterprise management frameworks.

Affordable resources: The cost of resources is dramatically reduced for two reasons. There is no requirement for capital expenditures on fixed purchases. Also, the economy of scale of the service providers allows them to optimize their cost structure with commodity hardware and fine-tuned operational procedures that are not easily matched by most companies.

Multi-tenancy: The cloud is used by many organizations (tenants) and includes mechanisms to protect and isolate each tenant from all others. Pooling resources across customers is an important factor in achieving scalability and cost savings.

Service-level management: Cloud services typically offer a service-level definition that sets the expectation to the customer as to how robust that service will be. Some services may come with only minimal (or non-existent) commitments. They can still be considered cloud services, but typically will not be "trusted" for mission-critical applications to the extent that others (which are governed by more precise commitments) might.

Service Models (SaaS, PaaS, IaaS)

One salient aspect of cloud computing is a strong focus toward service orientation. It is quite common to hear mention of it in conjunction with expressions like "anything, or everything, as a service" (XaaS). In other words, the cloud is not a single offering but instead an often fragmented amalgamation of heterogeneous services.

Rather than offering only packaged solutions that are installed monolithically on desktops and servers, or investing in single-purpose appliances, you need to decompose all the functionality that users require into primitives, which can be assembled as needed.

Unfortunately, it is difficult to aggregate the functionality in an optimal manner unless you can get a clear picture of all the services that are available. This is a lot easier if you can provide some structure and a model that illustrates the interrelationships between services.

The most common classification uses the so-called SPI (Software, Platform and Infrastructure as a Service) model (NIST, 2011). Amazon Elastic Compute Cloud (EC2) is a classic example of IaaS (Infrastructure as a Service). Google App Engine is generally considered to be a PaaS (Platform as a Service). And Salesforce.com represents one of the best known examples of SaaS (Software as a Service).

ANALYZE

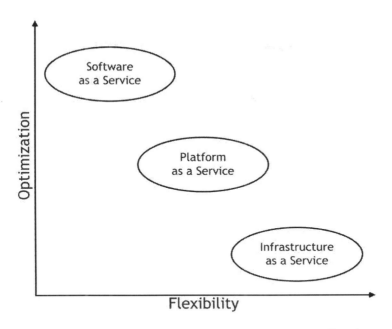

Figure 1-1: Software, Platform and Infrastructure Services

The three approaches differ in the extent of sharing that they provide to their consumers. Infrastructure services share the physical hardware. Platform services also allow tenants to share the same operating system and application frameworks. Software services generally share the entire software stack. As shown in Figure 1-1, these three approaches represent different tradeoffs in a balance between optimization, which leverages multi-tenancy and massive scalability, on the one hand, and flexibility to accommodate individual constraints and custom functionality, on the other.

The SPI model is a simple taxonomy that helps to present a first glimpse of the primary cloud-related services. However, as is often the case with classification systems, the lines are not nearly as clear in reality as they may appear on a diagram. There are many services that do not fit neatly into one category or the other. Over time, services may also drift between service types. For example, Amazon is constantly enhancing its AWS (Amazon Web Services) offering in an effort to increase differentiation and add value. As the product matures, some may begin to question if it wouldn't be more accurate to consider it a platform service.

Software as a Service

Software as a Service is arguably the archetypical delivery model for cloud computing, attaining most of the claimed benefits. It benefits from the easiest enterprise implementation and is perhaps the most mature model. For those or-

ANALYZE

ganizations wanting to focus on their core competencies it is the first place to look.

SaaS provides the full stack of cloud services, and ideally presents these to the end-user in a fashion that is not radically different from how users expect to use their applications. There may be some user interface changes that ripple through to the users, but the main difference is the deployment, licensing and billing model, which should be invisible to corporate end-users.

Consistent with the basic notion of cloud computing, SaaS is a model whereby the customer licenses applications and provisions them to users on demand. The services run on the provider's infrastructure and are accessed through a public network connection. Applications may be made available through the Internet as browser applications, or they may be downloaded and synchronized with user devices.

Some of the characteristics of SaaS services are that they are centrally managed and updated. Typically, they are highly standardized although they may vary in their configurability as well as their efficiency and scalability. The most common pricing model is based on the number of users, but there may be additional fees based on bandwidth, storage and usage.

There are many similarities between SaaS and the services offered a few years ago by application service providers (ASPs). However, there are also stark differences in the approaches to multi-tenancy, the pay-as-you-go model and the ability to provision on demand.

SaaS offers several compelling benefits. It simplifies licensing. In fact, the customer doesn't need to acquire (or directly pay for) a software license at all. This is a task of the provider. There is also no need to calculate maximum capacity. It outsources the tedious task of application maintenance and upgrades and ties customer costs to usage, which lowers fixed costs and capital investment.

However, it does so at the price of restricting customer flexibility in terms of configuration options and update schedules. It also entails a significant commitment to the provider since it isn't trivial to switch from one SaaS vendor to another (or back on-site). There may be APIs for extraction and loading but there are no standards on the semantics of these interfaces, so it requires significant effort to automate a migration process.

Platform as a Service

Cloud platforms act as run-time environments that support a set of (compiled or interpreted) programming languages. They may offer additional services such as reusable components and libraries that are available as objects and application programming interfaces. Ideally, the platform will offer plug-ins into common development environments, such as Eclipse, to facilitate development, testing and deployment.

ANALYZE

There has been a marked increase in the number of web hosting services that support a variety of active server-side components, ranging from Microsoft ASP.NET and Java to scripts such as PHP, Python and Ruby on Rails. Compared to infrastructure services, these platforms reduce the storage requirements of each application and simplify deployment. Rather than moving virtual machines with entire operating systems, the application only requires the code written by the developer. An additional benefit is the increased ease for the service provider to sandbox each application by only providing functions that cannot disrupt other tenants on the same system and network.

Platforms may also offer further functions to support the developers, for example:

Integrated Development Environment to develop, test, host and maintain applications

Integration services for marshalling, database integration, security, storage persistence and state management

Scalability services for concurrency management and failover

Instrumentation to track activity and value to the customer

Workflow facilities for application design, development, testing, deployment and hosting

User Interface support for HTML, JavaScript, Flex, Flash, AIR

Visualization tools that show patterns of end-user interactions

Collaboration services to support distributed development and facilitate developer community

Source code services for version control, dynamic multiple-user testing, rollback, auditing and change-tracking

Infrastructure as a Service

Infrastructure as a Service (IaaS) is the simplest of cloud offerings and the one most relevant to initial deployments of OpenStack. It is an evolution of virtual private server offerings and merely provides a mechanism to take advantage of hardware and other physical resources without any capital investment or physical administrative requirements. The benefit of services at this level is that there are very few limitations on the consumer. There may be challenges including (or interfacing with) dedicated hardware but almost any software application can run in an IaaS context.

We can divide IaaS services into three categories: Servers, Storage and Connectivity. Providers may offer virtual server instances on which the customer can

ANALYZE

install and run a custom image. Persistent storage is a separate service which the customer can purchase. And finally there are several offerings for extending connectivity options.

Usually all three are combined as part of a more complete infrastructure service.

Deployment Models (Public, Private, Community, Hybrid)

The previous section classified services according to the type of content that they offered. It can also be useful to examine the types of providers that are offering the services. In an ideal world, designed according to a service-oriented architecture, this distinction would not be meaningful. A service description should cover all relevant details of the service, so the consumer would be independent of the provider and therefore have no reason to prefer one over another.

Sadly, however, this is not the case. There are many implications in the choice of provider relating to security, governance, invoicing and settlement. It is therefore still very relevant to consider if the provider should be internal or external and the delivery should include an outsourcing partner, a community (such as the government) or a public cloud service.

Public Cloud

In the earliest definitions of cloud computing, the term referred only to solutions where resources are dynamically provisioned over the Internet from an off-site third-party provider who shares resources and bills on a fine-grained utility computing basis. This computing model carries many inherent advantages in terms of cost and flexibility, but it also has some drawbacks in the areas of governance and security.

Many enterprises have looked at ways that they can leverage at least some of the benefits of resource pooling while minimizing the drawbacks, by only making use of some aspects of cloud computing. These efforts have led to a restricted model of cloud computing, which is often designated as a Private Cloud. In contrast, the fuller model is often labeled the Public Cloud. NIST (2011) have expanded on these two deployment options with the notion of Community Cloud and Hybrid Cloud.

Most experts would still consider Public Cloud as the quintessential paradigm for cloud computing. Nonetheless, the other options will be the focus of this book. They are not only rising in importance throughout the industry but are also a core element of the value proposition of OpenStack.

ANALYZE

Private Cloud

The term Private Cloud is disputed in some circles as many would argue that anything less than a full cloud model is not cloud computing at all but rather a simple extension of the current enterprise data center. Nonetheless, the term has become widespread, and it is useful to also examine enterprise options that also fall into this category.

In simple theoretical terms, a private cloud is one that only leverages some of the aspects of cloud computing (Table 1-1). It is typically hosted on-premise, pools resources across departments, scales "only" into the hundreds or perhaps thousands of nodes, and is connected to the using organization through private network links. Since all applications and servers are shared within the corporation, the notion of multi-tenancy is minimized.

From a business perspective, you typically also find that the applications primarily support the business but do not directly drive additional revenue. So the solutions are usually financial cost centers rather than revenue or profit centers.

	Private	Public
Location	On-premise	Off-premise
Connection	Connected to private network	Internet-based delivery
Scale direction	Scale out (applications)	Scale up (users)
Maximum scale	100-1000 nodes	10 000 nodes
Sharing	Single tenant	Multi-tenant
Pricing	Capacity pricing	Utility pricing
Financial center	Cost center	Revenue/Profit center

Table 1-1: Private and Public Clouds

Given the disparity in descriptions between private and public clouds on topics that seem core to the notion of cloud computing, it is valid to question whether there is actually any commonality at all. The most obvious area of intersection is around resource pooling. As mentioned earlier, resources are shared across customers in a public environment and across departments or cost centers in a private implementation. The increased scale allows for better allocation and utilization, which contributes to additional benefits.

Virtualization can also play a central role in both scenarios. By enabling higher degrees of automation and standardization, it is a pivotal technology for many cloud implementations. Enterprises can certainly leverage many of its benefits

ANALYZE

without necessarily outsourcing their entire infrastructure or running it over the Internet.

Depending on the size of the organization, as well as its internal structure and financial reporting, there may also be other aspects of cloud computing that become relevant even in a deployment that is confined to a single company. A central IT department can just as easily provide services on-demand and cross-charge businesses on a utility basis as could any external provider. The model would then be very similar to a public cloud with the business acting as the consumer and IT as the provider. At the same time, the security of the data may be easier to enforce and the controls would be internal.

A black-and-white distinction between private and public cloud computing may therefore not be realistic in all cases. In addition to the ambiguity in sourcing options mentioned above, other criteria are not binary. For example, there can be many different levels of multi-tenancy, depending on the scope of shared resources and the security controls in place.

There are also many different options an enterprise can choose for security administration, channel marketing, integration, completion and billing. Some of these may share more similarity with conventional public cloud models while others may reflect a continuation of historic enterprise architectures.

What is important is that enterprises must select a combination that not only meets their current requirements in an optimal way but also offers a flexible path forward with the ability to tailor the options as their requirements and the underlying technologies change over time. In the short term, many corporations will want to adopt a course that minimizes their risk and only barely departs from an internal infrastructure. However, as cloud computing matures, they will want the ability to leverage increasing benefits without redesigning their solutions.

Regardless of whether the cloud is hosted internally or externally, it needs to leverage a great deal more than virtualization in order to achieve maximum value. There are a host of other improvements related to cloud computing ranging from fine-grained metering for usage-based cost allocation to rigorous service management, service-oriented architecture and federated access controls. An organization that implements these systematically has the most flexibility in selecting from private and public offerings or combining them for their business processes.

Partner Delivery

The distinction between internal and external delivery of cloud computing is not always clear. Depending on whether these delivery modes are determined on the basis of physical location, asset ownership or operational control, there may be three different perspectives on the source of a cloud service.

For the sake of completeness, it is also important to mention that there are more hosting options than internal/private versus external/public. It is not imperative that a private cloud be operated and hosted by the consuming organization itself. Other possibilities include co-location of servers in an external data center with, or without, managed hosting services.

A similar solution to a private cloud might be to enlist the services of an outsourcing partner, such as IBM, HP, or UNISYS. Since outsourcing is primarily an enterprise offering, the solutions provide a high degree of isolation and privacy. They also accommodate stringent service levels and an allowance for customization that is typically not available in the public cloud.

They will typically use some of the software and services of a private cloud. In addition, they often leverage a broad set of management tools and considerable experience in consolidation, standardization and automation. Their differentiation in these areas, along with a significant economy of scale, allows them to create a compelling value proposition to enterprises. They may be much more expensive than public cloud offerings due to the enhanced service levels and customization options they offer. Nonetheless, they represent significant potential for costs savings for many enterprises.

The implications of using an outsourcing partner for developing a cloud architecture need not be great. The same products and technical infrastructure could underpin a private or partner implementation. However, it is very important to ensure the contracts and service agreements are compatible with the preferred choice of development tools and run-time services. If the partner excludes these tools, for example in an effort to maximize standardization, then they are no longer viable. On the other hand, it is quite possible that a large outsourcing partner would be able to support a larger array of platform options than many customers could provide on their own.

In some ways, you can consider these "partner" clouds as another point on the continuum between private and public clouds. Large outsourcers are able to pass on some of their benefits of economy of scale, standardization, specialization and their point in the experience curve. And yet they offer a degree of protection and data isolation that is not common in public clouds.

Community Cloud

Another delivery model that is likely to receive increased attention in the future is a community cloud. It caters to a group of organizations with a common set of requirements or objectives. The most prominent examples are government clouds that are open to federal and municipal agencies. Similarly, major industries may have an incentive to work together to leverage common resources.

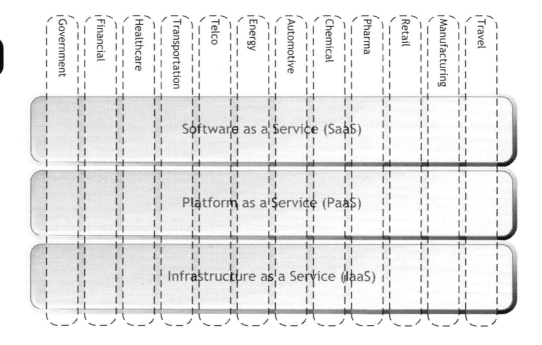

Figure 1-2: Community Clouds

The value proposition of a vertically-optimized cloud is initially based on the similarity of their requirements. Companies operating in the same industry are generally subject to the same regulations and very often share customers and suppliers who may impose additional standards and interfaces. A provider that caters to these specific demands can offer platforms and infrastructure with default service levels that meet all participants' obligations at a reasonable price.

However, the real benefits begin to accrue when a critical mass of industry players build a co-located ecosystem. When providers and consumers of software and information services are protected behind common security boundaries, and are connected with low-latency network links, the potential to share resources and data is greatly improved. The synergy that develops in this kind of cloud can spawn a virtuous cycle that breeds both additional functionality and efficiencies, and thereby allows the industry to advance in concert.

Hybrid Cloud

The categorization of cloud providers in the previous section into private, public and community deployments is a great simplification. Not only is there no clear boundary between the three delivery models, but it is very likely that customers will not confine themselves to any given approach. Instead, you can expect to see a wide variety of inter-cloud constellations (Figure 1-3).

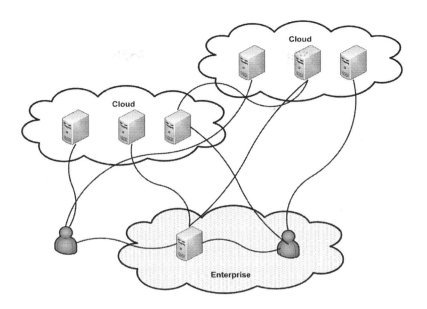

Figure 1-3 : Hybrid Delivery Model

Hybrid models can implement sourcing on the basis of at least four criteria.

Organizational: The simplest distinction would be that some business units use one source and other parts of the organization use another. This might be the case after a merger or acquisition, for instance.

Application: Another point of segregation would be the application. CRM, Email, ERP and Accounting may run from different delivery points for all applicable users in the organization.

Service: It is also possible that some services, such as Identity Management or a monitoring tool, are not immediately visible to the users but are transparently sourced from disparate cloud providers.

Resource: Virtual private clouds offer a means of extending the perimeter of the organization's internal network into the cloud to take advantage of resources with more elastic capacity than the internal systems. This extension is also invisible to end users.

Multi-sourced delivery models are inherently complex and therefore require careful planning. A framework such as eSCM (eSourcing Capability Model), developed by ITSqc, can be useful to ensure the design is systematic. It defines a set of sourcing life-cycle phases, practices, capability areas and capability levels as well as their interrelationships and suggests best practices both for the service providers and the customers who consume the services.

Value Proposition

ANALYZE

A detailed analysis of the business case for cloud computing is outside the scope of this book. Nonetheless, it is vital to understand the basic value proposition of the technology in order to gauge the impact of its risks. Some of the primary benefits of cloud computing derive from improvements in cost, risk, security, flexibility, quality and focus. Let's look at each of them briefly.

Cost

The most apparent advantages of cloud computing are around cost. In order to quantify the return, you will need to perform a complete financial analysis of both a cloud model and any alternative options. There can be a significant reduction in up-front investment since there is no need to purchase extensive hardware infrastructure or software licenses. Instead you can align your costs to actual usage. This means that you can allocate costs to the contributing revenue much more easily and accurately.

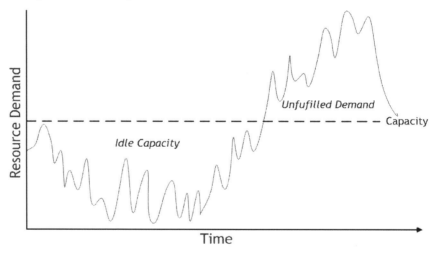

Figure 1-4: Fixed Capacity Utilization Curve

You also no longer need to over-provision resources in order to meet spikes in demand (Figure 1-4). High-end industry server utilization rates currently run at 15-20%. In the cloud, you do not pay for idle capacity which further reduces costs.

And finally, some benefits that the providers have acquired in terms of economies of scale and their place on the experience curve will translate into cost savings for the customer. Certainly, the providers will try to retain most of their advantage as profit; but, in a competitive environment with other efficient providers, you can also expect some savings to be passed on to customers.

Risk

Cloud computing can offload some risks from the customer to the service provider. By contractually stipulating data protection and disaster recovery provisions, and attaching them to indemnities in the case of failures, the company can mitigate its own risks.

It also reduces the likelihood of under-provisioning. Since it is not possible to accurately predict customer demand, there is always the possibility that there will be sudden unanticipated spikes of resource utilization. If the company owns its own resources, then there are limits to the amount of idle capacity that they will procure on the off-chance of a sudden increase in activity. On the other hand, the elastic capacity of a cloud provider should not often be exceeded.

It would be hard to over-emphasize this point. Scalability disasters can cause both direct and indirect costs. Lost revenues through unplanned downtime cost enterprises an average of over a hundred thousand dollars an hour and can exceed a million dollars an hour[1] (Forrester 2004). In addition, there are numerous other consequences. The company may lose potential customers who are irked by the unpleasant experience of losing a transaction. Employees cannot work which increases their hourly costs. There may be compensatory payments. The brand damage can hurt relations with customers, suppliers, financial markets, banks, business partners and investors.

There may even be an impact on financial performance through interruptions in billing or investment activities. Revenue and cash flow recognition may be delayed and distort the financial picture and there are risks of lost discounts from accounts payable, which can also damage the credit rating. If that isn't enough, then consider the contractual payment obligations to temporary employees, schedules for equipment renewal, overtime costs, shipping costs and travel expenses, which can all be adversely impacted.

Rogue clouds represent another potential risk that an authorized cloud service can mitigate. Historically, when a technology is not deployed in an organization the likelihood of an unauthorized deployment increases. A stark example was that of WLANs (Wireless Local Area Networks). Companies that prohibited wireless technologies often found that employees were adding personal access points to the corporate network creating a huge attack surface. By implementing authorized WLANs, many organizations removed the incentive for unauthorized WLANs and were thereby able to control the risks more effectively.

Similarly, there is an incentive for many users or departments to leverage cloud-based services for personal and group use. It is extremely easy for them to access these on their own since many of the providers offer free functionality or credit-card-based payment. Their rogue use may jeopardize sensitive company infor-

---

[1] Estimates in U.S. dollars.

mation or expose the business to severe sanctions for non-compliance with industry regulations.

It is impossible to completely remove the threat of departmental cloud use. However, if the functionality is available on an authorized and supported basis, then the incentive for unauthorized and unmonitored usage declines.

Security

Security is usually portrayed as a challenge for cloud computing, and rightfully so. Nonetheless there are several benefits that cloud computing may offer with respect to security. That is not to say that these benefits are necessarily exclusive to cloud computing, merely that they align very well with its implementation.

Cloud providers typically undergo very strict security audits. An enterprise may also institute the same audits but, on average, many businesses do not enforce the same level of rigor as a cloud provider. On a similar line, the cloud providers have access to the best-of-breed security solutions and procedures. They have been forced to inculcate a deep sense of security concern in their administrative staff. Again, this is not typically matched by smaller organizations.

The cloud also offers a platform for many security functions ranging from disaster recovery to monitoring, forensic readiness and password assurance or security testing. Its location makes it ideal for centralized monitoring. It is easier to isolate customer and employee data if they are managed in different environments. It might therefore increase security to segregate the data such that customer information is housed in the cloud while employee information is processed on the internal network.

Virtualization carries with it the inherent advantage that it is much easier to deploy preconfigured builds. It is possible to pre-harden these by locking down all traffic, eliminating unnecessary applications and features and applying the latest security patches.

There is some arguable advantage to the fact that the cloud obfuscates the physical infrastructure. Since virtual images may be brought up anywhere in the cloud and tend to move frequently, it makes it much more difficult for a hacker to launch a topology-based attack.

Finally, the constant presence of cloud services has an advantage in pervasive enforcement. Especially end-user devices tend to rely on connectivity to a central server for updates that address the most recent threats. Cloud resources are exposed on the Internet and therefore easily reachable from a wide variety of networks. Cloud services can also draw on the scale of security providers who gather threat intelligence globally and share the newest threats and protection mechanisms in real time.

Flexibility

ANALYZE

A cloud infrastructure adds considerable flexibility and agility to an enterprise architecture. It makes it much easier to roll out new services as they become necessary and to retire old applications when they are no longer needed. There is no need to procure hardware for the former or to cost-effectively dispose of the equipment in the case of the latter.

Similarly, a particular service can scale up and down as needed. There are cases where resource demand has spiked ten-fold overnight only to fall back to its original level shortly afterward[1]. The elasticity of a cloud allows the enterprise to exactly match the resources to the demand without overpaying for excess capacity or losing an opportunity to address market demand.

The flexibility also facilitates a faster time to market. When resources can be provisioned on demand, the usual lead time for procuring necessary equipment can be compressed to a few minutes. Ultimately, the speed and reduced commitment also lower barriers to innovation, which can encourage a more agile organizational culture.

A globally replicated cloud facilitates access from any place using any device at any time and therefore contributes to user flexibility and productivity. This advantage becomes even more visible when there is a need to integrate with business processes with suppliers, partners and customers. The absence of a firewall makes it easier to authorize fine-grained access to services and data without compromising or exposing other organizational assets.

Quality

Quality of service in all dimensions is a major concern around cloud computing. But in many cases, it is actually a benefit. Cloud service providers have great economy of scale and specialization. They have developed rigorous processes and procedures to maximize uptime and optimize performance. They run best-in-breed software to monitor and manage the infrastructure; and they employ some of the most skilled practitioners to oversee the management tools.

An on-demand model also differentiates itself from purchased and installed software in that the service provider can distribute new functionality and apply patches without any IT intervention. As a result, users can benefit from more frequent updates and newer functionality.

Cloud services also have the potential to deliver high availability since the provider's scale can offer multiple levels of redundancy with replication from the physical devices to the entire data center across large geographical distances.

---

[1] Animoto is a popular example: They scaled from 50 Amazon Servers to 3500 Servers in three days (16-19 April 2008)

Focus

The fact that some of the IT services are outsourced to a cloud provider reduces the effort and administration that is required by the corporate IT department. These responsibilities extend from user provisioning and support to application management and troubleshooting. Once service evolution is automated, experts can refocus on activities and opportunities that help to solidify the core competencies of the firm.

Practical Recommendations

Cloud computing and, by implication, OpenStack come in many different flavors. They can be built privately or sourced publicly. They can deliver basic infrastructure or serve as the foundation for sophisticated platforms and applications. They can offer an exciting array of opportunities for information technology to demonstrate value to the business. However, they also present substantial obstacles, so their adoption requires careful planning.

In order to achieve long-term success, it is critical that customers identify opportunities for cloud computing as early as possible and submit them to extensive evaluation. They will need to build business cases, perform risk analyses and develop comprehensive technical designs, which all take considerable effort.

In many cases, the ultimate goal is not within immediate reach for financial, security or technical reasons. It is therefore necessary to plan an evolution through private and hybrid cloud computing before achieving a fully-fledged public cloud solution.

Chapter 2

Gauge your Maturity

Almost everything related to IT has been rebranded as "Cloud Computing" in the past few years. Many experts argue that the labels are merely an example of leveraging marketing hype to sell old technology. Without diving too deep into this very heated topic, let's just say that adoption can come at varying speeds.

Cloud has a number of benefits, but it is also very disruptive. Large organizations cannot simply rip out their existing infrastructure and replace it with something entirely new, no matter how much better it might be. Instead, we need to look at the emerging trend as a journey more than a destination. Each step should take the customer closer to achieving the full benefits of cloud computing.

Enterprise Cloud Adoption Path

Service providers often have a highly standardized and homogenous data center. Rolling out cloud services and infrastructure is a logical extension of their existing operational model. This doesn't mean it is easy, but it is feasible to implement broad upgrades and roll-outs as long as there is a compelling value proposition. Businesses, on the other hand, face a different set of challenges based on the complexity of their legacy environment.

While a hybrid model is the most likely end-point for many enterprises, a realistic look at the industry today reveals that we still have a way to go before we achieve it. It is not uncommon to find small startups today that are fully committed to cloud computing for all their service requirements. Large organizations, on the other hand, have been very cautious, even if they recognize the value that cloud computing can bring to them.

Corporate reluctance comes as no surprise to anyone who has followed the adoption path of emerging technologies over the past few years. Legacy applications, infrastructural investment, regulatory concerns and rigid business processes represent tremendous obstacles to change. Even if there are obvious early opportunities, the transition is likely to take time.

ANALYZE

However, this doesn't mean that enterprises are completely stationary. In their own way, most of them began the journey to a private cloud years ago and they are gradually evolving in the direction of a public cloud. We can break down this path by identifying three steps, which are each associated with an increasing level of efficiency.

> ***Resource efficiencies*** are usually the first objective of a private cloud implementation. Standardization of components sets the scene for data-center consolidation and optimization. Each level of resource abstraction, from server virtualization to full multi-tenancy, increases the opportunity to share physical capacity, and thereby reduces the overall infrastructural needs.

> ***Operational efficiencies*** target human labor, one of the highest cost factors related to information technology. Ideally, all systems are self-healing and self-managing. This implies a high degree of automation and end-user self service. In addition to a reduction of administration costs, these optimizations also enable rapid deployment of new services and functionality.

> ***Sourcing efficiencies*** are the final step and represent the flexibility to provision services, and allocate resources, from multiple internal and external providers without modifying the enterprise architecture. This agility can only be attained if all systems adhere to rigorous principles of service-orientation and service management. They must also include fine-grained metering for cost control and a granular role-based authorization scheme that can guarantee confidentiality and integrity of data. On the plus side, the benefit of reaching this level of efficiency is that applications can enjoy near infinite elasticity of resources, and costs can be reduced to the minimum that the market has to offer.

Once the businesses have full sourcing independence, they are flexible in terms of where they procure their services. They can continue to obtain them from IT or they may switch to an external provider that is more efficient and reliable. However, this independence can work in both directions (Figure 2-1).

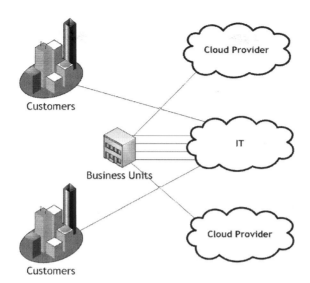

Figure 2-1 : Multi-source and Multi-target Services

If IT develops its services in a generic and modular form, then the organization also has the flexibility to offer parts of the functionality on the external market, and therefore monetize the investment in ways that were not possible before.

Software-Defined Data Center

As mentioned above, the SPI stack presents a simplified picture of how cloud services relate to each other. It facilitates the discussion by providing a common reference model. However, in reality, the lines are blurred, as many services (such as Identity Management) span multiple categories, and a complete solution involves additional components.

For example, in addition to the software and applications that run in the SPI model, and support a cloud application in its core functions, both the enterprise and service provider need to address core challenges, such as Implementation, Operation and Control, in order to successfully keep the solution going (Figure 2-2).

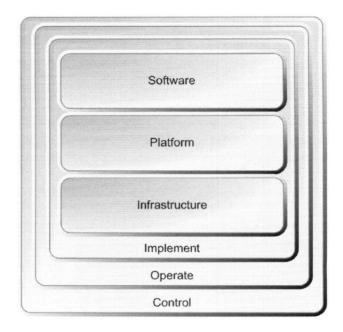

Figure 2-2: Implementation, Operation and Control

Implement: It is necessary to select and integrate all the components into a functioning solution. There are a large, and ever increasing, number of cloud-based services and solutions on the market. It is no simple task to categorize and compare them. And once that is done, it would be naïve to expect them all to work together seamlessly. The integration effort involves a careful selection of interfaces and configuration settings and may require additional connectors or custom software.

Operate: Once the solution has been brought online, it is necessary to keep it running. This means that you need to monitor it, troubleshoot it and support it. Since the service is unlikely to be completely static, you need to also have processes in place to provision new users, decommission old users, plan for capacity changes, track incidents and implement changes in the service.

Control: The operation of a complex set of services can be a difficult challenge. Some of the challenge may be reduced by working with solution providers and outsourcing organizations who take over the operative responsibilities. However, this doesn't completely obviate the need for overseeing the task. It is still necessary to ensure that service expectations are well defined and that they are validated on a continuous basis.

Fortunately, many of these capabilities are also in the process of being automated and delivered as services. The trend is to abstract the control plane (i.e. the administrative tools) from the service plane, where the workloads execute. This abstraction makes it easier to automate operational functions, such as provisioning, configuration and policy enforcement.

It is commonly referred to as the Software-Defined Data Center (SDDC) since it makes it possible to automate and flexibly deploy not only the workloads themselves but also the entire infrastructure that supports them. As with many emerging technologies, not everyone uses the SDDC label in the same way, but separation of control and service plane is usually a primary element in its definition. And this distinction is very relevant to the way we look at the data center.

In fact, we shall see that in many ways OpenStack is a means of implementing a software-defined data center and some of its core components, including Software-Defined Networking (SDN), Software-Defined Storage (SDS) and Software-Defined Compute (SDC).

Flexible Cloud Sourcing

One of the benefits of standardized cloud services is that the customer can easily and quickly change providers to optimize costs and functionality as the market and user requirements change. The broad industry adoption of OpenStack is a major advantage in this respect.

However, even with OpenStack, the current status is that not all implementations are interchangeable. Unfortunately, this incompatibility between providers makes the goal of seamless re-sourcing unrealistic without significant investment or complementary solutions. Nonetheless it is a big step in the right direction of reducing switching costs and we can expect the flexibility of moving from one provider to another to improve over time, either through increased standardization or the commoditization of brokering solutions.

Hybrid Cloud Design

Once an organization decides to embark on the journey of hybrid cloud, the task is not only to selectively source an increasing number of services from public providers. The bigger challenge is to integrate them dynamically with other services running internally and externally.

Figure 2-3: Hybrid Silos

ANALYZE

To illustrate, consider some of the integration options for hybrid cloud computing. The first step of a hybrid cloud is for the services to run in independent silos without any interaction (Figure 2-3). For example, an organization might run Microsoft Exchange internally and use Salesforce.com as their publicly procured CRM service. If the two do not interact, this is not a difficult achievement.

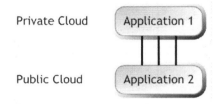

Figure 2-4: Static Hybrid Integration

The next step would then be to integrate them where possible (Figure 2-4). There might be a connection from Salesforce.com to the internal Active Directory for single sign-on or the service might leverage Microsoft Exchange to deliver email notifications and schedule tasks. This integration needs careful planning to ensure compatibility and safeguard any sensitive data.

Figure 2-5: Dynamic Hybrid Integration

The last step is support for dynamic workload distribution (Figure 2-5). This means that there must be equivalent internal and external services and they need interface compatibility. One reason for this approach would be to establish a disaster recovery facility. In the event of catastrophic failure of the internal data center, the company could shift the workload to the cloud and restart the service there.

An even more ambitious goal is cloudbursting, which can be used to optimize costs and flexibility. If the organization is able to shift workloads in real-time, then it is possible to run services internally as a standard practice. However, if there are spikes in activity or the service grows faster than anticipated, the company can off-load any processing that exceeds its internal capacity.

Let's look at these two notions in more detail.

Disaster Recovery

In Chapter 20, we will cover short-term resilience, which is the first line of defense for business continuity. If the environment is resilient, then there will be no need for an expensive and disruptive recovery. A large part of resilience relies on redundancy. If information, systems, processes, infrastructure and personnel are fully redundant, then the likelihood of an outage will be minimal.

In practice, it is usually not cost-effective, and sometimes not technically feasible, to ensure absolute redundancy.

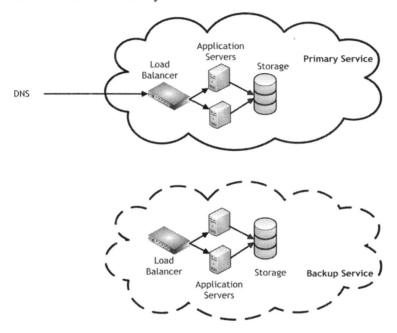

Figure 2-6: Cold Disaster Recovery

The simplest recovery scenario involves what is called a cold site (Figure 2-6). The entire environment is replicated to another location, which may be a cloud service. The service including both computational and storage instances is fully configured but it is not actually running. In the event of a disaster, there is a need to load the storage with current data and then activate the components.

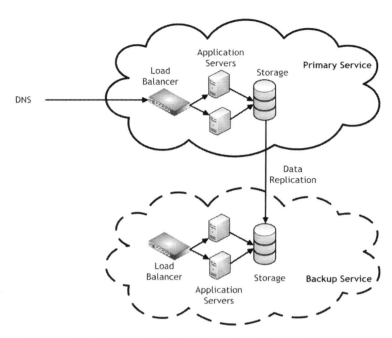

Figure 2-7: Warm/Hot Single-active Disaster Recovery

A more sophisticated option is a warm site. Its main technical difference is that the data is continuously replicated to the backup storage (Figure 2-7). This reduces the time it takes to launch the service when it is needed. In the case of a hot disaster recovery, the full service is also always operational, even if it is receiving no traffic. When a disaster strikes, someone just needs to redirect the DNS entry to point to the backup solution and it will take over without any delays.

The disadvantage of this design, where only one service is active at any given time, is that it wastes valuable resources and can be very costly to implement.

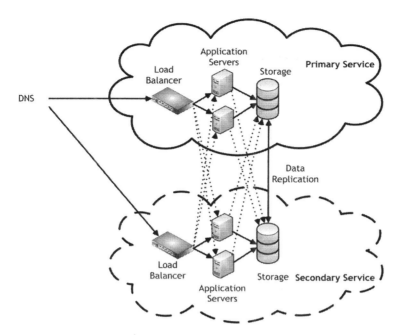

Figure 2-8: Dual-Active Redundant Services

In order to achieve greater efficiency, some organizations implement a dual-active scenario (Figure 2-8). In this setup, both services are fully operational and distribute the load between them. All end-user requests are shared, either through a global load balancer or DNS round robin. It is also vital that the storage be synchronized between the services to ensure consistency in the data.

In some cases, the entire architecture may be integrated so that the load balancers and application servers are pooled between data centers. The level of interconnection will vary depending on the solution and the infrastructure being used. It is particularly important to consider the cost and security ramifications of any network connections that need to traverse the public Internet.

After all, the service should ideally be replicated to a geographically remote location so that it is unlikely to be affected by the same disaster. The more distant the two locations are, the better the chances that the second will survive a disaster of the first. A different continent is therefore ideal, but that level of precaution may not be necessary in every case.

An additional level of independence can be achieved if a backup is hosted by a second provider. In this case, an incident (e.g. large-scale intrusion or malware attack) cannot easily affect both the backup and the primary system. Note that redundant systems are only effective if they can failover. Once they are set up, they should be tested during a "dry run" to ensure that they will switch over properly during an outage.

Cloudbursting

An even more ambitious goal is cloudbursting, which can be used to optimize costs and flexibility as long as the organization is able to shift workloads in real-time. It is usually cheapest to run the services internally as a standard practice. However, if there are spikes in activity or the service grows faster than anticipated, the company can off-load any processing that exceeds its internal capacity. Let's look at this concept in more detail.

When faced with static workloads, some large organizations can match and beat the costs of cloud services since they can achieve similar efficiencies through their own economy of scale. In these cases, the financial analysis requires a deeper study.

The calculation is fundamentally different for periodic workloads. If the resources are only used part of the time, then the customer bears the full cost with a fixed investment but only pays a fraction for a variably priced service.

Before we let the pendulum swing too far in the other direction, however, we need to consider the case of a private cloud. The fact that a particular service has an irregular usage pattern doesn't immediately lead to the need for a public service. If workloads are complementary, many organizations can achieve similar benefits through virtualization.

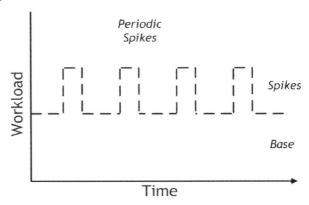

Figure 2-9: Periodic Incremental Workload

The picture in Figure 2-9 is typical for some workloads. Furthermore, when application consumption is aggregated through virtualization, almost all private clouds will manifest an uneven usage pattern over time. For organizations that are able to run a static workload more efficiently internally, the combined pattern presents a new opportunity.

Conventional wisdom would recommend an approach of "owning the 'base' and renting the 'spikes'" (Weinman & Lapinski, 2009). For example, if the workload represents the sum of the two previous examples, then we would invest in an internal implementation of the minimum workload and source the additional periodic requirements from the public cloud.

Cloudbursting is the capability of the platform to call on other resource providers (processing, storage or networking resources) when internal resources run short and additional resources are available from other internal or external cloud platforms.

Enterprises may be able to satisfy some of their needs on premise, but still be interested in tapping into the cloud to handle peak loads for internal applications. This approach, often called 'cloudbursting' (Perry, 2008), involves extending an existing enterprise application, written on a private platform, to be able to leverage external services once internal capacity has been exhausted.

The most ambitious form of resource allocation exploits all available private assets, but combines these with the elasticity of public resources (Figure 2-10). When it is well designed and orchestrated, cloudbursting can minimize costs and maximize agility. However, while the approach sounds elegant in theory, it is difficult to achieve in practice.

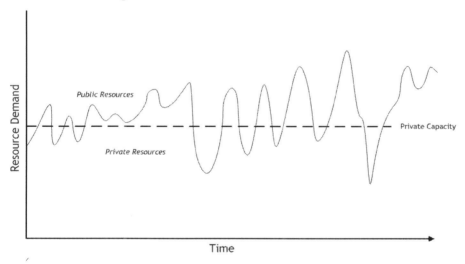

Figure 2-10: Cloudbursting

In order to shift load effectively, three prerequisites are needed: a trigger mechanism, capacity to launch public instances, and capacity to shift associated data. We will return to this topic in Chapter 21 to see how it might apply to OpenStack.

Practical Recommendations

The first steps toward an enterprise cloud rely on standardization, consolidation and virtualization. Beyond these, it is possible to achieve operational efficiencies

ANALYZE

and optimized sourcing options through a highly abstracted software-defined data center and well-defined service-oriented architecture.

OpenStack can be very helpful in implementing these phases with its extensible framework and standardized functions that facilitate hybrid operations, such as disaster recovery and cloudbursting.

Assess

Before implementing OpenStack, it is worthwhile to look at the alternatives. There are many commercial offerings for each type of cloud from IaaS to SaaS. The choice of OpenStack depends to a large extent on the value proposition of an open-source infrastructure service that caters to both private and public service providers. But there are also other open-source frameworks that are almost directly comparable, so the selection process should also consider them.

Chapter 3

Explore the Landscape

In Chapter 1, we gave a theoretical explanation of what cloud computing is and why it is so popular. But the concept is so broad and there is so much variety in the actual options that it only comes to life when we look at a few of the widely adopted services and technologies.

If you are interested in pursuing a cloud-based solution, you might ask yourself what delivery model you need. Should it be SaaS, PaaS or IaaS? You will also need to make a decision on a deployment model. Do you need a private, public or hybrid cloud?

OpenStack is best positioned as an infrastructure service, which can be consumed from either private or public sources. But it is not the only technology that you could use to build out your infrastructure. Before you build out your own service, you will be well advised to consider what is on the market. It may fully satisfy your requirements. And even if it doesn't, it will give you a baseline with which to compare your service and some good ideas on how to design your architecture.

This chapter will look at a cross-section of the commercially available offerings to consider as you make your selection. We will then look at the tradeoffs in the next chapter as well as what tools, including OpenStack, you might want to consider in creating a private or hybrid infrastructure service.

Software Services

One of the most popular and most publicized areas of Software as a Service is Customer Relationship Management (CRM) and in particular, sales-force automation. It includes functions such as account management, opportunity tracking and marketing campaign administration.

Chapter 3: Explore the Landscape

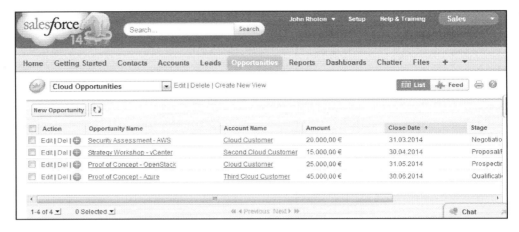

Figure 3-1: Salesforce.com

Arguably, the best known SaaS offering comes from Salesforce.com which provides a CRM solution consisting of several modules: Sales, Service & Support, Partner Relationship Management, Marketing, Content, Ideas and Analytics. It is available in over 20 languages and can be accessed from almost any Internet device including mobile platforms such as Android, iPhone and Windows Mobile.

NetSuite is another popular CRM package. Its base service is called NetSuite 2007.0 while NetSuite and NetSuite CRM+ are the two primary product options. Other options and services include NetSuite Global CRM, Dedicated Server Options, OpenAir and Payroll.

Human Resources (HR), or Human Capital Management (HCM), includes administration processes to support personnel functions such as recruiting, developing, retaining and motivating employees. Service providers include Workday and Taleo.

Workday, Netsuite, Intuit and others offer a variety of financial applications ondemand, ranging from accounting to procurement and inventory management.

Since collaboration involves establishing connectivity between people it is natural to also use a technology that is built on networking and utilizes a common infrastructure. There are a growing number of Web 2.0 services that are almost exclusively delivered over the Internet. But even some of the more traditional applications such as desktop productivity (e.g. from Google Apps, Microsoft Online Services and Zoho) and conferencing (Cisco Webex. Citrix GoToMeeting) can benefit from cloud computing.

Platform Services

Platform services lend themselves well for building new applications based on cloud-optimized infrastructure. In some cases, the boundary to infrastructure services is blurred, but platforms typically offer more programmer-oriented services, such as code libraries and development environments.

Google App Engine

Google App Engine is one of the best known platform services. In addition to a basic run-time environment, it eliminates many of the system administration and development challenges involved in building applications that can scale to millions of users. It includes facilities to deploy code to a cluster as well as monitoring, failover, automatic scaling and load balancing.

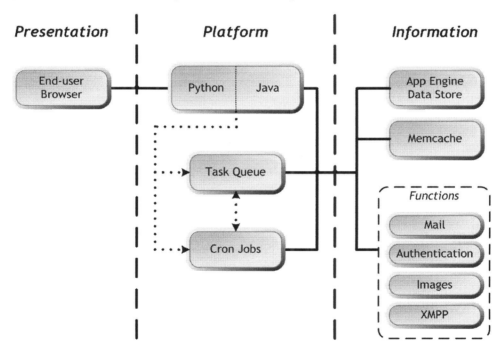

Figure 3-2: Google App Engine Architecture

Figure 3-2 offers a simple view of the Google App Engine Architecture. Users access the application through a browser, which connects to a hosted application written either in Python or Java. In addition to the run-time environment, batch jobs may run in the background either through a task queue or as scheduled "cron" jobs. The compute instances can access a persistent data store as well as a high-speed distributed cache.

The App Engine Datastore supports queries, sorting and transactions using optimistic concurrency control. It is a strongly consistent distributed database built

ASSESS

on top of the lower-level BigTable with some added functionality. Unfortunately for legacy code, the App Engine Datastore is not like a traditional relational database. In particular, the datastore entities are schemaless. Two entities of the same kind are not required to possess the same properties, nor do they need to use the same value types if they do share properties. Instead, the application is responsible for ensuring that entities conform to any schema required by the business logic. To assist, the Python SDK includes a data modeling library that helps enforce consistency.

Google App Engine's query language (called GQL) is similar to SQL in its SELECT statements however with some significant limitations. GQL intentionally does not support the Join statement and can therefore only accommodate single table queries. The rationale behind the restriction is the inefficiency that queries spanning more than one machine might introduce. However, Google does provide a workaround in the form of a ReferenceProperty class that can indicate one-to-many and many-to-many relationships.

Microsoft Azure

Windows Azure is Microsoft's Platform as a Service. Similar in concept to Google App Engine, it allows applications based on Microsoft technologies to be hosted and run from Microsoft data centers. Its fabric controller automatically manages resources, balances load, replicates for resilience and manages the application lifecycle.

The Windows Azure platform is built as a distributed service hosted in Microsoft data centers and built on a special-purpose operating system called Windows Azure. It is implemented as three components: Compute, Storage and a Fabric to manage the platform.

The *Compute* instances are exposed to the customer as role types that specify tailored configurations for typical purposes. The Web Role instances generally interact with the end user. They may host web sites and other front-end code. On the other hand, Worker Role instances cater to background tasks similar to Google App Engine cron jobs.

While Web and Worker role types are the most popular, Windows Azure provides additional templates for specific needs. For example, the CGI web role supports the FastCGI protocol and thereby enables other programming languages including PHP, Ruby, Python and Java. The WCF (Windows Communications Foundation) service is a web role that facilitates support of WCF services.

Azure *Storage* provides services that host three kinds of data:

- Blobs
- Tables

- Queue

A blob is simply a stream of unstructured (or at least opaque) data. It can be a picture, a file or anything else the application needs. There is a four-level hierarchy of blob storage. At the highest level is a storage account, which is the root of the namespace for the blobs. Each account can hold multiple containers, which provide groupings (e.g. similar permissions or metadata). Within a container can be many blobs. Each can be uniquely identified and may hold up to 50GB. In order to optimize uploads and downloads (especially for very large files) it is possible to break a blob into blocks. Each transfer request therefore refers to a smaller portion of data (e.g. 4MB) making the transaction less vulnerable to transient network errors.

Tables are used for structured data. As you might expect from the name, they typically hold a set of homogenous rows (called entities) that are defined by a set of columns (called properties). Each property is defined by a name and type (e.g. String, Binary, Int). Despite the conceptual similarity there are important distinctions to make between Windows Azure storage tables and relational tables. Azure does not enforce a schema nor does it support SQL as a query language. While this may lead to portability challenges for many legacy applications, Microsoft's strategy is similar to that of Google and reflects the importance of ensuring the new technology is optimized for the scalability requirements of cloud-based services.

Queues provide a mechanism for applications to communicate and coordinate asynchronously. This is an important requirement when applications are geographically distributed over high-latency links. Synchronous communication can severely degrade performance and introduces stability risks that must be minimized. Like Blobs and Tables, Queues are associated with a Storage Account. They hold a linear set of XML messages. There is no limit to the number of messages per queue but they typically will be removed from the queue if they are not processed within seven days (or earlier if requested).

Similar to Amazon S3, it is possible to specify a region for any storage requirements in order to ensure compliance with local data privacy laws and minimize latency between applications and users. If performance is critical, the Azure CDN (Content Delivery Network) also provides distributed delivery of static content from Azure Storage from Microsoft's worldwide network of data centers.

The *Fabric*, in Azure terminology, refers to a set of machines running the Azure operating system that are collectively managed and generally co-located in the same region. The Fabric Controller is the layer of code that provisions all the user instances (web and worker roles) and performs any necessary upgrades. It also monitors the applications, re-provisioning and reallocating resources as needed to ensure that all services remain healthy.

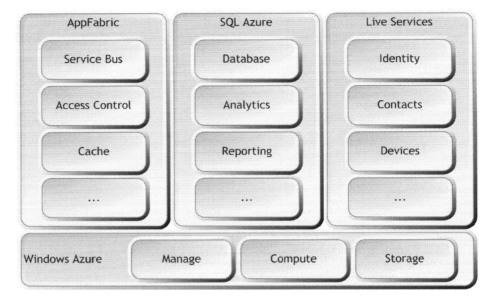

Figure 3-3: Azure Services

Azure also provides a set of services that can be consumed both from the Internet (including the Azure platform itself) and on-premise applications. These include HDInsight, Backup, Cache, Messaging, Notification, Active Directory, and Multi-Factor Authentication.

Other Platform Services

Salesforce.com also delivers a Platform-as-a-Service which is called Force.com. It is very different from both Google's and Microsoft's offerings in this space. It does also offer hosting services based on its technology with the usual features of redundancy, security and scalability. But Force.com is much more data-oriented than code-oriented.

Engine Yard Cloud provides a Ruby on Rails technology stack, including web, application and database servers, monitoring and process management. The Linux distribution is optimized for Rails and includes in-memory cache.

Salesforce.com's Heroku is another cloud application platform for Ruby. It is a managed multi-tenant platform and hosting environment. Each service consists of one or more dynos, or web processes running code and responding to HTTP requests.

A key differentiator of Facebook applications is that they revolve around a "social graph", which connects people with other people and their interests. One way to conceptualize the potential of the Facebook Platform is by thinking of it in terms of a three-tier model: Presentation, Application Logic and Data.

Intuit offers a platform service, called the Intuit Partner Platform (IPP), which focuses on the development, sale and distribution of multitenant SaaS applications. Initially it consisted of an Adobe Flex-based development environment with functions to target the large installed base of QuickBooks users. It has since expanded into a set of APIs that can be leveraged from any platform, notably including Microsoft Azure, a strong partner of Intuit.

Pivotal One is an enterprise PaaS built on Cloud Foundry. It is an open-source platform that can also run on OpenStack, which is a topic we will cover again in Chapter 23.

Infrastructure Services

One distinguishing factor of IaaS, as opposed to PaaS or SaaS, is that there are many more private and hybrid options available in addition to the public services on the market.

Amazon Web Services

The de facto standard for infrastructure services is Amazon. While they are not unique in their offerings, virtually all IaaS services are either complements to Amazon Web Services or else considered competitors to them. We therefore find it useful to structure the analysis of IaaS along the lines of what Amazon's offerings.

Figure 3-4: Amazon Web Services

Amazon EC2 (Elastic Compute) is the core service, which falls into the category of Shared Virtual machines, each based on an Amazon Machine Image (AMI). The customer can use pre-packaged AMIs from Amazon and 3rd parties, or they can build their own. They vary in resources (RAM, compute units, local disk size), operating systems (several Windows versions and many Linux distributions) and the application frameworks that are installed on them (e.g. JBoss, MySQL, Oracle).

Figure 3-5 gives an overview of some of the main services that are available from AWS. As you can see, the offering is very broad. There are many options for computation, storage, integration and scalability, not to mention functions for management and billing that are not even represented on the diagram.

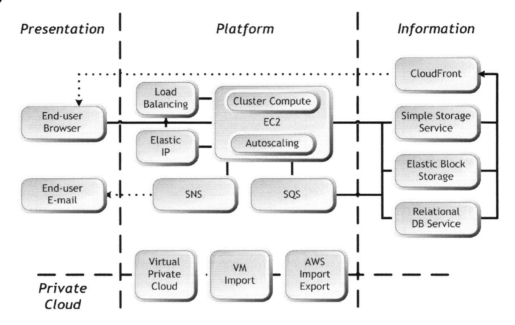

Figure 3-5: AWS Architecture

To help Amazon Web Services novices, we have tried to assemble the elements into one conceptual framework. However, although they are portrayed here in unified form, keep in mind that it is possible to consume almost every Amazon service independently of the others.

Microsoft Azure Virtual Machines

Microsoft Azure initially focused on platform services as described above. However, they have since introduced a service called Microsoft Azure Virtual Machines, which fits more closely to the characteristics of an infrastructure service comparable to Amazon EC2. It supports both Windows and Linux Virtual machines.

Additionally, the Windows Azure Virtual Network enables logical isolation in Windows Azure coupled with secure connections to on-premise datacenters.

And the Windows Azure Drive allows applications to mount a blob which they can use to move VMs between private and public clouds.

It is worth noting that Microsoft also has a strong private cloud offering based on System Center and Windows Server 2012. Since these products are based on the same underlying code as Windows Azure, it is relatively easy for customer to build hybrid environments that span both their internal data center as well as the Windows Azure public cloud.

Google Compute Engine

Similarly, Google also extended its App Engine with compute capabilities in the form of Google Compute Engine, an infrastructure service that lets large-scale computing workloads run on Linux virtual machines hosted on Google's infrastructure.

As would be expected, there are also load balancing services, object storage accessible through a REST API, the capability to reserve static IP addresses, and customizable firewall rules defining access to external traffic.

GoGrid

Figure 3-6: GoGrid Dedicated Server

GoGrid offers dedicated server configurations (Figure 3-6) as well as prein-stalled images of Windows and Linux with Apache, IIS, MySQL and several other applications. It also provides free hardware-based load balancing to opti-mize the performance of customer instances.

Flexiscale

ASSESS

Flexiscale is an infrastructure service comparable to Amazon EC2 or Rackspace Cloud (discussed later). Similar to its competition, it supports Linux and Win-dows operating systems and facilitates self-provisioning of Cloud servers via the Control Panel or API. Customers can start, stop and delete instances and change memory, CPU, Storage and Network addresses of cloud servers.

They offer extensive firewall rules based on IP addresses and protocols, and each customer has their own dedicated VLAN. Unlike some IaaS providers, their virtual machines offer persistent storage, which is based on a virtualized high-end Storage Area Network.

CSC

CSC's cloud services consist of a multi-tiered approach in which CSC manages the complete ecosystems of cloud service providers, including platform-as-a-service, infrastructure-as-a-service and software-as-a-service. Orchestration helps clients manage data and collaborate across public and private networks.

These are complemented with a private cloud solution, called BizCloud, which runs on customers' premises behind their firewall, and BizCloud VPE, which is hosted in CSC data centers, but runs on isolated networks using dedicated re-sources.

Verizon Terremark

Verizon became a major cloud player with its acquisition of Terremark, a global provider of IT infrastructure services. In addition to collocation, they offer VMware-based infrastructure services, such as utility hosting and enterprise-cloud virtual data centers. Terremark's data centers are built to stringent security standards with one location specialized for serving U.S. federal government needs.

The Enterprise Cloud from Terremark is an enterprise-class, Internet-optimized computing platform. A managed platform gives customers the ability to config-ure and deploy computing resources for mission-critical applications on-demand. The Enterprise Cloud gives control over a pool of processing, storage and memory resources to deploy server capacity. It's built around Terremark's Infin-istructure utility computing platform, top-tier datacenters and access to global connectivity.

Savvis

Savvis is an outsourcing provider of managed computing and network infrastructure for IT applications. Its services include managed hosting, co-location and network connectivity, which are supported by the company's global datacenter and network infrastructure. Savvis offers enterprise customers three primary variants of its Symphony services: Dedicated, Open and Virtual Private Data Center (VPDC).

Savvis Symphony Dedicated is a fully dedicated virtualized compute environment that is hosted and managed in Savvis data centers. The solution can be partitioned into multiple self-contained virtual machines (powered by VMware), each capable of running its own operating system and set of applications. Once deployed, customers can add instances automatically through the SavvisStation Portal.

Savvis Symphony Open is built on a scalable, multi-tenant infrastructure and delivers a secure, enterprise-class cloud environment with built-in high availability and automated resource balancing. It uses a purchase-by-the-instance cost model with flexible month-to-month terms for each instance.

Savvis Symphony VPDC introduces an enterprise-grade virtual private data center solution. Data center provisioning is facilitated through a self-service, web-based, drag-and-drop topology designer or through an application programming interface (API). The VPDC supports enterprise-grade security, platform redundancy, and high-performance information lifecycle management (ILM) storage as well as multi-tiered QoS levels with policy enforcement. A VPDC can contain a complete set of enterprise data center services, including compute instances of varying sizes, multiple tiers of storage, redundant bandwidth and load balancing.

VMware

VMware's cloud-oriented activity comes largely under the umbrella of its vCloud initiative. It represents a set of enabling technologies including vSphere, the vCloud API and the vCloud service provider ecosystem.

The *vSphere* platform, VMware's flagship product, is a virtualization framework that is capable of managing large pools of infrastructure, including software and hardware both from internal and external networks.

The *vCloud API* is a REST interface for providing and consuming virtual resources in the cloud. It enables deployment and management of virtualized workloads in private, public and hybrid clouds. The API enables the upload, download, instantiation, deployment and operation of virtual appliances (vApps), networks and "virtual datacenters". The two major components are the User API, focused on vApp provisioning, and the Admin API, focused on platform/tenant administration.

ASSESS

The ***vCloud service provider ecosystem*** is a common set of cloud computing services for businesses and service providers – with support for any application or OS and the ability to choose where applications live, on or off premise. It includes a set of applications available as virtual Appliances and is delivered by service providers, such as Savvis, T-Systems, AT&T, and Dell Cloud.

Beyond these infrastructure-oriented offerings, VMware vFabric offers a viable private platform service. It combines the Spring Java development framework with a set of integrated services including an application server, data management, cloud-ready messaging, load balancing and performance management.

Joyent

Joyent offers infrastructure services for both public and private cloud deployments as wells as their own web application development platform. For their infrastructure services, they use the term 'Accelerators' to refer to their persistent virtual machines. They run OpenSolaris with Apache, Nginx, MySQL, PHP, Ruby on Rails and Java pre-installed and the ability to add other packages. A feature called "automatic CPU bursting" provides reactive elasticity.

Joyent also offers a private version of their framework called SmartDataCenter for enterprise data centers. SmartDataCenter is software that runs on top of your existing hardware, or on new dedicated machines. It manages physical networking equipment and virtualized compute instances that are hosted within traditional physical servers and storage servers.

Red Hat

For those who resist the lock-in of a converged architecture such as Oracle Exadata, VCE Vblock, Dell vStart, HP CloudSystem Matrix and IBM PureSystems, the first port of call is open source. Red Hat, in addition to being a major contributor to OpenStack, provides its own stack, which is not backed by any consortium but has the advantage of being open.

Red Hat Hybrid IaaS Solution removes the complexity of building a hybrid cloud with open source tools. All the software to enable cloud computing is included in one product. The solution lets customers create a hybrid cloud spanning both private and public cloud resources. Since the design is modular, customers can use Red Hat's included infrastructure-management tools or another vendor's management tools.

An IT-governed, self-service portal facilitates application deployment and policy-based usage gives control over which applications can be run, where they can run, who can use them, and how they should be optimized.

For those who need to build their own applications, Red Hat OpenShift Enterprise Platform-as-a-Service (PaaS) is an enterprise cloud application platform providing a development and execution environment for enterprise applications. OpenShift provides a preconfigured, auto-scaling, self-managing application platform in the cloud that lets developers develop, deploy, and run their applications.

Rackspace

Rackspace is another very well-known IaaS provider with many managed hosting options, in addition to virtual server offerings covering a number of Linux distributions (such as Ubuntu, Fedora, Centos and RedHat Enterprise Linux). It has a large pool of dedicated IP addresses and offers persistent storage on all instances.

Rackspace was originally called Mosso, which is a label still occasionally seen in reference to its services. As mentioned earlier, they are one of the co-founders of OpenStack and one of the biggest contributors. In fact the OpenStack Object Storage service (Swift) is derived from a Rackspace offering called Cloud Files.

In addition to their public infrastructure service, Rackspace also offers an on-premise version of their technology called Rackspace Private Cloud, which is similarly based on OpenStack.

HP Cloud

HP is similar to Rackspace in offering both public and private versions of Open-Stack technology. The HP public cloud is available at www.hpcloud.com and it includes most of the OpenStack projects. Additionally, HP has also aligned its converged infrastructure product suite with their OpenStack strategy. HP Cloud OS provides the foundation for a common architecture across private, public, and hybrid cloud delivery. It facilitates enterprise-grade OpenStack with optimized workload portability, enhanced service lifecycle management and simplified installation and upgrades.

IBM SoftLayer

IBM SoftLayer is a hosting environment running both bare metal and virtual servers on demand. It is one of the largest hosters offering services to small, medium and large businesses for Big Data, Disaster Recovery and web applications. Although it is currently based on proprietary technology, IBM has announced that SoftLayer will eventually transform into an OpenStack operation.

ASSESS

Practical Recommendations

OpenStack has its benefits, but it is neither the easiest nor the quickest cloud service to deploy. Any organization should begin its technology selection process by looking at what is available on the market and has already been successfully implemented in the industry.

ASSESS

There are countless software, platform and infrastructure services that cater to a variety of needs. Even if you choose to continue with OpenStack, you will have a better understanding of what is architecturally possible in the cloud after exploring these options.

Chapter 4

ASSESS

Make the Selection

The choice of OpenStack as the underlying technology for a cloud deployment relies on several decisions that enterprises (and their service providers) must make.

In a nutshell, these are:

- Keep it simple: start with the infrastructure
- Play it safe: minimize disruption and risk profile changes
- Maximize long-term flexibility: look for standard solutions
- Find the best fit: match external offerings to internal capabilities and requirements

Let's look at these in sequence.

Start with the Infrastructure

The first decision in adopting a cloud solution is what kind of service to select. As we saw in Chapter 1, most offerings can be classified as SaaS, PaaS or IaaS. The choice of which depends on the need of the business.

Figure 1-1 illustrated the primary tradeoffs between flexibility and efficiency. If we look at the three service models as a stack, then we can say that the higher we go, the more efficient we become. Since efficiency is one of the main benefits of cloud computing, it is usually desirable to go as high up the stack as we can.

Infrastructure services are relatively inefficient. Certainly they waste fewer resources than dedicated physical machines, but they do not allow tenants to share much more than the physical resources. Software services, on the other hand, have the advantage that they allow tenants to share not only the hardware but also the operating system and even the application. In the long term, we can expect most services to evolve towards the top of the stack where they can achieve the greatest efficiency.

However, flexibility is also an important factor. In this context, we don't mean flexibility in the sense of agility to scale up and down quickly. Instead it is the latitude to use the service for a variety of applications. In spite of their benefits in efficiency, an effective SaaS model is not trivial to implement particularly for a set of customers with greatly differing requirements. And software services usually only offer a very narrow spectrum of functionality with little, if any, ability for the customer to extend the feature set.

The advantage of infrastructure services is that they are much easier to deploy. Most applications that were designed for a x86 architecture will run in a virtual machine without any modifications. This makes IaaS a logical first step for organizations with significant investment in legacy software.

Leverage Private Assets

A second important consideration is whether to build or buy. Large organizations can develop and deploy their own cloud services. But this doesn't mean that it is necessarily the best, or even the cheapest solution.

Service providers are typically in the business of implementing their own infrastructure. This is generally a core competence and their scale makes them attractive for highly scalable resource pools. If usage is volatile or unpredictable, it can be worthwhile for enterprises to consume the services externally.

The biggest drawback of a private cloud is that you don't automatically gain any benefits related to cloud computing. You can replicate many of the advantages internally, but it requires significant effort as well as a level of investment that may only be realistic for large enterprises.

The main financial considerations will be the scale of operation and the patterns of utilization. Typically large-scale deployments have a smaller unit cost which may be competitive with the services of an external provider. If the applications running on the infrastructure have a constant load, or the peaks and valleys tend to balance each other out across the portfolio, then the pay-as-you-go pricing model is not as compelling.

In addition to the costs, customers need to consider security and risk. External services rely on another organization, which may increase risk or insecurity or unavailability. However, the same risks also apply for an internal implementation. The main tradeoff is visibility and direct control versus trust and reliance on contractual agreements.

The choice to host your applications in a private data center gives the customer most control and flexibility. For example, after they install Apache or Microsoft IIS on the hardware of their choice with any necessary web frameworks, they can upload applications developed in their own environment.

They can choose any programming language and have complete freedom to implement any interfaces that may be necessary to connect to legacy or partner systems. It is only a matter of installing PHP, Python/Django, Ruby/Rails or a complete set of Java tools.

For those that do decide to implement a private cloud, there are tools, product and services that can be instrumental to attaining benefits in performance, utilization and automation. OpenStack is one of those options, but not the only one.

ASSESS

Maximize Flexibility with Open Source

For internal solutions, another critical question is whether to rely on their own code, purchase licenses of commercial software or leverage open source solutions. They may even want to combine elements of two or all three of these models to build the solution.

In the past, the case for open source was often considered to revolve around licensing costs. The implied guideline was that if you could afford it, commercial software was your best bet but, if you were on a tight budget, then open source might be an option.

However, software licensing is usually only a small portion of the full cost of a business service. In addition to the hardware and other infrastructure, you need to consider the human effort to deploy, manage and support the solution as well as the financial impact any application downtime may cause.

Poorly coded applications reduce user productivity and acceptance, which lead to higher indirect costs. At the same time, direct costs can explode through additional hotline calls and troubleshooting efforts. As such, they are likely to lead to much higher total cost of ownership in a production environment than more polished equivalents.

Fortunately for open source, licensing is not the only benefit it offers. The very nature of the easily accessible and publicly scrutinized code can also increase reliability and security. The pivotal factor is really the size and dedication of the team creating and refining the software.

Open source projects can often leverage a global community that far exceeds the scale any individual software vendor can dedicate to development. If they are willing to invest a significant effort to fixing the code and expanding its functionality, the results of crowdsourcing can be unbeatable.

A large development effort can mean faster roll-out of new functionality. The very fact that the source is publicly visible also exposes it to in-depth scrutiny. With enough experts involved, it is easier to find any significant vulnerability and fix it immediately rather than trying to keep it secret. Similarly, open-source software goes through a wider peer-review than proprietary software, which adds to its maturity and lays the foundation for high reliability.

Furthermore, open source yields benefits in terms of flexibility for the end customers. If the software doesn't fulfill all the requirements out-of-the-box, they can customize it or extend the foundation in order to plug in other services or write their own extensions. In many cases, they will also make these modifications available to the community thereby again increasing the pace of development.

ASSESS

This doesn't mean that open source is without any drawbacks. The lack of accountability in a community-driven program constitutes a significant risk. It can be difficult to find anybody who will accept responsibility if something doesn't work and support can hinge on the whim and other priorities of good-natured developers. It is possible to reduce these concerns by entering into a business arrangement with a distributor or other open-source specialist. However, open source is really a mindset. Unless an organization is comfortable with the general approach, they may be better off with the well-defined agreements common to commercial software.

This book mainly targets readers who gravitate toward open-source, private implementations of cloud computing at the infrastructure layer for some of the reasons outlined above. But even this choice doesn't lead unambiguously to OpenStack. There are still other options that merit consideration.

Open-Source Cloud Landscape

To protect customer investment and reduce the risk of lock-in, there is a strong and growing demand for convergence and many standards bodies have tackled cloud computing from varying perspectives. The best-known initiatives have concentrated on IaaS, but are gradually adding functionality that qualifies as PaaS. At a high level, they have adopted two different approaches:

Eucalyptus, CloudStack and OpenNebula strive for compatibility with AWS and thereby facilitate hybrid clouds with Amazon. The choice of Amazon carries with it two complementary benefits. The interfaces are well known and AWS has huge capacity to absorb temporary spikes in resource requirements. However, the fact that Amazon owns the APIs and can choose to develop them in any direction they choose implies that they are not completely open.

OpenStack is a collection of open-source technology projects co-sponsored by a broad consortium of industry leaders that provides an operating platform for orchestrating clouds on a massive scale. It is hypervisor-independent and includes software to provision virtual machines on standard hardware. It also provides a distributed object store. Other features include a scheduler, network controller and authentication manager.

We will look at each of these first three a little more closely.

Eucalyptus

Eucalyptus (Elastic Utility Computing Architecture for Linking Your Programs To Useful Systems) is a software platform implementing private and hybrid IaaS compatible with the Amazon EC2 and S3 services. The software, sponsored by Eucalyptus Systems, also implements support for VMware, Xen and KVM hypervisors.

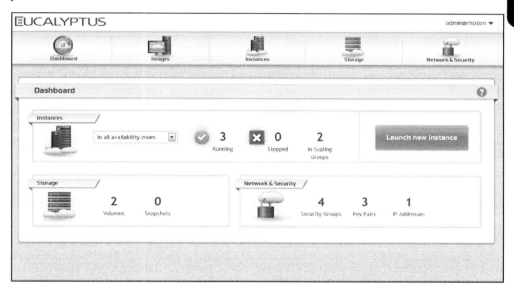

Figure 4-1: Eucalyptus Dashboard

The platform can be used to build clusters in a private cloud with configurable scheduling policies and SLAs. Eucalyptus supports the most popular Linux distributions including Ubuntu, Red Hat Enterprise Linux (RHEL), CentOS, SUSE Linux Enterprise Server (SLES), openSUSE, Debian and Fedora as well as Microsoft Windows images.

The platform is modularized to support multiple interfaces simultaneously with internal process communications via REST/SOAP and WS-Security. A single user interface administers resources (compute, network, and storage) available in Eucalyptus-based private clouds and public resources available externally.

Eucalyptus exports APIs via a modular web-services-based architecture. In addition to the Amazon Web Services (AWS) API, Eucalyptus provides Euca2ools a set of command line tools that can interact internally between private cloud installations and externally with public cloud offerings, including Amazon EC2.

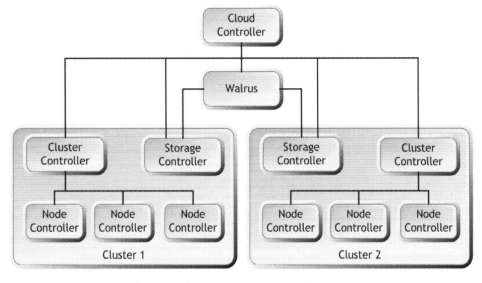

Figure 4-2: Eucalyptus Architecture

The system is based on five independent high-level components (Figure 4-2): Cloud Controller (CLC), Cluster Controller (CC), Walrus, Storage Controller (SC) and Node Controller (NC).

- Cloud Controller (CLC) manages virtualized resources (servers, network, and storage) with a web-based user interface and Amazon EC2 API.

- Walrus is scalable storage compatible with Amazon's S3 (a get/put interface for buckets and objects), for persistent storage and access control of user data including virtual machine images.

- Cluster Controller (CC) controls execution of virtual machines (VMs) and manages the virtual networking internally between VMs as well as between VMs and external users.

- Storage Controller (SC) provides block-level network storage modeled on Amazon Elastic Block Storage (EBS) that can be dynamically attached by VMs.

- Node Controller (NC) controls VM activities, including the execution, inspection, and termination of VM instances.

Each is implemented as a stand-alone web service with a WSDL (Web Services Description Language) document that describes its interface.

CloudStack

CloudStack is another open source cloud computing software platform, supporting common hypervisors such as XenServer, KVM and vSphere for virtualization. It is mostly written in Java with some elements, like CloudMonkey (its command-line utility), in Python.

The software was initially developed by Cloud.com which was acquired by Citrix in 2011. It had been made available under the GNU General Public License, version 3 (GPLv3), but after the acquisition, Citrix changed the license to the Apache License version 2.

The solution is a turn-key stack for running public, private, hybrid cloud. It can be scaled for carrier-grade needs but is also in use by several large companies, including Zynga.

Similar in many ways to Eucalyptus, it implements an extensible architecture that supports the Amazon EC2 and S3 APIs. In fact some of the Eucalyptus tools should work with CloudStack. Additionally it has its own API, which implements the vCloud API.

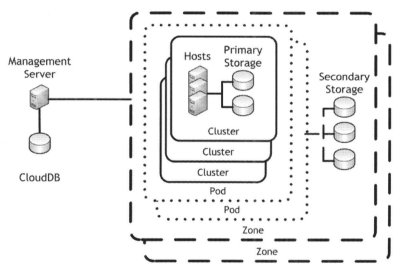

Figure 4-3: CloudStack Deployment

To understand the topology of a CloudStack deployment it is important to be aware of the three-level container structure for host machines (Figure 4-3). Individual hosts are grouped into a server pool that may be managed by XenServer, vCenter or KVM/libvirt. These hosts share their primary storage via a Storage Area Network (SAN), Network Attached Storage or Direct Attached Storage (DAS) using technologies such as LVM, iSCSI and Ceph.

One or more clusters can also be logically grouped together into a pod, which might be physically implemented as a rack or aisle in the data center. The pods, in turn, can be joined together a zone, which is typically a complete data center or a physically isolated location with a dedicated power and network connection.

Zones also host secondary storage that can be shared by all its hosts and which is used to store common templates and disk images. In addition to NFS, secondary storage supports GlusterFS and OpenStack Swift.

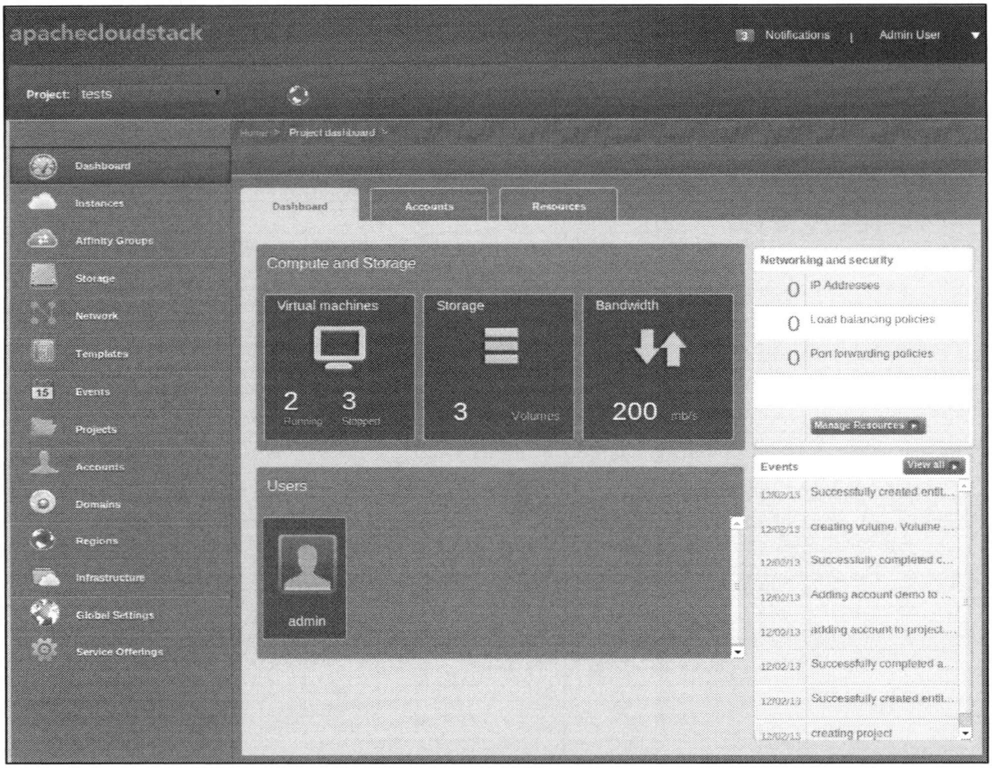

Figure 4-4: CloudStack Dashboard

CloudStack is designed to be relatively easy to implement. In addition to an administrative dashboard and self-service portal (Figure 4-4), which are almost universal in cloud implementations, the initial installation provides a wizard to set up and deploy a basic configuration. The solution also includes some more advanced features, such as load balancers, firewalls, identity management and metering.

OpenNebula

One other open-source cloud platform that receives less attention, but is also a strong offering is OpenNebula. It is most entrenched in scientific communities, where it is being used for research by FermiLab, the European Space Agency and others.

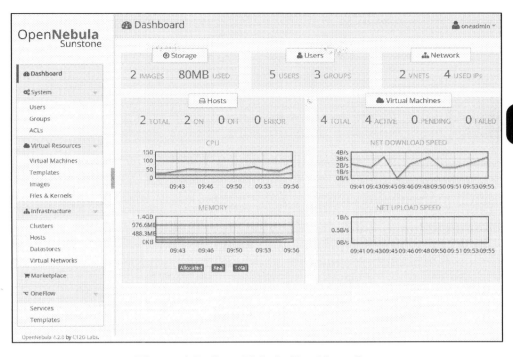

ASSESS

Figure 4-5: OpenNebula Dashboard

Most of the functions are very similar to the other cloud platforms we have seen and will look at in more detail for OpenStack in this book. Its dashboard (Figure 4-5) offers an administrative view for user management with authentication based on SSH, X.509 and LDAP and infrastructure management to assign the physical machines and configure the underlying networks.

Users have the ability to launch virtual instances from images, which may be based on templates. And they can manage data using various storage technologies, such as Ceph, LVM and iSCSI. Although it can be used for any general-purpose workloads, the approach is particularly appealing for supercomputing and high-performance computing, since it can work on a combination of physical and virtual resources and facilitates integration with common job management systems, such as Torque and Open Grid Engine.

Find the Best Fit

We will look at the components and architecture of OpenStack in more detail in the coming chapters, but for now let's just say that it is not that dissimilar to Eucalyptus, CloudStack or OpenNebula. With so many options available, making the selection is not an easy task. In some cases, a feature analysis will lead to a clear favorite. But in many situations, there will be no clear winner.

Most organizations could probably implement any one of those three to satisfy their current requirements. OpenStack's clearest differentiation is its long-term trajectory. It is an excellent example of a project carried forward by a very large open-source community. With over a hundred members including technology leaders like IBM and HP and cloud services pioneers, such as Rackspace, the consortium is unparalleled as an open-source cloud service.

As such, OpenStack can potentially enjoy many of the benefits of open source, such as improved reliability, security and speed of development. Compared to historical infrastructure services that were not much more than a hypervisor, OpenStack is a relatively complete offering including storage, provisioning, identity management and self-service administration.

The fact that it is widely endorsed and adopted also helps to address one of the biggest concerns around cloud computing: vendor lock-in. Cloud providers, such as Rackspace, HP Cloud and many others, offer standard interfaces so that customers can freely move their deployments between providers as well as between internal implementations and services.

Gaps

This is not to say that OpenStack is entirely complete and addresses every conceivable need. Probably the biggest concern is its maturity. It is a relatively new effort that has undertaken a huge challenge.

As such, it is not quite as polished as some commercial offerings, like Amazon Web Services, VMware vCloud or Microsoft Azure. Some would claim that it also trails behind CloudStack in this respect. It takes more effort to deploy and manage than these other services. And one could argue that the overall reliability is still work in progress.

At the same time, there is also the fact that this is an infrastructure service and many organizations are looking for a platform or software service. This doesn't automatically exclude OpenStack but does mean that there would be a need to extend it with additional software.

For example, it is possible to build an open-source PaaS by layering Stackato on top of OpenStack, or more generally by creating a run-time environment with a web server and open-source tools supporting the programming languages of choice.

SaaS is much more specific to the actual services that are required. Someone who needs a CRM solution might add SugarCRM for sales-force automation, marketing campaigns and customer support as well as collaboration and reporting functionality. For a Content Management System they might choose WordPress, Joomla or Drupal. There are also open-source ERP OpenERP, Openbravo, ADempiere) and HRM (SimpleHRM, Orange HRM, Waypoint HR) solutions, all of which can run in an OpenStack environment.

In summary, OpenStack is unlikely to ever yield a complete solution. But it can be a component of many solutions to any common problem.

Use case for OpenStack

Given that the hurdles for OpenStack adoption are substantial, it won't be an automatic choice for many businesses. There are three factors that influence how well it will match an organization's requirements.

ASSESS

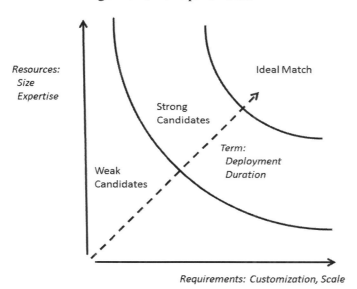

Figure 4-6: OpenStack Match Criteria

The first consideration is the capability of the team responsible for designing and deploying the cloud infrastructure. This is both a function of size (e.g. budget and number of employees) and expertise (historic focus of this team and the skills of its members). A large group that has considerable experience with infrastructure management as well as the underlying technologies (e.g. Linux, Python, Django) will find it much easier to adopt OpenStack and resolve any issues they have in deploying, operating or extending the environment.

Another consideration is the set of requirements. Someone with relatively simple and modest needs can probably find a commercial solution that fits the bill. On the other hand, an organization with advanced requirements will almost invariably need to add some functionality themselves. Open-source is extensible almost by definition. By providing the results back to the community, users may even be able to share some of the development and support effort.

The scale of the implementation is also an important requirement, particularly from a financial perspective. The larger the deployment, the more significant the variable costs become with respect to the fixed costs. As the installation grows,

ASSESS

the licensing fees are likely to become a major element of the marginal costs. At the same time, the fixed costs associated with designing and bootstrapping the new technology will carry less relative weight.

The third axis to consider is time. OpenStack is rapidly maturing and its industry acceptance seems to be growing. What this means is that for projects with a short time frame, both in terms of how soon they need to be deployed and how long they are likely to remain in production, OpenStack might not necessarily be the best fit. On the other hand, solutions that won't launch for years and may need to run indefinitely will benefit from both the increased stability and broader adoption of the future. Over time, benefits will increase while the costs decrease.

Taking these factors into consideration, it is natural to find that most early adoption is from top-tier service providers and some large enterprises. Some software vendors may also consider it as a means of offering a packaged infrastructure solution. These organizations have the resources to overcome any short-term obstacles in deploying OpenStack and they have the large-scale workloads to justify the investment.

There is a good match for service providers at all tiers once the software matures to a point where they can deploy and manage it without investing heavily in specialized expertise. Over time, we can expect the value proposition to become more compelling for smaller and less sophisticated customers.

Enterprises may trail in internal implementation initially, but as they adopt services from OpenStack cloud service providers, they will become more familiar with the interfaces and its administration. They will also find it attractive that by deploying a private cloud based on the same technology, they will be able to reduce provider lock-in and possibly evolve to a hybrid cloud that facilitates cloudbursting and other promising forms of tapping the potential of standardized services. Organizations that are looking for a scalable, long-term strategy may find that OpenStack is their best choice.

Practical Recommendations

The value proposition for an open-source private infrastructure service in the enterprise is rapidly evolving. It is most compelling for organizations with complex requirements and sophisticated capabilities, but as the technologies mature, we can expect smaller businesses to take advantage of the same tools.

There is no riveting technical difference between OpenStack and similar projects, such as Eucalyptus, CloudStack or OpenNebula. Each deserves individual, but not necessarily equal, consideration. OpenStack currently has the most industry attention and is evolving most quickly making its future trajectory very appealing. It would be foolish to ignore it in defining any long-term technical strategy.

ASSESS

Initiate

The first step in getting started is to construct a clear picture of how the system should work. This means getting the system working in a pilot scenario with a minimum set of standard components. But you also need to make sure that you will eventually be able to address your requirements and integrate with your legacy environment. You might need more complex topologies or you may need to create linkages to additional components or ecosystems.

Chapter 5

Construct the Framework

INITIATE

Now that we have covered the high-level functions of a cloud infrastructure and compared OpenStack to other industry offerings, it is time to take a closer look at what it is. You already know that OpenStack is a collection of open-source technology projects co-sponsored by a broad group of industry leaders.

Their objective is to develop an operating platform for orchestrating clouds on a massive scale. The implementation includes hypervisor-independent software to provision virtual machines on standard hardware. Additionally, there is a distributed object store and a wide range of optional functionality including a network controller, authentication manager, management dashboard and block storage.

Note that OpenStack is an abstraction layer that leverages many other tools and services, which it integrates into one cohesive environment. In other words, the value proposition is not the individual functions that OpenStack offers. You can accomplish most of them directly with the underlying technologies. But you would need to familiarize yourself with these applications and then figure out how to set them up, integrate them and manage them. OpenStack uses a plug-in architecture that standardizes the human interfaces and simplifies deployment and management while, at the same time, offering an easily extensible set of technical implementation options.

Even if the installation process is largely automated, we need to pull together all the elements to make the system work. So it is useful to understand the structure. To gain a better understanding of its architecture, we need to look at each of the individual components that it includes. One way to begin is with some historical perspective on how the project has evolved.

Historical Perspective

OpenStack was initiated by Rackspace Cloud and NASA in 2010 by integrating code from NASA's Nebula platform as well as Rackspace's Cloud Files platform. The first core modules were built on these technologies and were called Compute and Object Storage, but are more commonly referred to by their codenames Nova and Swift, respectively.

One of the most exciting things about OpenStack is that it continues to grow dramatically and quickly with often two or more releases per year. As a result, much of the information available on the technology is soon out-of-date, so it is important to keep straight which versions any documentation describes.

INITIATE

OpenStack uses a YYYY.N notation to designate its releases based on both the year of release and the major version of the release that year. For example, the first release of 2011 (Bexar) had the 2011.1 version number, while the next release (Cactus) was labelled 2011.2. Minor releases extend the dot notation further (e.g. 2011.3.1).

Developers often refer to the release by its codename, which is assigned alphabetically. Austin was the first major release, followed by Bexar, Cactus, Diablo, etc. These codes are chosen by popular vote at the OpenStack design summits and generally identify geographical entities near the location of the summit.

INITIATE

Release Name	Number	Date
Austin	2010.1	2010-10-21
Bexar	2011.1	2011-02-03
Cactus	2011.2	2011-04-15
Diablo	2011.3	2011-09-22
	2011.3.1	2012-01-19
Essex	2012.1	2012-04-05
	2012.1.1	2012-06-22
	2012.1.2	2012-08-10
	2012.1.3	2012-10-12
Folsom	2012.2	2012-09-27
	2012.2.1	2012-11-29
	2012.2.2	2012-12-13
	2012.2.3	2013-01-31
	2012.2.4	2013-04-11
Grizzly	2013.1	2013-04-04
	2013.1.1	2013-05-09
	2013.1.2	2013-06-06
	2013.1.3	2013-08-08
Havana	2013.2	2013-10-17
	2013.2.1	2013-12-16
Icehouse (Planned)	2014.1	2014-04-17
Juno (Planned)	2014.2	2014

Table 5-1: OpenStack Releases

Each release has incorporated new functionality, added documentation and improved the ease of deployment in an incremental fashion. But the roadmap has also enlarged the number of projects that form part of the initiative.

As mentioned above, the Austin release consisted only of two core projects: OpenStack Compute (Nova) and OpenStack Object Storage (Swift). Bexar complemented these with an Image Service (Glance) that in many ways forms the intersection of compute and storage. The images represent template virtual machines that are stored in OpenStack in order to rapidly launch compute instances on demand.

The Essex release added two more core projects. OpenStack Identity (Keystone) isolated the user management elements previously handled by Nova. And an OpenStack Dashboard (Horizon) was introduced to standardize and simplify the user interface, both for individual tenants and the OpenStack administrators.

Folsom increased the count two further notches. The team decided to split off the networking components (also previously included in Nova) into a separate service, initially called Quantum and later renamed to Neutron. In the same release, a separate team developed an OpenStack Block Storage component, which was branded Cinder.

At the time of writing, Havana is the most recent release. It includes additional functionality for Orchestration (Heat) and Metering (Ceilometer) as well as improvements in the other projects. The developers are now working toward an April 2014 delivery of Icehouse to be followed by a Juno release by the end of the year.

It is worth pointing out that in addition to the public releases, which usually form the basis of the official distributions, there are more frequent milestone releases, on approximately a monthly basis. Since all versions of the code are openly available, it is also possible to obtain the "trunk" release at any given time, which will include all modifications that have been committed and validated.

Keep in mind that the milestone and trunk releases undergo less beta testing than the code in the distros, so you may want to be careful about applying them directly to production. They are mainly useful for exploring the most recent functionality in a test or development environment.

OpenStack Programs

As of the Havana release, this makes seven core services[1]:

- Compute (Nova)
- Networking (Neutron/Quantum)
- Object Storage (Swift)
- Block Storage (Cinder)
- Image Service (Glance)
- Identity Management (Keystone)
- User Interface Dashboard (Horizon)

These are supplemented with two non-core projects:

- Instrumentation (Ceilometer)
- Orchestration (Heat)

We will look at each of these briefly and cover them in more depth in subsequent chapters.

---

[1] You can find the most current list of official programs at: https://wiki.openstack.org/wiki/Programs

OpenStack Compute (Nova) controls the cloud computing fabric (the core component of an infrastructure service). Written in Python, it creates an abstraction layer for virtualizing commodity server resources such as CPU, RAM, NICs and Hard drives, with functions to improve utilization and automation.

Its live Virtual Machine (VM) management has functions to launch, resize, suspend, stop and reboot through integration with a set of supported hypervisors. There is also a mechanism to cache VM images on compute nodes for faster provisioning. Once the images are running, it is possible to store and manage files programmatically via an API.

Networking (Neutron), formerly called Quantum, includes the capability to manage Local Area Networks (LANs) with capabilities for VLAN, DHCP and IPv6. Users can define networks, subnets and routers to configure their internal topology and then allocate IP addresses and VLANs to these networks. Floating IP addresses allow users to assign (and re-assign) fixed external IP addresses to the VMs.

INITIATE

OpenStack Identity (Keystone) manages a directory of users and provides a catalog of OpenStack services. Its purpose is to expose a central authentication mechanism across all OpenStack components. Rather than providing the authentication itself, it can integrate with a variety of other directory services, such as PAM, LDAP or OAuth. Through these plug-ins, it is able to facilitate multiple forms of authentication ranging from simple username/password credentials to sophisticated multi-factor systems.

OpenStack Identity makes it possible for administrators to configure centralized policies that apply across users and systems. They can create projects and users assign them to administrative domains and define role-based resource permissions. A catalog contains a list of all of the deployed services in a single registry. Users and tools can retrieve a list of the services they can access either through programmatic requests or by logging into the dashboard, which they can also use to create resources and assign them to their account.

OpenStack Object Storage (Swift) is based on the Rackspace Cloud Files product and is a redundant storage system ideal for scale-out storage. Swift is a distributed storage system for primarily static data, such as virtual machine images, backups and archives. The software writes files and other objects to a set of disk drives that can be distributed on multiple servers around one or more datacenters. This ensures data replication and integrity across the cluster.

OpenStack takes responsibility for data replication and distribution across the devices in its pool. So, users can employ commodity hard drives and servers rather than more expensive equipment. In the event of a component failure, Open-Stack is able to replenish the content from other active systems to new cluster members. The architecture also enables horizontal scalability since it is easy to extend storage clusters with additional servers as required.

INITIATE

OpenStack Block Storage (Cinder) manages block-level storage used by compute instances. Block storage lends itself well to scenarios with strict performance constraints, such as databases and file systems.

The most common storage back-ends to use with Cinder are standard Linux volumes, but there are also plugins for other platforms including Ceph, NetApp, Nexenta and SolidFire. Cloud users can manage their storage requirements through the dashboard. The system provides interfaces to create, attach and detach block devices from/to servers. It is also possible to back up Cinder volumes with the snapshot capability.

OpenStack Image Service (Glance) provides support for virtual machine images, primarily including the system disks to be used in launching virtual machine instances. In addition to discovery, registration and activation services, it has capabilities for snapshots and backups.

Glance images can function as templates to roll out new servers quickly and consistently. The API server exposes a REST interface with which users can list and fetch virtual disk images that are assigned to an extensible set of back-end stores, including OpenStack Object Storage.

Users can provide both private and public images to the service in a variety of formats, including: VHD (Hyper-V), VDI (VirtualBox), VMDK (VMWare), qcow2 (Qemu/KVM) and OVF (Open Virtualization Format). There are functions to register new virtual disk images, query for information on publicly available disk images, and stream virtual disk images.

OpenStack Metering (Ceilometer) is a mechanism for centralized collection of metering and monitoring data. It delivers a single point of contact for billing systems to obtain all the usage information they need across the suite of OpenStack components. It supports an extensible set of counters that are both traceable and auditable.

OpenStack Orchestration (Heat) is a template-based orchestration engine for OpenStack. It allows developers to define application deployment patterns that orchestrate composite cloud applications via a REST API. The templates can accommodate most OpenStack resource types (e.g. Nova instances and floating IP address ranges, Cinder volumes, Keystone users). There are also capabilities for advanced functionality including high availability, auto-scaling and nested stacks.

High-level Interrelationships

A typical OpenStack implementation will integrate most, if not all of the projects leading to a highly interconnected system (Figure 5-1).

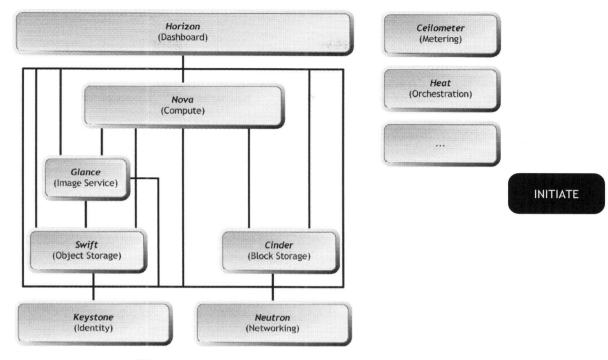

Figure 5-1: OpenStack Architecture

Three elements interact with all the components in the system. Horizon is the graphical user interface that administrators can most easily use to manage all the projects. Keystone handles the management of authorized users and Neutron defines the networks that provide connectivity between the components.

Nova can arguably be considered the heart of OpenStack. It handles the orchestration of workloads. Its compute instances usually require some form of persistent storage which can be either block-based (Cinder) or object-based (Swift). Nova also requires an image in order to launch an instance. Glance handles this request, whereby it can optionally use Swift as its storage backend.

The OpenStack architecture has endeavored to make each of the services as independent as possible. This gives users the option to deploy only a subset of the functionality and integrate it with other systems and technologies that offer similar or complementary functions.

Nonetheless, this independence shouldn't mask the fact that a fully functional private cloud is likely to require virtually all the functionality in order to operate smoothly. And the elements will need to be tightly integrated.

As mentioned above, two new projects were added in the Havana release that many had been looking forward to for some time: OpenStack Metering (Ceilometer) and OpenStack Orchestration (Heat). These are optional components.

So, none of the core modules are dependent on them. However, they are able to orchestrate and measure any of the other software packages as needed.

Roadmap

In understanding OpenStack, it is important to keep in mind that the system is still work in progress. It is possible to implement it in its current form. But there is a lot more coming down the line. These projects are first developed externally (usually in Stackforge). They are then proposed, incubated, and may eventually be integrated in the OpenStack core.

As with any product or technology, the roadmap is very fluid. Some of the services will change names, others will take on a different focus and a few may abort or merge with other initiatives. So you wouldn't want to stake your OpenStack strategy on any of this functionality. But it is still worthwhile to have a good understanding of what else is happening, so you can understand the references to these services and have some insight into the direction of OpenStack as a whole.

OpenStack Database as a Service (Trove)

Trove is Database as a Service for OpenStack. It has also gone by the name of Red Dwarf. The idea is to allow users to leverage the features of a relational database without the administrative overhead. Cloud users can provision and manage multiple database instances as needed.

The initial scope is automation of complex administrative tasks including deployment, configuration, patching, backups, restores, and monitoring while ensuring resource allocation and efficient performance. By default, it has been developed to use MySQL but the design is open to additional database implementations.

OpenStack Data Processing (Savanna)

For those who have more advanced database needs than SQL can handle, the Savanna service provides a means to elastically provision a Hadoop cluster on top of OpenStack. In a sense, it is similar to Heat but is specifically tailored to Hadoop. As such it has semantics for the Hadoop processes and the notion of Hadoop clusters. It functions as an abstraction layer that can accommodate multiple installation engines with a pluggable architecture.

The user can fill in relevant parameters, such as Hadoop version, cluster topology and node hardware details upon which Savanna deploys the cluster automatically and subsequently allows the user to scale the running cluster or add and remove nodes as needed.

OpenStack Bare Metal (Ironic)

Ironic is a hypervisor driver for OpenStack that facilitates the provisioning of bare metal machines. It uses common technologies such as PXE boot and IPMI to cover a wide range of hardware and thereby allows OpenStack to manage physical, in addition to virtual, machines.

In the same way that typical hypervisors offer functions to create virtual machines, load the operating system and manage power state, Ironic exposes functions for managing the physical hardware.

OpenStack on OpenStack (TripleO)

One service that is leaning heavily on Ironic is OpenStack on OpenStack (TripleO). The objective of TripleO is to manage OpenStack infrastructure as an OpenStack workload by layering the technology in two tiers called the undercloud and overcloud.

The result is a relatively static undercloud deployed on bare metal along with a versatile overcloud that can be automatically installed, upgraded and operated.

OpenStack Data Center as a Service (Tuskar)

Tuskar is another initiative aimed at automating the whole data center. Administrators can classify the hardware into groups that allow for elastic expansion according to demand. Tuskar components also assist with SLA governance, performance monitoring, health statistics, usage metrics, capacity planning and hardware procurement decisions.

OpenStack Integration Test Suite (Tempest)

Tempest is a series of tools to run functional integration tests against OpenStack installations. It is used as a gate on upstream commits to OpenStack, but it is designed so that anyone should be able to use it to validate their OpenStack deployment, whether it is the trunk release pulled from source or a production implementation of any size.

Tempest is based on the unittest2 framework using nose test runner. A configuration file describes the test environment and specifies a series of tests. The framework then makes the corresponding API calls against OpenStack service endpoints and validates the responses from the endpoints.

OpenStack DNS as a Service (Designate)

Designate is a DNS as-a-service project, formerly called Moniker. Given that users frequently operate their own virtual networking within an OpenStack deployment, they may also have the need for tenant-specific namespaces.

Designate provides an abstraction layer for creating, updating and deleting DNS data through its REST API. It is multi-tenant, integrated with Keystone for authentication and has a framework in place to integrate with Nova and Neutron notifications for auto-generated records.

It should be possible to plug in any DNS server that the organization uses, but only PowerDNS and Bind9 currently have support out of the box.

OpenStack Queuing and Notification Service (Marconi)

There is also work on an OpenStack Queuing and Notification Service (named Marconi) that would expose web-scale message queuing and pub-sub capabilities to the tenants, similar to Amazon SQS and SNS.

Large and complex applications require a web-scale message queuing service to support the asynchronous and distributed nature of cloud-based applications. Marconi is designed to fill this need with both producer-consumer and publish-subscribe usage models. It defines a REST API and gives users the option to customize it to achieve a wide range of performance, durability, availability, and efficiency goals.

Some of the supported use cases include:

- Distribute tasks among multiple workers (transactional job queues)
- Forward events to data collectors (transactional event queues)
- Publish events to any number of subscribers (pub-sub)
- Send commands to one or more agents (point-to-point or pub-sub)
- Request an action or get information from an agent (RPC)

OpenStack Common Libraries (Oslo)

Oslo is primarily an internal service, so it is not something that an OpenStack user is likely to see, but you will find references to it in the documentation. It is an effort to facilitate development and improve software quality. Its objective is to maximize code re-use across OpenStack services by assembling a set of Python libraries containing general-purpose code. The APIs should reflect a rough consensus across the project on the requirements and design for that use case.

Modules, Connections and Interfaces

In the upcoming chapters, we will look at the individual OpenStack services in a little more detail including their architecture and components. But before we get into the specifics, it's worth becoming familiar with the typical design of the elements.

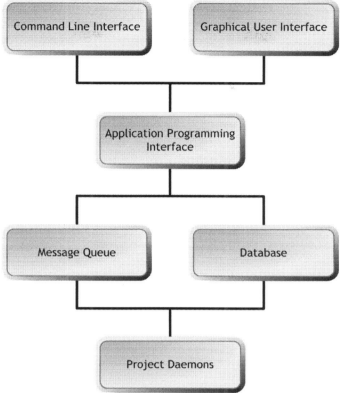

Figure 5-2: OpenStack Architectural Paradigm

As you can see in Figure 5-2, there are actually three interfaces to most services. The most user-friendly is the graphical user interface that is exposed as elements on the OpenStack Dashboard (Horizon). There is also a command line interface that is useful for administrators working at the console and for incorporation into shell scripts.

Both of these call the application programming interface internally. End users will not typically use the API directly, but it is the primary interface for interaction between services. Similarly, external tools (such as cloud brokering platforms like Rightscale and Enstratius) will usually write directly to the APIs. The API is HTTP-based and supports both JSON and XML payloads. REST/JSON is generally the first choice for new applications but many enterprise tools are still based on XML and require support for compatibility.

The programming interface then converts the requests to data, which it places on the message queue, and stores any persistent configuration information in the database. Note that these are internal components needed for OpenStack operation and not to be confused with the services in the previous section (e.g. Marconi or Trove) intended for tenant workloads.

INITIATE

The default queue is RabbitMQ but it is also possible to use alternatives. For example, Red Hat uses QPID, while Cloudscaling implements ZeroMQ. The database can be implemented with SQLlite, MySQL, PostgreSQL or any other back end supported by SQLalchemy.

The actual service-specific work is executed in daemons. These fetch their tasks from the message queue and interact with the database for any supplementary configuration information. Most daemons use the Paste (python) library with WSGI middleware that is configured through *-paste.ini files.

Practical Recommendations

INITIATE

New OpenStack projects appear frequently – some would argue too frequently. It is easy to be overwhelmed by what is going on and to lose sight of the forest for the trees.

To get started, you are well advised to focus on the core functionality and make sure you understand the part each component plays in the overall solution. Every application will need compute, storage and networking. Once you have a good grasp of how the primitives work, the other services will begin to fall into place.

Chapter 6

Get Started

INITIATE

There was a time, not so long ago, when getting started with OpenStack was very challenging. Unless you were blessed with a seasoned Linux administrator, an experienced Python programmer and a lot of patience, it was difficult to get the software up and running just to try out the most basic of operations.

Fortunately, we've come a long way from there. There are several options for familiarizing yourself with the project, such as:

- Hosted Service – you can try one of the many OpenStack public clouds in production
- Automated Setup – you can install a preconfigured environment
- Manual Installation – you can install the tools manually

Which one you choose is largely a function of your objective. If you just want to see the user components, then a hosted service is the easiest and quickest option. In order to see the whole installation, including administrative components, you would need to install the software, which is also not that difficult with some of the preconfigured packages.

However, if you have very specific requirements that don't form part of the standard builds, such as integration with third-party solutions, then you may need to install the components yourself. This is certainly the most difficult option, so you may want to try one of the other two as an interim step until you are at least familiar with the technology.

Hosted Service

For a quick user-based view of OpenStack, you can register an account with one of the public clouds in production across the world, including Rackspace, HP Cloud (Figure 6-1), Cloudwatt, DreamCompute, eNocloud, and Ulticloud. You will need to provide a credit card, but some of them offer limited trial accounts for free or at reduced rates.

INITIATE

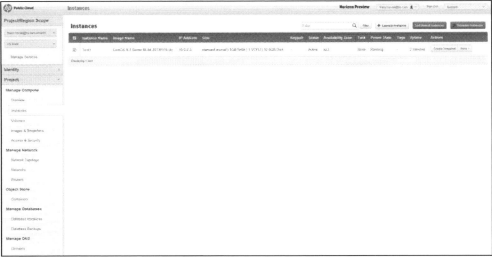

Figure 6-1: HP Cloud

As mentioned above, you will only have access to the user operations and will have no visibility of the underlying physical infrastructure. This also means that you cannot use the command line - you are limited to the graphical user interface and some functions of the API. You may also only see a subset of the full OpenStack services. For instance you will notice that the Rackspace interface (Figure 6-2) is quite different from the other screenshots in this book, which is because Rackspace doesn't use the Horizon interface although the operation of the system is still very similar.

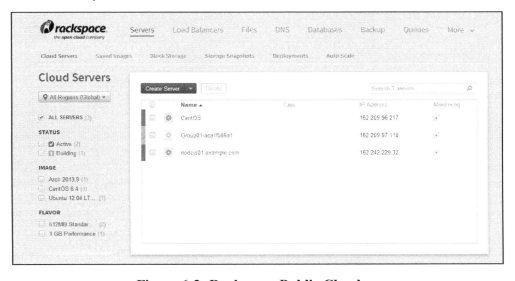

Figure 6-2: Rackspace Public Cloud

On the plus side, the public implementations may have other value-add functions. And they definitely have the benefit that they require no planning, no installation and entail no ongoing management and operations.

Hardware Requirements

If you want to run the software yourself, then you will need to have access to physical resources where you can install it. The hardware requirements will vary according to the load. If you just want to see OpenStack in operation or perform a functional demo, you can run it in a VM on a laptop with 8GB of RAM or even less with enough patience. But once your requirements become more significant, you will want to scale up and out.

In terms of scaling out, there are two directions to consider: separating the components and replicating them.

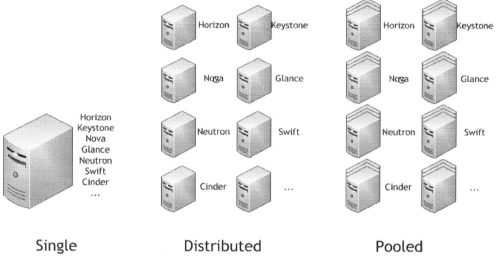

Figure 6-3: Scaling Out

You can move some of the components onto their own dedicated hardware, thereby distributing the load along functional boundaries. But you can also put any given service onto multiple servers creating resource pools within each function. Figure 6-3 illustrates this concept in its extreme form, which is a little simplistic. You probably want to start replicating before you put each module on a dedicated server.

In practice, the design usually includes one or more controller nodes and as many compute nodes as needed to handle the anticipated workload. They may be front-ended by a load balancer and back-ended with storage (Figure 6-4).

INITIATE

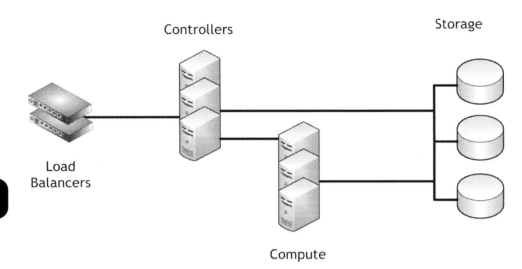

Figure 6-4: Controller-Compute Topology

This is just one example of how to distribute the OpenStack components. You could also use dedicated servers for other services, such as storage or networking. However, remember that OpenStack is primarily an abstraction layer. It shouldn't consume a large portion of the resources itself. It is really the workloads (compute and storage) that will require the bulk of resources. Bearing this caveat in mind, let's take a look at how the individual items might look.

Controller

The controller hosts the cross-service components, mainly the database and message queue. Additionally, it may include any of the services that don't have a dedicated server – which means all services other than compute and perhaps storage.

To ensure high availability, it is wise to have at least two, and ideally three, instances of the controller node. To distribute traffic evenly between the controllers, you can add a set of load balancers. These can be hardware appliances or software implementations (e.g. HAproxy) as we shall see in more detail in Chapter 20.

Compute

The number of compute nodes will depend directly on the load they are expected to process. You can make a quick estimate by multiplying the number of virtual machines with their average CPU and memory requirements. But you will need to make some adjustments for better accuracy.

On the one hand, the hypervisors will generate some overhead, typically in the range of 5%-10%, so you must add this buffer to the projection. However, you can also reduce the requirements my overcommitting processors and memory.

The overcommit rate is the ratio of virtual to physical resources. These are based on the fact that virtual machines are not always using all of their allocated resources. By default, OpenStack Compute uses a CPU allocation ration of 16 and a RAM allocation ration of 1.5. This means that a host with four physical cores and 4GB of physical RAM can run virtual machines with a total of 64 virtual cores and 6GB of virtual RAM concurrently. You may need to adjust these figures to your actual workloads, in which case you would also want to revise the calculations for your capacity planning.

INITIATE

OpenStack relies on a 64-bit x86 architecture, but otherwise it is designed for commodity hardware, so the minimal system requirements are modest. One important consideration for the Compute nodes is that they must support the Intel 64 or AMD64 CPU extensions, and enable the AMD-V or Intel VT hardware virtualization extensions.

Storage

It is a good idea to separate storage devices from the rest of the infrastructure for the simple reason that it makes the compute nodes and controllers stateless and therefore easier to load-balance.

This doesn't necessarily mean all the storage services are consolidated in separate systems. They could be on a network file system or storage area network. On the other hand, you could very well also run some of the OpenStack components (Swift, Cinder, Glance) on dedicated systems, too.

The key design considerations for storage will be resilience and performance. For the former, you need a configuration that is redundant and able to survive both localized component failures as well as natural disasters that precipitate the outage of an entire data center. This means ensuring redundancy through replication without compromising the integrity of atomic transactions.

The first element of performance is latency, which is largely a function of data placement. The closer the information is to the compute services, the faster it can be read. You can also consider specific technologies to improve performance, such as RAID-5 / RAID-10 for large sequential reads/writes, or SSDs for high IOPS requirements that you might have with Glance or with Swift Account and Container servers.

You also need to consider how you will scale out the infrastructure to meet your anticipated maximum needs. Rackspace puts up to ninety 3TB SATA hard disks on each Swift Object server, so it is possible for a large service provider to allocate quite a lot of capacity, but most organizations will be able to make do with much less.

INITIATE

Networking

There is considerable management and security benefit in isolating traffic onto up to four separate physical networks. This means the individual machines should have four NICs. But you will also need to make sure you have the infrastructure in place to connect the systems.

This would mean switches with 4 ports per server (ideally running with 10 Gbps Ethernet) plus high-speed upstream ports (40 Gbps) to the core switches. The OpenStack Networking (Neutron) server can run on the controller, but it is equally possible to deploy it on a separate server. In any case, you need physical network switches between the physical machines.

Bill of Materials

Based on your specific workload requirements, you can develop your own formulas and match them to the hardware catalogs of your preferred vendors. A good reference point is the BoM calculator from Mirantis[1]. It is based on some of the considerations described above and offers some sample product specifications for the chosen hardware vendors based on the user-supplied parameters (Figure 6-5).

---

[1] http://www.mirantis.com/openstack-services/bom-calculator/

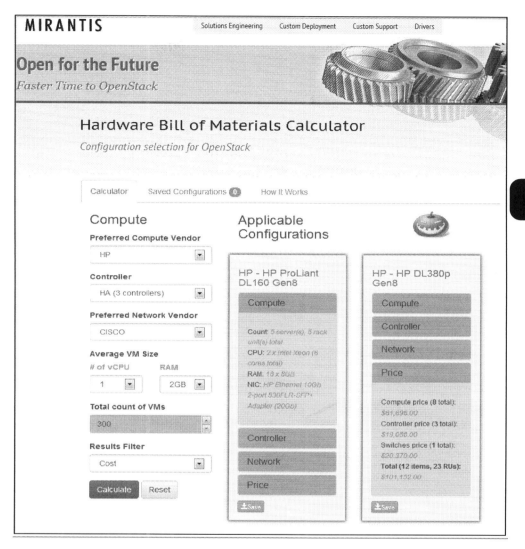

Figure 6-5: Mirantis Hardware Bill of Materials Calculator

Automated Setup

Once you have all the hardware in place, you need to install the software. The most straightforward way to get OpenStack running in your own environment is to use a distribution. OpenStack distributions provide their differentiation through supplementary software, validated configurations, support and documentation. The most important benefit for anyone wanting to get going quickly is that they generally supply automated installation procedures.

Some of the distributions include Cloudscaling, Debian, Fedora, Piston Cloud Computing, Red Hat, SwiftStack, SUSE, Ubuntu and Stackops. If you are just testing the waters, there are options to boot from USB or load the software into a VM. Basically all you need to do is download the distro from the web sites and follow its instructions.

We will just illustrate with a few options.

HP Cloud OS

HP offers a free deployment tool for OpenStack called Cloud OS (Figure 6-6). It allows the user to specify a configuration of physical nodes and uses Crowbar to provision OpenStack on to these systems.

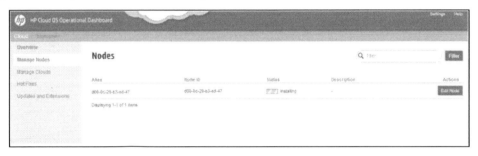

Figure 6-6: HP Cloud OS Operational Dashboard

In addition to OpenStack, Cloud OS includes a number of HP enhancements, such as Eve, Graffiti and Focus. Eve is a TOSCA-based infrastructure topology provisioning service. Graffiti is a resource pool registry and capability tagging service. And Focus is a topology design registry and repository service.

The software is preconfigured with specifications for HP hardware, but it is possible to tailor and add to these as needed.

Red Hat RDO

RDO is a community-supported distribution of OpenStack that runs on Red Hat Enterprise Linux, Fedora, and their derivatives (e.g. CentOS). The three letter name seems like it should be an acronym for something, but according to the Red Hat FAQ, it is not. Regardless, it is a well-crafted installation package that is remarkably easy and quick to use.

In fact, assuming you have a qualifying Linux operating system running, it requires only three commands, which you can find at: openstack.redhat.com/Quickstart

Install the Software repositories:

```
sudo  yum  install  -y  http://rdo.fedorapeople.org/openstack-havana/rdo-
release-havana.rpm
```

Note that you will want to update this command with the most recent release. Look at the RDO documentation for the most recent URL.

Install Packstack Installer:

```
sudo yum install -y openstack-packstack python-netaddr
```

Run Packstack to install OpenStack:

```
packstack --allinone
```

The installer will ask you to enter the root password for each host node. That is really all there is to it unless you want to create a more elaborate environment.

INITIATE

Mirantis Fuel

It's hard to imagine an installation process that is much simpler than RDO, but Mirantis Fuel certainly comes close and has the added benefit that it is very flexible in terms of the configurations it offers. It uses Cobbler for the baremetal installation of the operating system on each system and then leverages Puppet with MCollective to orchestrate the provisioning of the OpenStack components. For those who shy away from the command line, it has the added benefit of a comprehensive GUI and step-by-step configuration using a wizard.

For the simplest configuration, you do need to have VirtualBox, but that is about the only constraint. Fuel is a downloadable ISO along with some VirtualBox scripts. All you really need to do is get them from the Mirantis web site[1], put them in the correct folders and launch the script. It will create a set of VirtualBox machines (one master and three slave nodes).

A wizard will then take you through the process of creating one or more OpenStack environments (Figure 6-7). You can define the cluster with one of two reference architectures (Multi-node, Multi-node with HA). Multi-node in this case, usually means one controller, one compute node and one cinder node, but you can extend or modify the cluster to suit your requirements. The GUI also allows you to specify the network configuration and shows how drive space will be allocated.

---

[1] http://software.mirantis.com/

INITIATE

Figure 6-7: Mirantis Fuel Wizard

The tool will validate configuration for obvious errors (e.g. incompatible network parameters) and then allows you to deploy the systems with the touch of a button. You can use the same console to manage multiple environments if you need to run multiple clusters.

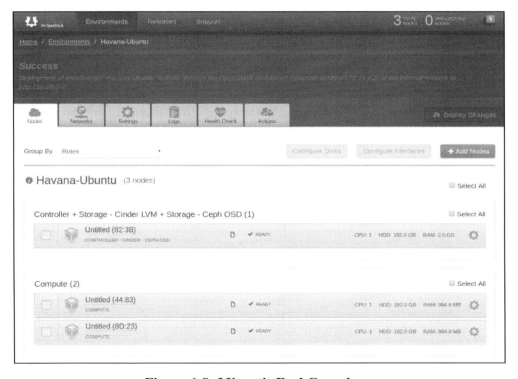

Figure 6-8: Mirantis Fuel Console

Once the systems have been deployed, Fuel allows you to monitor the status of the systems and run proactive health checks to verify that all the components are functioning correctly (Figure 6-8).

The amount of effort it takes to set up your environment will vary according to the complexity of your design, but it is possible to get a simple multi-node configuration running in less than an hour starting from the initial launch of the VirtualBox script.

DevStack

Red Hat RDO and Mirantis Fuel are safe options for launching production-grade services as they have been well tested and typically run on a very stable release of OpenStack. If you are more adventurous and want to see the newest features at the risk of some potential challenges, DevStack may be a good choice for you. And if you are a developer planning on contributing code upstream, then there is really no way around DevStack.

INITIATE

You should have at least elementary Linux admin skills and some familiarity with OpenStack before you try it, but it generally works very well. If all goes well, it should only take a few minutes.

Whether you are running on a physical or virtual machine, install a minimal version of a supported Linux distribution (Ideally Ubuntu LTS, but other versions of Ubuntu, Fedora, CenOS/RHEL should also work) and then download the DevStack source from GitHub:

```
git clone git://github.com/openstack-dev/devstack.git
```

The DevStack repo contains a script that installs OpenStack and templates for configuration files. Just switch to the correct directory and start the install:

```
cd devstack; ./stack.sh
```

That's all there is to it. In some ways, this is the easiest installation of all, but you need to have a solid understanding of OpenStack to make any fundamental changes to the environment since you need to manually edit the configuration files and launch the applicable commands from the console.

If you are going to be doing a lot of DevStack testing, you should consider automating the provisioning of your development environment with Vagrant. You then only need to specify your system attributes (e.g. memory) in a so-called Vagrantfile and Vagrant can take care of provisioning, managing and connecting to the VMs.

For example, you can use these commands to download and set up the base system:

```
vagrant box add precise32 http://files.vagrantup.com/precise32.box
```

```
vagrant init precise32
```

Then edit the configuration and open a shell in the server image:

```
vagrant up && vagrant ssh
```

Once you are in the shell, you can issue the DevStack commands mentioned above. You can find more detailed instructions for using DevStack with Vagrant on Anita Kuno's blog[1] but this gives you the basic idea.

Manual Installation

INITIATE

Your last recourse for installing OpenStack is to load and configure the individual components. We will provide some sample commands but our objective is just to give you a taste for what is involved in manually deploying OpenStack components. This is not an authoritative source for set-by-step instructions which you can find in the official OpenStack documentation.

Declare repository

The full installation procedure will hinge on the desired configuration and will depend on the exact release of OpenStack in question. The instructions will also depend on the distribution and, more specifically, on the package management utility that is selected.

As mentioned above, you will want to look at the installation guide for the authoritative instructions. For the purpose of illustration, below are the primary commands for Ubuntu (and many other Debian derivatives), Red Hat (e.g. RHEL, CentOS, Fedora) and OpenSUSE.

In many cases, it is necessary to declare the repository. So, for example, in the case of zypper, we announce to libzypp with zypper ar.

```
# zypper ar -f
http://download.opensuse.org/repositories/Cloud:/OpenStack:/Grizzly/SLE_11
_SP3/Cloud:OpenStack:Grizzly.repo
```

Nova

We then install the required nova packages on both the controller and compute nodes, and the package management utility should automatically install any dependencies.

Ubuntu

To install Keystone on a Debian-based system, such as Ubuntu:

---

[1] http://anteaya.info/blog/2013/09/01/installing-devstack-with-vagrant/

```
sudo apt-get install nova-novncproxy novnc nova-api nova-ajax-console-
proxy nova-cert nova-conductor nova-consoleauth nova-doc nova-scheduler
nova-network
sudo apt-get install nova-compute
sudo apt-get install glance
```

Red Hat

On Red Hat systems, the commands would be:

```
sudo yum install openstack-nova
sudo yum install openstack-glance
```

OpenSUSE

And on OpenSUSE:

```
sudo zypper install openstack-nova openstack-glance
```

Nova configuration involves several files, but the most important is nova.conf, which is installed in /etc/nova. A default set of options will work fine for a standard installation, but it will be necessary to edit the configuration for any special requirements.

You can find a sample on the OpenStack documentation site[1].

Storage

We then install the required Swift and/or Cinder packages.

Ubuntu

```
sudo apt-get install python-swift
sudo apt-get install swift
sudo apt-get install swift-auth
sudo apt-get install swift-proxy
sudo apt-get install swift-account
sudo apt-get install swift-container
sudo apt-get install swift-object
sudo apt-get install cinder-api
sudo apt-get install cinder-scheduler
sudo apt-get install cinder-volume
```

Red Hat

```
sudo yum install openstack-swift
sudo yum install openstack-swift-proxy
sudo yum install openstack-swift-account
sudo yum install openstack-swift-container
sudo yum install openstack-swift-object
sudo yum install openstack-swift-doc
```

---

[1] http://docs.openstack.org/trunk/openstack-compute/admin/content/sample-nova-configuration-files.html

```
sudo yum install openstack-cinder
sudo yum install openstack-cinder-doc
```

OpenSUSE

```
sudo zypper install openstack-swift
sudo zypper install openstack-swift-auth
sudo zypper install openstack-swift-account
sudo zypper install openstack-swift-container
sudo zypper install openstack-swift-object
sudo zypper install openstack-swift-proxy
sudo zypper install openstack-cinder-api
sudo zypper install openstack-cinder-scheduler
sudo zypper install openstack-cinder-volume
```

INITIATE

Configuring your Object Storage installation involves tailoring the configuration files for each of the four packages:

- account-server.conf
- container-server.conf
- object-server.conf
- proxy-server.conf

The configuration files are installed in /etc/swift/. A default set of options will work fine for a standard installation, but it will be necessary to edit the configuration for any special requirements.

Networking

Next, we move on to the Neutron packages.

Ubuntu

Install neutron-server and the client for accessing the API:

```
sudo apt-get install neutron-server python-neutronclient
```

Install the plugin you will be using

```
sudo apt-get install neutron-plugin-<plugin-name>
```

For example:

```
sudo apt-get install neutron-plugin-openvswitch-agent
```

Red Hat

Similar to Ubuntu you must install both the Neutron server and the plugin, for example:

```
sudo yum install openstack-neutron
sudo yum install openstack-neutron-openvswitch
```

OpenSUSE

```
sudo zypper install openstack-neutron
sudo zypper install openstack-neutron-openvswitch-agent
```

Most plugins require a database to be installed. The Fedora packaging for Open-Stack Networking includes server-setup utility scripts that will take care of the full installation and configuration of the database:

```
sudo neutron-server-setup --plugin openvswitch
```

But it is also possible to configure these manually. For example, on Ubuntu, you can install the database with:

INITIATE

```
sudo apt-get install mysql-server python-mysqldb python-sqlalchemy
```

If there a database is already installed for other OpenStack services, you only need to create a neutron database:

```
mysql -u <user> -p <pass> -e "create database neutron"
```

It is necessary to specify the database in the plugin's configuration file. Find the plugin configuration file in the Neutron plugins folder (e.g., /etc/neutron/plugins/openvswitch/ovs_neutron_plugin.ini) and set the connection string:

```
sql_connection = mysql://<user>:<password>@localhost/neutron?charset=utf8
```

Keystone

We then install the required Keystone packages.

Ubuntu

```
sudo apt-get install keystone
sudo apt-get install python-keystone
sudo apt-get install python-keystoneclient
```

Red Hat

```
sudo yum install openstack-keystone
sudo yum install python-keystone
sudo yum install python-keystoneclient
```

OpenSUSE

```
sudo zypper install openstack-keystone
sudo zypper install python-keystoneclient
```

The primary Keystone configuration file is named keystone.conf and it is located in /etc/keystone/. It identifies all the authentication plugins are specified in the [auth] section.

- methods – lists all the authentication plugin names
- <plugin name> - specify the class for each of the authentication methods

For example:

```
[auth]
methods = password,token,oauth1
password = keystone.auth.plugins.password.Password
token = keystone.auth.plugins.token.Token
oauth1 = keystone.auth.plugins.oauth1.OAuth
```

INITIATE

There is no standard mechanism for the plugin to register its own configuration options but it is common for it to have its own section in the configuration file.

OpenStack Integration Test Suite (Tempest)

Regardless of the deployment mechanism you used, you will probably want to validate that OpenStack installed correctly. If you are just trying it out for yourself, then you may not need to run a comprehensive test suite since you will discover soon enough if something isn't working.

However, if you are getting ready for production or even expect to run a full beta test, you will save time by making sure you have everything set up correctly. One OpenStack service that may help is Tempest. It defines a set of functional integration tests intended to be run against actual OpenStack deployments.

Tempest is actually also used internally to validate any commits to the trunk release.

Logging In

Once the process is complete, you can log in to the OpenStack web interface by pointing your browser at the dashboard on the Horizon node[1]. Most of the interface is intuitive, but we will explore it in more detail in Chapter 13 as well as the relevant service sections.

---

[1] Usually at http://xxx.xxx.xxx.xxx/ or http://xxx.xxx.xxx.xxx/dashboard, where xxx.xxx.xxx.xxx is the IP address of your Horizon node.

Practical Recommendations

If you have never seen OpenStack in operation before, you really need to get some hands-on exposure to it before reading much further. For those who don't want to spend much time on it, a hosted service is your quickest option. But if you have a spare PC or a virtual environment on your laptop, you'll get a much better idea of what OpenStack is by installing the software yourself.

The commands and configuration options may appear daunting at first, but don't let that deter you. Start with a packaged distribution and it should take care of the hard parts, so you can focus on the functions that are available in operation.

INITIATE

Chapter 7

Broaden your Scope

As you just saw, it shouldn't be too difficult to get OpenStack up and running. That is the best way to start. You can always expand later with additional components and more complex topologies, but it is easiest to get a feel for the technology with the default options, core components and a simple network.

Unfortunately, you do need to realize that the easy days will eventually come to an end. Greenfield installation of OpenStack may be able to use default settings, but default installations with simple components are not optimal for scaling or high availability.

In most environments there are also a number of legacy applications that need to be integrated; and default configurations are not likely to be compatible with existing infrastructure and applications. You will want to consider other special requirements such as security and compliance; and suppliers, partners or customers may mandate interfaces with additional/external systems that are based on other technologies.

Some options to consider include more advanced networking technologies, specific configurations, replacing the default plug-ins with vendor-specific alternatives, and potentially even modifying the code. You can take it slowly. The first instance of your production system should focus on the minimum viable configuration. Over time, you can expand this offering and integrate it with the rest of your architecture leading you to the best levels of operational efficiency and sourcing flexibility.

In this chapter, we will look at some of the more common ways for an enterprise to extend a simple installation. Typically this means interoperability with market-leading enterprise technologies from companies like IBM, HP, Microsoft, VMware, Cisco and EMC. It may also involve integrating across data centers and brokering across providers.

Converged Infrastructure

Many companies have now reached a point where a confusing sprawl of IT resources prevents them from maximizing their efficiency and effectively administering their infrastructure. At the same time, the business demands on IT have grown dramatically. The combination of uncontrolled internal growth on the one hand, and more demanding requirements, on the other, make it painfully obvious that there is a need for a more structured approach.

INITIATE

Converged Infrastructure is a new buzzword that promotes the notion of aggregating resources for better utilization and easier management. Instead of architecting each service individually and physically provisioning the resources it requires, the organization creates resource pools that can be used for a variety of applications. The system allocates resources to each application as needed and relinquishes the resources when they are no longer used.

This concept can extend to a variety of components. In the data center, the focus is usually on servers, storage and networks. The servers are actually aggregates of CPU, memory and local storage. Servers also rely on central shared storage, and there is networking equipment that ties these together and allows users to access the services. On top of these primary IT resources, we can also look at floor-space, power and cooling, as well as the physical cables that connect the equipment.

This may sound very familiar to you as it describes almost the same concept as cloud computing, more specifically private cloud computing. As such, you could apply the expression "converged infrastructure" to any kind of virtualized and automated environment including an OpenStack-based cloud.

However, the usage of the term tends to be different. It is usually associated with bundled hardware, software and management that may be available as a single line item from one of the larger technology vendors. It is often based on premium (i.e. not commodity) components, but its value proposition is that it is pre-configured and pre-tested making it easier to install, operate and support.

Since most enterprises are heavily invested with these large technology vendors, there is a strong need to be able to interoperate with these systems. Some of these reference architectures and pre-integrated solutions include:

- IBM PureSystems is a product line of pre-configured components and servers that can host five hypervisors (VMware, Hyper-V, KVM, Xen, PowerVM) and four different operating systems (Windows, Linux, AIX, IBM i) on two different hardware architectures (IBM Power and x86) simultaneously.
- The Cisco Unified Computing System (UCS) is a platform composed of computing hardware, virtualization support, switching fabric, and man-

agement software. Cisco UCS supports several hypervisors including VMware ESX, ESXi, Microsoft Hyper-V, Citrix XenServer. Along with UCS, Cisco offers two preconfigured solutions:

- o FlexPod consists of NetApp FAS storage, Cisco Systems Inc. Unified Computing System (UCS), either VMware or Microsoft Hyper-V, Cisco Nexus switches, and NetApp unified storage systems running Data ONTAP.
- o ExpressPod is a similar but simpler solution targeting customers with smaller workloads and less IT expertise. In order to keep the product affordable, simple to deploy, and easy to manage, it offers two standard and tested configurations with an open ecosystem of infrastructure management software available to streamline management.

INITIATE

- VCE, a joint venture between VMware, Cisco and EMC, offers a set of preconfigured systems called Vblocks:
  - o EMC provides storage and provisioning with VNX, VMAX, Ionix UIM/P.
  - o Cisco provides compute and networking with UCS, Nexus.
  - o VMware provides virtualization with vSphere.
- HP CloudSystem combines the storage, servers, networking and software for an organization's IT department to build complete private, public and hybrid cloud computing environments. It combines the HP Matrix Operating Environment, which manages, monitors and provisions servers for physical and virtual resources and HP Cloud Service Automation software, a set of system management tools used to provide and manage the lifecycle of IT services. The BladeSystem Matrix supports HP ProLiant x64 blades running Microsoft Windows and Linux, and HP Integrity blades running HP-UX.
- Dell Active System Portfolio includes PowerEdge Blade chassis, blade servers as well as rack servers along with EqualLogic and Compellent storage along with Dell Active System Manager, which centrally manages the various solution elements, automating workload delivery and end-to-end converged infrastructure management.
- Oracle Exalogic is a computer appliance with a software suite. All servers have an installed cluster configuration of Oracle WebLogic Server and Oracle Coherence, an in-memory distributed data grid. To run Java applications on a machine there is a choice of HotSpot or JRockit. Management of the appliance is available in the Oracle Enterprise Manager

toolset, which is also pre-installed on the appliance. Two related technologies from Oracle are:

INITIATE

    o Exabus, a high-performance communications backplane

    o Exadata, a database appliance with support for both OLTP (transactional) and OLAP (analytical) database systems

Also consider that the software often goes far beyond the simple administration of the hardware to a full-scale service management solution. To conceptualize the scope of the overall infrastructure, we find it helpful to borrow from HP's Reference Architecture (Figure 7-1), which divides cloud-based service management into three layers.

Figure 7-1: HP Cloud Reference Architecture

At the top, the Demand layer models demand, including user and access management, order processing and reports on usage, billing, service-level conformance and legal compliance. The Delivery layer is responsible for Service monitoring, capacity allocation and service instance lifecycle management. And at the bottom, the Supply layer manages the physical and virtual elements while overseeing the resource metering.

All of these components are directly related to the management of the cloud system and therefore need to be integrated into a full OpenStack deployment.

Microsoft

Since OpenStack is built on principles of open source, Microsoft may seem like a direct antithesis to it. However, since most organizations have invested heavily in Microsoft technologies, any comprehensive implementation is likely to need integration with some of the products.

It isn't only a question of incorporating legacy tools or acceding to business demands. Microsoft has a solid and extensive product suite that very often meets corporate needs better than anything else. For many organizations, it is critical not only to be able to integrate with the existing Microsoft products but to open up to the whole ecosystem. They must interface with the on-premise Microsoft Server products and the Azure cloud. They may have a suite of internal .NET applications, which need to be maintained and enhanced. Often their programmers will have acquired extensive experience with Microsoft tools and wish to protect their investment.

The simplest form of interface would be to accommodate Windows guest machines within an OpenStack infrastructure. You might want to extend the facility to provision entire Windows environments. Another step would be to incorporate Hyper-V as one of the OpenStack hypervisors. And finally, you can simplify administration and identity management if OpenStack integrates with the Microsoft Active Directory.

Windows Guests

INITIATE

There is no fundamental difference between running a Linux or Windows image on OpenStack infrastructure. It is just a question of obtaining a suitable disk image and launching it. For Microsoft operating systems, you cannot easily use Amazon Machine Images (since there is no kernel or ramdisk), but VHD and VHDX work well.

In a test environment, you would want to be careful of using a Multiple Activation Key (MAK) since you may run your activation count up, due to different perceived hardware. However, Microsoft has made evaluation editions of Windows 8, and Windows Server 2012 available as a downloadable image that can be directly deployed to KVM, Hyper-V and XenServer.

All you need to do is download the image, which is currently available from Cloudbase[1], upload it into Glance (Figure 7-2) and it should be ready to deploy.

---

[1] http://www.cloudbase.it/ws2012r2/

INITIATE

Create An Image   ✕

Name *

Windows Server 2012

Description

Windows Server 2012

Image Source *

Image File   ▼

Image File

Choose File   windows_server_...31117.qcow2.gz

Format *

QCOW2 - QEMU Emulator   ▼

Minimum Disk (GB)

Minimum Ram (MB)

Public
☐

Protected
☐

Description:

Specify an image to upload to the Image Service.

Currently only images available via an HTTP URL
are supported. The image location must be
accessible to the Image Service. Compressed image
binaries are supported (.zip and .tar.gz.)

Please note: The Image Location field MUST be a
valid and direct URL to the image binary. URLs that
redirect or serve error pages will result in unusable
images.

Cancel   Create Image

Figure 7-2: Upload Windows Image

It becomes more challenging when you want to create your own pre-built image since you need to use sysprep. Sysprep is a tool to prepare a Windows image to be distributed, typically on a large scale. It is run before distributing any Windows operating system and does generalization (replaces the SID at next boot) and is a prerequisite for WSUS. Although there is a prevailing myth that Active Directory would become confused with multiple SIDs in its environment, the real reason for running sysprep is that Microsoft will not support any software that was distributed without it.

Sysprep uses unattended XML to allow for a silent boot that doesn't ask the users for configuration details. Cloudbase also provides a tool called cloudbase-init that will extend this capability[1]. When you boot instances in an OpenStack cloud, you can use user data or cloud-init to automatically configure instances at

---

[1] http://www.cloudbase.it/cloud-init-for-windows-instances/

boot time. You might want to install some packages, start services, or manage your instance.

Windows Application Catalog (Murano)

Launching individual Windows guests is a first integration step that provides the correct image. But enterprise applications often require coordination between many different systems. Building and launching these environments is not fundamentally different to general-purpose orchestration, which you can perform with OpenStack Heat, using templates for Active Directory, Exchange, Share-Point, SQL Server and IIS.

INITIATE

To pull these together the Murano service introduces an application catalog, where administrators can publish cloud-ready applications. It is a new service helping new users to deploy reliable Windows-based environments in Open-Stack. It provides interfaces enabling the deployment and operation of Windows Environments at the Windows Services abstraction level. The service then rolls out complex topologies using Heat to orchestrate Windows environments with multiple dependent services.

The solution provides a higher level of abstraction for manipulating Windows environments. Some of its key concepts are:

- Windows Service - a service such as Active Directory, Microsoft SQL, or IIS, which usually consists of multiple virtual machines (VM) and has multiple dependencies.
- Windows Environment - a logical unit for all Services and represents a classical Windows data center.
- Windows VM instance - a VM which hosts a Windows Service, whereby a Windows Service might be deployed over several Windows VM instances.

The first step in using Murano is to register any Windows images, so that it is able to use them. After uploading an image (Figure 7-2), you also need to mark it in the Murano dashboard (**Murano**, **Manage**, **Images**) (Figure 7-3).

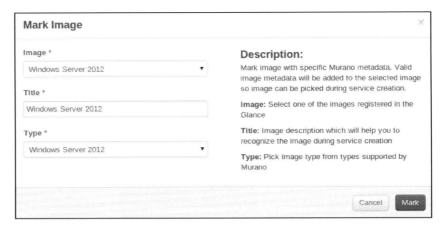

Figure 7-3: Mark Image for Murano

Once you have uploaded and marked all the images, the next step is to create a Murano environment (**Murano**, **Deploment**, **Environments**) (Figure 7-4).

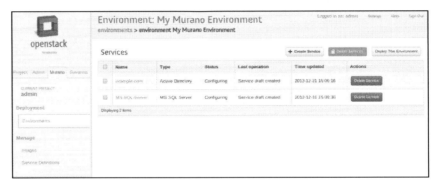

Figure 7-4: Murano Environment

You will need to populate the environment with services. For example, one of the services you are most likely to require is Active Directory (Figure 7-5).

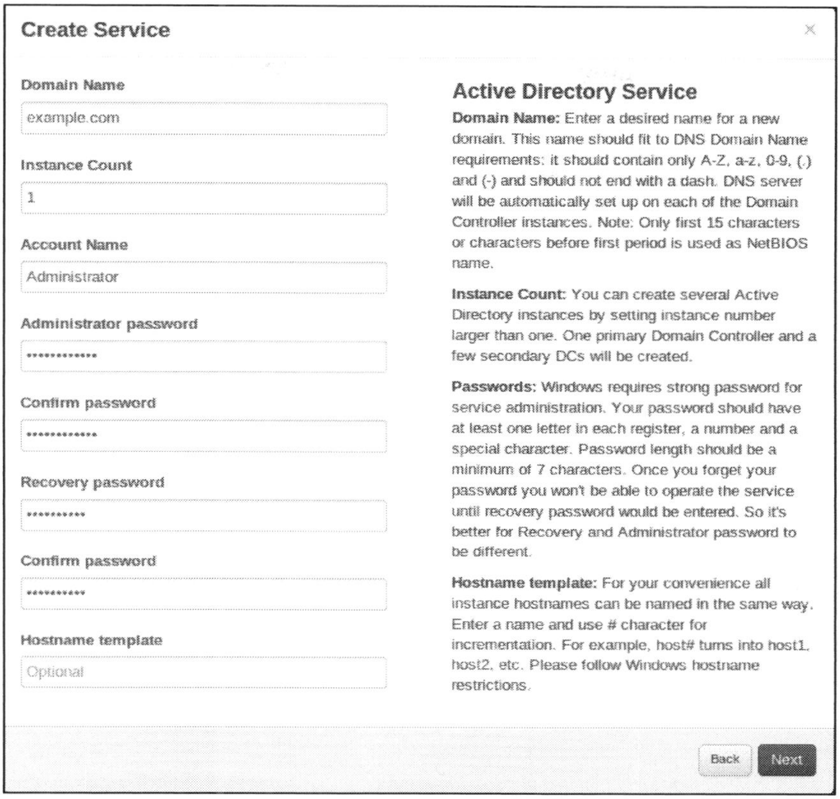

Create Service ✕

Domain Name

example.com

Instance Count

1

Account Name

Administrator

Administrator password

••••••••••••

Confirm password

••••••••••••

Recovery password

••••••••••

Confirm password

••••••••••

Hostname template

Optional

Active Directory Service

Domain Name: Enter a desired name for a new domain. This name should fit to DNS Domain Name requirements: it should contain only A-Z, a-z, 0-9, (.) and (-) and should not end with a dash. DNS server will be automatically set up on each of the Domain Controller instances. Note: Only first 15 characters or characters before first period is used as NetBIOS name.

Instance Count: You can create several Active Directory instances by setting instance number larger than one. One primary Domain Controller and a few secondary DCs will be created.

Passwords: Windows requires strong password for service administration. Your password should have at least one letter in each register, a number and a special character. Password length should be a minimum of 7 characters. Once you forget your password you won't be able to operate the service until recovery password would be entered. So it's better for Recovery and Administrator password to be different.

Hostname template: For your convenience all instance hostnames can be named in the same way. Enter a name and use # character for incrementation. For example, host# turns into host1, host2, etc. Please follow Windows hostname restrictions.

Back   Next

Figure 7-5: Create Active Directory Service in Murano

You can also use the dashboard to create additional Windows or Linux services or to modify the existing definitions (Figure 7-6).

Figure 7-6: Murano Service Definitions

Hyper-V

The previous section covered use cases where we wanted to insert Windows within an OpenStack deployment. Now, let's look at the opposite scenario – using Microsoft technologies to build the OpenStack infrastructure.

In theory the hypervisor and guests should be completely independent of each other. Windows applications should run on any hypervisor and any guest platforms should be able to operate within Hyper-V. However, just because these are possible, doesn't mean they make sense.

From a financial perspective there is little difference on the surface. Microsoft offers attractive deals for running Windows workloads on Hyper-V, and use of Hyper-V for non-Windows (Linux, FreeBSD) workloads is free, so the hypervisor costs are not likely to be the deciding factor.

However, the total cost of ownership also includes support. Microsoft doesn't support Windows guests unless they are running on a fully certified stack, which is easiest to confirm if it is based on Hyper-V. And Linux machines are more likely to run smoothly on KVM or XenServer than Hyper-V.

Assuming you have sufficient Windows machines to make the distribution efficient and no compelling reasons to decide otherwise, your best bet will be to place the Windows guests on Hyper-V and the Linux guests on Linux hosts.

What does this actually mean in practice? Hyper-V is a role of Windows and OpenStack is designed to run on Linux. In other words, the default OpenStack modules are not natively compatible with Hyper-V. In order to integrate these, you need to install some Nova drivers on the Hyper-V (or full Windows Server) host.

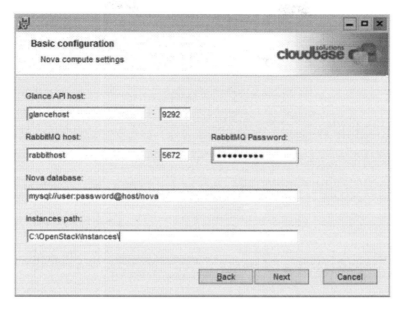

Figure 7-7: Cloudbase Installer

Cloudbase offers a free installer[1], which is wizard-based, generating the configuration files based on parameters provided by the user (Figure 7-7). It then connects to the controller to register the driver and any required networking components.

Active Directory

Active Directory (AD) is generally a core component of any Windows environment since domain-wide policies and management form a significant part of the Microsoft value proposition. At a minimum, this means that any domain-joined virtual machines must be able to resolve the DNS name of its domain controller. The machines will need unique names and must be able to join the domain by rebooting after provisioning.

Beyond the guest integration with Active Directory there is also a further opportunity for alignment. For example, it may make sense to use AD as the backend user store for Keystone since this will help to streamline the identity management in the enterprise.

---

[1] http://www.cloudbase.it/openstack/openstack-compute-installer/

VMware

The case for VMware integration is similar to that of Microsoft. VMware has a huge installed base at the virtualization layer, so it will simplify management to merge it into the OpenStack installation. In some ways, VMware is very similar to OpenStack. vCenter supplies functionality comparable to OpenStack Dashboard Identity Management, while ESX delivers capabilities similar to Compute, Network and Block Storage.

You might be tempted to consider the VMware ecosystem to be competitive to that of OpenStack since you could accomplish similar objectives with either. However, VMware has made a huge effort to bring the two closer together and is one of the most active contributors to the OpenStack project.

In fact, VMware is perhaps more often complementary than competitive to OpenStack. In this context, you will often hear a comparison with the distinction between cattle and pets. The point of this analogy is that while we have a strong emotional bond to individual pets, we are more concerned with cattle in terms of the whole herd. A rancher is accustomed to losing a few head of cattle and may even be forced to put down some animals with infectious diseases in the interests of the greater good.

Without diving too deeply into the morality of these attitudes, let's just say that the OpenStack approach is more akin to that of cattle. We assume that workloads have application-level resilience, so that they are able to sustain the loss of individual virtual machines.

The VMware approach is to implement resilience at the infrastructure layer. This is useful for workloads that are very important to us (pets) and that we do not want to simply substitute for a secondary instance. Instead we must ensure that they remain operational without interruption.

If we combine these two, as companies such as Intel and Paypal have done, we can optimize the environment to take advantage of the inherent elasticity of a horizontally scalable solution while still ensuring the high-availability requirements of specific mission critical applications. And we can continue to manage them through a single integrated framework.

To facilitate this integration, VMware provides plugins to the core OpenStack modules. There is a vSphere driver for Nova, an NSX network driver for Neutron and a vSphere block storage driver for Cinder.

Being able to integrate vSphere into Nova has several advantages. It brings the availability features (such as vMotion, and vSphere High Availability) to critical production workloads. It also adds advanced resource management (DRS, SDRS) capabilities to protect workloads from noisy neighbors and better utilize the underlying hardware.

Similar to the arrangement with Hyper-V above, there is a need to connect the hypervisor with OpenStack Compute, but rather than Nova running ESX directly, it connects through vCenter. This means that it is possible to perform all the VM orchestration tasks (create, destroy, start and stop) through the Nova interfaces.

When VMware acquired Nicira, they became the owners of one of the first and most robust network virtualization solutions to run on OpenStack. NSX integrates with many hardware switch vendors to allow OpenStack to manage workloads, but it doesn't rely on physical networks and can manage VLANs, firewalls and other components from a variety of vendors. It provides high tunneling performance and high availability across distributed network services in addition to troubleshooting tools that help visualize how virtual networks are built and model the impact of physical network failures.

You can connect OpenStack to any shared storage that works with VMware through the Cinder block storage driver. This means you can enable virtual SANs to access the directly attached storage on ESX hosts and apply policy-driven data placement across the cluster without needing any hardware-based features, such as RAID. You can auto-tier between SSD and rotating disks (SSD for high IOPS, HDD for high capacity) or accelerate low-cost storage devices with a local SSD cache allowing you to support extremely high IOPS for data-intensive workloads.

Virtual Volumes further give you the ability to abstract VMDKs into a SAN so that existing SAN/NAS systems can become VM-aware.

One final intersection point between vSphere and OpenStack is the VMware vCloud Automation Center (vCAC), a high-level cloud broker and self-service portal that can aggregate services from heterogeneous resource pools, including OpenStack components.

Amazon

Amazon already dominates the public infrastructure services market and their lead shows no sign of abating. Any company tackling cloud computing today would be foolish to ignore them. Unless an organization's culture accepts the totalistic rule of the IT department, there is a good chance that some businesses are already using Amazon Web Services. But even if there is no rogue IT effort using these services, there may be a great opportunity to use them either for point solutions, as part of a multi-sourcing strategy to reduce risk of internal lock-in, or as a way to add elasticity to some solutions whose future utilization is hard to predict. You could even use AWS to deploy OpenStack configurations that you would like to test outside your environment.

Regardless of your motivation, your options are the same. Many OpenStack technologies are based on Amazon equivalents and therefore reduce the switching costs at least a little. There are AWS-compatible APIs; you can import and export Amazon Machine Images; and the OpenStack Orchestration templates are based on Amazon CloudFormation – just to name a few examples.

Some implementation options therefore do provide a degree of commonality with Amazon. However, it would be naïve to expect the interoperability to be seamless. You can either implement a federated cloud management platform, such as Rightscale, Dell Enstratius or Scalr, or you can develop your own tools to handle the transitions between the two clouds.

Service Intermediation and Aggregation

INITIATE

The decision to consider multiple cloud providers is not limited to Amazon. Whether we use Amazon Web Services, Microsoft Azure or Google Cloud Platform, the challenges and solutions remain the same.

The complexity increases in a hybrid cloud environment where many services are provisioned from a variety of different sources. Service intermediation, aggregation and cloudbursting are essential mechanisms for the service brokering and dynamic resourcing capabilities of a hybrid cloud solution.

Service intermediation and aggregation refer to the capability of an organization's internal cloud platform to include services and/or service elements provided by another cloud provider in its service catalog and provide service access to its cloud platform users.

As we described earlier, cloudbursting is the capability of the platform to call on other resource providers (processing, storage or networking resources) when internal resources run short and additional resources are available from other internal or external cloud platforms.

In a hybrid cloud, service intermediation, aggregation and cloudbursting must be secured throughout their lifecycles.

The phases of service intermediation and aggregation involve a heavy security and governance focus, including:

- During the assessment, the organization evaluates the controls provided by the external service provider.
- Service integration involves adding the service to the cloud platform service catalog.
- When services are used, the intermediation must secure communication mechanisms.
- When the service is removed from the cloud platform's service catalog, all existing integrations must be disabled, deleted and/or de-provisioned.

The phases of secure cloudbursting include:

- As with services aggregation, an assessment involves evaluating the security of the external service provider. All resource requests must be protected by mutual authentication and authorization.
- Workload data must migrate from the cloud platform to the environment of the provider.
- Resource usage notifications must exchange between the cloud platform's users and administrators and the resource provider.
- Reverse payload migration is necessary to transfer the virtual payload from the environment of the provider back to the customer.
- Resource liberation should also be complete and verifiable.

INITIATE

Practical Recommendations

There is a reason why there are very few good enterprise architects. Large organizations have a wide variety of applications, systems, resources and processes. Integrating a broad set of disparate technologies is a very difficult skill to master.

Cloud computing doesn't reduce this complexity. In fact, in some ways it makes it worse as there are now a set of cloud technologies that augment, rather than replace, existing infrastructure.

OpenStack can mask some of the heterogeneity, but to do so it must be configured and integrated with each of these external components. It shifts some of the ongoing operational effort to a one-time design and implementation task. It is beyond the scope of this book to provide detailed instructions on any of the common scenarios, but hopefully we have shared enough to give you an idea of what is involved.

Assemble

The design of an OpenStack-based solution begins with the OpenStack services themselves. While it is possible to replace the individual modules, it is generally a good idea to start with the base solution and see to what extent it meets the business requirements. In particular, the core components of an infrastructure service include compute, storage and networking.

Chapter 8

Build the Workload

In this chapter we will look at Compute, which represents the core of any workload. Even though there are cloud services without computation, they can represent static storage at best. All dynamic activity involves some element of computation.

A workload could be a simple LAMP (Linux, Apache, MySQL and PHP) website. It might be a content-management system like WordPress, Joomla or Drupal. Or it could be running a business application, such as SugarCRM. Our goal will be to create an environment where we can easily launch, operate and manage a set of these services.

But first, let's back up and reflect on what it takes to create a shared pool of compute resources.

Software-Defined Computation

The primary elements of a computer are a Central Processing Unit (CPU), Random Access Memory (RAM) and an Input/Output (I/O) subsystem. The CPU executes instructions using its own internal registers and RAM to receive and store data. The I/O subsystem provides the interfaces to peripheral components, such as persistent storage and human interface devices, as well as network connectivity to remote systems.

Server Virtualization

The first step in optimizing efficiencies through cloud computing is virtualization. By sharing resources across individual physical machines, we can accommodate increased workloads as each instance has different usage profiles and these are, at least partially, complementary. In other words, when one application is I/O bound another may have high CPU needs and another may be consuming most of the RAM, with this balance shifting over time.

To be clear, virtualizing these elements is not a new trend. For decades, all mainstream operating systems have included functionality for process scheduling, virtual memory and I/O virtualization. However, when we speak about virtualization in the data centre today, we usually mean server virtualization. Rather than being a component of the operating system, server virtualization abstracts both the operating system itself and the underlying physical resources and presents these as a set of virtual machines, each of which appears to its applications and users as though it were a physical system.

ASSEMBLE

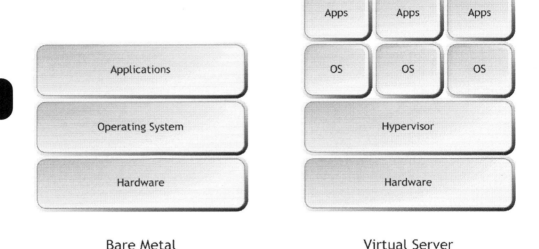

Bare Metal   Virtual Server

Figure 8-1: Server Virtualization

There are two kinds of management layers (or hypervisors) that facilitate the abstraction. Type 1 hypervisors (such as Microsoft Hyper-V, VMware ESX/ESXi or Citrix XenServer) run on the bare hardware (Figure 8-1). Type 2 hypervisors (such as Microsoft Virtual Server, VirtualBox or VMware Workstation) run on a host operating system. While the latter can be useful for developers or for building a test environment, the former is most efficient and is the most common technique used in a data centre. We will therefore focus on Type 1 hypervisors.

There are many reasons why server virtualization has become so popular. The virtual machine can provide instruction set architectures that are independent of the physical machine thereby enabling platforms on hardware for which they were not necessarily designed. It improves the level of utilization of the underlying hardware since guest applications can be deployed with independent (and ideally complementary) resource demands.

Probably the most important driver is the fact that virtual machines can be launched from a virtual disk independent of the hardware on which they were configured. It is simply a matter of copying the virtual machine to a new machine that is running the same hypervisor. This encapsulation makes it very easy to load-balance, redeploy applications or provision new instances as usage requires. It also enforces a level of standardization in configuration between similar instances of the same application.

Operational Efficiencies

Once encapsulation and standardization are in place, we can take these benefits even further by automating the entire management layer. Most cloud services, for example, offer an image catalog that facilitates self-service. They may also include mechanisms to automatically scale resources up and down in response to the service loads.

One final feature of infrastructure services is metering and billing. One of the reasons that cloud computing is becoming popular now is that capabilities have evolved to allow the service provider to recuperate its costs easily and effectively. Fine-grained instrumentation provides the foundation by accounting for usage and delivering accurate information that can be used for internal cross-charging or fed into a billing and payment system for external collection.

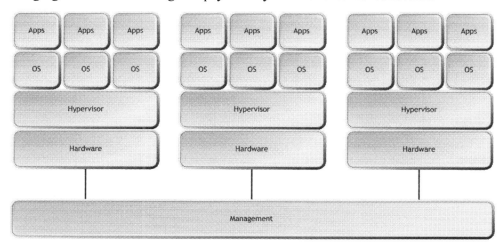

Cloud

Figure 8-2: Software-Defined Compute

A fully software-defined data centre would include these capabilities. But, most importantly, it needs to offer a simple management interface that covers all this functionality and is able to collectively administer resources across heterogeneous hypervisors and hardware (Figure 8-2).

OpenStack Implementation

The name "OpenStack Compute" refers to a specific service, also called "Nova", but there are really two services that relate to computation and the software that runs it: Image and Compute. The OpenStack Image Service (Glance) manages static disk images, which contain the executable code as well as the operating environment. OpenStack Compute (Nova) manages the running instances.

Nova controls the cloud computing fabric, and as such it forms the core of an infrastructure service. Nova is also the most complex component of the Open-Stack family. It runs in numerous processes, potentially spans many physical systems, and offers a range of over four hundred configuration options.

Nova interfaces with several of the other OpenStack services: It uses Keystone to perform its authentication, Horizon as its administrative interface and Glance to supply its images. The tightest interaction is with Glance, which Nova requires to download images for use in launching images.

OpenStack Image Service (Glance)

Before going into more detail on Nova, let's take a closer look at the Image Service, which, chronologically, represents the beginning of the Compute workload. Glance is the service name for the OpenStack Image Service, which registers, lists, and retrieves virtual machine images.

Glance manages the images in an OpenStack cluster but is not responsible for the actual storage. Rather it provides an abstraction to multiple storage technologies. A local file system provides minimal latency and is easy to configure making it attractive for small deployments, but it is also more constrained in terms of space. Network file systems or object-storage are more common for larger implementations. Some of the supported back-ends include OpenStack Object Storage (Swift), OpenStack Block Storage (Cinder), Ceph, Sheepdog and even Amazon S3.

The OpenStack Image Store is a central repository for virtual images. Along with the actual disk images, it holds metadata and status information describing the image. Glance supports a range of container and disk formats. Some of the more popular ones include the Amazon Machine Image (AMI) and qcow2, a compressed format supported by the QEMU emulator that offers good performance.

Users and other services can store both public and private images, which they can access to launch instances. They can request a list of available images, retrieve their configuration information and then use them as a basis for starting Nova instances. It is also possible to take snapshots from running instances as a means of backing up the virtual machines and their states.

Nova comes into action after the image is created. It typically uses an image to launch an instance, or virtual machine. Although it does not include any virtualization software itself, it can integrate with many common hypervisors through drivers that interface with the virtualization technologies.

From a practical perspective, launching an instance involves identifying and specifying the virtual hardware templates (called "flavors" in OpenStack). The templates describe the compute (virtual CPUs), memory (RAM) and storage configuration (hard disks) to be assigned to the virtual machine instances. By default, the installation includes a set of five flavors, which administrators can modify or extend.

OpenStack Compute (Nova)

Nova then schedules the requested instance by assigning its execution to a specific compute node (called a 'host' in OpenStack). Each system must regularly report its status and capabilities to nova-scheduler, which uses the data to optimize its allocations.

ASSEMBLE

The whole assignment process consists of two phases. The *filtering* phase applies a set of filters to generate a list of the most suitable hosts. As mentioned above, every OpenStack service publishes its capabilities, which is one of the most important considerations. The scheduler will narrow the selection of hosts to meet the parameters of the request.

A *weighting* phase then uses a special function to calculate the cost of each host and sorts the results. The output of this phase is a list of hosts incurring the least cost to satisfy the user's request for a given set of instances.

After the scheduler determines the appropriate host, it passes the request on to Nova-compute, which interacts with the corresponding hypervisor. The daemon accepts actions from the queue, creates/terminates instances through hypervisor APIs and subsequently updates the state in the database.

Nova also carries out a number of additional functions, many of which interact closely with other OpenStack services covering networking, security and administration. Nova generally handles the instance-specific aspects of these, such as attaching and detaching storage, assigning IP addresses or taking snapshots of running instances.

Architecture

Nova uses a shared-nothing architecture (Figure 8-3), so that all major components can run on separate servers. The distributed design relies on a message queue to handle the asynchronous component-to-component communications.

Nova stores the states of virtual machines and instance types in a central SQL-based database that is used by all OpenStack components. Any database supported by SQLAlchemy can be used.

ASSEMBLE

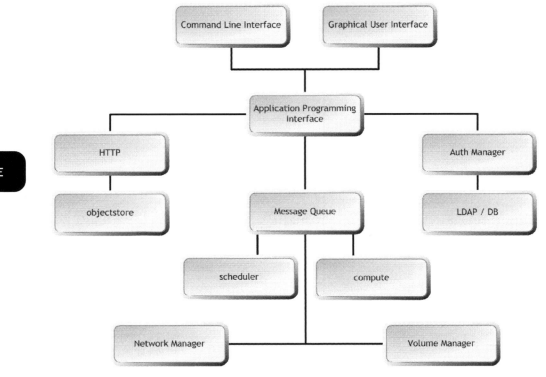

Figure 8-3: Nova Architecture

Web Dashboard

The primary user interface to OpenStack Compute is via the web dashboard (OpenStack Horizon). This central portal for all OpenStack modules presents a graphic interface of all the services and makes API calls to invoke any requested services.

API

The API Interface is based on REST. It's a Web Server Gateway Interface (WSGI) application that routes URIs to action methods on controller classes. The application programming interface receives HTTP requests, processes the commands and then delegates the task to other components via the message queue or HTTP (in the case of the ObjectStore). The Nova API supports the OpenStack Compute API, Amazon's EC2 API and also an Admin API for privileged users. It initiates most of the orchestration activities and policies (like Quota).

Auth Manager

Each HTTP Request requires specific authentication credentials using one of the authentication schemes the provider has configured for the Compute node. The Authorization Manager is not a separate binary. Instead it is a python class that any OpenStack component can use for authentication. It exposes authorized APIs usage for Users, Projects and Roles and communicates with OpenStack's Keystone for details. The actual user store can be a DB or LDAP backend.

ObjectStore

The ObjectStore is a simple HTTP-based object-based storage (like Amazon's S3) for images. It can be, and usually is, replaced with OpenStack's Glance.

Message Queue

The message queue provides a means for all of the components in OpenStack Nova to communicate and coordinate with each other. It's like a central task list shared and updated by all Nova components.

All these components run in a non-blocking message based architecture, and can be run from the same or different hosts as long as they use the same message queue service. They interact in a callback-oriented manner using the AMQP protocol. By default, most distributions implement RabbitMQ accessed via the Kombu library, but there are also plug-ins available for Apache Qpid and ZeroMQ.

Nova components use RPC to communicate with each other via Message Broker using PubSub. More technically, Nova implements rpc.call (request/response, API acts as consumer) and rpc.cast (one way, API acts as publisher).

Nova API and the scheduler use the message queue as the Invoker, whereas Network and Compute act as workers. An Invoker sends messages via rpc.call or rpc.cast. The Worker pattern receives messages from the queue and responds back to each rpc.call with the appropriate response.

Daemons

The two main daemons to consider for Nova are the scheduler and compute daemons. The *scheduler* decides which compute host to allot for a virtual machine request. It uses the filtering and scheduling algorithms described above and considers a variety of parameters, including affinity (co-locating related workloads), anti-affinity (distributing workloads), availability zone, core CPU utilization, system RAM, and custom JSON schedules. Note that it makes this decision at provisioning time only and does not redistribute running instances.

Nova compute is a worker daemon that manages communication with the hypervisors and virtual machines. It retrieves its orders from the message queue and performs virtual machine create/delete tasks using hypervisor's API. It also updates the status of its tasks in the central database.

For the sake of completeness, there are also some daemons that cover functionality originally assigned to Nova that is slowly moving to other services.

- The Network Manager administers IP forwarding, network bridges, and VLANs. It is a worker daemon picking network related tasks from a message queue. These functions are now also covered by OpenStack Neutron which can be selected in its place.
- The Volume Manager handles the attachment (and detachment) of persistent block storage volumes to virtual machines (similar to Amazon's EBS). This functionality has been extracted to OpenStack's Cinder. It's an iSCSI solution utilizing the Logical Volume Manager.

Hypervisors

OpenStack is hypervisor-agnostic but you do have to choose some virtualization technology behind the abstraction layer.

The dawn of cloud computing was dominated by the Xen hypervisor. Both Amazon and Rackspace based their infrastructure on it; and it was also the most popular hypervisor in the first OpenStack deployments. However, since then Citrix ceased their involvement in OpenStack, Red Hat switched from Xen to KVM, and KVM has gained a considerable share of the open-source hypervisor market.

For these reasons, and perhaps a few others, KVM is now by far the most common hypervisor in current OpenStack deployments. It is the default choice for DevStack and it is used in most reference implementations.

A second popular option is QEMU (Quick EMUlator). The QEMU hypervisor is very similar to the KVM hypervisor in that they are both controlled through libvirt. This means that they are compatible with the same virtual machine images and have the same level of support from OpenStack. The main difference is that QEMU does not support native virtualization.

QEMU therefore has worse performance than KVM and isn't optimal for deployment into production. However, it does have its use cases. It is very popular among developers for running compute services within virtual machines. And it is well suited for older systems that lack hardware virtualization support.

Another option for hosts without hardware virtualization support is Linux Containers (LXC), which typically offer better performance than QEMU. LXC is similar to a chroot, but offers more than filesystem isolation. Control groups provide process isolation with resource control and accounting options (quotas). Network namespaces allow each virtual environment to use a dedicated network stack. But, because they still use the host operating system, the applications can access any specialized hardware (e.g. interface cards or GPUs) more easily than in a fully virtualized system.

However, LXC should be used with caution in a multi-tenant environment since it has no inherent protection against exploits that allow a user to become root. At a minimum, it is wise to improve the default isolation between the containers using additional containment technologies, such as AppArmor.

An extension to Linux Containers is Docker, which is currently riding a wave of popularity. It is not a replacement for LXC but builds on top of the containers with several enhancements:

ASSEMBLE

- Portability across machines with a format for bundling an application and its dependencies into a single object
- Tool for developers to automatically assemble a container from their source code
- Full control over application dependencies, build tools and packaging
- Git-like capabilities for tracking successive versions of a container
- Re-use of any container as a base image for more specialized components
- API for automating and customizing the creation and deployment of containers
- Public marketplace (called the registry) for sharing useful containers

These benefits along with the lightweight nature of containers have made Docker very attractive for dense application deployments. However, there are also some constraints that customers should recognize. Linux containers and Docker packages share the host operating system. There is no way to insert another guest layer. This means that the application must be compatible with the underlying host platform.

There are also some limitations in the OpenStack operations supported. For example, there is no support for suspending and resuming instances or for attaching volumes.

Two other hypervisors that are very important in corporate deployments are ESXi and Hyper-V, as both technologies have high penetration in most enterprise data centers. Both VMware and Microsoft offer their own cloud ecosystems, so there is no absolute requirement to integrate these with OpenStack. However, it does simplify operations in a heterogeneous environment if it is possible to merge the deployments and manage them centrally as we described in Chapter 7.

Usage Scenario

To get a high-level view of Nova, you can begin with the administrative interface.

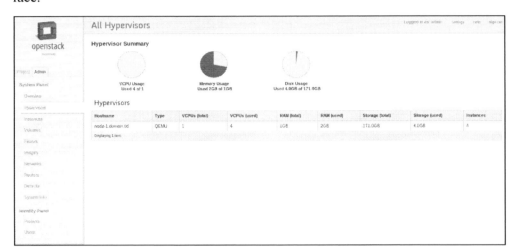

Figure 8-4: Hypervisors

You can see a list of the compute nodes along with their hardware specifications and utilization in the **Hypervisors** section (Figure 8-4) of the **System Panel**.

ASSEMBLE

ASSEMBLE

Figure 8-5: Flavors

Another system-wide configuration is the set of **Flavors** available to compute instances (Figure 8-5).

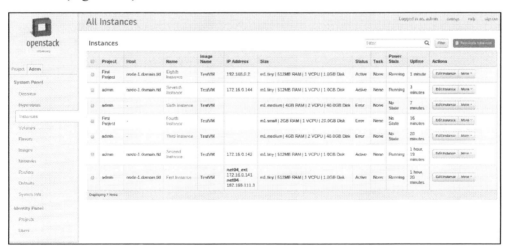

Figure 8-6: Instances

You can also see an overview of all the **Instances** across the OpenStack deployment (Figure 8-6).

To get an idea of how OpenStack Compute might be used in practice, imagine that you have a base image that you would like to launch in OpenStack. After configuring the system and making some personalized customizations, you may want to take a snapshot of the running instance so that you can accelerate the provisioning process to execute the same task again. Once you have completed the project, you will want to stop the instance and eventually delete the image.

To begin with, you would need to login to the OpenStack Dashboard as a user with a Member role. You would then click **Images & Snapshots** in the **Manage Compute** menu. And press the **Create Image** button.

ASSEMBLE

Figure 8-7: Create An Image

You will see the **Create An Image** dialog (Figure 8-7) and can configure the settings that define your instance. Here you can enter a name for the image and point to an image that you have previously created or downloaded. You need to specify the format of the image file but there is no need to indicate the minimum disk size or RAM unless you would like to supply them.

After creating the image, you can select **Instances** in the **Manage Compute** menu and press the Launch Instance button.

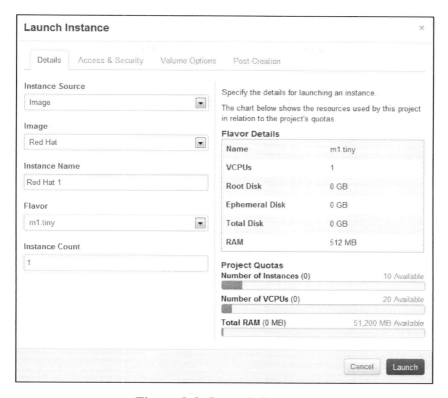

Figure 8-8: Launch Instance

You will see a dialog that confirms your configuration and allows you to specify the required Flavor, or basic hardware configuration. Once you press the **Launch** button, the instance should be up and running (Figure 8-8).

As a next step, you may want to take a snapshot. Again, you would click **Instances** in the **Manage Compute** menu and then press the **Create Snapshot** button on the row associated with the instance of interest.

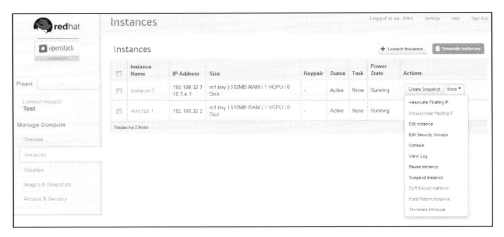

Figure 8-9 : Instances

ASSEMBLE

Some of the other tasks you can execute from this screen include editing, pausing, suspending and rebooting the instance. It is also the place to go in order to terminate the instance once you have finished using it (Figure 8-9).

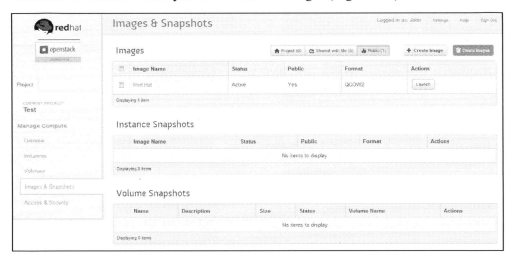

Figure 8-10: Image & Snapshots

To delete the image and/or any snapshots, you would go back to the **Images & Snapshots** menu, where you have the option to delete the objects you no longer need (Figure 8-10).

Practical Recommendations

Nova is one of the most powerful OpenStack services but also the most complex. Fortunately, you don't need to know the details to be able to use it. The base functionality is easy to understand and use. It's straightforward to create a few images, launch instances based on them and take some snapshots to save intermediate states.

You can build on these tasks from the user side with functions to pause, suspend and reboot the instances. As an administrator, you can experiment with additional compute hosts and different flavors. If you are really ambitious, you can try different hypervisors and scheduling algorithms.

ASSEMBLE

Chapter 9

Store the Information

In this chapter we will look at Storage, which offers persistent storage for other OpenStack services. As noted in OpenStack Compute, computation is the core of a computational workload. In some cases, a virtual machine may be all that is required. Every Nova instance has access to ephemeral storage that contains the operating system and can cache temporary files. However, this data disappears when the instance terminates.

Often there is a need for durable storage that persists beyond the life of an instance. This might be documents, media files (audio/video), structured business data, configuration information or even system images.

Storage is one of the few OpenStack services that offer a compelling value proposition on its own even without OpenStack Compute. In fact there may be cases where applications running outside an OpenStack environment require replicated, scalable and reliable storage and OpenStack storage services meet their requirements.

Software-Defined Storage

The key objectives of any storage system are performance and reliability. Performance may be determined by latency, which is critical for high I/O per second workloads, or throughput which is important for operations involving large amounts of data. Reliability is also a function of two factors: availability of the data storage when it is needed, and integrity of the data that is stored there.

Most storage systems differ primarily in how they attempt to address these two dimensions. But they must also consider how to minimize both the cost and administrative burden associated with them; and they must ensure that all sensitive data is properly secured.

In terms of conceptual components, we could argue that the earliest implementations were physical (Figure 9-1). They involved storage units that were connected to the CPU through a hardware interface supported by software drivers. Using these, the applications could read and write data without any special knowledge of the hardware.

So, for example the storage media might be tape libraries, optical media, or more commonly today, rotating Hard Disk Drives (HDDs) and Solid State Disks (SSDs). These might be connected through interfaces such as the Small Computer Systems Interface (SCSI), Serial Advanced Technology Attachment (SATA), FibreChannel or Infiniband.

The first step in abstracting these resources was to create a logical interface to the storage subsystem. Logical Units (LUNs) are actually a primitive form of storage abstraction/virtualization and a prerequisite for advanced storage technologies such as Redundant Array of Independent Disks (RAID).

ASSEMBLE

The ultimate objective of RAID is really just to improve performance and availability. It can enhance performance with RAID 0 (Striping) and availability with RAID 1 (Mirroring) or it can combine the two with RAID 5 (Striping with Parity) or RAID 10 (Mirrored Striping).

On a single host, you can simplify the management of logical devices with the Logical Volume Manager such as LVM, which is shipped as part of the Linux kernel. It allows organizations to manage large hard disk farms by adding and replacing disks without any service disruption and it makes it easier to resize the file system when partitions change. It also supports the creation and management of RAID logical volumes to stripe or mirror as needed.

Storage Virtualization

You could argue that the logical storage abstraction is already a primitive form of storage virtualization, but it takes on a much more recognizable shape when you introduce the notion of shared network storage (Figure 9-1). Rather than using host-based Direct Attached Storage (DAS), the storage series connect over the network using protocols like Common Internet File System (CIFS), Internet SCSI (iSCSI) and FibreChannel over Ethernet (FCoE) to Storage Area Networks (SANs), Network Attached Storage (NAS) or a Network File System (NFS).

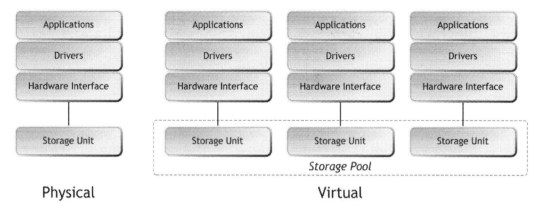

Figure 9-1: Storage Virtualization

There are admittedly downsides to this approach which can come at the price of degraded performance and increased complexity. But there are also some great benefits. The primary motivation of networked storage is to increase availability by including redundancy and to increase the scale through distribution. It also makes tasks such as archiving, back-up, and recovery easier and faster.

ASSEMBLE

Storage virtualization helps to achieve location independence. The technology presents a logical space for data storage and handles the process of mapping it to the actual physical location. The virtualization software re-directs incoming I/O requests containing information based on a logical disk location and translates them into new requests based on a physical disk location.

This abstraction makes storage consolidation much easier since it is possible to migrate data without disrupting access. The host can manipulate the logical disk associated with a guest. So the physical data can be moved or replicated to another location without affecting the operation of any client.

Resource pooling can also increase utilization. When physical storage is logically aggregated, additional drives can be added as needed and the virtual storage space will scale up transparently. This allows users to avoid over-buying and over-provisioning storage solutions.

Operational Efficiencies

Finally, the storage virtualization software can act as a centralized console for managing all volumes in the environment. Multiple dispersed and independent storage devices appear as a single monolithic storage device. Administrators can then configure policy-based storage management (Figure 9-2).

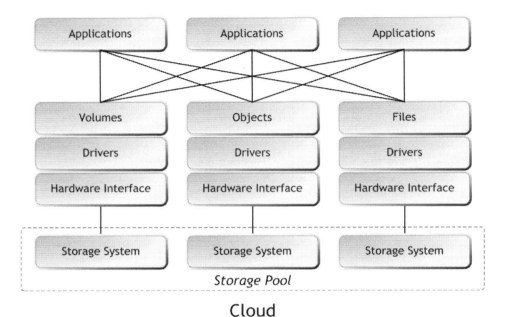

ASSEMBLE

Cloud

Figure 9-2: Software-Defined Storage

There are three different ways applications typically access network storage.

Block storage appears to the operating system like ordinary storage volumes. The drivers typically implement protocols like iSCSI and FCoE that hide the network from both the application and the underlying platform.

File storage is accessible via a network path, for example using CIFS or NFS. Applications can read and write files just as if they were local, but they do not have access to the actual volume. So, for example, they would not be able to format the drive or perform any other low-level operations.

Object storage is generally exposed via an API and is not visible to the operating system at all. It therefore requires no client configuration, but the application must be coded to the storage API for it to work.

Centralized management makes it possible to automatically enforce per-machine SLAs for all applications across different types of storage. The policies can specify such parameters as availability, throughput rate, latency, backup schedule and disaster recovery point/time objectives.

All of these benefits make virtual storage very attractive. At the same time, it is important to plan the virtualization exercise carefully. It can be very difficult to rollback if the migration encounters problems or to switch between vendors if the technology strategy changes. The technology can also be quite complex and may suffer from performance or scalability issues, so it should be analyzed and tested carefully before being implemented.

OpenStack Implementation

There are currently two fundamentally different storage services in OpenStack. OpenStack Swift is an example of object storage, which is similar in concept to Amazon S3. OpenStack Cinder, on the other hand represents block storage similar to Amazon EBS.

It is also worth mentioning that there is an OpenStack service, called Manila, in the works for file storage. It provides an API for management of shared filesystems with support for multiple protocols (such as NFS and CIFS) and pluggable back-end implementations.

Swift is the more mature of the two offerings as it has been a core service since the inception of OpenStack. It functions as a distributed, API-accessible storage platform that can be integrated directly into applications or used for storing virtual machine images, backups and archives as well as smaller files such as photos and mail messages.

There are two main concepts to the Object Store: objects and containers.

An *object* is the primary storage entity. It consists of the content and any optional metadata associated with the files stored in the OpenStack Object Storage system. The data is saved in uncompressed and unencrypted format and consists of the object's name, its container and any metadata in the form of key-value pairs.

Objects are spread across multiple disk drives throughout the data center, whereby Swift ensures data replication and integrity. The distributed operation can leverage low-cost commodity hardware while also enhancing scalability, redundancy and durability.

A *container* is similar to a Windows folder, in that it is a storage compartment for a set of files. Containers cannot be nested, but it is possible for a tenant to create an unlimited number of containers. Objects must be stored in a container so there is a need for at least one container in order to use the Object store.

Unlike a traditional file server, Swift is distributed across multiple systems. It automatically stores redundant copies of each object in order to maximize availability and scalability. Object versioning offers the user additional protection against inadvertent loss or overwriting of data.

The second service is Cinder, which provides persistent block storage to guest VMs. Block storage is often necessary for expandable file systems, maximum performance and integration with enterprise storage services as well as applications that require access to raw block-level storage. The system can expose devices and manage their attachment to servers. The API also facilitates snapshot management, which can back up volumes of block-storage.

So, which should you use, Swift or Cinder? It really depends on your application. If you need to run commercial or legacy applications, you will rarely have a choice. They are unlikely to be coded to take advantage of the Swift APIs, but you can easily mount a Cinder disk that will behave just like direct attached storage for most applications.

You can certainly use Cinder for new applications too. But you wouldn't get the benefits of resiliency and redundancy that automatically accompany Swift. If your programmers are up to the challenge, the distributed and scalable architecture of Swift is definitely a feature worth considering.

OpenStack Object Storage (Swift)

Servers

The swift architecture is very distributed to prevent any single point of failure and to provide virtually unlimited horizontal scale. At Rackspace, for instance, it controls more than 85 petabytes of raw storage[1].

It includes the following four servers:

- A Proxy server
- Object servers
- Container servers
- Account servers

The *Proxy* Server presents a unified interface to the remainder of the OpenStack Object Storage architecture. It accepts requests to create containers, upload files or modify metadata and can also provide container listings or present stored files. When it receives a request, it determines the location of the account, container, or object in the ring and forwards the request to the relevant server.

An *Object* Server is a simple server that can upload, modify and retrieve objects (usually files) stored on the devices it manages. The objects are stored in the local file system using extended attributes to hold any metadata. The path is based on the object name's hash and a timestamp.

A *Container* Server is essentially a directory of objects. It handles the assignment of objects to specific containers and provides listings of the containers upon request. The listings are replicated across the cluster to provide redundancy.

An *Account* Server manages accounts using the object storage services. It operates similarly to a Container Server in providing listings, in this case enumerating the containers that are assigned to a given account.

---

[1] http://www.openstack.org/assets/presentation-media/Swift-at-Scale.pdf

Processes

There are also a number of scheduled housekeeping processes that manage the data store, including replication services, auditors and updaters.

Replication services are the most essential of these processes. They ensure consistency and availability throughout the cluster. Since one of the primary drawing points of the Object Store is its distributed storage, there is a need to ensure a consistent state in the case of transient error conditions like power outages or component failures. This is accomplished by regularly comparing local data with its remote copies and ensuring that all replicas contain the latest version.

To minimize the amount of network traffic needed for comparison, the services create a hash of each partition subsection and compare these lists. Container and account replication also use hashes but supplement these with shared high water marks. The actual updates are pushed, generally using rsync to copy objects, containers and accounts.

The replicator also performs garbage collection to enforce consistent data removal when objects, containers or accounts are deleted. Upon deletion, the system marks the latest version with a tombstone, which signals to the replicator to remove the item from all replicated nodes.

Even the best replication design is only as effective as the components that implement it. Production environments need to be able to cope with failure, whether they are due to hardware or software failures, or merely the result of insufficient capacity. In Swift, this is accomplished with Updaters and Auditors.

Updaters are responsible for ensuring the integrity of the system in the face of failure. When the replication services encounter a problem and cannot update a container or account, there will be a period of inconsistency where the object exists in storage but is not listed on all the container or account servers. In this case the system queues the update on the local file system, and an updater process will regularly retry the updates.

Auditors provide an additional level of protection against inconsistency. They regularly scan the local repository verifying the integrity of the accounts, containers and objects. When they identify any corruption, they quarantine the element and replace it with a copy from another replica. If they discover an inconsistency that they are not able to reconcile (e.g. objects that do not belong to any container), they record the error in a log file.

Rings

Users and other OpenStack services reference storage entities by their logical name. However, ultimately all requests, whether for reading or for writing, need to map to a physical location. To accomplish this, the Proxy server and the background processes, including replication services, need to be able to map logical names to physical locations.

This mapping is called a *ring*. Accounts, containers, and objects are assigned to separate rings. The ring describes this mapping in terms of devices, partitions, replicas and zones.

The term partition, in this context, refers to logical subsets of the content stored in the ring. The recommendation is to allocate one hundred partitions for each participating device. The partitions are distributed evenly among all the devices assigned to OpenStack Object Storage. If a cluster uses drives of varying sizes, it is also possible to assign weights which will balance the distribution of partitions across devices.

ASSEMBLE

By default, each partition will be replicated three times. It is possible to use a higher number in order to optimize availability but obviously this will also increase storage consumption. The ring also specifies which devices to use for handoff in failure scenarios and how to redistribute partitions when devices are added to (or removed from) the cluster.

The last element of the ring mapping is the zone, which is used to enable data affinity and anti-affinity. A zone can represent a storage device, a physical server or a location, such as a rack, aisle or data center. It is a logical concept that users can employ to suit their needs but it usually reflects physical elements such as location, power source and network connectivity.

OpenStack Block Storage (Cinder)

Cinder is significantly simpler than Swift since it doesn't provide automatic object distribution and replication. Similarly to other OpenStack services, its functionality is exposed to both the dashboard and the command line via an API. It incorporates authentication to Keystone with a python class called the Auth Manager (Figure 9-3).

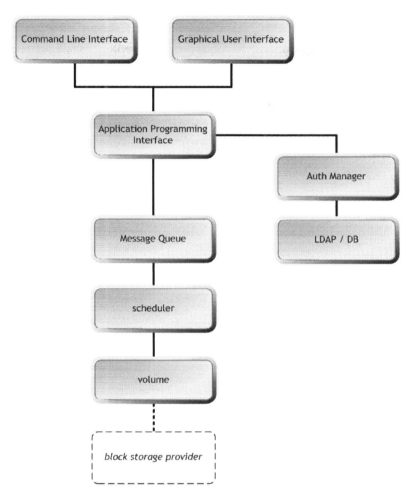

Figure 9-3: Cinder Architeture

The API parses and forwards all incoming requests to the message queue where the scheduler and volume service perform the actual work. When new volumes are created, the scheduler decides which host should be responsible for it. By default, it will select the node with the most space available.

The volume manager manages the dynamically attachable block storage devices, called volumes. They can be used as the boot devices of virtual instances or attached as secondary storage. Cinder also provides a facility for snapshots, which are read-only copies of a volume. These snapshots can then be used to create new volumes for read-write use.

Volumes are usually attached to the Compute nodes via iSCSI. The Block Storage also requires some form of back-end storage, which by default is LVM on a local Volume Group but can be extended via drivers to external storage arrays or appliances. Some of the back-end options include NFS and a range of high-end iSCSI devices as well as Ceph, GlusterFS and Sheepdog, which we will look at next.

Ceph, GlusterFS and Sheepdog

There are a few other open-source storage aggregation technologies that have gained favour over the past years independently of OpenStack. They also offer Object, Block and File storage services, so you might consider them competitive offerings to Swift, Cinder and eventually Manila. But they provide interfaces to OpenStack and are probably more accurately seen as complementary back-end systems.

Ceph, in use at Best Buy and others, is currently the most popular of these but there are also other options, such as GlusterFS and Sheepdog, which function similarly. The main value proposition is that they offer multiple forms of storage (i.e. object, block and file) in one integrated package.

ASSEMBLE

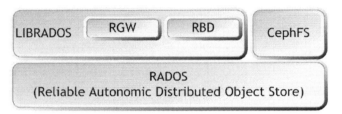

Figure 9-4: Ceph Architecture

The Ceph architecture is based on an object store layer called RADOS (Reliable Autonomic Distributed Object Store) (Figure 9-4). There are several ways for applications to access RADOS. They can use the LIBRADOS library with bindings for C, C++, Python and other languages. Or they can call the bucket-based REST gateway (RGW) using S3 and Swift compatible APIs. Alternatively they can interface with the fully distributed RADOS Block Device (RBD), which offers thin provisioning, full and incremental snapshots, and copy-on-write cloning. Finally they can access the POSIX-compliant CephFS filesystem.

OpenStack applications are free to access any of these interfaces directly. However, this would bypass the centralized storage management that OpenStack provides. Fortunately, it is also possible to combine the benefits of OpenStack with those of Ceph by simply declaring Ceph as a back-end driver for Swift or Cinder. Ceph supports Keystone authentication, so it can integrate tightly into any OpenStack deployment.

Even though the implementation details of GlusterFS and Sheepdog are quite different, the principles are the same. Red Hat is a strong backer of GlusterFS which is in use at Amadeus and other large customers. Sheepdog is running at NTT and Taobao and offers similar functionality.

In summary, you can run Cinder and Swift using LVM and local storage and you may find it easier to keep the architecture simple as long as you have no need to expand beyond this environment. But there is also something to be said for being able to satisfy a wide number of use cases (big data, web applications, multimedia and archival) within one distributed and highly redundant cluster.

Usage Scenario

To get an idea of how you might use OpenStack storage, imagine a scenario where you have a project that runs both legacy software using a filesystem and new code where you would like to use distributed object storage. The environment for this project should include both Swift and Cinder.

Let's start with Cinder. It's really quite simple to use. First you would need to login to the OpenStack Dashboard as a user with a Member role. You would then click **Volumes** in the **Manage Compute** menu and press the **Create Volume** button (Figure 9-5).

ASSEMBLE

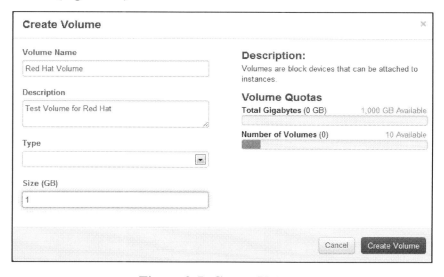

Figure 9-5: Create Volume

The volume should appear in the list for your project (Figure 9-6).

Chapter 9: Store the Information

Figure 9-6: Volumes

You can then use the **Edit attachments** button to connect the volume to one of your Compute instances (Figure 9-7).

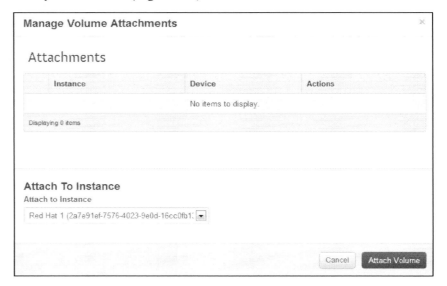

Figure 9-7: Manage Volume Attachments

OpenStack creates a unique iSCSI IQN and exposes it to the compute node, which now has an active iSCSI session. The instance will then be able to use the Cinder volume just as if it were local storage (usually a /dev/sdX disk).

In order to use Swift with your project, the first step would be to create a container. Log in to the OpenStack Dashboard as a user with a Member role. You would then click **Containers** in the **Object Store** menu and press the **Create Container** button (Figure 9-8).

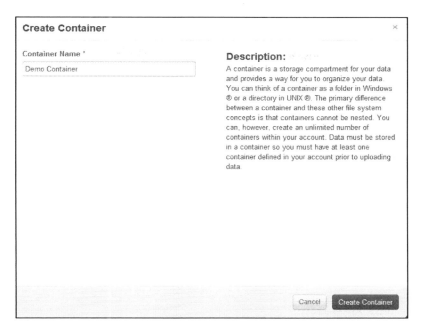

Figure 9-8: Create Container

It's a simple operation that doesn't involve supplying any data at all. It is literally just a name. Once you have the container, then it is usually up to the application to populate it with objects and retrieve these as needed using a programmatic interface. You can then see a list of containers in **Object Store / Containers** (Figure 9-9).

Figure 9-9: Containers

However, you can also upload objects from the dashboard. Simply press the **Up-load Object** button and supply a file with the stored content (Figure 9-10).

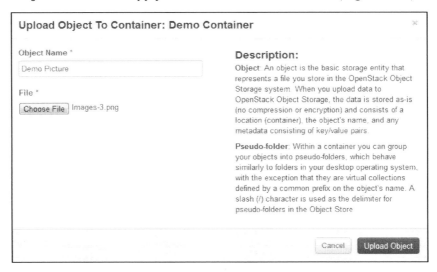

Figure 9-10: Upload Object

This is just one example. You can also use the interface to copy, download or delete objects.

Practical Recommendations

Storage is a relatively easy place to get started with OpenStack since it is self-contained and you don't even need to move your applications in order to use it.

If you do have legacy applications that you want to move to OpenStack, the easiest storage service to use is the OpenStack Block Store (Cinder). All you need to do is create the volumes, attach them to the instances and you are ready to go.

OpenStack Object Storage (Swift) is able to provide much better performance and reliability, but your application also needs to be Swift-aware. It needs to write to the OpenStack APIs to post and retrieve data, so it is more suited to new applications that are being developed now and should be optimized for the cloud.

ASSEMBLE

Chapter 10

Connect the Pieces

In this section we will look at Networking, which manages the connectivity between other OpenStack services. Let's start with its objective. It would be possible to develop an elastically scalable workload management system without including any network-specific functionality. Certainly the compute nodes would need connectivity between them and access to the outside world. But, it would be possible to leverage the existing networking infrastructure to allocate IP addresses and relay data between nodes.

ASSEMBLE

The biggest problem with such an approach in a multi-tenant environment is that the network management system in place would not be able to isolate traffic between users efficiently and securely. And this is a big concern for organizations building both public and private clouds.

One way to address this problem would be for OpenStack to build an elaborate network management stack that handles all network-related requests. The challenge with this strategy is that every implementation is likely to have a unique set of requirements that include integration with a diverse set of other tools and software.

OpenStack has therefore taken the path of creating an abstraction layer, called OpenStack Networking which presents a unified interface but can also accommodate a wide range of plugins to handle the integration with other networking services.

To better understand the rationale for this design choice, let's step back and refresh our memories of how networks have evolved over the last decades.

Software-Defined Networks

The simplest and earliest form of computer connectivity was a point-to-point connection between host machines, but this implied a separate interface and link for each additional peer. This kind of full mesh topology doesn't scale very well beyond two or three systems. So the idea of a network was born.

A physical packet-switched network consists of a set of hosts, links and network devices, whereby the network devices forward (and optionally process) traffic between the links. The links could be point-to-point or bus-oriented. The topology could be based on hub-and-spoke, token rings or a variety of other models. All of these designs have in common that the hosts send data in packages through their network interfaces. The network equipment receives this traffic on one interface and forwards it through another interface, optionally processing (e.g. segmenting, aggregating, compressing, decompressing, encrypting, decrypting) the contents in the process.

However, physical networks have their limitations in terms of security and scalability. Let's consider the security first. We may have sensitive data that we do not want to expose to all other hosts on the network but instead should be confined to a small subset of systems. Broadcasting all traffic throughout the network may have an impact on scalability too, since it can generate capacity bottlenecks on some of the links and these could reduce the availability of mission critical systems.

Network Segmentation

To achieve better confidentiality and availability, we need to segment the network. The most common segmentation mechanism in modern data centers is the Virtual Local Area Network (VLAN). These networks run over the same physical infrastructure but appear logically isolated. They use special tags to segment traffic and provide a degree of isolation by compartmentalizing the network.

On the host side, it is also possible to implement a degree of isolation through namespaces. Namespaces allow multiple instances of a routing table to co-exist within the same physical system. This is important for virtualized environments that are running applications belonging to different owners.

Most Linux kernels today support namespaces. In fact, Linux Containers (LXC) depend on the concept. The namespaces make it possible to separate network domains (network interfaces, routing tables, iptables) into completely separate and independent domains. It is therefore possible to have overlapping IP addresses (re-used between tenants) and multiple virtual routers per compute node.

Network Virtualization

Fragmenting the network into smaller segments addresses the security concerns but it doesn't help with scalability. We need a way to join the isolated pieces together as new "virtual" networks. Virtual Private Networking (VPN) can achieve the opposite of network segmentation. It allows the user to join or extend networks. This aggregation can be for remote access or for site-to-site connectivity. When referring to a VPN, we also often use the terms "tunnel" and "overlay" (Figure 10-1). Some may imply subtle differences between these concepts, but here we are using the expressions interchangeably.

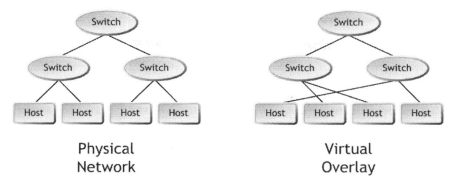

Figure 10-1: Network Virtualization

This simplest, and most common, form of overlays in most data centers are VLANs. We can call these Layer-2 (L2) overlays since they work at the second layer of the OSI stack. VLANs work with a notion called "trunk" that allows network switches to bridge traffic associated with the same VLAN between discontiguous areas on the network.

Standard VLANs have some drawbacks that reduce their effectiveness in a data center operating at cloud scale. They cannot span multiple subnets, which limits their flexibility. They have limited scalability since they are restricted to a finite number of VLAN IDs (4096). Furthermore, any movement in virtual machines or isolation boundaries requires reconfiguration of the switches.

To overcome these limitations, it is necessary to resort to Layer-3 (L3) tunnels. The endpoints to these tunnels encapsulate all the traffic with their own protocol and forward it to remote endpoints for delivery to the destination. Decoupling the logical tenant topologies from the physical data center topology creates the illusion of a dedicated IP address space for each customer. This simplifies network resource use and also facilitates VM deployment and network migration with a minimum of reconfiguration or service interruption.

By encapsulating the traffic into overlays, tunnels achieve the same benefits that compute virtualization provides through encapsulating virtual machines into files: it is possible to abstract the application from the hardware, re-locate the service and fully automate provisioning as we shall see shortly.

The idea is to create a layer that exposes virtual networks, implemented in software at the edge, having the same properties as physical networks, such as access control lists, firewall rules, higher-level (OSI Layer 4-7) services and support for dynamic routing updates.

The overlay can be based on various technologies. GRE (Generic Routing Encapsulation) has been very common in the past. But we also often see VXLAN and IPsec tunnels in many data centers.

Outside the data center, they may be complemented with SSL VPNs or technologies like Microsoft DirectAccess to allow the end users to access secure services from their PCs and mobile devices. The latter is necessary to facilitate hybrid cloud connections.

VPNs can create a secure connection between cloud entities and enterprises, end-users or even other cloud providers. These allow applications to operate in a trusted mode whereby they can treat the cloud service as an extension of the private network.

There are several intersections between virtualization and networking technologies. Virtual servers use virtual network interfaces. Virtualization can be used to segment networks. And virtualization can be used to connect discontiguous networks.

Establishing secure connectivity between an enterprise data center and components is not trivial. When you compound the complexity of discovering network resources, addressing them and ensuring all traffic is protected as it passes through public networks, the result is a challenge some organizations choose to forego.

One means of facilitating the task, and thereby seamlessly extending legacy applications into the cloud is through the use of a so-called Virtual Private Cloud (Figure 10-2).

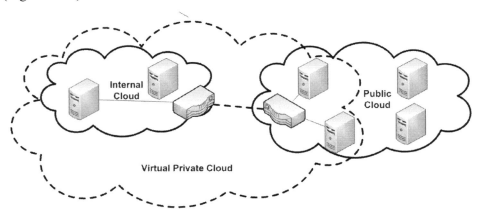

Figure 10-2: Virtual Private Cloud

Amazon runs a service by the same name, which essentially provides secure connectivity into a segment of Amazon's EC2 cloud. Other solutions, such as CohesiveFT's vns-cubed, provide similar functionality across cloud service providers. CloudSwitch also offers facilities to migrate virtual machines from the enterprise data center into the cloud. Layer-two bridging ensures that the network environment, including host names, IP and MAC addresses, remains intact thereby making it relatively easy to migrate legacy applications into a secure hybrid environment.

Network Function Virtualization

Another intersection between networking and virtualization is Network Function Virtualization (NFV). The idea of NFV is to leverage server virtualization technologies to consolidate many network equipment types, thus allowing providers to replace custom-built hardware with commodity systems.

Network operators are facing a proliferation of proprietary hardware appliances in their networks. Each time they launch a new service, they need to find the space and power to service the new systems. They also need to maintain a comprehensive set of skills and operational processes to design, integrate, administer and support these components.

A consortium of service providers have joined together to reduce this challenge. The European Telecommunications Standards Institute (ETSI) has commissioned an NFV Working Group with the charter of virtualizing network functions that were previously performed by proprietary dedicated hardware. The objective is to reduce the cost of network devices by running them on commodity platforms.

ASSEMBLE

Some of the network functions worth virtualizing might include routers, switches, security appliances and network management systems. The basic traffic forwarding functions can run in a virtual machine, managing traffic from both physical and virtual ports using a combination of L2 and L3 overlays. Physical machines that host security functions, such as firewalls, proxies, intrusion prevention and detection systems can be replaced with virtual appliances. You might even want to include traffic analysis, network monitoring tools and load balancers as some of the virtualized functions running on a pool of physical resources.

Standard IT virtualization is able to support the consolidation of many network equipment types onto industry-standard high-volume servers, switches and storage. And these could be located in the data center, on the carrier networks or on customer premises.

Virtualization also enables the separation of control and forwarding functions. By centralizing the control, it is possible to program the behavior of the network using well-defined interfaces, thus eliminating the need to constantly install new equipment and greatly simplifying network management.

Operational Efficiencies

Software Defined Networks (SDN) is a technology that abstracts the network while providing programmatic control. As such, it not only lends itself to the cloud objective of resource efficiency but also facilitates automation for opera-

Chapter 10: Connect the Pieces

tional benefits. To achieve this objective, it fundamentally changes the administrative perspective. The controller obtains a complete inventory of all components including switches, routers and firewalls. It then provides an abstracted flow-based view of all network connections and services that the applications require.

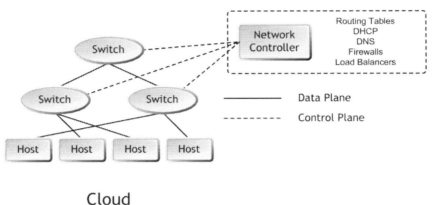

Cloud

Figure 10-3: Software-Defined Networking

The goal of SDN is to separate the control plane from the data forwarding plane in the network architecture (Figure 10-3). This increases flexibility in deploying and managing networks makes it possible to deploy network functions on industry-standard x86 servers. The controller centrally manages the overall network.

The initial interest in SDN came from the academic community, where researchers were developing and analyzing new protocols. The fact that networking functions were built into hardware made it very difficult for them to test and validate their experiments. They therefore had a very compelling reason to develop programmable network devices, which they could update according to their needs.

The momentum behind SDN today comes from large data centers. Corporations and service providers spend huge amounts on high-end switching equipment and are nonetheless running into limitations with what they can do, due to the limitations of 4096 VLANs and scaling problems of the Spanning Tree Protocol (STP). To support their legacy infrastructure, traditional data centers require a complex physical fabric with support for L2 switching, large numbers of L3 overlays, a suite of security (e.g. ACLs, firewalls) and network (e.g. load balancers) functions. This complexity makes it very difficult to operate an agile architecture.

With SDN, the customer can relegate the administration of this complexity to the the SDN controller and therefore use lower cost, less feature-rich switches. SDN also reduces hardware dependencies and accelerates provisioning, thereby minimizing operational overhead.

Since some of the benefits of SDN sound similar to those of NFV, it is worth clarifying the relationship between these two technologies. They are both a kind of network virtualization, which by definition means that they seek to decouple the logical network from its physical hardware, so that they can use commodity hardware and automate on top of it. However, there are important differences in their approach.

NFV originates with service providers and targets operator networks while SDN has its beginnings in research networks and enterprise data centers. The main objective of NFV is to relocate the network functions from dedicated appliances to generic servers while SDN is about centralizing control and increasing network agility. Consequently NFV focuses on routers, firewalls, gateways and other network elements while SDN is used for cloud orchestration.

As such NFV and SDN are best seen as complementary rather than competitive. NFV is certainly possible without SDN but the separation of control and data planes as implemented by SDN enhances performance and simplifies operations. NFV can support SDN since it provides the infrastructure that SDN controllers will manage. SDN can accelerate adoption of NFV technologies by providing programmatic access to provision and configure them.

ASSEMBLE

OpenFlow

The Open Networking Foundation is the most prominent industry initiative involved with software-defined networking. Its membership includes Google, Facebook, Microsoft and many network equipment manufacturers. Their jointly developed standard, OpenFlow, is a generalized network tunneling protocol with programmatic interfaces to create control and management schemes based on an organization's application requirements. For example, OpenFlow can dynamically extend a private cloud into a hybrid model by masking the enterprise-specific IP addresses from the cloud provider's infrastructure. The protocol can also assist service providers by dynamically provisioning WAN services, potentially across multi-provider/multi-vendor networks.

The essence of the OpenFlow architecture is the decoupling of data and control planes as we mentioned above. The network state is centralized in the control plane and fully abstracted from the applications and end systems, which operate in the data plane (Figure 10-4).

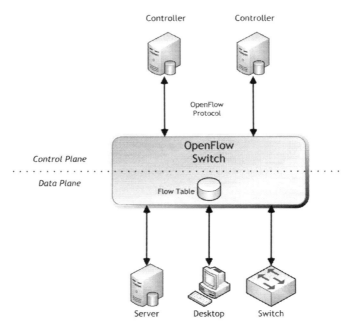

ASSEMBLE

Figure 10-4: OpenFlow Control and Data Planes

Each OpenFlow switch communicates in both planes. It routes traffic between the nodes in its data plane based on instructions in its flow table. Updates to the flow table come from controllers, which use the OpenFlow protocol to disseminate changes in topology and other network attributes.

The flows themselves consist primarily of rules and actions. The rules represent criteria, such as physical ports, MAC addresses, IP addresses and TCP ports that trigger the rules. The actions can include the option to forward the packets to a given port, drop the packets for security reasons or encapsulate the data and forward it to a controller for further processing.

The ability to dynamically reconfigure switches using an open standard offers enterprises and carriers many benefits. It simplifies control in multi-vendor environments, reduces complexity and allows faster innovation. At the same time it increases network reliability and security. These functions are particularly critical for large-scale multi-tenant environments, where it is vital to be able to frequently and rapidly re-provision loads across a dispersed pool of resources while also maintaining strict network isolation.

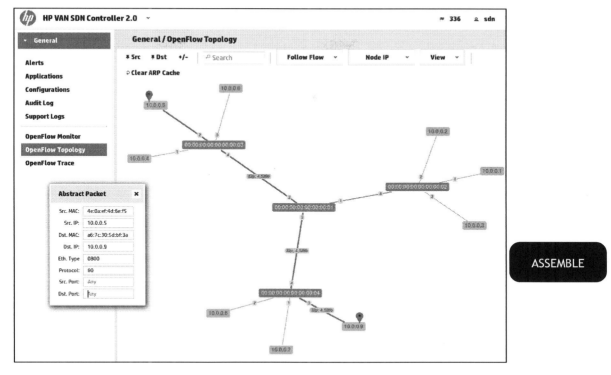

Figure 10-5: HP VAN SDN Controller

Major industry players such as HP, Juniper, Cisco, VMware and Microsoft are promoting SDN and OpenFlow. HP, Juniper and Cisco provide OpenFlow-capable networking devices and controllers (Figure 10-5). VMware acquired Nicira – an important SDN player – for extending its vSphere virtual networking and SDN capabilities. Microsoft is working with partners such as Nec to provide OpenFlow-based monitoring extensions for its Windows Server 2012 Extensible Virtual Switch.

OpenDaylight

OpenFlow is perhaps the best known SDN initiative, but it is not the only one. Microsoft has built its own Hyper-V Network Virtualization. VMware developed VXLAN which has seen broad industry adoption. Path Computation Element Protocol (PCEP) and Interface to the Routing System (I2RS) are yet other ways to approach SDN. Each caters to different scenarios and has its own challenges and benefits.

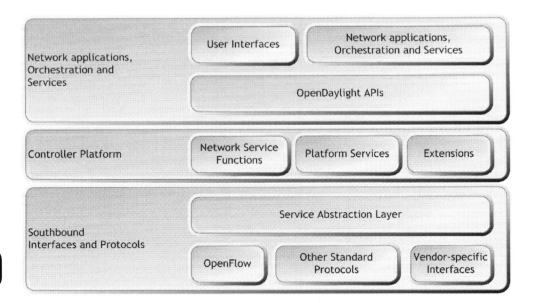

Figure 10-6: OpenDaylight

OpenDaylight (Figure 10-6) is an effort to bridge all of these protocols, providing a single REST API to the network application. The controller platform itself is primarily an interface layer. It offers some common abstractions, such as topology discovery and tracking of network elements. But ultimately it passes the execution to any one of several standard protocols (including OpenFlow) or vendor-specific interfaces through a Service Abstraction Layer (SAL).

OpenStack Implementation

Once it reaches a certain scale, networking is almost always a difficult topic. So, it should come as no surprise that it is typically the biggest customer challenge for organizations implementing OpenStack. Starting with the physical cabling and top-of-rack switch configuration to the VLAN tagging and implementation of upstream gateways and overlay networks, there are many different elements to consider.

Most of this configuration is external to OpenStack. As mentioned above, OpenStack has created an abstraction layer, called OpenStack Networking which can accommodate a wide range of plugins that handle the integration with other networking services.

Historically, the networking components of OpenStack were situated in the Nova (Compute) service. Most of these were split out into a separate service with the Folsom release. The new service was initially called Quantum but later renamed to Neutron to avoid any trademark confusion with the company Quantum

Corporation. So, don't be surprised to see the names Nova, Quantum and Neutron all appear in references to OpenStack Networking.

OpenStack doesn't perform networking functions itself but provisions networking configuration to the components (compute instances and network elements). For example, Open vSwitch can implement multiple VLANs in an OpenStack deployment and trunk them across the physical network to provide basic segmentation. Neutron provides the API to cloud tenants with which they can configure flexible policies and build sophisticated networking topologies, for example to support multi-tier web applications.

The principle is to enable third parties to write plugins that introduce advanced network capabilities at multiple layers of the OSI stack. These include L3 capabilities by creating Routers, defining Floating IP ranges and configuring Network Address Translation (NAT). With some of the services in development, they can also create higher-level (L4-L7) services, such as load balancing, VPN or firewalls that plug into OpenStack tenant networks.

ASSEMBLE

For instance, there is a service for Load Balancing as a Service (LBaaS) that we will cover in Chapter 20. We will talk about Firewall as a Service in Chapter 17. There is also a VPN as a Service (VPNaaS) and work on DNSaaS.

The initial focus of VPN as a service is a reference implementation for IPsec-based VPNs using static routing. But the long-term goal is to support multiple tunneling and security protocols for both static and dynamic routing.

DNS as a Service (Designate) is designed to provide a standard interface to DNS regardless of the underlying technology (e.g. BIND9 or PowerDNS). It is fully distributed with both command-line and programmatic interfaces for creating, updating and deleting zones and records.

You could consider OpenStack to be a form of software-defined networking on its own. But it also integrates well with the other SDN standards and initiatives in development. For example, OpenStack doesn't directly support NFV but an open initiative (called CloudNFV) using SDN to build a prototype of NFV based on OpenStack technology.

Some of the main networking plugins for OpenStack (e.g. Open vSwitch or VxLAN) are OpenFlow compliant, which make them the easiest path to adopting OpenFlow within an OpenStack implementation.

Chapter 10: Connect the Pieces

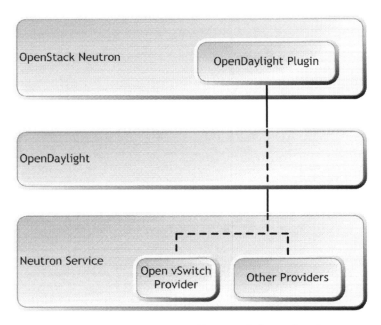

Figure 10-7: OpenDaylight and OpenStack

Similarly, there is ongoing work to deliver OpenDaylight as a Neutron plugin (Figure 10-7). It is currently limited to core functionality, but there are plans for full L4-L7 integration on the roadmap.

OpenStack Networking (Neutron)

The OpenStack Networking API is based on a simple model of virtual network, subnet, and port abstractions to describe networking resources.

Network is an isolated Layer-2 segment, analogous to a VLAN in the physical networking world. More specifically, it is a broadcast domain reserved to the tenant who created it unless it is explicitly configured to be shared. The network is also the primary object for the Neutron API. In other words, ports and subnets are always assigned to a specific network.

Subnet is a block of IPv4 or IPv6 addresses and their associated configurations. It is an address pool from which OpenStack can assign addresses to virtual machines. Each subnet is specified as a Classless Inter-Domain Routing (CIDR) range and must be associated with a network. Along with the subnet, the tenant can optionally specify a gateway, a list of DNS name servers and a set of host routes. Virtual machine instances on this subnet will then automatically inherit the configuration.

Port is a virtual switch connection point. A virtual machine instance can attach its NIC to a virtual network through this port. Upon creation, a port receives a fixed IP address from one the designated subnets. API Users can either request a specific address from the pool or Neutron will allocate an available IP address. OpenStack can also define the MAC addresses that the interface should use. After the Port is de-allocated, any allocated IP addresses are released and return to the address pool.

Plugins

The original OpenStack Compute network implementation assumed a very basic model of performing all isolation through Linux VLANs and IP tables. OpenStack Networking introduces the concept of a plugin, which is a back-end implementation of the OpenStack Networking API. A plugin can use a variety of technologies to implement the logical API requests.

Some OpenStack Networking plugins might use basic Linux VLANs and IP tables. These are typically sufficient for small and simple networks. But larger customers are likely to have more sophisticated requirements, such as multi-tiered web applications and internal isolation between multiple private networks. They could require their own IP addressing scheme (which could overlap with addresses used by other tenants), for example to allow applications to be migrated to the cloud without changing IP addresses. In these cases, there may be a need for more advanced technologies, such as L2-in-L3 tunneling or OpenFlow.

ASSEMBLE

The plugin architecture offers a great deal of flexibility for the cloud administrator to customize the network's capabilities. Third parties can supply additional API capabilities through API extensions, which may eventually become part of the core OpenStack Networking API.

The Neutron API exposes the virtual network service interface to users and other services, but the actual implementation of these network services resides in the plugins, which provide isolated virtual networks to the tenants and may also offer other services like address management. The API network should be reachable by anyone on the Internet and, in fact, may be a subnet of the external network.

As described above, the Neutron API exposes a model of network connectivity consisting of networks, subnets and ports, but it doesn't actually perform the work. The Neutron plugin has the responsibility for interacting with the underlying infrastructure so that traffic is routed in accordance to the logical model.

There are a large, and growing, number of plugins with different features and performance parameters. The list currently includes:

- Open vSwitch Plugin
- Cisco UCS/Nexus Plugin
- Linux Bridge Plugin
- Nicira Network Virtualization Platform (NVP) Plugin

- Ryu OpenFlow Controller Plugin
- NEC OpenFlow Plugin

In addition to these technology-specific plugins, starting with the Havana release, there is a new Modular Layer 2 (ML2) plugin which serves as the default. It consolidates code that was previously redundant between multiple plugins and allows for the deployment of multiple technologies within OpenStack and even on the same logical networks.

It works with the existing L2 agents (e.g. Open vSwitch, LinuxBridge, Hyper-V) and supports both multiple network segmentation types (local, flat, VLAN, GRE, VXLAN) and mechanism drivers (Arista, Cisco Nexus, Hyper-V Agent, L2 Population, Linuxbridge Agent, Open vSwitch Agent, Tail-f NCS).

Architecture

neutron-server is the main process of the OpenStack Networking server. It is a Python daemon that relays user requests from the OpenStack Networking API to the configured plugin. OpenStack Networking also includes three agents that interact with the main Neutron process through the message queue or the standard OpenStack Networking API. neutron-dhcp-agent provides DHCP services to all tenant networks. neutron-l3-agent does L3/NAT forwarding to enable external network access for VMs on tenant networks. There is also an optional plugin-specific agent (neutron-*-agent) that performs local switch configuration on each hypervisor.

It is important to be aware of the interaction between OpenStack Networking and the other OpenStack components. As with other OpenStack services, OpenStack Dashboard (Horizon) provides a GUI for administrators and tenant users to access the functionality, in this case to create and manage network services. The services also defers to OpenStack Identity (Keystone) for the authentication and authorization of any API request.

The integration with OpenStack Compute (Nova) is more specific. When Nova launches a virtual instance, the service communicates with OpenStack Networking to plug each virtual network interface into a particular port.

Network Design

A typical OpenStack Networking setup can be very complex, with up to four distinct physical networks. A management network is used for internal communication between OpenStack Components. A data network handles data communication between instances. The API network exposes all the OpenStack APIs to tenants. There is also usually a need for an external network that grants Internet access to the virtual machines.

On top of these physical networks, there are many ways to configure the virtual networks required by the tenants. The simplest scenario is a single flat network. There may also be multiple flat networks, private per-tenant networks or a combination of provider and per-tenant routers to manage the traffic between the networks.

The next choice is the plugin or plugins to use for network configuration. The simplest setup involves Linux Bridges, which is also the embedded solution used by many low-end hardware switches. Open vSwitch is another open-source solution that is slightly more powerful than Linux Bridges. It includes some limited flow control (Netflow, sFlow) and is a good choice for smaller deployments.

For high scalability, as well as faster speed to deployment, there is a need for a more sophisticated SDN, such as VxLAN, a standardized overlay technology for encapsulating Layer-2 traffic on top of an IP fabric. It breaks through the 4096 VLAN limitation and solves MAC address scaling. It also has the support of many network ASICs giving it an edge in performance for high-throughput requirements.

ASSEMBLE

Usage Scenario

To get an idea of how OpenStack Networking might be used in practice, let's just go through a very simple scenario where a tenant creates a network, defines a router to forward traffic from the private network, associates a subnet with the network and launches an instance that is to be associated with the network.

To begin with, you would need to login to the OpenStack Dashboard as a user with a Member role. If you click **Networks** in the **Manage Network** menu, you will see the list of networks already defined (Figure 10-8).

Figure 10-8: Networks

You can add to these by pressing the **Create Network** button and will first be asked to enter your choice of network name (Figure 10-9).

Figure 10-9: Create Network

You also need to specify a first subnet, meaning the network address range (e.g. 10.2.0.0/16) and the default gateway (Figure 10-10).

Figure 10-10: Create Subnet

And, if applicable, you can configure DHCP and DNS for that subnet (Figure 10-11).

Chapter 10: Connect the Pieces

Figure 10-11: Subnet Detail

As a next step, you might create a router by going to the **Router** section of the **Manage Network** menu and pressing the **Create Router** button. You can then connect the interfaces of the router to define how the traffic should flow (Figure 10-12).

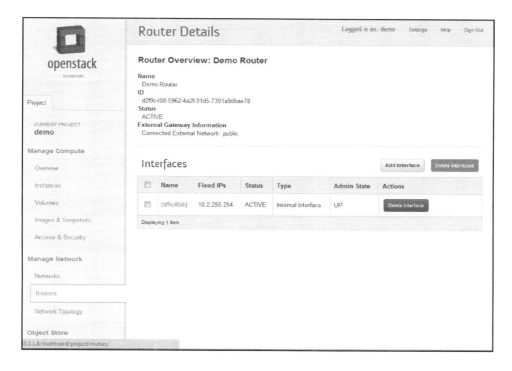

Figure 10-12: Network Router

The IP address port assignment will happen when you launch an image. Nova will contact Neutron to create a port on the subnet. Every virtual instance automatically receives a private IP address. You can optionally assign public IP addresses to instances using OpenStack's concept of "Floating IP address" (Figure 10-13).

Figure 10-13: Manage Floating IP Associations

Once the project requests a floating IP from the pool, it owns the address and is free to disassociate it from that instance and attach it to another (Figure 10-14).

Figure 10-14: Access & Security

Practical Recommendations

Software Defined Networking is a powerful concept that may revolutionize the data center. But it requires in-depth knowledge and careful planning to implement. Before you go there, make sure you are ready.

Most enterprises can at least begin with simple topologies. Make sure your OpenStack environment will run on a flat network before you attempt anything more advanced.

Your next step is to make sure it is secure. If any of the applications or data are sensitive, segregate the traffic either with separate physical links or cryptographic encapsulation.

As you become more proficient, you can tackle some of the more challenging tasks like integration of heterogeneous network appliances and replacement of the standard plugins.

Deploy

After the initial design and implementation work is complete, you may have demonstrated the feasibility of the technology but that is a far cry from ensuring it will work in production, particularly for highly scalable workloads. The first task is to roll out the OpenStack software itself onto the bare machines in the data center. The second is to design the orchestration of the workloads so that they are able to launch easily and automatically.

DEPLOY

Chapter 11

Bootstrap the Infrastructure

Part of the value proposition of cloud computing is the benefit that users don't need to deal with physical infrastructure. Many organizations prefer to focus on their core business and minimize the effort they place in supporting the underlying technology. After all, setting up the hardware is generally neither a differentiating skill nor closely aligned to their business objectives.

DEPLOY

However, this doesn't mean that we can avoid the infrastructure completely. Someone will need to design the data center, take care of power and cooling and fill the space with computing, networking and storage equipment. As long it is only a few systems, we can approach these ad hoc. The same engineer might be able to order the equipment, fit it into the racks, connect all the cables and load all the software on to it.

This doesn't work so well when you try to scale. When there are hundreds, thousands or even tens of thousands of hardware components, manual effort is error-prone and generally very expensive. We may want to consider pre-loaded data center containers for rapidly deploying large numbers of physical servers. There are also a number of interesting efforts in data center automation involving robotics, which may eventually lead to truly lights-out operation.

Regardless of how we get there, at some point the equipment will have been racked and stacked and the next step will be to deploy OpenStack on top of it. Certainly we can manually install each machine, but this requires physical access and is very human-intensive. It is ok for a demonstration or proof of concept, but will not scale efficiently to an enterprise or carrier-grade production deployment.

The challenge is a little like a chicken-and-egg problem. OpenStack makes it easy to deploy infrastructure services without any consideration for the hardware. Once it has been installed, it is almost trivial to roll out new software.

However, until some virtualization layer is in place, OpenStack itself cannot leverage any of these benefits.

As we shall see at the end of this chapter, one option is to first install a virtual substrate (TripleO) and then put OpenStack on top of it. This doesn't solve the fundamental problem since we still need to find a way to put the virtualization on the base infrastructure. But it does bring with it a number of additional benefits that we will point out.

Network Boot

The best remote way to bootstrap the infrastructure is via the network. The only hardware prerequisite for this approach is that all servers must be capable of network boot. This means the firmware needs to support PXE and ideally the systems should include an IPMI interface.

Using some bare-metal provisioning tools like Razor or Cobbler, we can then proceed to tailor the systems and hand-off to a configuration management system for ongoing operations. Before we go on to these, let's summarize what IPMI and PXE actually do.

DEPLOY

The easiest way to think of the Intelligent Platform Management Interface (IPMI) is that it is a KVM (Keyboard, Video and Mouse) implementation that runs over Ethernet. It is used for out-of-band system management and often is the only way to connect to a remote computer that is powered off or unresponsive.

The main component of an IPMI subsystem is the Baseboard Management Controller (BMC). It manages the interaction between the network interface and the platform hardware, which may include specialized sensors (temperature, voltage) and hardware controls (e.g. fan speed, power).

Administrators can use any of several utilities to manage the physical hosts. These will connect to the BMC via the network interface. Two of the most common include:

- **IPMItool** – a Linux command-line application
- **IMPI View** – a multi-platform Java GUI application distributed by SuperMicro

With these tools, it is possible to perform the console functions over the network. So, for example, the administrators can power the machines on and off or configure the BIOS parameters. They can also examine sensor values and query error logs. And – very important in this context – they can specify PXE as the source for the next boot cycle.

The Preboot Execution Environment (PXE) is an open industry standard. It was originally defined by Intel and Microsoft in 1998 as part of their PC System Design Guide – Wired for Management (WfM) specification. Its key objective is simply to allow a system to boot over the network instead of from system disks or external storage media (e.g. CD, DVD or USB Stick).

The PXE-enabled client system uses the Network Interface Card (NIC) to send a request to the DHCP server, which returns the address of a Trivial File Transfer Protocol (TFTP) server that hosts all necessary files for booting and configuring the system.

It is a simple process with essentially these steps:

1. When the bare metal client boots, its Network Interface Card (NIC) broadcasts a BOOTP request via DHCP.
2. A DHCP server responds with the IP address of a TFTP server.
3. The client sends a request to TFTP server to obtain the boot image.
4. TFTP server sends the boot image (pxelinux.0).
5. The client executes the boot image.
6. The client downloads all the files it needs (configuration files, Linux kernel and root file system), and then loads them.
7. The client reboots.

DEPLOY

So, you can use IPMI to specify PXE boot, assuming it wasn't already part of the pre-configured boot sequence, and then restart the machine. That's really all there is to it on the machines themselves. But you still need to create the boot files, set up the TFTP server and take care of the rest of the system configuration.

Fortunately, there are a number of tools to help. Not all of them will work equally well, so especially if you are only setting up a relatively small environment (e.g. less than a thousand nodes), you may want to stick with projects that are widely adopted or even commercially supported. On the other hand, if you plan to scale to huge dimensions, there is a better case for investing the time and effort to identify the best possible solution for your environment.

Some criteria to consider are automated system discovery, prerequisite checking, installation validation, logging, notifications, integration with configuration management systems as well as general principles such as the ability to customize and the availability of programmatic interfaces.

Let's look briefly at a few popular options:

Cobbler is designed as a small and lightweight application that is easy to use. It was originally developed by Red Hat but has since been packaged for Ubuntu and is used by Canonical for automating tests of OpenStack.

It is written in Python and offers three interfaces: the command line, a web interface, and an API. Its objective is simplicity, so it doesn't come with a lot of bells and whistles, but it does provide some limited functionality out of the box. For example, it can assign DHCP configuration (e.g. IP address) or software profiles based on MAC addresses and can reinstall systems using a helper called koan.

It uses Red Hat's Kickstart to furnish responses for unattended installation and to call custom scripts before/after install. For more advanced needs, it supports integration with configuration management systems, such as Puppet.

Razor is a relatively recent provisioning system from Puppet Labs that is written in Ruby. It uses iPXE, which extends PXE with the ability to retrieve data through other protocols like HTTP, iSCSI, ATA over Ethernet (AoE), and Fibre Channel over Ethernet (FCoE) and allows it to operate over Wi-Fi rather than requiring an Ethernet connection.

Its biggest additional feature is the ability to auto-discover server hardware. It boots into a Razor Microkernel that runs Puppet Labs Facter, which takes an inventory of CPUs, hard disks, memory and other interfaces and provides them to the Razor server in real-time[1]. Razor is tightly integrated with Puppet enabling a seamless hand-off. Once Razor finishes deploying the operating system, it installs the Puppet agent and transfers control to it for the configuration of the operating system and applications.

DEPLOY

The fact that Razor is developed by Puppet Labs and is tightly integrated with Puppet doesn't mean that other configuration management systems won't also work with it. For example, Rackspace uses Chef with Razor to provision their Rackspace Private Cloud offering.

Foreman also uses Puppet for configuration management and application deployment. Its strength comes to bear in a very distributed deployment model. The installation is driven from a central Foreman instance that provides the web interface and hosts all the configuration details.

But it is possible to distribute the workload to a set of smart proxies that are located on or near machines performing specific functions, such as TFTP, DHCP, DNS, and Puppet. Placing the proxies closer to the target nodes helps reduce latencies in large deployments spanning multiple data centers.

Crowbar was one of the first OpenStack-focused deployment frameworks. It was spearheaded by Dell and is also in use as the foundation of SUSE private clouds. It uses PXE boot to bootstrap a minimal CentOS image that launches Chef, its preferred configuration management tool.

---

[1] https://github.com/puppetlabs/Razor-Microkernel/wiki/An-Overview-of-the-Razor-Microkernel

It also includes native monitoring capabilities through Nagios and Ganglia and has strong configuration capabilities for OpenStack since many project parameters are exposed in the Crowbar UI.

The tools work with any vendor hardware but, not unsurprisingly, there is better integration with Dell products, where there are options to configure BIOS/Firmware and set up RAID.

CloudBoot is a system orchestration framework from Piston. It really only makes sense with the Piston distribution of OpenStack, where it is an elegantly bundled solution. The framework detects hardware using IPMI, boots the nodes to a hardened, embedded Linux operating system using PXE, and then passes off system control to Piston's Moxie high availability framework for configuration and service management.

MAAS (Metal as a Service) from Canonical is another bare-metal provisioning framework. It provides strong lifecycle management, which means that it can discover and deploy both virtual and physical servers, dynamically re-allocate physical resources in response to changing workloads and retire servers when they are no longer needed.

It is built for high-volume, scale-out deployments with built-in support for a cross-region controller. Unfortunately, this also means that it is not really suitable for small installations. It requires at least a ten-node configuration for a clean deployment.

DEPLOY

Fuel from Mirantis was already covered in Chapter 6. We won't repeat the description here but would like to reinforce the point that Fuel is not only an option for a quick proof of concept in a virtual environment. The same GUI-based tool can also be used to deploy and manage a set of bare metal servers.

Compass is s pluggable deployment framework developed by Huawei. It is relatively new but worth noting as an option for a comprehensive tool that manages everything from server discovery to OS provisioning and configuration management. It doesn't replace the other tools in this list as much as it provides a unified interface to orchestrate them.

So, for example, it includes modules to control servers via IPMI, networking gear through SNMP and hardware configuration modules for specific vendors that can be substituted or augmented. It relies on software like Cobbler and Razor for OS provisioning and can integrate with the configuration management of Chef, Puppet, Ansible, Salt and others.

This list is nowhere near exhaustive. You may come across dnsmasq, pxedust or xcat, for example. The main consideration, particularly for tools that nobody has yet used to deploy OpenStack, is that it may take considerable effort to make them work. It will probably be possible, but unless you have an overriding reason to choose the path less traveled, you will want to make sure you know what you are in for.

Configuration Management

Automating the bare metal installation has its clear advantage in reducing the need for physical access to the hardware. But even once the operating system has been deployed, there is still a compelling value proposition for a tool that simplifies the manual interaction required to configure the platform and all installed applications.

Let's reflect on how these tasks are performed without a configuration management system. When you have two or three systems, you can go to the console, install any software packages from the command line and manually edit configuration files. If you scale up to a couple of dozen systems, most administrators will see a benefit in a remote login, for example via SSH, to save themselves a lot of walking around. They may want to script their installations and configuration edits. In a deployment of this size, partial automation is sufficient; they can always intervene manually when there are problems or some machines have atypical configurations.

DEPLOY

However, when you reach into the thousands of nodes, these ad hoc scripts tend to break down. The machines have a wide variety of combinations of different hardware and installed software making it difficult to test any scripts and validate their success.

It is at this scale that it becomes almost mandatory to have a tool that can automate a consistent deployment across many different configurations. We often say that the operations are idempotent, borrowing from the mathematical notion of an operation that does not change result when it is re-applied multiple times. In this model, the administration specifies a stateful configuration, or describes how the system should look, and the software ensures that the systems converge to that state.

Puppet

Puppet is the most widely adopted open source data center automation and configuration management framework today (Figure 11-1). In that sense, it is the baseline that others measure against. It provides system administrators with a platform that allows consistent, transparent, and flexible systems management.

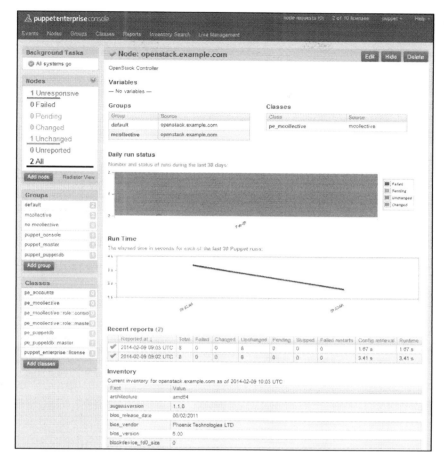

Figure 11-1: Puppet

DEPLOY

Some of the key elements of Puppet include:

Puppetmaster: central manager that can configure thousands of nodes

Dashboard: console to visualize, explore and command puppet infrastructure

Secure infrastructure: built-in SSL-based public key infrastructure

Puppet Modules: reusable units of puppet configuration including some free community-developed modules

A declarative language describes the system configuration, so that administrators can reproduce any configuration on other systems. The framework can help enforce configuration policies and automatically correct systems that drift from their baseline. Puppet also provides an audit trail of all systems, which can be kept in version control for compliance purposes.

PackStack[1] is a command line utility used, for example, by Red Hat RDO. It uses Puppet modules to support rapid deployment of OpenStack on existing servers over an SSH connection. PackStack is suitable for deploying both single node proof-of-concept installations and more complex multi-node installations. Deployment options are provided either interactively, via the command line, or via a text file containing preconfigured answers to the questions PackStack asks.

Chef

Opscode's Chef is very similar to Puppet in its objectives but is a newer system and therefore not quite as widely known or used although they do have some big-name customers, like Facebook. Even though both are written in Ruby, Puppet's domain-specific language hides it more than Chef, which expects users to be familiar with Ruby. Depending on your organization's familiarity with Ruby, you may consider this a benefit or a drawback.

Chef defines its configuration in units called cookbooks. Each cookbook defines a task, such as the components necessary to install a software package. It contains templates, files, metadata and collections of resources, called recipes.

DEPLOY

There are community-supported cookbooks for each OpenStack project available on GitHub[2], so it is relatively easy to use Chef to build an OpenStack environment. Opscode also offers a hosted version of the Chef open-source configuration management software, which is interesting if you want to minimize your in-house footprint.

Ansible

You can write Ansible modules in any language you like, including simple bash scripts. One of its advantages is that you don't need to install an agent on the managed nodes. The client needs SSH and Python, but that is it. Ansible then uses SSH to push commands to the remote systems.

In addition to the initial setup and provisioning of the server and the deployment of layered applications, it is also able to execute any ad hoc commands on remote systems either individually or based on defined selection criteria, which many administrators find useful for troubleshooting and debugging.

Ansible isn't currently widely used for OpenStack deployments but there has been some work in this area. You can find Ansible playbooks on GitHub if you would like to try it out yourself[3].

---

[1] https://wiki.openstack.org/wiki/Packstack
[2] https://github.com/stackforge/openstack-chef-repo
[3] https://github.com/openstack-ansible/openstack-ansible

Salt

Saltstack is written in Python and, like Ansible, is both a configuration management system that can maintain remote nodes in defined states, and a distributed remote execution system used to query data on remote nodes. One of the main champions of Saltstack is LinkedIn.

One difference between Ansible and Salt is that the former uses SSH by default, while Saltstack uses ZeroMQ as the communications protocol. When making requests to hundreds of remote systems simultaneously, this distinction can have a significant performance impact. To address the potential bottleneck, Ansible has also developed a mechanism, called fireball mode, that sets up a ZeroMQ listener on the target systems and improves its handoff performance in a similar fashion to Ansible.

As with Ansible, you can find SaltStack formulas for deploying OpenStack on GitHub[1].

Juju

Juju, from Canonical, is another interesting tool for packaging applications. In some ways, it is a higher-level abstraction since you can create 'charms' using Puppet, Chef, Ansible, Salt or any other configuration management assets.

DEPLOY

Juju provides both a command-line interface and a web application to design, build, configure, deploy and manage infrastructure. In addition to charms available for popular applications like Apache or WordPress, Juju facilitates the deployment of applications to Amazon EC2, Microsoft Azure, and of course any OpenStack cloud[2].

Selection Criteria

One of the initial challenges in evaluating these tools is that even though they largely incorporate similar concepts, they use different metaphors and therefore different names to describe their objects. You could say that a Puppet manifest is similar to a Chef cookbook or Ansible playbook. A Salt master corresponds to a Chef server and a Salt minion to a Chef client.

Once you get beyond the terminology, there are a few subtle differences that may have some bearing on your selection. As you look at the above and numerous other packages that provide similar functionality, including Cfengine, Bcfg and LCFG, there are several criteria to consider such as size of the developer base, commercial track record, documentation, range of use cases and platform support. There are also philosophical differences around dependency manage-

---

[1] https://github.com/saltstack-formulas/openstack-standalone-formula
[2] https://juju.ubuntu.com/docs/config-openstack.html

ment. Puppet, for instance declares these explicitly, while with Chef they are implied through the order of the commands.

You should look at the configuration languages both in terms of how familiar your developers are with them and how well they handle your requirements. There is a significant difference between the domain-specific language that Puppet uses and straight Ruby from Chef, or Python from Fabric. You might also care about the transport mechanism, which could be based on ZeroMQ, SSH or HTTP, and whether the packages are formatted with JSON, YAML or any other notation.

OpenStack Bare Metal (Ironic)

OpenStack Bare Metal (Ironic) is only indirectly related to bare-metal provisioning. It is actually a variant of OpenStack Compute and so you could argue we should have covered it in Chapter 8. However, we will describe it here simply because we are on the topic of bare metal. Our next provisioning mechanism, TripleO, depends on Ironic. And Ironic itself will also need to be provisioned on bare metal.

DEPLOY

Let's back up just a moment. What is Ironic? It is a hypervisor driver for OpenStack Nova that allows guest machines to run directly on physical hardware rather than requiring a virtualization layer. Now, if virtualization is so great, you may wonder why anyone would want to do this.

There are a few benefits or use cases for Ironic. Bare metal is more efficient than a virtualized system. Admittedly the overhead of a hypervisor is minimal, but it still has an impact which might be significant for high-performance computing applications. Other applications may require support for specific hardware that is not available in a virtual environment. Some hosting customers may insist on dedicated machines for security reasons, whereby they need to be very careful since bare metal can expose other threats such as firmware attacks. And finally, it is an enabler for TripleO as we mentioned above.

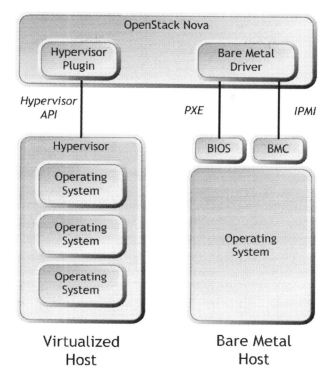

Figure 11-2: OpenStack Bare Metal Driver

So, how does it work? Ironic has the same role as the drivers for other hypervisors (e.g. libvirt, Xen, Hyper-V) (Figure 11-2). Since it doesn't have an intermediate virtualization layer to handle Nova requests, it connects directly to the hardware interfaces we mentioned earlier, PXE and IPMI.

For illustration, the sequence for launching a single instance would be something like

1. Nova pulls image from glance.
2. IPMI turns the machine on.
3. The machine boots via PXE.
4. A small bootable RAM disk exposes local disks via iSCSI.
5. Nova copies images to hard disk.
6. Machine boots and runs image.

There are some prerequisites to using Ironic. The hardware (BIOS, RAID) must already be configured and an inventory (MAC address, IPMI credentials, CPU/RAM specifications) must be registered with Nova. There are also some limitations, since it is impossible to allocate partial resources of a physical system, for example. However, by and large, it is possible to manage both a physical and virtual infrastructure with a degree of consistency even if the actual operation is quite different.

OpenStack on OpenStack (TripleO)

OpenStack on OpenStack (TripleO) is a program that leverages OpenStack to install, upgrade and operate OpenStack. At first glance, this may seem very odd and inefficient. After all, how can it be easier to roll out two OpenStack deployments than it is one?

The simple answer is that if you were only concerned with quickly launching an OpenStack service, there would probably be little benefit. But in reality, the initial deployment is just the tip of the iceberg. With new releases, bug fixes and changes in workload, you need to continuously update the infrastructure and if this infrastructure is tied to the physical hardware, it can be a very tedious process.

DEPLOY

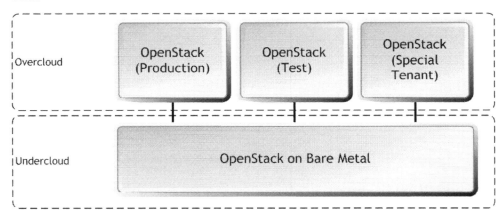

Figure 11-3: Overcloud and Undercloud

TripleO addresses this problem by separating the OpenStack infrastructure into two separate layers, or "clouds", called the undercloud and overcloud (Figure 11-3). The undercloud is relatively static and is deployed on bare metal. The overcloud runs on top of the undercloud and can leverage OpenStacks's orchestration capabilities for installation upgrades and updates.

The undercloud runs the Glance, Nova Keystone and Heat services and requires at least two machines for a high-availability control plane. Any additional nodes are then available for the overcloud tenants, which incidentally do not all need to belong to the same overcloud. There could be multiple undercloud tenants (i.e. multiple overclouds), either for testing purposes or in order to implement additional resource allocation boundaries.

Practical Recommendations

When you are setting up a lab to try out OpenStack, the easiest way to get started is to configure the hardware by hand. You can even keep to a manual setup for trials and small production deployments.

But once you start to scale to hundreds of physical nodes, you need to find a way to roll out new machines automatically. There are quite a few tools that will take you from a PXE-based network boot to a configuration management system that sets up your basic software, so you can take your pick.

In the long term, you should consider TripleO with an Ironic undercloud to give you a stable infrastructure that is consistent with OpenStack technologies. It is still work-in-progress, but worth keeping an eye on.

DEPLOY

Chapter 12

Provision the Applications

The overriding objective of any information technology is to support the business by providing insight and automating manual processes. Once the OpenStack infrastructure is in place, the deployment focus can shift from the underlying technology to the business services.

DEPLOY

The complexity and types of resources required by these services may vary greatly depending on who requests them. Consider some common organizational roles and the types of IT requests these users might have (Table 12-1).

Role	Request	OpenStack Impact
Project Manager	Create collaboration site	Direct
	Set up portal	Direct
Research Team	Create environment for simulation or grid workload	Direct
Application Developer	Test and state application	Direct
Line Manager	Create account	Indirect
	Set up workplace	Indirect
Business Manager	Grant access to accounting system	Indirect

Table 12-1 : Resource Requests

Requests to create sites or allocate resources are great use cases for OpenStack since they map direction to OpenStack-managed elements. But many other provisioning requests may have an indirect impact. For example, there will be situations where adding a single account or providing additional quota from a shared resource pool reaches a threshold that triggers the need for additional IT resources (e.g. another server, more storage).

In our quest for a software-defined data center, we want to automate as much as possible throughout the infrastructure. We can look at the provisioning process at two levels. We need to configure the individual resources (primarily the virtual machines), but we also need to look at complete business services, which typically consist of a multiple interdependent resources.

On any individual level, we have the same bootstrapping challenge as we did for the infrastructure in the previous chapter. This task is similar to what we already covered in the sense that it also requires a two-step process. We must first obtain the image with the base operating system and then ensure that it stays current using some kind of configuration management tools. However, the fact that we now have a virtual environment in place makes the initial provisioning much easier.

DEPLOY

Coordinating the resources to deliver value-added business services is quite a different task – one that is potentially very complex. The application layer is much less homogenous and predictable than the infrastructure layer. For example, each business service will requires different sets of resources and these sets of resources will change over time.

We will begin this chapter with the individual resource configuration and then move on to the task of building business services from the resources.

Image Generation

The starting point for a virtual workload is the disk image that will be used to start the virtual machine. In OpenStack, this would be the image that is loaded into Glance and then passed to Nova when launching a new instance (Figure 12-1).

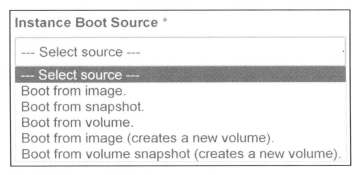

Figure 12-1: Nova Boot Source

At a minimum, the virtual image must contain the operating system. However, it may also be desirable to include some additional software. Alternatively, we can only include a bare minimum into the disk image and install the rest after launching the instance.

How much to pre-install comes down to a basic trade-off. The more we include in the base image, the faster we can deploy the instance into production. However, we also reduce the flexibility to change configuration. And, even if we have pre-installed some software, we may need to upgrade it to ensure it is fully up-to-date.

Oz is a popular python-based utility, used by Rackspace Cloud Builders for example, to create virtual machine images from ISOs by automating the installation process. VeeWee was designed for creating Vagrant base boxes, but it can also build VM images for VMware and KVM. It runs inside Ruby and, similar to Oz, creates a disk image, starts up a virtual machine and installs any required software using a VNC session if necessary.

BoxGrinder is another tool for creating virtual machine images, which it calls appliances. BoxGrinder can create Fedora, Red Hat Enterprise Linux, or CentOS images which can run under KVM, Xen or VMware. However, one limitation of BoxGrinder is that it runs inside of a chroot jail. It is therefore necessary to use a host machine running the same distribution and version of the operating system as is needed for the guest image that is being created.

DEPLOY

Other tools for creating images for multiple hypervisors include imagefactory and VMbuilder. If you are targeting specific hypervisors, you may also want to consider VMware Studio, VMWare's solution for building virtual appliances or, Microsoft sysprep and cloudbase-init for creating Windows images.

Guest Configuration

Once the image is loaded into Glance, we can provision it to Nova as needed. But as we consider its ongoing management, we need to remember that cloud computing is very service-centric. Services are much more dynamic, complex and customizable than most infrastructural components. As a result, there is a stronger need to facilitate a diverse set of operational needs that can rarely be achieved through a set of static configuration values and instead requires active involvement of the operations team.

These requirements represent a break from the past, where operations took a passive role in software execution, manually installing standard software according to guidelines handed to them. Instead, there is a need for increased collaboration between the development and operations teams to optimize and automate application deployments. This new approach is often called DevOps.

By avoiding isolated decisions it makes it much easier to re-locate applications between environments, such as a public and private cloud. The simplest way to encapsulate configuration instructions with an application is to package a shell script with it. The problem with this approach is that while scripts contain a list of actions to achieve their goal, they normally lack any way of checking if the system is in the correct initial state and whether the desired outcome has been achieved.

A declarative configuration-management system, like Chef or Puppet, covered in the previous chapter, allows the user to specify the desired system state and then takes the necessary action to push the system into this state. It can probe the current state of the system, and deploy changes when the state needs to be corrected. If a system is already in the desired state, it may or may not redeploy the changes. The tools can also regularly examine the target systems and detect when they have diverged from the desired state.

In theory, we could hard-code the instructions straight into the base image. If we have pre-installed the CM software, it could launch the agent on boot and take over the management from there. However, this approach does tie us down and makes it difficult to change any operational details without re-building the image.

DEPLOY

A better approach is to be able to specify some instructions that should execute at boot-time. OpenStack offers two techniques we can use to help with this task: user data and cloud-init.

- User data is simply an unstructured blob that can be passed as a parameter to the instance with a nova boot call. Typically it would be a local file that contains configuration information or shell commands to be executed.
- Cloud-init is a tool maintained by Canonical that runs a service on boot to retrieve user data and take action based on its contents. The package is pre-installed on Ubuntu cloud images but has also been ported to other distributions.

In addition to the user data, the cloud-init service may also require other instance-specific data. To obtain any of this information it can query a so-called metadata service, which is accessible at http://169.254.169.254 and returns information in JSON format. Instances can also access the meta data using a Config Drive (available as a nova boot option) which is exposed as a partition with all the metadata and can be attached to the instance when it boots.

Cloud Automation

At this point, we have established how to launch and configure individual virtual machines. This helps us to achieve one of the benefits of cloud computing. We can deploy services that are consistent and self-contained (don't require manual configuration), thereby making operations much more scalable. We also reduce operational costs, achieve quicker time to market and potentially improve security and compliance.

But there is still a missing piece. We are still looking at each of the resources individually. An administrator needs to plan and launch each configuration manually. An ideal cloud service entails the ability for the infrastructure to heal itself. When a server crashes, it can launch a new instance. Or if there is an increase in demand, the service should be able to scale elastically and automatically.

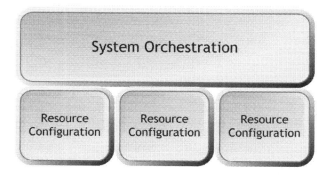

Figure 12-2: System Orchestration

DEPLOY

We must also contend with a new challenge as we automate complex workflows (Figure 12-2). A major element of this orchestration is the encapsulation of multiple resources into bundles that can be treated as a single unit. A business user should be able to deploy a multi-tier application with a single click, without seeing any of the dependent workflows that coordinate execution across all the required components.

OpenStack Orchestration (Heat)

OpenStack Orchestration (Heat) is a service that facilitates workflow orchestration and indirectly supports self-healing and auto-scaling capabilities. It borrows heavily from Amazon's implementation of their CloudFormation service. The service is based on templates that define application environments in terms of the resources they require.

Heat operates on units called stacks, which are comprised of sets of connected cloud resources such as machine instances, volumes, floating IP addresses, security groups and can be extended with additional orchestration capabilities such as auto-scaling groups and load balancers.

Each stack is specified in a template file, which is text file that is formatted with JSON or YAML and based on the AWS CloudFormation template syntax[1]. Each file contains five elements:

- Description: text description of templates
- Parameters: Input values
- Mappings: conditional values evaluated like switch statement
- Resources (e.g. SecurityGroup, Alarm, DBInstance, AutoScalingGroup, LoadBalancer, SNS Topic)
- Outputs: custom values returned in console outputs tab (e.g. URL of website created in template)

The stacks can be nested and are the basic building block for auto-scaling and high availability at all levels.

Both the API and the templates come in Amazon-compatible and native variants. In other words, it is possible to use many of the same tools and templates for building both Amazon and OpenStack stacks with only minor changes. However, if there is no foreseeable requirement to be able to span both of these technologies, users may find the native interfaces to be easier and more efficient.

DEPLOY

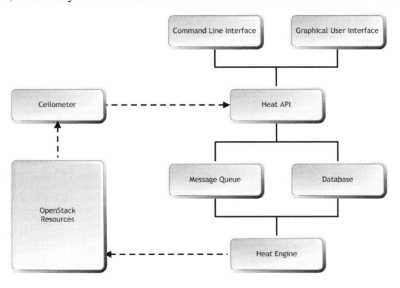

Figure 12-3: Heat Architecture

---

[1] http://docs.aws.amazon.com/AWSCloudFormation/latest/UserGuide/template-reference.html

The architecture of Heat is similar to other OpenStack components in that the Heat API accepts requests from the CLI or dashboard and passes them on to the message queue where the Heat engine processes them (Figure 12-3). The engine makes requests to the appropriate services (e.g. Nova to launch VMs) and stores any persistent information in the database.

An interesting distinction of Heat is that there is also an interaction with Ceilometer, particularly for alarming and auto-scaling. Ceilometer gathers telemetry data from the resources and can be used to trigger events when either upscaling or downscaling thresholds are met.

Usage Scenario

The easiest way to understand OpenStack Orchestration is to look at a specific case. To illustrate the concept, let's go through a simple template. You can find the WordPress Single Instance in Appendix B; or you can download the most current version from Github[1].

As mentioned above, it consists of five elements.

The *Description* is quite straightforward. It is free-form text that serves primarily as a means of internal documentation.

```
"Description" : "AWS CloudFormation Sample Template Word-
Press_Single_Instance: WordPress is web soft
```

The *Parameters* indicate user-supplied values. In this example we can see there are seven parameters: KeyName, InstanceType, DBName, DBUsername, DBPassword, DBRootPassword, LinuxDistribution.

They all have a description and type. Some specify a default value and it is possible to indicate some constraints, such as length, input values and input patterns.

```
"Parameters" : {

  "KeyName" : {
    "Description" : "Name of an existing EC2 KeyPair to enable SSH access
to the instances",
    "Type" : "String"
  },

  "InstanceType" : {
    "Description" : "WebServer EC2 instance type",
    "Type" : "String",
    "Default" : "m1.small",
    "AllowedValues" : [ "m1.tiny", "m1.small", "m1.medium", "m1.large",
"m1.xlarge" ],
    "ConstraintDescription" : "must be a valid EC2 instance type."
  },
```

---

[1] https://github.com/openstack/heat-templates/blob/master/cfn/F18/WordPress_Single_Instance.template

DEPLOY

```
  "DBName": {
    "Default": "wordpress",
    "Description" : "The WordPress database name",
    "Type": "String",
    "MinLength": "1",
    "MaxLength": "64",
    "AllowedPattern" : "[a-zA-Z][a-zA-Z0-9]*",
    "ConstraintDescription" : "must begin with a letter and contain only
alphanumeric characters."
  },

  "DBUsername": {
    "Default": "admin",
    "NoEcho": "true",
    "Description" : "The WordPress database admin account username",
    "Type": "String",
    "MinLength": "1",
    "MaxLength": "16",
    "AllowedPattern" : "[a-zA-Z][a-zA-Z0-9]*",
    "ConstraintDescription" : "must begin with a letter and contain only
alphanumeric characters."
  },

  "DBPassword": {
    "Default": "admin",
    "NoEcho": "true",
    "Description" : "The WordPress database admin account password",
    "Type": "String",
    "MinLength": "1",
    "MaxLength": "41",
    "AllowedPattern" : "[a-zA-Z0-9]*",
    "ConstraintDescription" : "must contain only alphanumeric characters."
  },

  "DBRootPassword": {
    "Default": "admin",
    "NoEcho": "true",
    "Description" : "Root password for MySQL",
    "Type": "String",
    "MinLength": "1",
    "MaxLength": "41",
    "AllowedPattern" : "[a-zA-Z0-9]*",
    "ConstraintDescription" : "must contain only alphanumeric characters."
  },
  "LinuxDistribution": {
    "Default": "F18",
    "Description" : "Distribution of choice",
    "Type": "String",
    "AllowedValues" : [ "F18" ]
  }
},
```

If you were to launch the stack from the command line, you would be able to supply these parameters as arguments to the command.

```
$ heat stack-create "My Stack"
    --template-file=/heat/templates/WordPress_Single_Instance.template
    --parameters="InstanceType=m1.large;
                  DBUsername=wp;
                  DBPassword=pswd;
                  KeyName=heat_key;LinuxDistribution=F17"
```

Similarly, if you launch the stack from the Horizon dashboard, you will be prompted for the parameters (Figure 12-4).

Figure 12-4: Launch Stack

Mappings are simply a lookup table that you can use later in the template in order to perform some simple transformations on the input values.

```
"Mappings" : {
  "AWSInstanceType2Arch" : {
    "m1.tiny"     : { "Arch" : "32" },
    "m1.small"    : { "Arch" : "64" },
    "m1.medium"   : { "Arch" : "64" },
    "m1.large"    : { "Arch" : "64" },
    "m1.xlarge"   : { "Arch" : "64" }
  },
  "DistroArch2AMI": {
    "F18"        : { "32" : "F18-i386-cfntools", "64" : "F18-x86_64-
cfntools" }
  }
},
```

The Resources section is the most complex. It lists each resource that needs to be launched along with the properties that describe its configuration. You will note, for example in the UserData property, that there are several intrinsic functions you can use to manipulate data. Join performs a simple string concatenation. Base64 converts binary to ASCII text using the Base64 encoding scheme.

DEPLOY

The most interesting function is FindInMap, which uses the Mapping described earlier. So, for example, if we refer back to the mapping table we can see that an instance type of "m1.small" would map to an Arch of "64". A LinuxDistribution of "F18" combined with an Arch of "64" would lead to a DistroArch2AMI of "F18-x86_64-cfntools", which is the ImageID that is generated.

In the example below, the only resource to create is an EC2 (i.e. Nova, in the case of OpenStack) instance. We can specify the instance type, a keypair and also some UserData to bootstrap the instance.

```
"Resources" : {
  "WikiDatabase": {
    "Type": "AWS::EC2::Instance",
    "Metadata" : {
      "AWS::CloudFormation::Init" : {
        "config" : {
          "packages" : {
            "yum" : {
              "mysql"        : [],
              "mysql-server" : [],
              "httpd"        : [],
              "wordpress"    : []
            }
          },
          "services" : {
            "systemd" : {
              "mysqld"   : { "enabled" : "true", "ensureRunning" : "true"
},
              "httpd"    : { "enabled" : "true", "ensureRunning" : "true"
}
            }
          }
        }
      }
    },
    "Properties": {
      "ImageId" : { "Fn::FindInMap" : [ "DistroArch2AMI", { "Ref" :
"LinuxDistribution" },
                          { "Fn::FindInMap" : [ "AWSInstanceType2Arch", {
"Ref" : "InstanceType" }, "Arch" ] } ] },
      "InstanceType"   : { "Ref" : "InstanceType" },
      "KeyName"        : { "Ref" : "KeyName" },
      "UserData"       : { "Fn::Base64" : { "Fn::Join" : ["", [
        "#!/bin/bash -v\n",
        "/opt/aws/bin/cfn-init\n",
        "# Setup MySQL root password and create a user\n",
        "mysqladmin -u root password '", { "Ref" : "DBRootPassword" },
"'\n",
        "cat << EOF | mysql -u root --password='", { "Ref" : "DBRootPass-
word" }, "'\n",
        "CREATE DATABASE ", { "Ref" : "DBName" }, ";\n",
        "GRANT ALL PRIVILEGES ON ", { "Ref" : "DBName" }, ".* TO \"", {
"Ref" : "DBUsername" }, "\"@\"localhost\"\n",
        "IDENTIFIED BY \"", { "Ref" : "DBPassword" }, "\";\n",
        "FLUSH PRIVILEGES;\n",
        "EXIT\n",
        "EOF\n",
        "sed -i \"/Deny from All/d\" /etc/httpd/conf.d/wordpress.conf\n",
        "sed -i \"s/Require local/Require all granted/\"
/etc/httpd/conf.d/wordpress.conf\n",
        "sed --in-place --e s/database_name_here/", { "Ref" : "DBName" },
"/ --e s/username_here/", { "Ref" : "DBUsername" }, "/ --e
s/password_here/", { "Ref" : "DBPassword" }, "/ /usr/share/wordpress/wp-
config.php\n",
        "systemctl restart httpd.service\n",
        "firewall-cmd --add-service=http\n",
        "firewall-cmd --permanent --add-service=http\n"
    ]]}}
    }
  }
},
```

DEPLOY

The Outputs provide a mechanism for Heat to return information back to the user after the resources have been provisioned. In this case, we use the GetAtt function to obtain the public IP address of the instance and use it to compose a URL pointing to the WordPress site.

```
"Outputs" : {
  "WebsiteURL" : {
    "Value" : { "Fn::Join" : ["", ["http://", { "Fn::GetAtt" : [ "WikiDa-
tabase", "PublicIp" ]}, "/wordpress"]] },
    "Description" : "URL for Wordpress wiki"
  }
}
```

Business Process Automation

Provisioning resources is an important part of automating IT, but it is only a part. We also need to validate what has been provisioned. For example, in the case of OpenStack, we may want to use the Tempest suite to run through a comprehensive set of quality assurance checks.

DEPLOY

Upgrades are another issue. The worst-case scenario would require rebuilding the complete environment for each software version. But in some cases it is sufficient to simply stop all the services, update them and restart them in sequence.

Probably the largest challenge in an enterprise is integrating the service into the rest of the IT landscape. As the enterprise needs to launch increasinglycomplex environments with auto-scaling, load balancing and self-healing capabilities not only at the operating systems, but also at the application or service layer, it is necessary to go beyond the basic orchestration capabilities of Heat with additional tools.

This task is made even more difficult when the workflow integrates with external systems. For example, there may be a need to register new systems with DNS, ensure that all deployed resources are being backed up and interface with security systems, such as firewalls or intrusion detection/prevention systems. The service desk needs to be updated when new systems are launched and the monitoring tools also need to be current with what they should be polling.

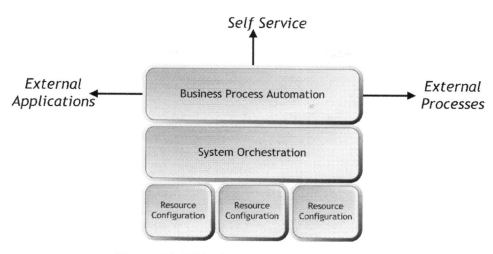

Figure 12-5: Business Process Automation

We can look at the automation as a multi-tiered system with three layers (Figure 12-5). At the lowest layer, we configure the individual resources (e.g. servers, storage and network). At the middle layer, we coordinate the deployment of each of the individual components. We enforce a strict sequence and validate that each element is configured successfully. We may even roll out policies to automatically bring up additional resources, or scale them down, based on external triggers.

DEPLOY

And at the highest layer, we integrate the service with the full business environment and make it accessible to end users. This means automating the interfaces to backup, failover systems, monitoring consoles, firewalls and load balancers. We also need to integrate with service management functions such as demand management and service desk.

OpenStack Orchestration manages the middle-level orchestration for bringing up the basic service stack. But, you will need your own custom scripts or layered automation solution like Chef or Puppet to fully configure all the resources in the bottom level. There are numerous other commercial cloud management services, such as Rightscale and Dell enStratius that also accomplish this function. Generally, they have either built their own DevOps scripting languages, or adopted others.

Heat also has its shortcomings in representing the higher-level business services that are using the resources. It is quite limited in its ability to integrate with external components that may be part of the overall workflow. You may choose to deploy specific software products like HP Operations Orchestration or IBM Smart Cloud Orchestrator to automate the entire process, but at present, there is no open-source technology that addresses this need. However, there is some progress on the standards front that may help in the future.

OASIS TOSCA

The Topology and Orchestration Specification for Cloud Applications (TOSCA) is a potentially complementary standard that is designed to capture the deployment and operational behavior of a service or application in an XML template using BPEL (Business Process Execution Language).

The specification is driven by the Organization for the Advancement of Structured Information Standards (OASIS) and is independent of OpenStack. However, there are several large organizations, including IBM, HP, Red Hat and Cisco, who are very active in both OpenStack and the TOSCA subcommittee and therefore bringing convergence between the two initiatives.

The advantage of a specification like TOSCA is that, in addition to orchestration at the instance level, it can also invoke specific workflows, dependencies and triggers at the application level. For instance, there might be a workflow for setting up a SugarCRM service that requires an operational MySQL instance running. It isn't sufficient for the node hosting MySQL to be launched – the actual database must be accessible and the SugarCRM must be able to connect to it before it can continue its configuration.

DEPLOY

Practical Recommendations

Once you have an OpenStack infrastructure in place, you'll need to give all the users a way to quickly and easily deploy their workloads.

A set of template images that are preconfigured with common applications are a big step. But many applications and business processes will need more than one component. Orchestrating the allocation and configuration of these resources can be confusing and cumbersome.

Heat will facilitate one-click provisioning stacks of related elements. You may also want to integrate other networking, security and service management functions. Automating business processes is not currently in the scope of OpenStack, so you are likely to need commercial management frameworks. However, it's worth monitoring TOSCA, and the work that's being done to incorporate it into OpenStack, since this effort could soon lead to a standards-based solution that addresses many of these challenges.

Operate

Once deployed, the administration chores begin. On the one hand, there are pro-active tasks to set policies, re-allocate resources and tailor the configuration of standard services based on user needs. On the other hand, it is also important to detect any unforeseen events. We must also keep an eye on trends in order to detect and resolve issues as they occur and to project where future problems may arise in order to prevent them.

OPERATE

Chapter 13

Administer the Software

After OpenStack has been set up in production, the responsibilities shift from deployment to operations. This chapter describes the main responsibilities of the administrator and the interfaces that OpenStack offers to assist with these tasks.

While a great deal of the service delivery may be outsourced in a cloud solution, this doesn't completely remove the continuous responsibility of checking and reporting on service health. Someone needs to take ownership for the stability of the system after it is operational. This involves both proactive planning to ensure business/service continuity as well as reactive processes for coping with any problems that occur. This chapter focuses on the former while the next will address the latter.

OPERATE

Cloud Administration

Ideally automation and self-service would take care of all the operational tasks so that the administrator would be free to do other work. But in reality there are still also some tasks that cannot be fully automated.

From an ITIL perspective, administration of OpenStack is largely focused on the Service Catalog. There are options to define which services should be available, allocate resources and tailor the configuration of standard services based on user needs. There is also some support for asset and configuration management, since it is possible to take an inventory of physical and virtual resources.

There are also other operational tasks that OpenStack administrators must address. They will need to integrate OpenStack into the backup and archival strategy, ensure it is included in the disaster recovery plan and take care of deploying the applications that run on top of OpenStack. But all of these tasks are largely outside the scope of OpenStack and depend very much on the environment where OpenStack is deployed. We will therefore be focusing on the capabilities that OpenStack offers to manage itself.

Chapter 13: Administer the Software

OpenStack Implementation

There are really three ways to administer both the infrastructure and the actual services that are running on it (Figure 13-1).

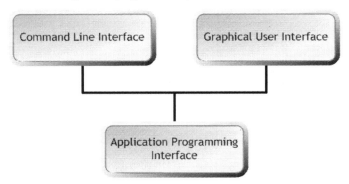

Figure 13-1: OpenStack Interfaces

Horizon is an OpenStack service that presents a graphical user interface (GUI) to manage most of the OpenStack system. It is the most intuitive way for humans to interact with the components since it presents the structure logically and visually.

There is also a command line interface (CLI), which is particularly useful for scripting and also provides a secondary option for administrators, who may log into the system via ssh to troubleshoot problems or make custom modifications. The CLI is less easy for a novice to use than the GUI since it requires some knowledge of the command syntax. However, it is more flexible and expert users may find it more efficient.

OPERATE

Lastly, there is a REST interface for developers to use if they need to integrate administrative functions into other tools. It is programmatic, so it isn't meant for end users but it is the most effective mechanism for repetitive and automated tasks that require complex business logic.

All three provide essentially the same capabilities, but the graphical interface is the easiest for most people to conceptualize and it is also the approach most operational personnel is likely to use in their initial exposure to OpenStack. So we will start with it.

OpenStack Dashboard (Horizon)

Horizon is where the earth meets the sky. So you could say that OpenStack Horizon is where earth-bound humans meet sky-based clouds. It is a modular Django web application that provides an end user ("Project Dashboard") and cloud operator interface ("Admin Dashboard") to OpenStack services.

Admin Interface

The administrative dashboard is used for system-wide configuration. It is accessible through the Admin tab in the navigation pane and consists of two main sections, the System Panel and the Identity Panel.

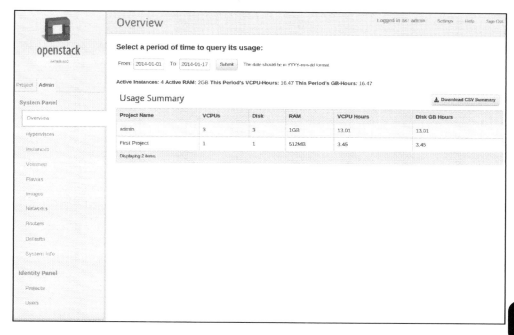

Figure 13-2: System Panel Overview

OPERATE

The system panel contains most of the configuration pages. In particular, it has an overview of the current system usage (Figure 13-2) and a page showing overall system configuration, with options to see which OpenStack services are running (Figure 13-3), to configure Nova availability zones and define host aggregates.

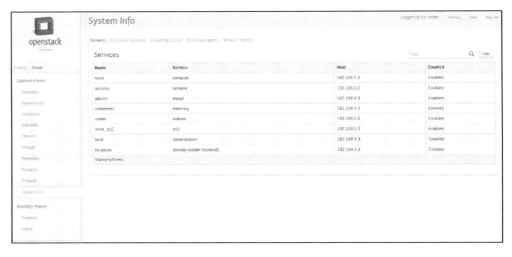

Figure 13-3: System Info

The administrator can also create and manage users and projects through the Identity Panel (Figure 13-4).

Figure 13-4: Project Administration

Project Interface

End users generally do not have access to the Admin Dashboard since many of the functions have system-wide impact. Instead most resources are assigned to projects and each user may have access to one or more projects. In earlier releases, projects were called tenants, so don't be confused if you encounter that term instead.

The subsections within the project interface will depend on which OpenStack services are implemented. We cover these in the respective chapters. For example, there is a section called **Manage Compute**, for administering Nova (Figure 13-5), which we looked at in Chapter 8.

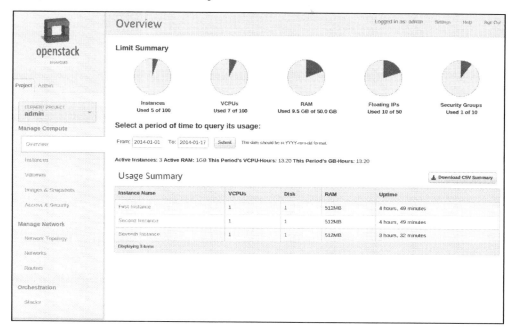

Figure 13-5: Compute Overview

Similarly, we can manage the networking configuration in the **Manage Network** section (Figure 13-6), covered in Chapter 10.

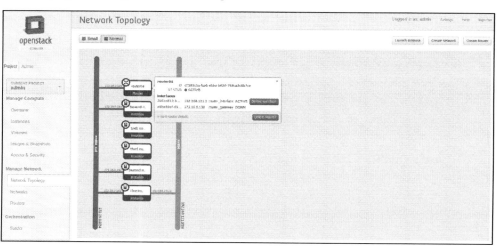

Figure 13-6: Network Topology

And, if we have installed OpenStack orchestration, there will be a section called **Orchestration** in the project interface (Figure 13-7), as we saw in Chapter 12.

Figure 13-7: Orchestration Stacks

Note that if users have access to a single project, Horizon will automatically se-lect that project when they log in. If they have received rights to manage multi-ple projects, then they will be able to switch between the projects by selecting the appropriate choice from the **Current Project** button (Figure 13-8).

OPERATE

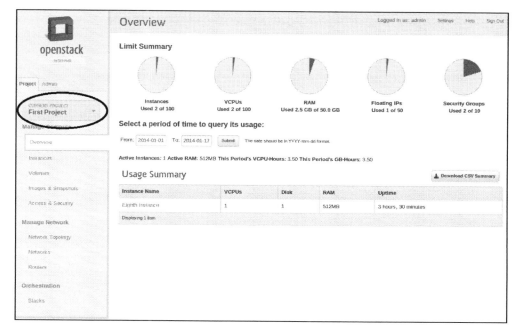

Figure 13-8: Project Selection

Additional Interfaces

Not all OpenStack services appear in the Project interface. Some use a separate panel instead. For example, Murano (covered in Chapter 7) is used to integrate OpenStack with Microsoft technologies (Figure 13-9).

OPERATE

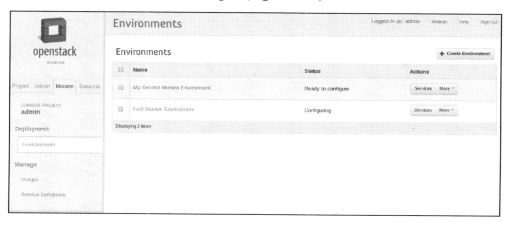

Figure 13-9: Murano Interface

And Savanna (see Chapter 24) extends OpenStack with automatic provisioning for Hadoop (Figure 13-10).

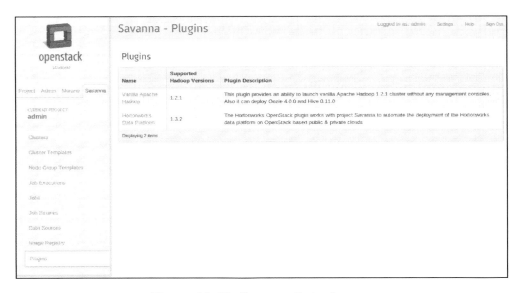

Figure 13-10: Savanna Interface

Architecture

Horizon uses the Django framework to expose the majority of the OpenStack APIs to a browser-based front end. Django is a high-level Python web framework that supports developers with a templating system, an object-relational mapper and other tools that facilitate web development.

The application is hosted with mod_wsgi, an Apache HTTP Server module that provides a standard Web Server Gateway Interface between web servers and Python applications.

In deploying Horizon to a multi-network topology, it is important to be aware that all tenants will need to be able to access its public APIs and that the service will need to be able to connect to the service endpoints for all OpenStack services.

For anyone familiar with Django, the architecture is quite straightforward. It is written with extensibility in mind, so it is possible for future OpenStack components or third parties to contribute additional dashboards in a consistent manner.

OPERATE

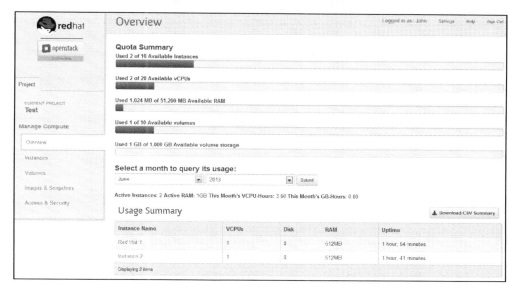

Figure 13-11: Customized Logo

Most enterprises will probably refrain from adding any new functionality to OpenStack but they may still want to customize its appearance (Figure 13-11). It is quite easy to re-brand the interface by modifying the local configuration settings to change the site title, logo image or logo hyperlink. By modifying the style sheets or adding some javascript, they can revamp the look and feel without compromising any of the underlying functionality.

OPERATE

Command Language

Horizon is easy to use for ad hoc queries, but as soon as you want to automate tasks or execute multiple actions at the same time, it hits its limits. It's a lot easier to create a few scripts that use the command language.

There is work underway for a unified OpenStack client that will provide a common and consistent command-line interface to OpenStack APIs[1] using the "openstack" command. However, in the interim, each OpenStack service implements its own client.

Basically, you can execute the same functions via the command line that you can from Horizon and, in some cases, a little more. Each one of the commands operates on a set of objects. The typical actions for each of these objects are: create, update, delete and list; but many also support additional operations.

The best way to get a picture of how they work is to look at some examples of the objects which you can see by listing them:

---

[1] http://docs.openstack.org/developer/python-openstackclient/

Chapter 13: Administer the Software

Cinder

Using the cinder command, we can create, rename, extend, migrate, show details and list volumes.

```
# cinder list
+--------------------------------------+-----------+---------------+------+-------------+-----------+--------------------+
| ID                                   | Status    | Display Name  | Size | Volume Type | Bootable  |            At-     |
tached to  |
+--------------------------------------+-----------+---------------+------+-------------+-----------+--------------------+
| c179833a-e268-4311-8050-9375355dc1df | available | Second Volume | 2    |    None     | false     |                    |
| c96c1207-09a3-425e-b9a2-3b9b5f9bd5a0 | in-use    | First Volume  | 1    |    None     | false     | 586d0368-ec89-     |
4f43-814e-2f7b5c838b11 |
+--------------------------------------+-----------+---------------+------+-------------+-----------+--------------------+
```

We can also operate on backups, encryption types, QoS specifications, quota classes, snapshots and volume transfers.

Glance

The glance commands lets us create, delete, download, update, show details and list images. We can also share and remove tenant access to the image.

```
# glance image-list
+--------------------------------------+--------+-------------+------------------+----------+--------+
| ID                                   | Name   | Disk Format | Container Format | Size     | Sta-   |
tus |
+--------------------------------------+--------+-------------+------------------+----------+--------+
| bfa25aa9-abeb-40d3-add2-0bdd4f29cbae | cirros | qcow2       | bare             | 13147648 | ac-    |
tive |
+--------------------------------------+--------+-------------+------------------+----------+--------+
```

Keystone

Keystone has subcommands to create, get details, delete and list roles.

```
# keystone role-list
+----------------------------------+---------------+
|                id                |     name      |
+----------------------------------+---------------+
| 74913175bd4f49a3bec1daf4a4ce43af |  First Role   |
| 15d9bf316f4b4f21baeea97f9a51951f |    Member     |
| b0c5dc6be6074c26b40da5207bf11465 | ResellerAdmin |
| 39db744265ee4d7db1d9f6cb00e074f3 | SwiftOperator |
| 9fe2ff9ee4384b1894a90878d3e92bab |    member     |
| 137bac21671a4b88a4ab6168b2978c58 |    admin      |
+----------------------------------+---------------+
```

Similarly you can create, delete, get details and list the services in the Service Catalog.

```
# keystone service-list
+----------------------------------+-----------+--------------+------------------------------+
|                id                |   name    |     type     |          description         |
+----------------------------------+-----------+--------------+------------------------------+
| 06bbd1babc9641c5a39d437b3c3c5ca0 | ceilometer|   metering   | Openstack Metering Service   |
| e8b5780bbd054bde9a446d01c1749aad |  cinder   |    volume    |      Cinder Service          |
| a4e9e7fc470a4302a26ecbf7b2e87941 | cinder v2 |   volumev2   |      Cinder Service v2        |
| 17526e0f7aab441b8f96cf3a5ae32080 |  glance   |    image     | Openstack Image Service      |
| f39c461d71074376a3ff884ec2fbe30c | keystone  |   identity   | OpenStack Identity Service   |
| b3bbf238f01e42f2a189476dd5504036 |  neutron  |   network    | Neutron Networking Service   |
| dfc4c6fafa634495a2e8d3e240a72765 |   nova    |   compute    | Openstack Compute Service    |
| 48a24d43bb5349eb8d9e9500c910f54b |  nova_ec2 |     ec2      |      EC2 Service             |
| 2312d535e17c41fd9543562e62399040 |   swift   | object-store | Openstack Object-Store Service|
| 9605a893349027cb80bf43921a708d1  |  swift_s3 |      s3      | Openstack S3 Service          |
+----------------------------------+-----------+--------------+------------------------------+
```

The commands to create, delete, get details and list the tenants refer to what are now called projects in the Horizon interface.

```
# keystone tenant-list
+----------------------------------+----------+---------+
|                id                |   name   | enabled |
+----------------------------------+----------+---------+
| 8d44504fbfb84ff59673a36e4504325c |  admin   |  True   |
| f1c33502827e473a854cf9d702d02608 | alt_demo |  True   |
| 01bc55a8c6ed41d98c698041ecafb430 |   demo   |  True   |
| cf47ae876b2e4b8c978cc59fcf2d881b | services |  True   |
+----------------------------------+----------+---------+
```

In addition to creating, deleting, getting details and listing users, you can also update passwords and add/remove roles.

```
# keystone user-list
+----------------------------------+-----------+---------+----------------------+
|                id                |   name    | enabled |        email         |
+----------------------------------+-----------+---------+----------------------+
| 6950daff4dbf467cae747d2cce35a5c0 |   admin   |  True   |    test@test.com     |
| 5515f6eb55fd40d6968a88a78d6dd3fa | alt_demo  |  True   |                      |
| 00e208e434c34950801c82a0190e2073 | ceilometer|  True   | ceilometer@localhost |
| 529c2017c1394ad7a5ad3a7e8775fa4d |  cinder   |  True   |   cinder@localhost   |
| ef72bee966284bbb9e2c0b8ee8e33772 |   demo    |  True   |                      |
| ac9ae740a42343c0a4e5bbb291ed508b |  glance   |  True   |   glance@localhost   |
| 8a49c75b055142f990bcf6698d6356f6 |  neutron  |  True   |  neutron@localhost   |
| 2688a6528a5646ebb53c25a6eea5bcf5 |   nova    |  True   |    nova@localhost    |
| 4a50fa5904224b94af0bffaafa661c2d |   swift   |  True   |   swift@localhost    |
+----------------------------------+-----------+---------+----------------------+
```

OPERATE

There are further commands to discover Keystone servers, create/delete endpoints and manage credentials.

Neutron

Neutron agents are launched automatically based on the configuration settings. But there are options from the command line to show, delete, update and list them.

```
# neutron agent-list
+--------------------------------------+------------------+------------------------+-------+------
----------+
| id                                   | agent_type       | host                   | alive | ad-
min_state_up |
+--------------------------------------+------------------+------------------------+-------+------
----------+
| 232237f3-36a8-4fec-946a-2dba8da4f055 | DHCP agent       | localhost.localdomain  | :-)   | True
|
| aee6a724-cf51-43bc-94d0-869c7b5ff493 | L3 agent         | localhost.localdomain  | :-)   | True
|
| e56f3ec2-7d30-46fe-802c-10f56e69098e | Open vSwitch agent| localhost.localdomain | :-)   | True
|
+--------------------------------------+------------------+------------------------+-------+------
----------+
```

As expected it is possible to create, delete, show and list Floating IP addresses. Additionally, there are commands to associate and disassociate them from internal IP addresses.

```
# neutron floatingip-list
+--------------------------------------+------------------+---------------------+---------+
| id                                   | fixed_ip_address | floating_ip_address | port_id |
+--------------------------------------+------------------+---------------------+---------+
| 01c98f20-3b26-4769-a5b7-21165b8cfe9d |                  | 172.24.4.228        |         |
+--------------------------------------+------------------+---------------------+---------+
```

You can create, update and list routers. Furthermore, you can set/remove external gateways, add/delete interfaces, and list the router ports.

```
# neutron router-list
+--------------------------------------+---------+----------------------------------------
--------------------------------+
| id                                   | name    | external_gateway_info
|
+--------------------------------------+---------+----------------------------------------
--------------------------------+
| f5faee34-ef75-476a-b65b-db7a368835a4 | router1 | {"network_id":   "e78d9372-a0b7-4e5d-b1f8-
d7645c87cb59", "enable_snat": true} |
+--------------------------------------+---------+----------------------------------------
--------------------------------+
```

Beyond creating, deleting, showing and listing security groups, it is possible to create/delete/list rules within the groups.

```
# neutron security-group-list
+--------------------------------------+------------------+-------------------------------+
| id                                   | name             | description                   |
+--------------------------------------+------------------+-------------------------------+
| 4c02bfef-bdd2-457b-b9b0-9ec46ff93451 | FirstSecurityGroup | Demo group to show featuers |
| 5d9ab208-57d9-4aa0-a9d3-d972dd1d3d8b | default          | default                       |
| 75bea1e4-309f-46d4-be0e-e2e3d580359c | default          | default                       |
| ea0e5f2d-7199-4201-87d2-f132b9280942 | default          | default                       |
+--------------------------------------+------------------+-------------------------------+
```

OPERATE

The standard create, delete, show, update and list commands also apply to subnets.

```
# neutron subnet-list
+--------------------------------------+----------------+----------------+------------------------
------------------------+
| id                                   | name           | cidr           | allocation_pools
|
+--------------------------------------+----------------+----------------+------------------------
------------------------+
| 2e1efee2-0112-4659-9a90-72bdeb36dfd4 | public_subnet  | 172.24.4.224/28 | {"start":
"172.24.4.226", "end": "172.24.4.238"} |
| 451ca5e1-c80f-4e7b-8d54-5e88501bb4d6 | private_subnet | 10.0.0.0/24     | {"start": "10.0.0.2",
"end": "10.0.0.254"}   |
+--------------------------------------+----------------+----------------+------------------------
------------------------+
```

There are many other options for VPN services, VPN IPsec and IKE policies, quotas, ports, load balancers, firewalls and DHCP agents.

Nova

Nova comes with a set of standard flavors. You can create, delete, show and list to view and change them. Additionally, you can add/remove tenant (project) access to specific flavors.

```
# nova flavor-list
```

```
+----+-----------+-----------+------+-----------+------+-------+-------------+-----------+
| ID | Name      | Memory_MB | Disk | Ephemeral | Swap | VCPUs | RXTX_Factor | Is_Public |
+----+-----------+-----------+------+-----------+------+-------+-------------+-----------+
| 1  | m1.tiny   | 512       | 1    | 0         |      | 1     | 1.0         | True      |
| 2  | m1.small  | 2048      | 20   | 0         |      | 1     | 1.0         | True      |
| 3  | m1.medium | 4096      | 40   | 0         |      | 2     | 1.0         | True      |
| 4  | m1.large  | 8192      | 80   | 0         |      | 4     | 1.0         | True      |
| 5  | m1.xlarge | 16384     | 160  | 0         |      | 8     | 1.0         | True      |
+----+-----------+-----------+------+-----------+------+-------+-------------+-----------+
```

The implemented hypervisors are defined in the Nova configuration files. But you can show and list them and view statistics and uptime.

```
# nova hypervisor-list
+----+-----------------------+
| ID | Hypervisor hostname   |
+----+-----------------------+
| 1  | localhost.localdomain |
+----+-----------------------+
```

The core function of Nova is to operate on instances (active servers), which you can boot, delete, rename, resize, resume, suspend, start and stop.

```
# nova list
+--------------------------------------+-----------------+--------+------------+-------------+-----------------------+
| ID                                   | Name            | Status | Task State | Power State | Networks              |
+--------------------------------------+-----------------+--------+------------+-------------+-----------------------+
| 586d0368-ec89-4f43-814e-2f7b5c838b11 | First Instance  | ACTIVE | None       | Running     | public=172.24.4.227   |
| 68b55e9c-9051-4a8e-b1a2-cd7039e9bd54 | Second Instance | ACTIVE | None       | Running     | public=172.24.4.229   |
+--------------------------------------+-----------------+--------+------------+-------------+-----------------------+
```

There are also commands for host aggregates, availability zones, keypairs, quotas, baremetal nodes as well as obsolescent options for volumes and networking that have since been split out into Cinder and Neutron.

OPERATE

Swift

Swift has a relatively simple interface. You can delete, list, post metadata, and display statistical information of containers.

```
# swift list
First Container
Second Container
Third Container
```

You can also list objects within a container.

```
# swift list "First Container"
First Object
Fourth Object
Second Object
Third Object
```

And it is possible to upload files/directories or download them.

Application Programming Interface

The API is necessary in order to execute complex program logic and can simplify automation across a set of distributed systems. It is also the most functional interface since both the command line and graphical user interface rely on the API to access the OpenStack resources.

In fact, you can see how any OpenStack commands use the API by adding the --**debug** option.

```
# keystone --debug service-list
```

The response is too verbose to list here, but it includes all of the REST API calls that the command invokes.

The easiest way to access the OpenStack API is to use the Python bindings.

```
# python
Python 2.6.6 (r266:84292, Feb 22 2013, 00:00:18)
[GCC 4.4.7 20120313 (Red Hat 4.4.7-3)] on linux2
Type "help", "copyright", "credits" or "license" for more information.
>>> import keystoneclient.v2_0.client as ksclient
>>> keystone = ksclient.Client(auth_url="http://openstack.example.com:35357/v2.0/",
...                            username="admin",
...                            password="23732317dee64019",
...                            tenant_name="admin")
>>> keystone.services.list()
[<Service {u'type': u'metering',
    u'description': u'Openstack Metering Service',
    u'name': u'ceilometer',
    u'id': u'06bbd1babc9641c5a39d437b3c3c5ca0'}>,
<Service {u'type': u'image',
    u'description': u'Openstack Image Service',
    u'name': u'glance',
    u'id': u'17526e0f7aab441b8f96cf3a5ae32080'}>,
<Service {u'type': u'object-store',
    u'description': u'Openstack Object-Store Service',
    u'name': u'swift',
    u'id': u'2312d535e17c41fd9543562e62399040'}>,
<Service {u'type': u'ec2',
    u'description': u'EC2 Service',
    u'name': u'nova_ec2',
    u'id': u'48a24d43bb5349eb8d9e9500c910f54b'}>,
<Service {u'type': u's3',
    u'description': u'Openstack S3 Service',
    u'name': u'swift_s3',
    u'id': u'9605a8933490427cb80bf43921a708d1'}>,
<Service {u'type': u'volumev2',
    u'description': u'Cinder Service v2',
    u'name': u'cinder_v2',
    u'id': u'a4e9e7fc470a4302a26ecbf7b2e87941'}>,
<Service {u'type': u'network',
    u'description': u'Neutron Networking Service',
    u'name': u'neutron',
    u'id': u'b3bbf238f01e42f2a189476dd5504036'}>,
<Service {u'type': u'compute',
    u'description': u'Openstack Compute Service',
    u'name': u'nova',
    u'id': u'dfc4c6fafa634495a2e8d3e240a72765'}>,
<Service {u'type': u'volume',
    u'description': u'Cinder Service',
    u'name': u'cinder',
    u'id': u'e8b5780bbd054bde9a446d01c1749aad'}>,
<Service {u'type': u'identity',
    u'description': u'OpenStack Identity Service',
```

```
    u'name': u'keystone',
    u'id': u'f39c461d71074376a3ff884ec2fbe30c'}>]
```

But this assumes that you are coding in Python. For other languages you can write your own bindings or else you can make the calls directly using a REST library. For example, you can even make REST calls directly from the command line using cURL.

```
#   curl   -si   -H"X-Auth-Token:$TOKEN"   -H   "Content-type:   application/json"
http://localhost:35357/v3/services
HTTP/1.1 200 OK
Vary: X-Auth-Token
Content-Type: application/json
Content-Length: 2217
Date: Mon, 27 Jan 2014 14:32:04 GMT

{"services": [
  {"id": "06bbd1babc9641c5a39d437b3c3c5ca0",
   "type": "metering",
   "name": "ceilometer",
   "links":                                                                {"self":
"http://localhost:5000/v3/services/06bbd1babc9641c5a39d437b3c3c5ca0"},
   "description": "Openstack Metering Service"},
  {"id": "17526e0f7aab441b8f96cf3a5ae32080",
   "type": "image",
   "name": "glance",
   "links":                                                                {"self":
"http://localhost:5000/v3/services/17526e0f7aab441b8f96cf3a5ae32080"},
   "description": "Openstack Image Service"},
  {"id": "2312d535e17c41fd9543562e62399040",
   "type": "object-store",
   "name": "swift",
   "links":                                                                {"self":
"http://localhost:5000/v3/services/2312d535e17c41fd9543562e62399040"},
   "description": "Openstack Object-Store Service"},
  {"id": "48a24d43bb5349eb8d9e9500c910f54b",
   "type": "ec2",
   "name": "nova_ec2",
   "links":                                                                {"self":
"http://localhost:5000/v3/services/48a24d43bb5349eb8d9e9500c910f54b"},
   "description": "EC2 Service"},
  {"id": "9605a8933490427cb80bf43921a708d1",
   "type": "s3",
   "name": "swift_s3",
   "links":                                                                {"self":
"http://localhost:5000/v3/services/9605a8933490427cb80bf43921a708d1"},
   "description": "Openstack S3 Service"},
  {"id": "a4e9e7fc470a4302a26ecbf7b2e87941",
   "type": "volumev2",
   "name": "cinder_v2",
   "links":                                                                {"self":
"http://localhost:5000/v3/services/a4e9e7fc470a4302a26ecbf7b2e87941"},
   "description": "Cinder Service v2"},
  {"id": "b3bbf238f01e42f2a189476dd5504036",
   "type": "network",
   "name": "neutron",
   "links":                                                                {"self":
"http://localhost:5000/v3/services/b3bbf238f01e42f2a189476dd5504036"},
   "description": "Neutron Networking Service"},
  {"id": "dfc4c6fafa634495a2e8d3e240a72765",
   "type": "compute",
   "name": "nova",
   "links":                                                                {"self":
"http://localhost:5000/v3/services/dfc4c6fafa634495a2e8d3e240a72765"},
   "description": "Openstack Compute Service"},
  {"id": "e8b5780bbd054bde9a446d01c1749aad",
   "type": "volume",
   "name": "cinder",
```

OPERATE

```
   "links":                                                        {"self":
"http://localhost:5000/v3/services/e8b5780bbd054bde9a446d01c1749aad"},
   "description": "Cinder Service"},
  {"id": "f39c461d71074376a3ff884ec2fbe30c",
   "type": "identity",
   "name": "keystone",
   "links":                                                        {"self":
"http://localhost:5000/v3/services/f39c461d71074376a3ff884ec2fbe30c"},
   "description": "OpenStack Identity Service"}],
   "links": {"self": "http://localhost:5000/v3/services",
   "previous": null,
   "next": null}}
```

This is particularly useful for debugging and accessing any functions that are only available via the API.

Figure 13-12: Google Chrome Advanced Rest Client

There are also browser-based graphical interfaces for REST for both Google Chrome (Figure 13-12) and Mozilla Firefox (Figure 13-13).

OPERATE

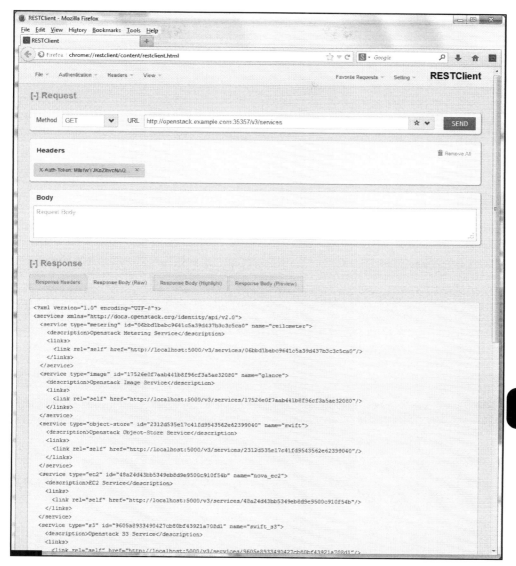

Figure 13-13: Mozilla Firefox RESTClient

Furthermore, the API is necessary for integrating into a wider framework that may manage everything from data center infrastructure to applications. It is the mechanism that cloud management platforms, such as Dell Enstratius and Rightscale use and also the way that you can plug into an ongoing monitoring solution, like the ones we will see in the next chapter.

OPERATE

Practical Recommendations

OpenStack offers three different management interfaces, each with its own set of use cases. The Horizon GUI is the most common starting point for new administrators. It is the easiest to use for familiarization and ad-hoc exploration of the product, as well as quick visual verification that the environment is in order.

The command language is helpful for quick targeted actions. It also has its use in scripting repetitive or scheduled tasks.

The programming interface is the most powerful management mechanism. It gives full access to the underlying functionality and is the best fit for complex logic or integration with external systems that also expose APIs.

OPERATE

Chapter 14

Monitor its Health

In addition to planned changes that you can trigger through the administrative interfaces, management responsibilities include making sure that the system is running as it should and fixing any unforeseen problems with it.

Cloud Monitoring

There are many different reasons to have a comprehensive, continuous and accurate view of the system state. We need to have access to any potentially relevant information in order to detect and resolve issues as they occur. But we also need to be able to project where future problems may arise so that we can try to prevent them. And it is often necessary to be able to reconstruct what has happened in the past either for forensic investigations or in order to determine the root causes of recurring problems.

OPERATE

In order to facilitate our monitoring activities, we can make use of three basic mechanisms that work together:

Logging: Recording all noteworthy activity allows us to assess the current state and reconstruct past events.

Alerts: Certain events, such as error messages or crossing of performance thresholds, can trigger notifications that draw attention to potential problems.

Trending: Analytics on logging data and other performance metrics can serve as the foundation for projecting where future problems may arise.

We will examine how all three can be addressed in a cloud environment.

OpenStack Implementation

At this point in time, OpenStack offers very little in the way of cloud resource monitoring. This is perhaps not so surprising since it primarily represents an abstraction layer and there are plenty of tools to monitor the individual components.

At a primitive, and very manual, level it is also possible to monitor the actual OpenStack components themselves using basic Linux commands. You could use the **ps** command to determine if required processes are running. So, for example, if you want to verify that all the Nova services are running on the Cloud Controller you can check them:

```
# ps aux | grep nova-api
nova 12786 0.0 0.0 37952 1312 ? Ss Feb11 0:00 su -s /bin/sh -c exec nova-api --
config-file=/etc/nova/nova.conf nova
nova 12787 0.0 0.1 135764 57400 ? S Feb11 0:01 /usr/bin/python /usr/bin/nova-api --
config-file=/etc/nova/nova.conf
```

You can use similar commands to see whether the processes for Keystone, Swift, Cinder, Glance and other OpenStack services are running.

Some of the OpenStack implementation components may also have monitoring capabilities. For example, Open vSwitch supports the sFlow standard making it possible to integrate OpenStack into a consistent and scalable network monitoring solution. It should work across most network vendor implementations giving visibility into network performance metrics, usage accounting and providing a defence against major security threats[1].

You can also make connectivity checks to the databases via SQL or to the REST interfaces with cURL commands to create your own checks. Or, as we will see later in this chapter, you can scan and analyse the log files for each of the OpenStack services to assess whether they are operating correctly.

But the bottom line is that you probably need to avail of additional tools in order to monitor all the components in a comprehensive way. Some of the most common choices are Nagios, Ganglia and Zenoss, whereby these each handle different functions and are therefore not mutually exclusive.

Nagios

Nagios is included in several popular Linux distributions. It provides monitoring and alerting for servers, switches, applications, and services as well as system metrics and network protocols. It can be configured to notify administrators of any important events, for example by sending alerts whenever infrastructure components fail.

Its reports consolidate all salient performance and availability metrics with details on outages, security breaches and other important events. It also provides trending and capacity planning projections, so that customers can upgrade their

---

[1] http://www.mirantis.com/blog/openstack-monitoring/

infrastructure or procure additional resources before any bottlenecks lead to degraded performance or failures.

Nagios is composed of a web interface, a server and a configuration that ties all of it together. Like OpenStack, Nagios uses a plug-in architecture to allow for greater extensibility. The plugins retrieve object/host information from both local and remote machines and report it back to the server. Plugins operate as standalone applications, providing low-level intelligence to Nagios Core. For example the check_by_ssh plugin can use ssh to execute commands on a remote host.

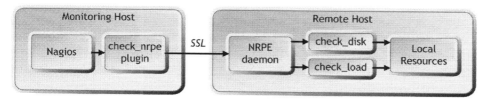

Figure 14-1: Nagios with NRPE Addon

Nagios also supports an interface called an addon, which can extend base functionality or integrate with other applications. Some of the most common add-ons include:

NRPE (Nagios Remote Plugin Executor) provides an interface for plugins that execute on remote Linux/Unix hosts (Figure 14-1). They can monitor remote resources/attributes such as disk usage, CPU load, memory usage and report their status back to Nagios. The addon is similar in objective to the check_by_ssh plugin, but imposes a smaller CPU load on the monitoring host.

OPERATE

NSCA (Nagios Service Check Acceptor) sends passive check results from remote Linux/Unix hosts to the Nagios monitoring server. Unlike NRPE, the NSCA server does not poll the remote agent. Instead the remote agent sends alerts to the server in reaction to significant events. Since Nagios is not actively checking the remote systems, this approach is very useful in highly scalable environments.

NDOUtils (Nagios Data Output Utilities) allows you to export current and historical data from Nagios to a MySQL database. Multiple Nagios instances can consolidate their information in a central database for centralized reporting.

Nagios is well equipped to provide monitoring and alerts for the OpenStack network and infrastructure, but it does need to be set up. The OpenStack Operations Guide provides instructions on how to configure it[1]. For example, a deployment with OpenStack distributed across several machines would require the installation of NRPE and the Nagios plugins on each remote machine.

You can create automated alerts for critical processes by using Nagios and NRPE. Or you may want to monitor resources, such as disk usage, server load, memory usage, network I/O and available vCPUs. For example, to ensure that the nova-compute process is running on all compute nodes and receive an alert when disk capacity appears to be reaching its limits, add the following to your Nagios configuration:

```
define service {
    host_name nova.example.com
    check_command check_nrpe_1arg!check_nova-compute
    use generic-service
    notification_period 24x7
    contact_groups sysadmins
    service_description nova-compute
}
define service {
    host_name nova.example.com
    check_command check_nrpe!check_all_disks!20% 10%
    use generic-service
    contact_groups sysadmins
    service_description Disk
}
```

The compute node would also need the following NRPE configuration:

```
command[check_nova-compute]=/usr/lib/nagios/plugins/check_procs -c 1: -a nova-compute
command[check_all_disks]=/usr/lib/nagios/plugins/check_disk -w $ARG1$ -c $ARG2$ -e
```

OPERATE

Nagios will raise an alert if the nova-compute process stops for any reason or if the disk reaches 80% of its capacity.

---

[1] http://docs.openstack.org/trunk/openstack-ops/content/logging_monitoring.html

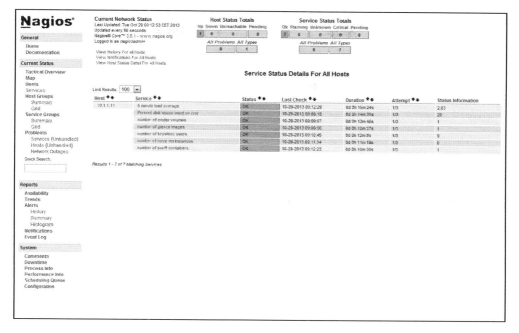

Figure 14-2: Nagios with RDO

Of course, this is just the tip of the iceberg of what you can do with Nagios. If you have the time and resources, you can develop a complete monitoring system for OpenStack. Alternatively, you can make use of some of the work that has already been done and incorporated into the distributions, such as Red Hat RDO, which includes Nagios and pre-configures it to monitor the OpenStack deployment (Figure 14-2).

OPERATE

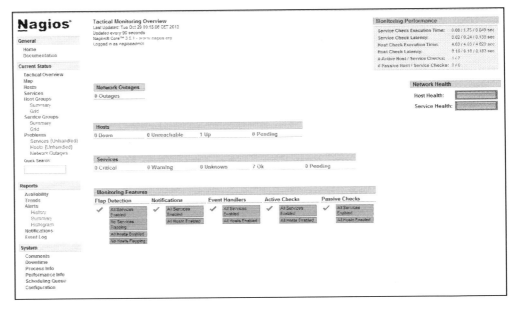

Figure 14-3: Nagios Tactical Monitoring Overview

The installation configures Nagios to provide a high-level monitoring overview (Figure 14-3). It is also possible to examine the state of individual services (Figure 14-4).

OPERATE

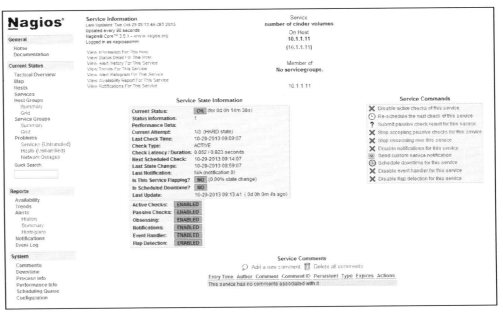

Figure 14-4: Nagios Service Information

Ganglia

Ganglia is a performance monitoring framework for distributed systems. It collects metrics on individual machines and forwards them to an aggregator that presents the global state of a cluster. Although there is some overlap between the functions of Nagios and Ganglia, it is best to look at them as complementary.

Nagios is focused on health checking and alerting while Ganglia's strengths are in monitoring and trending. Nagios sends alerts based on set criteria, so you can use it to determine if a system or service is unavailable. Ganglia could also perform this function but not as well. It excels in monitoring compute grids, such as clusters of servers that are operating on the same task. In these environments, it provides in-depth utilization monitoring and provides data to help with trend analyses and capacity planning.

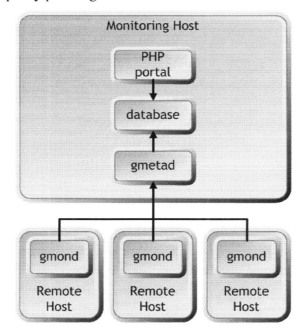

Figure 14-5: Ganglia distributed monitoring

OPERATE

As we said above, Ganglia implements a distributed monitoring system (Figure 14-5). Each host runs an agent (called *gmond*) that collects data and sends it across the network to a collector. The collector runs a process called *gmetad*, which receives *gmond* data and aggregates it in a file.

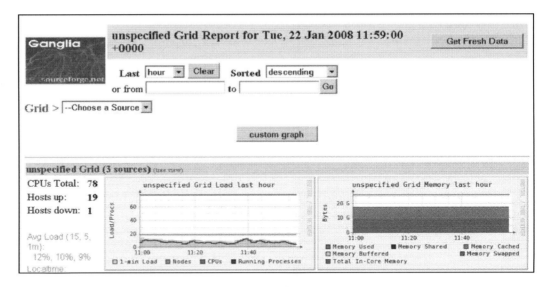

Figure 14-6: Ganglia Grid Report

Ganglia provides a PHP-based web interface to display the data (Figure 14-6 and Figure 14-7).

Figure 14-7: Ganglia Cluster Report

It is relatively simple to set up. There must be at least one collector on the network, which is running *gmond*, *gmetad* and the web interface. Each machine that is being monitored will also need *gmond* installed on it. By default the installation uses broadcast, so the hosts and collector will see each other automatically. This is probably not how you want to configure a large deployment on a multi-segment network. But it makes it very easy to get Ganglia running on a small installation.

Zenoss

Zenoss (Zenoss Core) is another free and open-source management platform. It is based on the Zope application server and provides a web interface to monitor availability, inventory/configuration, performance, and events (Figure 14-8). The graphical user interface is compelling with nice drill-down capabilities that expose data pulled from remote systems via log files, SSH commands or SNMP MIBs.

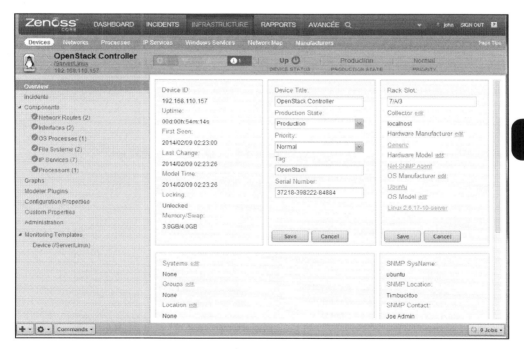

OPERATE

Figure 14-8: Zenoss Console

Like Ganglia it offers performance insight out-of-the-box, which Nagios does not. So it is well suited for trending and planning activities.

There has been some work to develop a deployable OpenStack monitoring kit, called a Zenoss Zenpack, which you can find by searching for the OpenStack Cloud Monitor ZenPack[1].

Monitoring Services

There are also many other tools, like Zabbix or Cacti, for example that offer very similar functionality to Ganglia, Nagios and Zenoss, each with their own strengths and weaknesses.

Red Hat CloudForms provides a single, unified management interface for an open hybrid cloud incorporating datacenter virtualization and RHEL OpenStack Platform capacity. It includes capability for discovery, event capture, provisioning and reporting across providers including Amazon Web Services and Openstack.

Note that these systems don't necessarily need to be installed and operated on premise. Zenoss offers its solution as a service with "Zenoss Service Dynamics as a Service (ZaaS)". Established enterprise management frameworks are also gradually adding capability to cope with cloud-based services. Some, such as Hyperic, offer plug-ins for Google Apps, Amazon Web Services and other cloud providers. HP Cloud Assure projects future cloud services availability by diagnosing and reporting on potential performance and security issues before they impact the business.

OPERATE

Pingdom is another network monitoring tool that tracks uptime, reachability, responsiveness and performance. It also has a means of sending SMS or email alerts when there are problems. When Pingdom does detect an error, it automatically performs additional tests to assist in troubleshooting.

Logging

As mentioned at the beginning of the chapter, a key part of any monitoring system is logging. It is vital for forensic reconstruction and is also essential for accurate forecasting of future requirements.

OpenStack does its part in providing event information. You can find a longer description of OpenStack logging in the OpenStack Operations Guide[2]. By default, the log files are widely dispersed across each of the servers and split up among the different OpenStack services. For example, on Ubuntu you can find the files in the subdirectories of the /var/log directory:

- nova-* /var/log/nova

[1] http://wiki.zenoss.org/ZenPack:OpenStack_Cloud_Monitor
[2] http://docs.openstack.org/ops/

- glance-* /var/log/glance
- cinder-* /var/log/cinder
- keystone /var/log/keystone
- horizon /var/log/apache2/
- misc (Swift, dnsmasq) /var/log/syslog

You can use the Linux tail command to view the most recent messages to any of the log files that are relevant to your troubleshooting. OpenStack services use logging levels, which are ordered according to their gravity:

- CRITICAL (FATAL) = 50
- ERROR = 40
- WARNING = 30
- AUDIT = 21
- INFO = 20
- DEBUG = 10

Only events with a severity of at least the current logging level will be recorded in the log file.

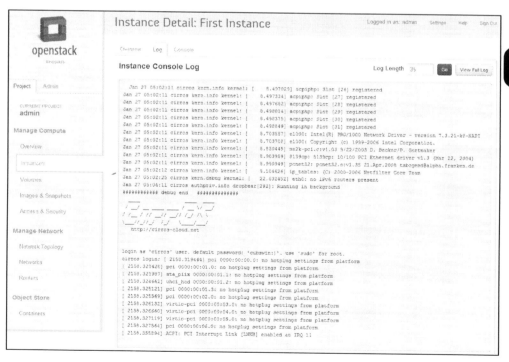

OPERATE

Figure 14-9: OpenStack Instance Logging

Sometimes the problems are not in the OpenStack infrastructure but in the workloads themselves. If you need to dive into the log files of the individual instances, you can access them from the Horizon dashboard (Figure 14-9). Just navigate to the **Instances** under **Manage Compute**, select the appropriate machine and go to the **Log** tab within the display area.

In order to easily correlate events from different services and servers, it is worthwhile to aggregate the log files in a central location. On Ubuntu, you can use rsyslog, the default logging service to send logs to a remote location in addition to their standard log file location. You can configure each component to log to a different syslog facility so that it is easier to track individual components on the central server.

Alternatively, you may want to look at a centralized logging framework to manage and visualize all your event information. Splunk is a popular commercial solution that is in use in many enterprises. There are also free and open-source solutions such as Logstash and Fluentd that provide similar functionality, especially when combined with the Elasticsearch search engine and Kibana visualization interface.

Trend analysis is critical for capacity planning since we need to be able to project future resource usage in order to procure systems, storage and networking equipment before it is needed. We also need to be able to specify the appropriate flavors, allocate the resources efficiently and design an optimal architecture.

OPERATE

In order to plan, we need some insight into the overall resource consumption and the trajectory of its growth (or in rare cases, its decline). This takes us to our next topic. In Chapter 15, we will be looking in more detail at measurement – which will give us more detail about who is using which resources.

Practical Recommendations

Monitoring the health of an OpenStack deployment is not trivial or intuitive. If you have major problems, you will probably notice that something is wrong from the Horizon dashboard, but the root cause won't usually be apparent. Since OpenStack runs on Linux, you can use common Linux tools to diagnose obvious problems, such as the absence of important processes and you can make ad-hoc queries to the services to drill down into specific components.

In a production environment, this is generally not sufficient. So you will either need to implement a commercial management tool or use an open-source package like Nagios, Ganglia or Zenoss.

Once you have discovered a problem, the log files are your best bet for troubleshooting. They are also an important resource for auditing and service-level monitoring. You may want to consider centralizing this function and running analytics across it to distill the most important data.

OPERATE

Account

Financial governance is a top concern of almost every business. It relies on ensuring visibility of what activities generate expenses and what trends these cost drivers are projecting. Whether the charges are invoiced to external parties, cross-charged to internal departments or merely reported to show value to the business, the numbers are critical in sustaining a compelling business case.

ACCOUNT

Chapter 15

Measure Usage

This chapter is about measuring resource usage, which is a fundamental requirement both for effectively managing the infrastructure and for allocating costs or billing customers.

Cloud Instrumentation

When we looked at cloud maturity in Chapter 2, we highlighted sourcing efficiencies as one of the key objectives of cloud computing. In an ideal world, an organization can alternate between resources in real time based on fluctuating costs and performance metrics. However, one prerequisite to this vision is that we need to be able to identify resource usage at a very granular level and allocate costs based on the results.

There are many other reasons why we need to measure resource consumption. Instrumentation is a key component of auto-scaling. It is helpful for auditing and troubleshooting. And its input into capacity planning and alarming can prevent overcapacity or resource bottlenecks.

ACCOUNT

Metering becomes particularly important when running multi-tenant solutions in the cloud. Supporting multiple users sharing common resources presents specific challenges, such as how to enforce quotas for tenants, identify any users who might be consuming excessive resources, or decide if the pricing tiers need to be redefined. Keep in mind that metering multi-tenant solutions is not only about determining or validating the usage bill of a cloud provider but also about optimizing resources in a deployment that guarantee the level of service tenants expect, typically expressed in a service-level agreement (SLA).

OpenStack Implementation

The OpenStack implementation of measurements is centered on Ceilometer. The idea is that all OpenStack services should feed their instrumentation information to Ceilometer, which consolidates and stores it and then makes it available to other services, such as OpenStack Orchestration, or to external applications, for example to billing and debugging tools.

OpenStack Metering (Ceilometer)

Unless you have a keen interest in meteorology, you may have never come across the word 'ceilometer' before. It is a blend of the words 'ceiling' and 'meter' and refers to a device that measures and records both the ceiling (altitude of lowest layer) and thickness of clouds through triangulation. It typically shines a laser at the cloud and measures the time elapsed before the reflected light is received. The name of the OpenStack service is a direct application of the cloud metaphor. OpenStack Ceilometer measures OpenStack clouds.

That is enough trivia and about as far as we can take the analogy. Ceilometer is an abstraction layer for gathering and distributing usage information. It is designed with a plug-in architecture so that other applications can both contribute metrics to the system and consume the consolidated data.

The goal of Ceilometer is to consolidate all measurement collection in one place for the purposes of efficiency and consistency. The original purpose was to create a framework for billing information, but it was designed to be expandable so that it collects usage for other needs, such as monitoring, benchmarking, debugging, statistics and graphing tools.

Some of its requirements included the ability to segment data for each customer, to produce signed and non-repudiable metering messages, and as mentioned above, the ability to include an interface with other systems through an open API and additional plugins.

ACCOUNT

Metrics

The main services that currently report to Ceilometer are: Compute (Nova), Network (Neutron), Image (Glance), Volume (Cinder), Object Storage (Swift) and Energy (Kwapi).

- Nova offers meters for the duration of instances, the CPU time used, numbers of disk reads and writes as well as incoming and outgoing network traffic.
- Neutron provides information on creation and update requests as well as duration of key objects including networks, subnets, ports, routers and floating IP addresses.
- Glance reports on duration and size of volumes.
- Swift measures the number and size of stored objects and containers as well as the incoming and outgoing traffic.

- Kwapi is an OpenStack service that focuses exclusively on measurement of power consumption. It is intended for wattmeters and includes a layer of plugins to support them. Its metrics include cumulative and current power consumption.

You can find a full list of currently provided metrics as well as their specifications in the OpenStack Ceilometer documentation[1].

As you explore the list, you will find that there are three types of meters: Cumulative, Delta and Gauge. Cumulative and Delta measurements both refer to resources that are being consumed. Cumulative metrics report the total usage with each measurement. Delta meters only report the amount that has been consumed since the last measurement. Gauge metrics refer to standalone values, such as CPU utilization.

The content of each measurement includes the user, project and resource as well as the name, type (cumulative, gauge, delta), volume (e.g. number of CPU cycles or transmitted bytes) and unit of the actual measurement (where possible using SI-approved units).

Architecture

The two main tasks of instrumentation are collecting data and publishing it to its consumers. We will look at them separately, beginning with the collection phase.

There are three different ways that services are able to deliver their instrumentation information to Ceilometer[2]. The preferred mechanism is to use the notification bus through the Oslo library. This is the easiest mechanism to implement and it automatically provides high availability.

However, to provide interoperability with legacy applications and services, there are also two further options. One of them is a push agent. It involves adding an agent to each monitored node, which will fetch the required information and send it back to the collector. The other is a polling agent, which regularly queries an external tool or interface for the required information.

---

[1] http://docs.openstack.org/developer/ceilometer/measurements.html
[2] http://docs.openstack.org/developer/ceilometer/architecture.html

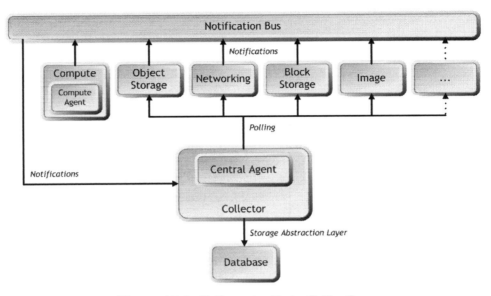

Figure 15-1: Ceilometer Data Collection

Ceilometer is realized as a set of at least four agents that communicate using the standard OpenStack messaging bus (Figure 15-1).:

- The Compute Agent runs on each compute node that is being monitored. It polls the hypervisor for performance data and resource utilization statistics.
- The Central Agent runs on a central management server where it polls for instrumentation information relating to resources that are not assigned to the compute nodes, such as storage and networking services.
- The Collector service also runs on one or more of the central management servers. Its role is to monitor the message queues for notifications, which it turns into metering messages and stores in the database.
- The API also runs on one or more central management servers. It provides a REST interface to the database and thereby presents aggregated metering data to billing engines and other external applications (Figure 15-2).

Tying these together is the Notification Bus, which receives AMQP notifications from all of the agents and passes them on to the Collector.

The persistent data store is implemented as an abstraction layer. In the simplest case, it could represent a simple file but in a typical production environment, a high-performance database is likely to be necessary since the store must process a large number of concurrent reads and writes (often hundreds per second) from multiple collectors and external applications. The recommended backend is

MongoDB, which is both highly scalable and well tested. Other options would be HBase or any SQLAlchemy-compatible databases.

Publishing

Once the data has been collected, it needs to be prepared for consumption. There are two ways that measurements can be retrieved. Ceilometer implements a Publishing Pipeline that will stream the metrics as they are processed. It is also possible to make ad hoc queries to the database through a REST API.

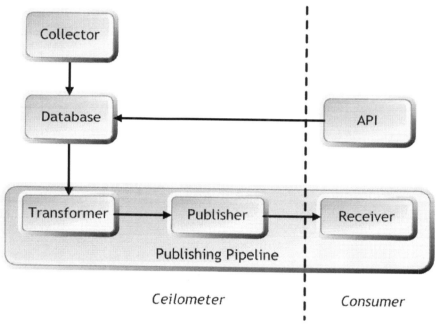

Figure 15-2: Ceilometer Data Publishing

The publishing pipeline includes a transformation stage where it is possible to convert or aggregate data. For example, a customer may want to take multiple discreet values for CPU utilization and average them over an extended time period.

Any given measurement may feed into multiple transformers and publishers. This is an extension from the original Ceilometer specifications which became necessary as the program scope widened from merely facilitating billing to other functions such as monitoring and debugging. Each publisher is able to specify different frequencies as well as transport parameters, such as link encryption and service quality.

An alternate interface to the measurement data is through the API. It can be used as a mechanism for a billing engine to obtain supplementary information. Or it could be the sole interface for an analytics tool to snapshot data that is subsequently used for trend analysis or capacity planning.

Alarms

Another function that was not implemented in the initial releases of Ceilometer was Alarms. These allow operators and users to trigger actions based on individual (or a combination of several) meters. This feature is fundamental to the auto-scaling capabilities that we will look at in Chapter 21.

An alarm consists of a set of criteria that must be met and an action that should execute. The criteria are typically specified as threshold values (e.g. CPU utilization is over 70% or memory usage is over 75%).

Ceilometer also supports multiple alarming mechanisms. You can simply log the condition. Or you can supply an HTTP callback. This means that you provide a URL to be called whenever the alarm has been set off. The payload of the request contains all the details of why the alarm went off.

Usage Scenario

If you want to try out metering, you need to make sure you are using an Open-Stack distro that includes Ceilometer or else have installed the modules yourself.

You can see a list of Ceilometer meters with a simple command.

```
# ceilometer meter-list
+----------------------------+------------+-----------+--------------+-----------+--------------+
| Name                       | Type       | Unit      | Resource ID  | User ID   | Project ID   |
+----------------------------+------------+-----------+--------------+-----------+--------------+
| cpu                        | cumulative | ns        | 586d0368-... | 6950d...  | 8d44504f...  |
| cpu_util                   | gauge      | %         | 586d0368-... | 6950d...  | 8d44504f...  |
| disk.ephemeral.size        | gauge      | GB        | 586d0368-... | 6950d...  | 8d44504f...  |
| disk.read.bytes            | cumulative | B         | 586d0368-... | 6950d...  | 8d44504f...  |
| disk.read.requests         | cumulative | request   | 586d0368-... | 6950d...  | 8d44504f...  |
| disk.root.size             | gauge      | GB        | 586d0368-... | 6950d...  | 8d44504f...  |
| disk.write.bytes           | cumulative | B         | 586d0368-... | 6950d...  | 8d44504f...  |
| disk.write.requests        | cumulative | request   | 586d0368-... | 6950d...  | 8d44504f...  |
| image                      | gauge      | image     | bfa25aa9-... | None ...  | cf47ae87...  |
| image.download             | delta      | B         | bfa25aa9-... | None ...  | cf47ae87...  |
| image.serve                | delta      | B         | bfa25aa9-... | None ...  | cf47ae87...  |
| image.size                 | gauge      | B         | bfa25aa9-... | None ...  | cf47ae87...  |
| instance                   | gauge      | instance  | 586d0368-... | 6950d...  | 8d44504f...  |
| instance:m1.tiny           | gauge      | instance  | 586d0368-... | 6950d...  | 8d44504f...  |
| ip.floating                | gauge      | ip        | 01c98f20-... | 6950d...  | 8d44504f...  |
| ip.floating.create         | delta      | ip        | 01c98f20-... | 6950d...  | 8d44504f...  |
| memory                     | gauge      | MB        | 586d0368-... | 6950d...  | 8d44504f...  |
| network                    | gauge      | network   | ddd25e25-... | 6950d...  | 8d44504f...  |
| network.create             | delta      | network   | ddd25e25-... | 6950d...  | 8d44504f...  |
| network.incoming.bytes     | cumulative | B         | instance-... | 6950d...  | 8d44504f...  |
| network.incoming.packets   | cumulative | packet    | instance-... | 6950d...  | 8d44504f...  |
| network.outgoing.bytes     | cumulative | B         | instance-... | 6950d...  | 8d44504f...  |
| network.outgoing.packets   | cumulative | packet    | instance-... | 6950d...  | 8d44504f...  |
| port                       | gauge      | port      | b0cb2bb0-... | 8a49c...  | 8d44504f...  |
| port.create                | delta      | port      | b0cb2bb0-... | 8a49c...  | 8d44504f...  |
| storage.objects            | gauge      | object    | 01bc55a8c... | None ...  | 01bc55a8...  |
| storage.objects            | gauge      | object    | 8d44504fb... | None ...  | 8d44504f...  |
| storage.objects            | gauge      | object    | cf47ae876... | None ...  | cf47ae87...  |
| storage.objects.containers | gauge      | container | 01bc55a8c... | None ...  | 01bc55a8...  |
| storage.objects.containers | gauge      | container | 8d44504fb... | None ...  | 8d44504f...  |
| storage.objects.size       | gauge      | B         | 01bc55a8c... | None ...  | 01bc55a8...  |
| storage.objects.size       | gauge      | B         | 8d44504fb... | None ...  | 8d44504f...  |
| storage.objects.size       | gauge      | B         | cf47ae876... | None ...  | cf47ae87...  |
| vcpus                      | gauge      | vcpu      | 586d0368-... | 6950d...  | 8d44504f...  |
| volume                     | gauge      | volume    | c179833a-... | 6950d...  | 8d44504f...  |
```

```
| volume.size              | gauge      | GB         | c179833a-... | 6950d... | 8d44504f... |
+--------------------------+------------+------------+--------------+----------+-------------+
```

You may notice that some of the meters (e.g. for storage objects) show up more than once. This is because there are separate meters for each Nova instance, Cinder volume, Swift object, etc.

You can create an alarm for any of the meters. For example, you might want to log an event whenever the CPU utilization exceeds a certain threshold (e.g. 80%).

```
# ceilometer alarm-threshold-create \
    --name cpu_high \
    --description 'High CPU Utilization' \
    --meter-name cpu_util \
    --threshold 80.0 \
    --comparison-operator gt \
    --statistic avg \
    --period 200 \
    --evaluation-periods 5 \
    --alarm-action 'log://' \
    --query resource_id=Instance_ID

+----------------------------+------------------------------------------+
| Property                   | Value                                    |
+----------------------------+------------------------------------------+
| alarm_actions              | [u'log://']                              |
| alarm_id                   | 31fc25e2-60a0-443d-8fc3-6390364b5614     |
| comparison_operator        | gt                                       |
| description                | High CPU Utilization                     |
| enabled                    | True                                     |
| evaluation_periods         | 5                                        |
| insufficient_data_actions  | []                                       |
| meter_name                 | cpu_util                                 |
| name                       | cpu_high                                 |
| ok_actions                 | []                                       |
| period                     | 200                                      |
| project_id                 | 8464a2938de24f5fa9a35f68af039c9f         |
| query                      | resource_id == Instance_ID               |
| repeat_actions             | False                                    |
| state                      | insufficient data                        |
| statistic                  | avg                                      |
| threshold                  | 80.0                                     |
| type                       | threshold                                |
| user_id                    | 91b506ed805d412abbe17eb4e5d6d944         |
+----------------------------+------------------------------------------+
```

ACCOUNT

There are a number of other command line options. Unfortunately, at present you can't do too much with the Horizon interface, but you will find the meters in the **System Panel** under **Resource Usage**.

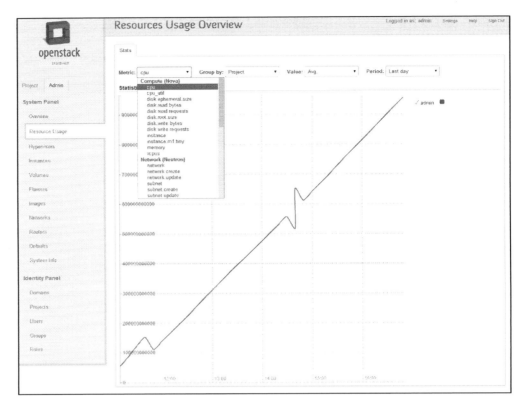

Figure 15-3: CPU Usage

You can select any of the metrics, such as Nova CPU usage (Figure 15-3) or Swift object storage size (Figure 15-4) over a designated period and visualize the results in a graph.

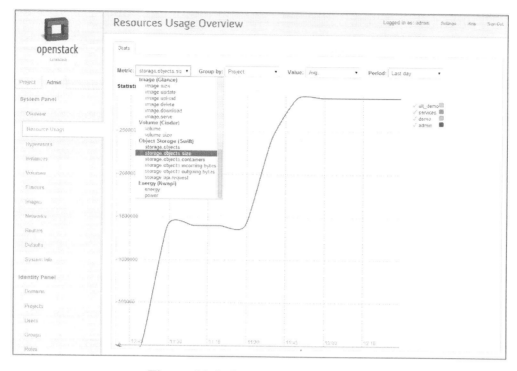

Figure 15-4: Storage Object Size

Integrating Instrumentation

Ceilometer is designed to be extensible both in facilitating additional instrumentation and in making the information accessible to other applications and services. The core of this extensibility is an architecture consisting of two types of plugins: pollsters and listeners.

Pollsters make it possible to integrate metrics for objects that are not natively monitored by OpenStack. They can retrieve any needed metering data from the rest of the infrastructure and construct a metering object from it. The agent daemons then periodically query each pollster for instances of these objects. The framework converts the objects to metering messages, which it places on the metering message bus.

Listeners provide an interface on the receiving side of the process. They consist of a filter and callback method. As Ceilometer processes messages from the queue, it identifies any messages that are appropriate for the listener and will call the associated method passing it the corresponding objects.

As we have already seen above, it is also possible to obtain information asynchronously from the database using the REST API.

Practical Recommendations

OpenStack Metering is largely a function that operates behind the scenes. It supplies data to the billing function. It can trigger events that log critical states. And it can launch orchestration activities.

These may not be your first priority, but it is still worthwhile to become familiar with the data Ceilometer supplies if for no other reason than to get a baseline of normal consumption levels, which you can use for forecasting and troubleshooting.

ACCOUNT

Chapter 16

Extract the Value

The absence of internal billing is often cited as one of the primary differences between public and private cloud implementations. However, this distinction may be misleading since it is not absolutely necessary. In fact, this is one area where cloud technologies can provide an opportunity for better accounting and transparency and thereby add more value to a private cloud than simple virtualization brings to the table. Regardless of whether there is a monetary cross-charge involved, it is always useful to show value and ROI on services. The better they can be quantified, the easier it is to justify. It is therefore just as important to meter and report on transactions and usage even in an internal environment.

A best practice in external billing is to attempt to align charges as closely as possible to your own costs. In other words, if you expect that most of your cost will come from storage, then you might base the customer-charged price on data volume or storage volume. On the other hand, if you anticipate a high computational load then it might be more sensible to base the price on the number of transactions. If support will be a big burden, you might charge extra for helpline calls. If customer acquisition cost is going to be significant (expensive campaigns or AdWords), you'll have to build that into the model.

ACCOUNT

As you select your billable units, you need to sum all the variable resource costs that are attributable to each unit. However, it is unlikely that you will be able match up your costs and incoming charges perfectly. So you also need to make sure you include a contribution margin that covers all the fixed costs to be allocated in order for you to reach overall profitability.

This becomes even more challenging if you bill according to multiple criteria or implement a differentiated pricing scheme. There is no magic formula as to how to distribute your fixed costs. As long as you ensure that your total costs are covered, it is up to you and your determination of what the market will bear.

Cloud Monetization

Every service needs to generate value and demonstrate it to its stakeholders. In some cases, the process is direct and explicit. For example customers may pay subscription and/or usage-based fees for consuming public services. Advertising-funded solutions, on the other hand, also generate money but the cash flow and funding model are much less obvious.

Internal clouds are often seen as free resources by the departmental users who request and use them. Nonetheless, even they must be funded either directly or indirectly from the other company divisions. And this form of internal tax will not be tolerated for long if the systems do not demonstrate sufficient value to the business.

There are three primary means of monetizing a public service. The two most common approaches are a direct-charge model and advertising. The former involves charging the user for the service while the latter gains revenue through sponsored ads on the web site. A third option is to offer a basic service for free, but charge for extended functionality or ancillary consulting and support services.

We will focus here on the first since it is more closely related to traditional forms of doing business. You can find out more about the other two strategies in *Cloud Computing Architected* (Rhoton, 2011). If you break down the direct-charge model, then you really face two different challenges. The first task is to determine how much to charge the user; and the second undertaking is to collect the money.

Pricing

ACCOUNT

The simplest forms of pricing involve one-time fees or flat subscription rates. These are easy to work with since they don't involve collecting and monitoring resource usage and are less likely to lead to a dispute with the customer. However, they are not always practical since one customer may impose very high costs on you while another only needs a minimal service. Subscriptions also transfer a fixed, rather than a variable, cost to the customer and thereby reduce one of the perceived benefits of cloud computing.

Utility-based services can be priced according to various factors including the number of users, transactions or support calls. Profitable monetization relies on effective alignment of internal costs to external pricing and fine-grained metering to substantiate the charges. Fortunately, OpenStack Ceilometer provides visibility on consumption across many of these metrics as we saw in the previous chapter.

A good starting point is a cost model that identifies the cost drivers and calculates the magnitude and shape of the associated cost curve. The most common internal components will be hardware-related and include computational resources (CPU cores), storage (memory and persistent stores), network bandwidth and infrastructure. Unless you rely exclusively on open-source (or in-house) software, licensing can also be a major cost driver. Most importantly, you need to factor in personnel costs for development (probably the biggest in the beginning, leveling off as your service matures), administration and support.

As you dig down into each of these you may be able to break down the costs even more precisely. For example, if writing data is significantly more expensive than reading it, both in terms of the directly attributable costs and indirect costs such as performance, then you will want to maintain that distinction. As you look at computation, you may also find that some transactions lend themselves to horizontal distribution better than others. If you can execute the software on low-cost instances, the cost per CPU cycle may be lower.

You may also need to factor in external costs based on hardware, software and services that you do not own but leverage from other providers. You can pass the charges through as they are. You may also choose to mark them up or, in some cases, subsidize them through a discount.

Initial scalability tests are vital as you start predicting your growing infrastructure costs. If you've already designed your application to run on PaaS from the start, it should scale without any huge surprises. Thoughtful planning mitigates the risk of a moment where you desperately need to re-architect your whole service because your database server is running out of capacity.

Settlement

After determining the amount each of your clients owes you, comes the often unpleasant task of getting them to pay. If you are offering internal cloud services, this usually means creating some interfaces to the Enterprise Resource Planning (ERP) system to cross-charge the amount from one cost-center to another, potentially involving some workflow for approvals.

The equivalent for automated external billing would be to create Electronic Data Interchange (EDI) relationships based on standards such as X12, EDIFACT or XML/EDI. These work great once they are in place; however, it takes significant effort to set them up. As a result they are not common for cloud-related billing and are likely to only be of interest to very large organizations that consume and centrally bill customized services.

For consumers, small and medium businesses, and even for departmental applications of large enterprises, it is much more common to use credit-card billing, which has become the de facto payment mechanism of the Internet, contributing directly to the eCommerce boom in recent years.

While it may be possible for you to build your own credit card processing system and establish relationships with the major credit cards, it would come with significant effort and risk. In particular, consider that if you store credit card details then you are likely to be a prime target for hacker and are obligated to demonstrate compliance with Payment Card Industry (PCI) standards. You are also potentially liable for any data leakage and certainly vulnerable to unfavorable publicity if there are any problems.

To fill this need, particularly for smaller merchants, there are a number of credit card processing systems and payment gateway services such as: Chargify, Flagship Merchant Services, Merchant Warehouse, goEmerchant Merchant Accounts, Chase Paymentech, Merchant One and First Data. They verify a customer's credit card information, judge the authenticity of the transaction, then either decline or process the credit card payment, crediting the merchant account with the payment. Many also offer additional services such as a Shopping Cart, Recurring Billing and Fraud detection (e.g. address verification, card verification value).

There are also a few offerings, such as PayPal, that make themselves available as trusted intermediaries for smaller merchants, who do not yet have the scale and visibility to establish public trust. PayPal is an account-based system that lets anyone use their credit card, or bank account, to securely send and receive online payments. It is the most popular way to electronically pay for eBay auctions and is also becoming a cheap way for merchants to accept credit cards on their online storefronts instead of using a traditional payment gateway. Users can also use PayPal to wire money to other people without requiring them to get a paid account.

ACCOUNT

PayPal supplies a set of standard buttons that nontechnical customers can add to their sites without any development expertise. It is augmented with an extensive set of HTML resources available to permit a custom shopping experience. For more sophisticated needs, PayPal exposes its services through an API called Adaptive Payments, which enables developers to build more complex applications that handle payments, preapprovals for payments and refunds. The payments can be ad hoc or pre-approved and can range from simple (sender makes a single payment to a single receiver) to parallel (sender makes a single payment to multiple receivers), as well as chained (sender makes a single payment to a primary receiver; who keeps part of the payment and pays the remainder to the secondary receivers).

While PayPal's target market may be smaller merchants, the service also has appeal for international business. It operates in over 190 countries and supports 20 major currencies. In addition to its mediation of payments, it also calculates overseas shipping, international taxes and facilitates currency conversions.

Amazon Flexible Payments Service (FPS) is a similar service, but it is considered by many to be easier than PayPal and allows more flexibility than PayPal's original Payments API. Amazon created FPS for developers, allowing them to integrate with Amazon's retail billing system. The customers can use the same identities, shipping details and payment information that they would for ordering directly with Amazon.

The metering and billing includes dynamic usage tracking and reports as well as an extensive array of payment options including one-time payments, periodic charges, delayed payments and aggregation of micropayments. These can all be set and changed through the API.

Google Checkout is Google's equivalent to FPS. Once users have signed up and entered their credit or debit card details, they can shop conveniently whenever they log into Google. The financial details and e-mail addresses are not shared with the merchant who simply receives confirmation of the payment. Customers have access to a history feature to track shipping information for all purchases.

On the merchant side, setting up the site involves adding some Google supplied code to let visitors shop via Checkout. As you would expect, Google takes a commission on the sales. Google Checkout is similar to Amazon FPS, and differs from PayPal, in that they do not operate a separate payment service; but rather they use the existing credit card infrastructure to enable payments and online transactions.

OpenStack Billing

Two very different mindsets prevail when it comes to OpenStack billing, and they derive directly from the deployment model of the OpenStack services. Service providers running public clouds typically have a standard process, which borrows heavily from the telecommunications industry.

Enterprises very often have no charging system in place at all. Their priority is usually to get the services up and running and worry about how to refine the cost allocation later. However, even these private clouds are under pressure to demonstrate value. As their adoption increases, the operational costs tend to explode and it becomes necessary to implement a system that is very similar to what public providers have been doing for many years.

ACCOUNT

This process is logically composed of three functions:

- Metering: collects and stores usage data on all actions that have taken place.
- Rating: transforms usage data into billable line items and calculates the associated costs. It needs to consider different price lists and pricing plans.
- Billing: creates an invoice, sends it to the customer and collects payment. It applies discount rules, formats the invoices, calculates taxes and either processes the payment or interfaces with a payment gateway.

OpenStack covers the first operation quite well through Ceilometer as we saw in the previous chapter. However, it doesn't offer any capabilities for Rating or Billing. This leaves a gap which you may try to fill with an open-source billing system such as jBilling[1] or you may choose to rely on a commercial offering like Aria Systems[2] or Zuora[3]. You may even want a SaaS solution, for example, Recurly[4] or Chargify[5].

The main challenge in implementing any billing system will be the integration with your OpenStack infrastructure. Stated differently, you need to find a way to feed the Ceilometer information to the billing process. Let's look at two solutions that already have working interfaces to Ceilometer making this a much easier task.

Talligent

Talligent is a rating and billing engine with interfaces to OpenStack, VMware and others. It is built as a Java application running on Tomcat using a Cassandra (or MySQL) database. It connects to Ceilometer endpoints and retrieves the metric names (Figure 16-1), which it can subsequently present as "Billable Features",

ACCOUNT

---

[1] http://www.jbilling.com/
[2] http://www.ariasystems.com/
[3] http://www.zuora.com/
[4] https://recurly.com
[5] http://chargify.com/

Figure 16-1: Talligent OpenStack Resource Manager

Each rate plan has a beginning and end date. These rate plans are assigned hierarchically to different organizational units of the customers. They are used to bill tenants based on their resource consumption and their persona (e.g. whether they are a trial user, reseller, from a specific location). They can pro-rate the charges (in the case of partial billing periods) and automatically calculate discounts, taxes and currency conversions (Figure 16-2).

ACCOUNT

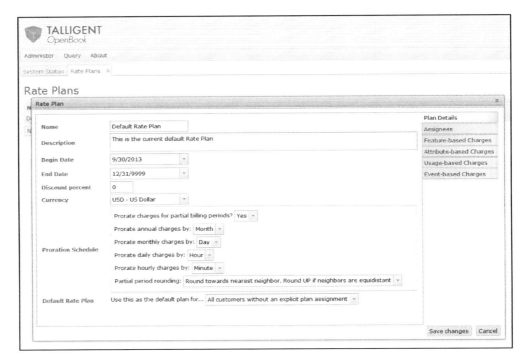

Figure 16-2: Talligent Rate Plan

The charges can be based on OpenStack elements including virtual machine instances, floating IP addresses, storage blocks, load balancers, applications, firewalls and backup services (Figure 16-3).

ACCOUNT

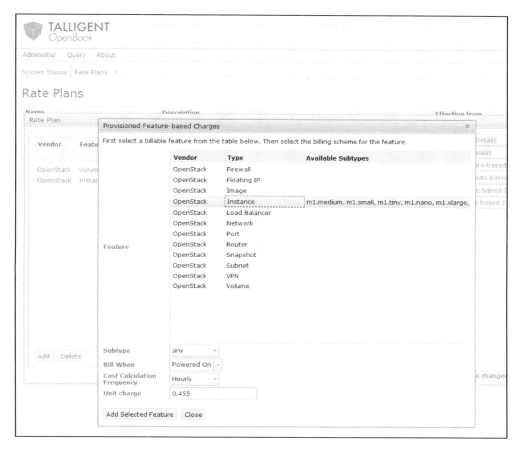

Figure 16-3: Talligent Feature-based Charges

For each of these elements, Ceilometer exposes a set of metrics that can be used as the basis for billing (Figure 16-4).

ACCOUNT

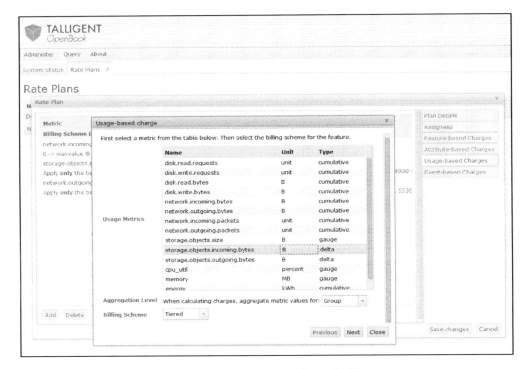

Figure 16-4: Talligent Usage-based Charges

Volume-based charges can be based on linear calculations (Figure 16-5).

Figure 16-5: Talligent Linear Cost Calculation

Alternatively, it is also possible to implement a tiered billing scheme (Figure 16-6), where, for example, the first ten gigabytes are free, the next 90 are at a discounted rate and the full price sets in over one hundred gigabytes.

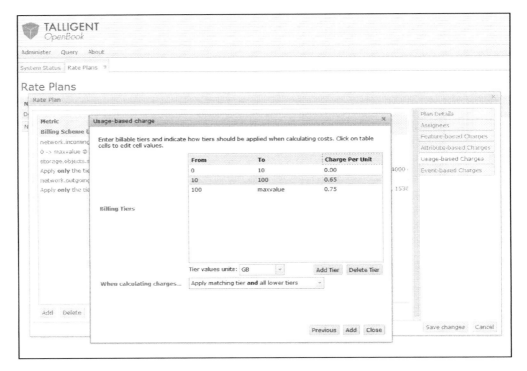

Figure 16-6: Talligent Tiered Pricing

The solution can generate the invoices and send them to the customers automatically or interface to a payment system for bill collection (Figure 16-7).

ACCOUNT

Invoice
Number: Sample
Date: Feb 01, 2014

Sample Customer

Billing Period: Jan 01, 2014 - Feb 01, 2014
Bill Amount: $2,326.14

Detailed Charges

Instances	$2,210.08
c1.2xlarge	**608.01**
Instance type c1.2xlarge @ $4.752 Hourly when Powered On, for 127 hours, 57 minutes	608.01
c1.large	**152.01**
Instance type c1.large @ $1.188 Hourly when Powered On, for 127 hours, 57 minutes	152.01
c1.medium	**76.00**
Instance type c1.medium @ $0.594 Hourly when Powered On, for 127 hours, 57 minutes	76.00
c1.xlarge	**304.01**
Instance type c1.xlarge @ $2.376 Hourly when Powered On, for 127 hours, 57 minutes	304.01
m1.large	**140.75**
Instance type m1.large @ $1.1 Hourly when Powered On, for 127 hours, 57 minutes	140.75
m1.medium	**57.71**
Instance type m1.medium @ $0.451 Hourly when Powered On, for 127 hours, 57 minutes	57.71
m1.xlarge	**230.82**
Instance type m1.xlarge @ $1.804 Hourly when Powered On, for 127 hours, 57 minutes	230.82
s1.2xlarge	**168.89**
Instance type s1.2xlarge @ $1.32 Hourly when Powered On, for 127 hours, 57 minutes	168.89
s1.3xlarge	**337.79**
Instance type s1.3xlarge @ $2.64 Hourly when Powered On, for 127 hours, 57 minutes	337.79
s1.large	**33.78**
Instance type s1.large @ $0.264 Hourly when Powered On, for 127 hours, 57 minutes	33.78
s1.medium	**16.89**
Instance type s1.medium @ $0.132 Hourly when Powered On, for 127 hours, 57 minutes	16.89
s1.micro	**3.71**
Instance type s1.micro @ $0.029 Hourly when Powered On, for 127 hours, 57 minutes	3.71
s1.small	**8.44**
Instance type s1.small @ $0.066 Hourly when Powered On, for 127 hours, 57 minutes	8.44
s1.xlarge	**67.56**
Instance type s1.xlarge @ $0.528 Hourly when Powered On, for 127 hours, 57 minutes	67.56
type	**3.71**
Instance type s1.micro @ $0.029 Hourly when Powered On, for 127 hours, 57 minutes	3.71

Usage-Based Charges	$0.00
Network Outgoing Bytes	**0.00**
0.00012763 GBs @ $0.00/GB	0.00
Object Storage Size	**0.00**

0.00008270 GBs @ $0.109/GB	0.00

Volumes	$116.06
Standard Volume	**19.34**
size=1024 GB @ $0.115 per GB Monthly, for 5 days	19.34
Standard Volume 5TB	**96.72**
size=5120 GB @ $0.115 per GB Monthly, for 5 days	96.72

Figure 16-7: Talligent Sample Invoice

Cloud Cruiser

Cloud Cruiser also offers integrated billing capabilities for OpenStack as well as other leading cloud platforms such as Amazon Web Services and Microsoft Azure. It can apply costs to any resource using flat, variable and tiered schemes based on schedule and resource-state and taking into consideration promotions and discounts (Figure 16-8).

Figure 16-8: Cloud Cruiser Integrated Billing

Its strengths lie in its deep analysis of usage and costs (Figure 16-9). The dashboard provides an overview of cloud resources, showing which customers or tenants are consuming the most.

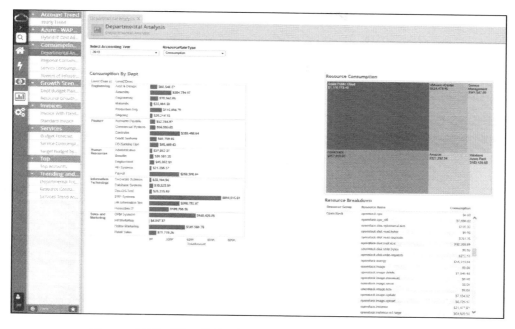

Figure 16-9: Cloud Cruiser Departmental Analysis

As a full-scale financial management system, it provides much more insight than a billing system. Its objective is complete cost transparency, mapping all costs to the resources that have been consumed. By placing fine-grained data in the hands of the customer, they can facilitate cost accountability and detailed analytics showing how IT customers are consuming services.

ACCOUNT

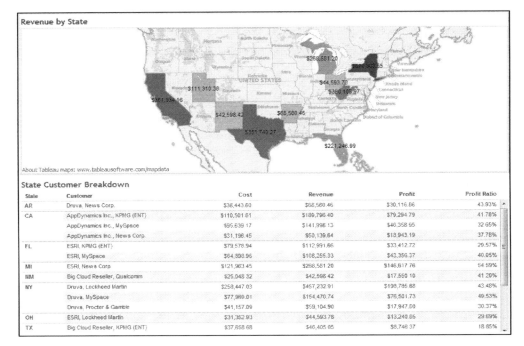

Figure 16-10: Cloud Cruiser Regional Analysis

For instance, they can break down the service provider revenue by geography (Figure 16-10) or by industry (Figure 16-11).

ACCOUNT

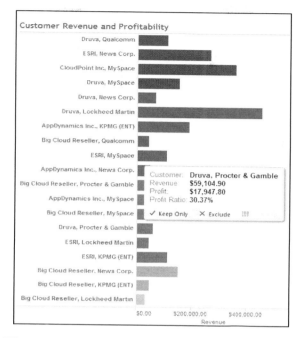

Figure 16-11: Cloud Cruiser Industry Analysis

It is also possible to analyze service performance by revenue, customer (Figure 16-12), geography or business function.

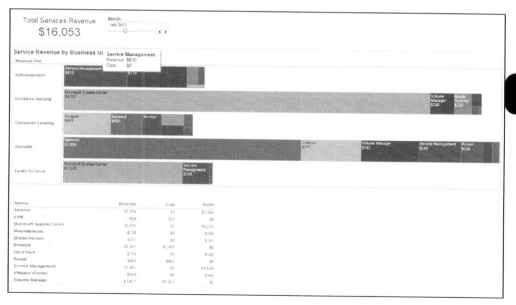

ACCOUNT

Figure 16-12: Cloud Cruiser Business Analysis

And service providers can see which services and resources most profitable (Figure 16-13).

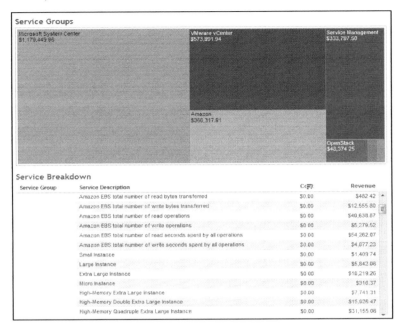

Figure 16-13: Cloud Cruiser Service Analysis

Budgeting is another financial function that is very important, particularly for the enterprises that set monthly spend limits to align with internal monthly budgets. Service providers may have similar requirements to enforce customer credit lines.

ACCOUNT

Practical Recommendations

Implementing any technology, including OpenStack, costs money and someone has to pay for it. Whether the expenses are shared by multiple business units or passed on to external customers only changes the actual collection processes.

In both cases, it improves accountability and facilitates forecasting if there is a verifiable mechanism in place to measure usage and calculate the costs that are associated with it.

OpenStack has made great strides in the area of the first, but there is a need to look at other solutions to fill the gap for the second. There are several options, but Talligent and Cloud Cruiser are well integrated into OpenStack, so they would be our first ports of call.

ACCOUNT

Secure

OpenStack itself is neither particularly secure nor insecure. Security is a discipline that requires systematic application. This means the first task of a risk analysis is simply to make sure all the components are implemented securely. After verifying that the configuration adheres to best practices, it is important to be vigilant of any newly found exploits and supplement the bare infrastructure with further layers of security. In addition to the base infrastructure, a key component of the overall security model is identity and access management and the enforcement of consistent policies governing user activity.

SECURE

Chapter 17

Protect the Assets

The introduction of any new technology should involve a risk analysis. Information technologies, in particular, have a tendency to alter the risk profile of the organization with potentially disastrous consequences. This study needs to go beyond a simple assessment of the products involved and extend into the technical, procedural and cultural ramifications that they may trigger.

OpenStack itself is not encumbered with any significant publicized vulnerabilities at this point in time. In fact, it has a big advantage over most commercial solutions since it is open source and therefore available to thorough scrutiny. But it also introduces a new way of building out infrastructure, which can lead to additional risks. Public implementations are based on a disruptively different trust model that needs to be solidly supported with contractual agreements and third-party audits. Private clouds also introduce resource abstractions that make it more difficult to monitor and troubleshoot the underlying physical layers.

This chapter will look at some of the major considerations as they might pertain to an OpenStack deployment. We've already discussed some of the networking issues in Chapter 10 and will look more closely at Identity Management in the next chapter and Availability in Chapter 20. If you want to dig deeper, you can also find a more extensive treatment of these and other security topics in Cloud Computing Protected (Rhoton, De Clercq, & Graves, 2013).

SECURE

Cloud Security

Security experts usually look at cloud computing with great skepticism. It is a disruptive change, but we should realize that its impact on enterprise risk can be both positive and negative. Let's begin with the benefits that it brings to table.

Reduced Risk

Increased specialization through the use of public cloud services may reduce risk. Every case of outsourcing changes the risk profile of the customer since it shifts some responsibilities (and therefore risks) from the company to the provider. Although the same problems may present themselves, the contractual transfer mitigates the customer risks by providing some form of indemnity that should compensate for any loss.

There may also be reason to expect fewer incidents to occur given the cloud providers' advanced position on the experience curve. With world-class processes and personnel, they can afford specialized staff and are in a position to rapidly provision and scale security resources both proactively and reactively (after an incident breaks out).

The economy of scale of the provider reduces the risk of exceeding capacity when demand surges. Cloud services can draw on a larger pool of resources, so they can absorb localized spikes much more easily. The wide geographical presence of many cloud service providers allows them to replicate remotely much more effectively thereby reducing the likelihood of a complete loss in the face of a natural or man-made disaster. Cloud providers may also improve content delivery through extensive geographical representation. Decreased latency and dependency on fewer network hops reduces the number and magnitude of service delivery failures to end customers.

Considered from a very different perspective, officially authorized cloud service solutions may reduce the number and usage of rogue clouds. Without an official cost-effective solution to trial new services in a timely manner, the businesses, some departments, or even individual users, may subscribe to their own external services. The impact of these 'Shadow IT' deployments can range from suboptimal resource allocation, to non-compliance with legal restrictions and a compromise of information security policies.

Finally, cloud computing provides a company with a means to reduce strategic risk. In a highly dynamic environment with regular market and industry shifts, the organization may need a way to react quickly and scale faster than it has been able to do in the past. On-demand activation and elasticity of resources give the company this flexibility.

SECURE

Increased Risk

Unfortunately, there are also some areas where cloud computing can increase the risk of a company. We will look at the risk drivers in general terms and then examine some specific threats.

Reduced Control: The aforementioned shift of some responsibilities from the company to the provider may reduce some risk to the customer through contractual transfer. However, it may also increase risk by diminishing the control of the end user over business-critical services. This means that customers cannot dictate the amount of effort that should be directed at solving a particular problem nor can they shape the direction of that effort.

Service-level agreements can cover broad performance indicators, but they only serve as an approximation of the enterprise needs. Outages, downtime and poor user experiences can have direct financial consequences in terms of failed transactions. Furthermore, they can diminish user acceptance and tarnish the image of the company. It is difficult to accurately quantify these effects and convince the service provider to compensate them fully.

Externalization: Storing data outside the corporate firewall will be seen by many security practitioners as a potential vulnerability. If the information is exposed to hackers or competitors, there is potential damage in terms of exposed intellectual property and competitive information, a loss of confidence from customers, suppliers and partners and, in some cases, potentially also legal liability for the damages that result.

Regulation: In the past few years, there has been an increase in the number and scope of regulatory provisions that govern information processing across the world. Violation of these articles can carry heavy financial penalties for companies, as well as for board members and senior management. Cloud computing obfuscates the location as well as the security provisions that protect it. While this lack of visibility may inhibit targeted attacks, it makes it very difficult for an enterprise to validate compliance with all relevant laws.

Complexity: The problems are only partially mitigated by standards and third-party auditing mechanisms, which are not yet fully refined for cloud computing and typically do not cover all components involved in service delivery. A comprehensive design requires mastery of servers, storages and networking in both physical and virtual environments. Furthermore, problems of control and accountability are complicated by the fact that the architecture caters to openness and heterogeneity with the consequence that there are often many different service providers and subcontractors involved in any solution.

SECURE

Uncertainty: Lastly, there is an inherent risk in adopting any new technology. By definition less is known about it and it is less mature than conventional mechanisms. Intuitively, it will almost always be easier and less risky to stay stationary with the existing products and processes than to embark on an unknown experiment. However, in a dynamic business environment staying stationary may no longer be an option.

The Cloud Security Alliance has identified seven top threats (Cloud Security Alliance, 2010)[1] which enterprises should specifically consider in the context of the risk assessment.

Abuse and Nefarious Use of Cloud Computing: Spammers, malicious code authors, and other criminals are able to abuse the anonymity behind cloud-based registration and usage models to distribute various forms of unwanted content and malware. In the future they may be able to extend these activities to password cracking, distributed denial of service (DDoS) and botnet operations.

Insecure Application Programming Interfaces: Cloud providers expose a broad set of programmatic interfaces to their services in order to facilitate tight customer integration and build a profitable ecosystem. The wide range of functions for provisioning, orchestration and monitoring, along with the complexity of the layered interfaces, increase risk to the customer.

Malicious Insiders: Malicious insiders can take advantage of the integrated management of IT services to maximize the scope of their impact. At the same time, the customer's lack of visibility into the provider process and procedure can help them to avoid detection.

Shared Technology Vulnerabilities: The shared technologies that host cloud infrastructure (e.g. disk partitions, CPU caches, GPUs) were not designed for strong compartmentalization. They do not offer the isolation properties necessary for a multi-tenant architecture and therefore present an inherent vulnerability.

Data Loss and Leakage: The risk of data leakage is the most publicized concern around cloud solutions which commonly share resources and access media among users. It is further compounded by the lack of control over physical assets and operational processes as well as the complexity of identity management and service integration.

Account, Service and Traffic Hijacking: If attackers are able to hijack user credentials, they can intercept all communications, manipulate transactions and block legitimate user access. The hacker may even use the accounts as a platform for further attacks and thereby compromise the reputation of users.

Unknown Risk Profile: Cloud providers offer copious information on the features and functionality of their services. But they are less forthcoming with details on their internal security procedures. Without specifics on software versions, vulnerability profiles and intrusion attempts, it is very difficult for a customer to assess and improve their security profile.

SECURE

---

[1] cloudsecurityalliance.org/research/top-threats/

Of these, generally Data Loss and Data Leakage receive the most attention. The terms actually represent two very different threats. Data loss refers to data that the user has lost access to (for example through a disk failure). Data leakage refers to data that has been illegitimately passed on to an unauthorized user. Many security professionals also refer to the second risk as data loss. The ambiguity can be confusing, but shouldn't stop us from covering both concerns.

Data Loss: The fact that the data is outside the enterprise's control makes it more difficult to impose availability constraints as well as backup and restore procedures. In the event of a disaster, or a human mistake, data can be irretrievably lost.

Multi-tenancy may further exacerbate the threat by exposing the enterprise to denial-of-service and malware attacks that are directed at co-tenants or launched from their platforms.

Data Leakage: The cloud delivery model entails enterprise data physically residing in data centers that are outside the customer firewall. This means that the data is exposed to competitors and hackers. The threat is accentuated through multi-tenancy, outsourcing and use of public communication links.

Multi-tenancy makes the boundaries between the enterprise and the outside more permeable. The borders may lack policy enforcement points and access control points that the enterprise can enforce and monitor. Outsourcing by the provider reduces the visibility and control that the enterprise has over hiring policies, role segregation and compartmentalization of job duties, customer assignment and need-to-know information security policies.

We would also like to cover a few additional risks that can have a significant impact on an organization adopting cloud services.

Service Loss: Independent of the data risks, there is also a concern about services that enterprises may require for the business processes of their employees or for revenue-generating transactions by customers.

There are several levels of possible service loss:

SECURE

> *Service termination* – If the cloud provider should declare insolvency, or if there is a fundamental and irresolvable conflict between the customer and provider (for example, unacceptable increase in costs for contract renewal), these may lead to permanent termination of the contract and service.

> *Service interruption* – A less severe problem is when the service is only temporarily unavailable, for example, due to network connectivity loss or technical problems inside the data center.

Partial service interruption – A service may be generally available but only portions may not work as needed. Depending on the criticality of the missing functionality, the severity of this case may vary.

Service Impairment – Even though a service may technically be available, it could still be suboptimal. If the service-level agreement focuses on availability and neglects performance, service quality, resolution times of non-critical bugs and on-time delivery of new/remediated services, then the enterprise will risk employee productivity and customer satisfaction losses.

Similarly, if the provider is physically unable to deliver increases in capacity, or refuses to do so, then the business loses the elasticity benefit of cloud computing. They may even be more restricted than in a fully insourced scenario where they do at least have some options to add capacity when it is needed.

Lock-in: The lack of standardization of cloud services can easily lead to a situation where the customer services and data cannot be moved to another service provider without significant effort. There are two drawbacks to this restriction.

On the one hand, the provider can hold the customers hostage and force them to accept increasingly disadvantageous terms since they have no viable exit strategy. On the other hand, if the service does terminate for any of the reasons listed earlier, then the customers have a significant problem in trying to find an alternative. As we shall see in Chapter 22, it can take considerable time, cost and effort to find a replacement and migrate all of the data.

Damaged Reputation: Data and service problems, if they are visible to the public, can have a cascade effect on the reputation of the company. Customers may be unwilling to do business with a company if they believe their financial, health or other private information is not adequately protected. Similarly they may be disgruntled if their services are not available or are cumbersome to use.

In a multi-tenant scenario, there is also the possibility that co-tenants may unfavorably influence the perception of an organization. If it is publicly known that the company shares resources with a high-profile target of attacks, it may reduce the confidence customers have in their services and data; or, if the data center is known to host services of unsavory businesses or extremist groups some customers may be apprehensive of allowing their information to be co-mingled on the same systems.

OpenStack Security Mechanisms

Perhaps the most distinctive feature of OpenStack with regard to security is that it is open source. There is a downside to making the code available to all potential attackers. They don't need to reverse engineer anything in order to analyse the program logic and look for vulnerabilities.

But the benefits generally outweigh the risks. The fact that the source is easily available means that many people have the opportunity to validate it and therefore minimize the number of vulnerabilities in the first place. As OpenStack adoption takes hold, we can expect the interest and public scrutiny to increase leading to even better software protection.

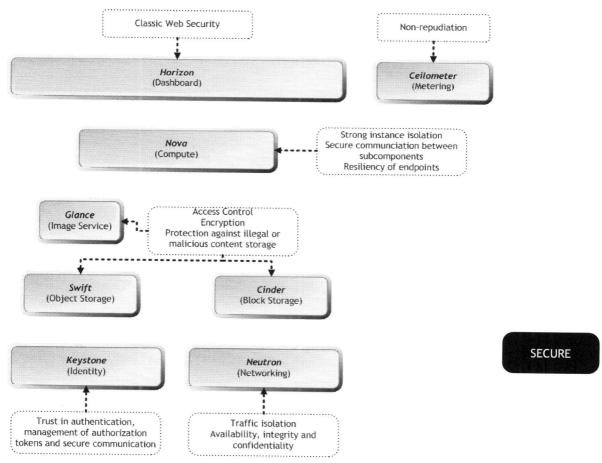

Figure 17-1: OpenStack Security Requirements

Security is a topic that needs to be addressed systematically. In other words, it is vital for every component to take responsibility for the security ramifications of the processes within its scope (Figure 17-1). For the most part, we can say that

OpenStack can facilitate a secure implementation of its technologies (Figure 17-2).

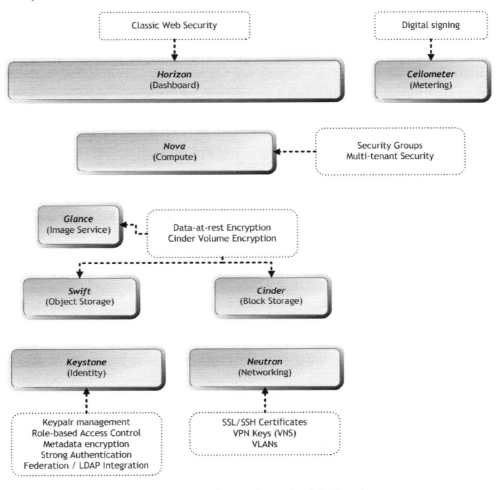

Figure 17-2: OpenStack Security Mechanisms

SECURE

The storage functions, Cinder, Swift and Glance can cover data at rest through file encryption. Neutron supports SSL certificates and VPN keys. Nova supports the management of SSH keys. Keystone encrypts metadata and user-level keys and provides hooks to support strong authentication. And Ceilometer implements digital signatures to enforce non-repudiation of metering messages.

You can find a wealth of specific guidance on setting up OpenStack securely in the OpenStack Security Guide[1]. And there is a set of OpenStack Security Advi-

---

[1] http://docs.openstack.org/sec

sories (OSSAs)[1] and OpenStack Security Notes (OSSNs)[2] to help you ensure that you are well protected against any known vulnerabilities.

OpenStack also includes some security-oriented features, such as security groups, firewalls and secure key storage, which we will look at below.

Keypair management

A critical security point in the use of cloud services is the connection. It is vital for the transmission between the user and the service to be protected. With respect to the compute instances, users will typically access the console via a secure shell (SSH).

It is a relatively simple matter to encrypt a transmission, so that a third party cannot read any part of the payload. However, it is much more challenging to authenticate both endpoints. Even with username/password authentication, it would be possible for an attacker to launch an insertion (man-in-the-middle) attack by hijacking the stream and forwarding it along a second connection to the legitimate target.

To protect the connection, it is necessary generate an asymmetric keypair. OpenStack assists in the management of these keypairs (Figure 17-3).

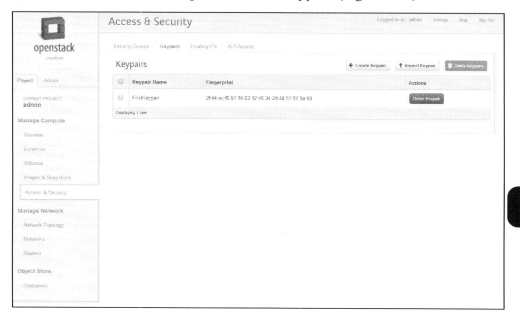

SECURE

Figure 17-3: OpenStack Keypairs

---

[1] https://wiki.openstack.org/wiki/Vulnerability_Management
[2] https://launchpad.net/ossn/

The user can generate a new keypair, only needing to supply the name (Figure 17-4).

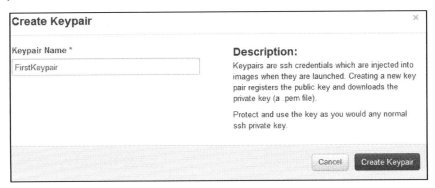

Figure 17-4: Create Keypair

OpenStack then injects the credentials into new images. The user can download the keypair (Figure 17-5) as a PEM (Privacy Enhanced Mail) file, which includes the private key.

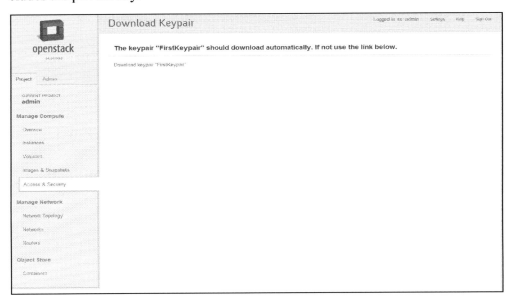

Figure 17-5: Download Keypair

Subsequent SSH connections to instances using this keypair will then authenticate the client endpoint.

SECURE

Security Groups

A second major security domain that is particularly important in multi-tenant environments is access control lists, which, in OpenStack, take the form of Security Groups (Figure 17-6).

Figure 17-6: Security Groups

Each Security Group consists of a set of rules that grant access to the instances belonging to the specific group (Figure 17-7).

SECURE

Figure 17-7: Security Group Rules

Users can specify whether the rule is inbound (ingress) or outbound (egress) as well as which TCP (or UDP) port and IP address ranges is refers to (Figure 17-8).

SECURE

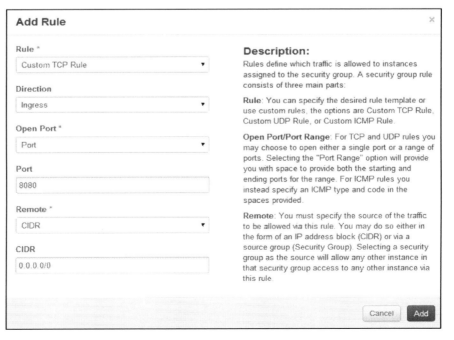

Figure 17-8: Add Security Group Rule

Any data packets matching these criteria will be allowed to/from the instance and all other traffic will be dropped.

FWaaS

There is an experimental service called Firewall-as-a-Service (FWaaS), which is conceptually very similar to security groups. Firewalls are able to handle more sophisticated access control lists with rules not only for allowing but also for denying specific patterns of traffic.

The fundamental difference between these two access control mechanisms is that security groups apply to the network ports of the instances while the firewalls apply to the network infrastructure, or more specifically, the routers. The initial implementation is a perimeter firewall, meaning that it applies to all routers of a particular tenant. However, there are plans for additional drivers that allow deployment in other modes (e.g. L2, bump-in-the-wire).

OpenStack Key Management (Barbican)

Another security feature of OpenStack that is still in development is Barbican, driven in large part by Rackspace. The term 'barbican' refers to a protective tower or wall on the perimeter of a medieval castle, often over the drawbridge or gateway. In OpenStack we can think of the service as a secure facility for storing keys or access credentials.

Barbican provides a mechanism for protecting commonly exposed settings, such as SSL, TLS, SSH and other encryption keys. It can interface to any PKCS-11-compliant Hardware Security Module (HSM) on the back end. A secure storage facility means that the other services don't need to worry about how to protect the encryption key. For example, when Swift needs to access encrypted data, it is able to obtain the key from Barbican.

Note that it doesn't prevent the other services from retaining the keys or abusing them in some way, but it means they don't have to write their own functions to securely persist the keys between user requests.

SECURE

In theory, all encryption keys could be placed in the HSM and each OpenStack service would obtain them via Barbican per user request. In practice, there are scalability limits to most HSMs that make it impractical to place all Data Encryption Keys (DEKs) in the HSM. Instead, Rackspace and others only store a tenant-level Key Encryption Key (KEK) in the HSM. Barbican stores all the DEKs after encrypting them with the KEK. So, Barbican can provide the DEKs to any authenticated service, if necessary first obtaining the KEK from the HSM.

Cinder Volume encryption

In outsourced and shared-services environments, volume encryption is often mandatory. It may be in order to achieve compliance with respect to industry regulations and norms, such as the U.S. Health Insurance Portability and Accountability Act (HIPAA) or Payment Card Industry Data Security Standard (PCI-DSS). Or it may just be to protect sensitive data and intellectual property in the case of lost and stolen disks, reused disk sectors or intercepted iSCSI commands.

It has always been possible to implement volume encryption manually by configuring full-disk encryption or an encrypted file system. However, these techniques can require complex key management especially if the volumes may be attached to different instances.

The Havana release introduced the capability for Cinder volume encryption. In this scenario, Cinder performs the encryption using any cipher, mode, hash, and key size supported by the kernel. When Nova attaches an encrypted volume to an instance, it retrieves the cryptographic metadata (key UUID, cipher, key size, provider, control location) from Cinder and then passes it on to the virtualization driver which transparently encrypts outgoing data and decrypts incoming data. All data in transit is automatically secure and the instance is able to work on the contents in plaintext without any additional effort.

All other Cinder features, such as snapshots, clones or booting from Cinder volumes, can be used in conjunction with encryption.

The pluggable architecture provides a choice of key managers to handle encryption keys. The current default is a single static key per tenant that is shared across all volumes. However, it is possible to include other key managers including OpenStack Barbican or third-party commercial systems (e.g. Safenet).

Complementary Security

We have seen some of the general areas of concern around cloud security and a few features that OpenStack implements to support security. Obviously, there is still quite a gap between them. This doesn't mean that OpenStack is insecure, but rather that it takes a lot more to implement it securely. For example, we need to look at the entire commercial and legal environment. We need to consider the human process components and we need to be meticulous in how we implement both OpenStack and any necessary supplementary components.

Security interacts with cloud computing at many levels. We have structured this part of the book according to the components shown in Figure 17-9. From outside the cloud we have the *Environment* that determines the general risk profile of cloud computing. It includes both *Threats* that continuously adapt to further put cloud at risk as well as *Regulation* that can dilute or exacerbate many risks. What these have in common is that they are largely outside of the control of the cloud provider and consumer.

SECURE

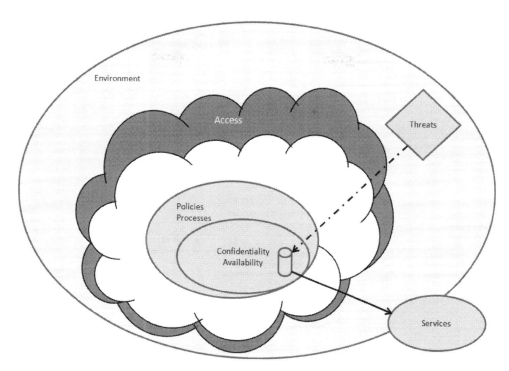

Figure 17-9: Cloud Security Model

The perimeter protects the cloud from some of these external risks but it must be at least partially permeable to be useful. It is this *Access* that is the first line of defense. The highest security objectives at the core of the cloud are the protection of *Confidentiality* and *Availability* of both resources and services. However, in order to achieve this effectively, we need *Policies* that govern user and service behavior as well as defined *Processes* to ensure that policies are implemented.

Finally, we need to look at how we can benefit from the service federation inherent in cloud computing. In many cases, there are security *Services* that we can leverage to protect our internal resources and these external services may be both more efficient and more effective than anything we can implement internally.

SECURE

Cloud Security Responsibilities

Another classification of cloud security is the alignment of focus areas to the cloud delivery model. Depending on whether the service involves software, a platform or infrastructure, it may be susceptible to separate risks and may require different safeguards. Even though the scope of OpenStack is primarily limited to IaaS, any operational solution will also include ingredients of PaaS and SaaS, so the design must also consider them.

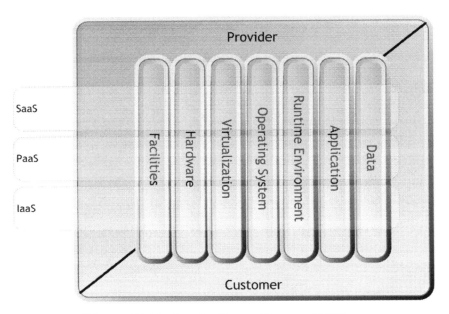

Figure 17-10: Service Layer Responsibilities

More specifically, the risks may fall under the responsibility of different entities depending on the level of cloud delivery (Reed & Bennet, 2011). Generally, services that fit into the bottom of the stack offer less functionality and more flexibility (Figure 17-10). As such, the consumer has greater responsibility, including provisions for security. Services at the top of the stack are fully functional and do not provide much customer flexibility. The provider must therefore take on the responsibility for security.

For example, software licensing is typically a high-level function. When software is delivered as a service, the provider will either own the software or at least take over this responsibility on behalf of the consumer. But when customers purchase an infrastructure service, they must make the effort to ensure all platforms and applications they use are fully licensed.

SECURE

Application security is also an ingredient of a shrink-wrapped software service. At the infrastructure level, the application is not visible to the provider, so the customer must take full responsibility for its security. PaaS lies between the two and involves shared responsibilities. The provider must ensure that the platform is fully secured and exposes no vulnerabilities while the consumer must carefully scrutinize the application code.

Network security and OS hardening are only visible to the customer at the infrastructural level where they are the responsibility of the customer. At the higher levels, the provider must transparently ensure that they do not expose any vulnerability that could impact the service.

Other areas, such as policy enforcement, encryption, monitoring and governance span all levels of the SPI stack, but they do not carry the same meaning at each. Instead they relate to their respective elements (services, platforms, infrastructure), which they must protect.

Security Best Practices

Security is such a comprehensive topic that it is often difficult to know where to begin. We've tried to distill a few of the core elements into actionable items that you can use to begin your assessment. We also list some pointers at the end of the chapter where you can find more comprehensive checklists.

Provider Assessment

A critical first step is a rigorous selection process of the cloud provider. The customer should review the provider's security processes and establish if they are sufficient and reflect the expected maturity level. The review should include provider documentation as well as an assessment of the contractual terms.

Clearly, the investigation will be easiest if the provider is willing to collaborate so that the risk assessment approaches are consistent between provider and user in their definition of impact and likelihood. The service-level agreements will give some insight into the provider's protection level, but it is important to externally verify the safeguards.

For obvious reasons, the provider may restrict broad vulnerability assessments and penetration testing, so other assessment options will be necessary. Published metrics and certifications or audits will be helpful in evaluating the provider's security posture. For example, the CSA STAR (Security, Trust and Assurance Registry) is a helpful place to find self-assessments, certifications and attestations that validate the controls in place at a large number of providers.

Lastly, it is very important to assess the risk of the vendors themselves. On the one hand, this refers to their interoperability with other services and the portability of their data and applications (to facilitate graceful exit). On the other hand, there is an inherent risk in the solvency of an outsourcer and this risk is made more pronounced by the fact that many cloud providers have not been operating for a long time.

SECURE

Contract Negotiation

As part of the provider selection, it will be necessary to evaluate, and possibly negotiate, the terms of the contract. At this stage, it is important to keep in mind that the service levels and their performance indicators will have a direct impact on the level of risk of successful service delivery.

The customer can reduce these risks with active service monitoring, but should also seek the best conditions including certifications, right to audit (or audit reports from a reliable third party), and financial compensation when the provider doesn't adhere to the contract.

Obviously, the same considerations also apply to the service providers who will have an interest in minimizing any potential liability and enforcing their rights in the case that a tenant contributes to risk, insecurity or performance problems either directly or indirectly.

Supplementary Backup

In addition to any backups taken by the service provider, the enterprise may want a supplementary disaster recovery strategy. The options include

- Co-located system that archives all critical information with the cloud service provider
- Process agreed with service provider to send periodic tape backups of systems to the customer
- Replication from within the service to another data center or cloud provider
- Customer-activated extraction of data from the service through available interfaces

The decision of which approach to use will depend on the availability of each of the options. It is also contingent on the amount of data, the price of bandwidth and the time criticality (both in terms of recovery point objective and recovery time objective) of the data.

Physical Isolation

Physical isolation is the IT security technique that has been most widely adopted in the past. Before the onset of wireless technologies, an air gap was virtually unassailable. Times have changed, but it can still be very useful to separate sensitive operations and data from the rest of the network where possible.

For instance, the administrative interfaces to OpenStack require very tight access control. If any guest can gain access to the message queue, they can inject messages that will destabilize the system and might be able to commandeer access to instances and storage of other tenants.

One way to reduce this risk is to implement a separate physical network for the OpenStack services and ensure that the guests cannot access the network.

SECURE

Logical Isolation

When physical isolation is impossible or impractical, we can resort to logical isolation. Traditionally, data centers have implemented logical isolation by segregating traffic at OSI Layer 2 (bridge level) via VLANs. It is certainly possible to use VLANs with OpenStack (Figure 17-11).

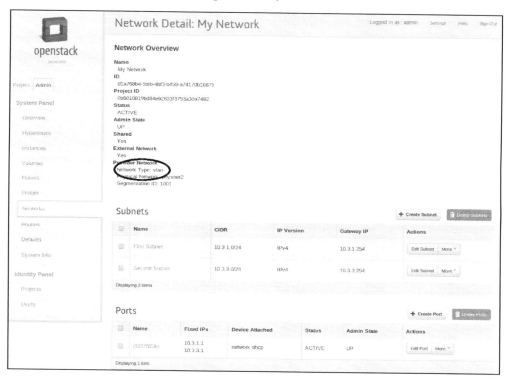

Figure 17-11: OpenStack VLAN

However, as we covered in Chapter 10, VLANs are less than optimal when operating at cloud scale since they are constrained to an absolute limit of 4096 VLANs, which may be insufficient for larger organizations. Instead OpenStack (and other cloud providers, such as Amazon) use security groups and firewalls, providing Layer-3 isolation.

SECURE

You can augment these access controls with firewall capabilities on the hosts themselves. For example, if RDP or SSH ports are not necessary, it might be wise to disable them completely. Dome9 even makes it possible to control these firewalls from a central management console, opening and closing the ports on demand to minimize exposure[1].

---

[1] http://www.dome9.com/security-challenges/openstack-security

Of course, none of these is sufficient if someone is able to break into the underlying network and manipulate the data on the network interface using promiscuous mode. The only way to address this risk is by encrypting the channel.

Encryption

OpenStack facilitates secure keypairs for SSH as described above. It is also possible to configure the majority of HTTP communications to run across SSL. However, a secure implementation of SSL will rely on a solid PKI with a trusted certificate chain, which is outside the scope of OpenStack and must be handled as a separate project.

Encryption of cloud-stored data also helps to mitigate the risk that it will be leaked. However, it needs to be clear that this limits the service of the provider. It cannot offer any high-level integrity checking or assist constructively in the case of electronic discovery unless it also has access to the encryption keys.

Generally, an enterprise will prefer the additional responsibility of information management and key management rather than risking the possibility that the key could be compromised. Nonetheless, it is a decision that must be made. Regardless of who performs the encryption, the enterprise must validate that the key management is handled in accordance with its policies and that the ciphers and key-lengths are sufficiently strong.

As mentioned above, Barbican is a good starting point for a secure key management implementation, ideally backed by a reputable HSM.

Infrastructure Automation

Automation can improve security by providing systematic audits of the infrastructure and applying consistent policies throughout the data centre. It can introduce a level of standardization, scalability and predictability that is impossible to match with manual, ad hoc processes. A solid implementation can facilitate auditing and tracking through comprehensive documentation.

SECURE

However, automation is also a double-edged sword since it makes the tools more powerful and these tools can just as easily be used for malicious purposes. Configuration management tools, like Puppet and Chef can be weaponized to distribute malware. A misconfiguration of the SDN controller can take out the entire network. So it is vital to carefully review all processes to ensure that they are ready for a virtualized or cloud environment. This includes diligent assessment of all workflows, controls, roles and responsibilities as part of a systematic change management process.

Virtualization Implications

Server virtualization offers inherent security advantages through isolation. It has the capacity to prevent cross-over interference from other applications with better defined memory space. This minimizes application instability and facilitates fault isolation and system recovery. Cleaner images contribute to application longevity. And automated deployment can increase redundancy and facilitate failover.

On the other hand, as complexity goes up, security goes down. Even though virtualization simplifies the application context, it adds more components to the overall stack, which introduces additional points of potential vulnerability. These include the hypervisor, the virtualization control layer and the internal virtual network.

To date there have been few breaches against the virtualization layer. The management control plane usually offers a very small attack surface making it difficult for attackers to target it. This reduces the threat considerably, but it doesn't completely eliminate it as buffer overflows and other vulnerabilities are still possible.

For example, at Black Hat 2009, Kostya Kirtchinsky described an exploit called "Cloudburst[1]" that allowed a VMware guest to escape to the host. VMware had already issued a patch, so it is unlikely that this particular problem will lead to a breach. Nonetheless, it highlights the importance for enterprises to constantly monitor for any suspicious activity.

At earlier Black Hat conferences, Joanna Rutkowska, Alexander Tereshkin and Rafal Wojtczuk presented several hypervisor attacks, specifically often targeted against Xen, including a rootkit, called the "Blue Pill Project", and in-place replacement of the hypervisor.

A more immediate concern in the short term is the network activity that the virtualization layer hides from the physical network links. It is critical that virtual network appliances monitor traffic crossing virtualization backplanes and make it accessible through hypervisor APIs since the virtual interfaces will be opaque to traditional network security controls.

Unless a rigorous authorization process oversees provisioning, there is a risk that default, or poorly hardened, images may be released onto the network. Virtualized operating systems should therefore be augmented by third-party security technology (e.g. layered security controls) to improve their robustness.

SECURE

Strong authentication should be integrated with the enterprise identity management system for access to the virtual operating system (especially the administrator interface). This would include tamper-proof logging and integrity monitoring tools.

---

[1] The "Cloudburst" exploit is unrelated to the concept of "cloudbursting", used to designate elastic resource utilization in a hybrid cloud.

It is also critical to have a comprehensive procedure for patching virtual machines with security and reliability updates. This process is much more challenging in a virtual environment where some machines may not be active when updates are released.

It is easy to confuse virtualization security with platform (operating system) security, but there is an important difference (Chauhan, 2012). An intrusion into a single (physical or virtual) system will only impact services running on that system. Virtualization introduces the notion of a host (also called the virtual machine manager or the hypervisor) and one or more guests (virtual machine instances running on the host).

An intruder who succeeds in gaining control of a hypervisor may be able to compromise the whole environment. VM (Virtual Machine) Escape is the term for malicious code that breaks out of the guest and executes on the underlying Host. Hackers may also launch a targeted attack at the hypervisor layer or take over a guest and use it to attack other guests.

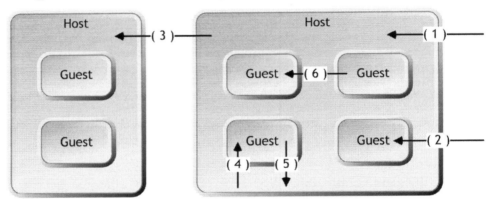

Figure 17-12: Virtualization Threat Vectors

As shown in Figure 17-12, threats can travel along several vectors. The most common source is the external environment, where hacks either target virtualization hosts (1) or guests (2). There is also a risk that a compromised host might be used to infect other hosts (3) or guests (4). Finally, particularly in a multi-tenant environment, there is a very real risk that other guests will be used as an instrument in an attack. They might begin with an attack of the host (5) or immediately target other guests (6).

Customers will be primarily concerned with threats that are directed to their guest machines (2, 4, 6). But that is not to say that the other threats are irrelevant. Sophisticated attacks may take a circuitous route before arriving at their destination. For example, they may originate externally, successfully compromise hosts and poorly secured guests and then use these as a platform to infiltrate hardened machines with the most valuable information.

Clearly one challenge in addressing these threats is the sheer complexity of vectors. It is a major problem if the IT staff loses control of the virtual machines because they do not see all the risks. There is some value in automating the testing process with tools such as VASTO (Virtualization Assessment Toolkit)[1] or VMinformer[2]. VASTO is a tool that assesses multiple virtualization solutions from an intruder's viewpoint including VMware, Oracle and Xen server and provides an audit of all layers of a virtual environment. VMinformer audits the virtual environment using policies and checks for misconfiguration, missing patches and other weaknesses in the management layers.

Guest Hardening

As mentioned earlier, the VM guests (both images and instances) represent a very different security profile from the hypervisor. While the former will be relatively consistent across the organization, the guests are as diverse as the applications that run on them.

Furthermore, the hypervisors are typically under the direct control of the IT staff and receive little interest from the business. On the other hand, the applications are immediately visible to users who may wish to impose their preferences on how they are presented and delivered. The fact that there are multiple interested parties can lead to internal governance issues.

The primary risks related to the guest VMs involve vulnerabilities in the platform. It is important to harden the systems with strict file permissions, user access controls, firewalls, host intrusion prevention and continuous patching as well as virus protection, file integrity checking and log monitoring.

Assuming an image has been created using a secure development and testing process, there are still two risks that need to be considered as part of the lifecycle. The first is image tampering. It is important for the image to be maintained in secure storage where only authorized users have access and any modifications are logged. There should also be a secure provisioning channel for delivering the image into production whenever a new instance is created.

The second risk is what is known as the instant-on gap that results when an image is created securely but, by the time it is provisioned, new threats and vulnerabilities have appeared and the image has not been patched to the most recent level. The problem is compounded by the proliferation of server images that develops due to both the simplicity of taking snapshots of running systems and the lack of a meticulous inventory of these images.

In many cases, there is no simple way to identify the patching history of an image; even when there is an accurate record, it is not possible to update the guest

---

[1] http://vasto.nibblesec.org/
[2] http://www.vminformer.com

without launching it periodically – a cumbersome and time-consuming process. Once the VM is in operation, the instance must be kept up to date with any subsequent patches and will require active monitoring for any security issues.

In a multi-tenant cloud environment, there must be reliable isolation between the guests, and the system needs to fairly arbitrate any resource contention between the users. Sensitive application environments may require the guest to be encrypted, which significantly increases security but puts a large performance burden on the infrastructure. The additional overhead reduces the value proposition for consolidation and must be carefully weighed against its benefits.

For detailed recommendations on guest hardening, you should look at some of the online resources:

- Center of Internet Security (CIS) Recommended Resources for System Hardening[1]
- Defense Information Systems Agency (DISA) Security Technical Implementation Guides (STIGs)[2]
- National Security Agency (NSA) Security Configuration Guides[3]

OpenStack Security Guide

With the above, we have tried to give you a general idea of how to go about securing OpenStack. When it comes down to a deployment, you'll need something more specific, so that you can make sure you haven't exposed any gaps.

The PCI-Cloud SIG put together set of recommendations on what can/cannot be done in cloud[4]. But for OpenStack specifically, a great place to start is the OpenStack Security Guide[5].

SECURE

---

[1] https://security.berkeley.edu/node/143
[2] http://iase.disa.mil/stigs/
[3] http://www.nsa.gov/ia/mitigation_guidance/security_configuration_guides/operating_systems.shtml
[4] https://www.pcisecuritystandards.org/pdfs/PCI_DSS_v2_Cloud_Guidelines.pdf
[5] http://docs.openstack.org/sec

Practical Recommendations

As an open-source program, OpenStack has the benefit of a very broad review process that minimizes vulnerabilities and exploits. However, that doesn't mean you can't misconfigure it so that it is insecure. You are also likely to include a large set of plugins and complementary products that may each expose additional attack surfaces.

The main points to take away from this chapter are that you can almost ignore security in an isolated lab setup, but there is a lot to consider if you are deploying OpenStack in a public or otherwise hostile environment. There is no way around going through all the available guidance to ensure every possible concern has been met.

SECURE

Chapter 18

Enable the Users

Unless a service provides anonymous access exclusively, it needs to manage its users. The service will need to identify each connection in order to analyze and personalize the user experience. There may also be a need to correlate usage to an identity in order to bill for a service or provide differentiated access to personal and other sensitive information.

This chapter examines several approaches to managing identities and associated credentials in order to provide secure and efficient authentication across an ecosystem of cloud-based services. To put it into perspective, authentication is really part of a more comprehensive access control system. In an independent system this involves Authentication, Authorization and Accounting (AAA).

In this context, *Authentication* describes the process of verifying an individual's identity. Typically the users supply credentials that are associated with their digital identity. These credentials are often classified into:

- Knowledge: What you know

- Ownership: What you have

- Inherence: What you are

Each of these has its strengths and weaknesses, so strong authentication systems will usually combine at least two mechanisms to overcome the most apparent vulnerabilities.

SECURE

Authorization refers to the mechanism to establish if the authenticated entity is permitted to execute a particular activity or access a given resource or service. In addition to the user's identity, the criteria may include a combination of physical location, time of day and previous access history.

The *Accounting* system tracks access and use of network resources by authenticated and authorized users for billing, capacity planning and security purposes. In addition to the identity of the user and time of access, an AAA system may also record more granular auditing that is specific to the actual service.

Cloud Identity

Authentication and authorization focus on determining who users are and which resources they can access. However, even if this information can be derived securely, it doesn't automatically mean that it will be enforced.

In a traditional, on-premise environment, it is possible to implement physical access controls. Applications and information may be confined to a location that is protected by a surveillance system with hardware authentication systems. Many enterprise services also assume a degree of trust toward employees. Those who have network access are not expected to abuse it.

Neither of these two approaches, physical or trust-based, work very well in a cloud environment. It is impossible to create physical controls when the location of the data is outside the control of the owner. Likewise, a trust-based attitude is not prudent when anyone in the world can gain access to the information. Therefore it is critical for the software to regulate access to sensitive information according to stringent criteria. It is also vital to audit and validate the algorithms that provide this protection.

Multi-tenancy

One of the biggest benefits of cloud computing is the increased utilization that results from the sharing of resources through multi-tenancy. However, this optimization also introduces significant risks since it implies that tenants of the same system may share access controls and information. This is particularly worrisome in the public cloud where another tenant may be a competitor or malicious user. But even in a private deployment, employees assigned to one tenant may not be authorized to access the sensitive resources of another department.

The first concern is that a common access control system may be susceptible to cross-authentication if it is not properly isolated. In this case, authentication through a co-tenant may allow a user to access an organization's resources. Similarly, a model that relies on the lowest common denominator may not provide the multi-factor authentication required by security-conscious enterprises.

SECURE

A second concern relates to co-mingled data. If the data of multiple tenants is shared in the same repository, it will maximize the efficiency of the system. However, this means that any software bugs or vulnerability exploits in the application could expose sensitive information to co-tenants.

In order to address these concerns, the application needs to be equipped with solid and flexible access controls. Customers should only be able to access their own information, with the system preventing one customer from viewing data from another customer. It is also necessary to take a vigilant and proactive stance in applying patches, monitoring anomalous activity and maintaining an activity log that is available for review upon request.

Strong Authentication

A first step toward cloud-ready access controls is to insist on strong authentication, not only of the users but also of the devices and applications that the user accesses. As mentioned above, there are three factors that can be used to verify a user's identities prior to granting them access. Some examples include:

- Knowledge: password, pass phrase or personal identification number (PIN), challenge response (the user must answer a question)
- Ownership: wrist band, ID card, security token, software token, phone, or cell phone
- Inherence: fingerprint, retinal pattern, DNA sequence, signature, face, voice, unique bio-electric signals, touch gesture

There are challenges with using any of these techniques in isolation. Physical tokens can be lost or stolen. Passwords and PINs can be broken through brute force or captured with a keystroke logger. Biometric readers can often be tricked.

Probably the most common authentication mechanisms at present are simple username/password credentials, which are also considered by many to be the weakest. There are some ways to mitigate these risks, for example with strong password policies and challenge responses. CAPTCHAs[1] and lockouts can also help prevent brute-force and dictionary attacks.

However, security practitioners typically refer to authentication as strong only when it verifies at least two, and ideally all three factors. Often this takes the shape of a credential that is composed both of a user-memorized passphrase and a one-time passcode that is generated by a physical device. RSA SecurID tokens are perhaps the best known example of this approach but other options include soft-tokens installed on a mobile device (Figure 18-1) or passcodes sent on demand via SMS.

---

[1] CAPTCHA (Completely Automated Public Turing test to tell Computers and Humans Apart) is a simple test to tell whether the user is human. It usually takes the form of a distorted image containing letters and digits, which the user must interpret and enter.

Figure 18-1: Mobile One-time Password

Implementing these systematically across a cloud environment can be challenging. To make it easier, a HyTrust Appliance can provide native support for two-factor authentication solutions, including RSA SecurID tokens across a virtual infrastructure without manual configuration of individual hosts.

Graded Authentication

Once users have been authenticated, the authorization rules will determine which resources they can access. This is particularly critical when it comes to administrative access, but the general rule is that it is wise to minimize the impact authenticated users can have. This might be through trusted network IP address ranges or with role-based access controls implemented in the applications.

Authentication and authorization are often seen as completely disjoint and sequential. When they are implemented as such, it is necessary to enforce the most stringent controls that any access could conceivably require. From a security perspective, that is not necessarily a bad principle but it can cause problems with user acceptance.

IT departments like strong authentication because they understand the importance of safeguarding vital assets, but users find it cumbersome and look for ways to circumvent it - often for good reason! Some user actions have so little impact that an awkward form of authentication is simply not warranted.

Graded (also often called risk-based) authentication is a dynamic system that takes into account both the context of the user and the target of the request when determining the authentication mechanism. Based on the user's connection profile (considering location, connection type, keystroke dynamics and other elements of user behavior) it calculates a risk profile.

For example, innocuous browsing may be permitted based only on device authentication that occurs automatically and is not visible to the user. Changes in preferences and formats may require a username and password. High-risk transactions that could lead to legal liabilities or financial damages might involve a one-time password that is delivered via SMS or a phone call.

The advantage of this approach is that it presents a less intrusive user experience. Users are not bothered by cumbersome login mechanisms when there is no need for them. At the same time, it is possible to protect the most sensitive and valuable assets with the safeguards that they require.

However, such a system is not trivial to design and implement. Complexity is a major risk in security systems. It requires diligent vigilance for new threats and careful verification of all configuration settings. If the system is not designed correctly, then minimal authentication can expose the environment to high-impact attacks that are not possible in a traditional system.

Identity Management

The biggest management challenge around authentication/authorization is identity management. Historically, each application was responsible for managing its users, authenticating them and granting them the appropriate rights relating to their role in the system. While this approach does provide some application autonomy and modularity, it is a nightmare to manage and use.

For IT, it means administering multiple identity repositories and keeping them synchronized as users join and leave the organization or pursue different job functions. In a multi-vendor cloud architecture, this can mean each user needs to remember and correctly enter multiple sets of credentials.

The core component of identity management is the store. Identity repositories, such as Microsoft Active Directory, hold information about the user. In addition to credentials, this usually includes personal details, like contact information or organizational roles.

Some of the primary responsibilities of an identity management solution include:

SECURE

- Attribute management
- Provisioning
- Workflow
- Administration

Attribute management is the mechanism the organization uses to update user details (including credentials, such as a password) in the directory. From an operational perspective, there is value in providing as much of this as possible through a self-service portal in order to reduce the workload for the helpdesk and other IT staff.

Provisioning is necessary when there are multiple identity stores in operation, or multiple applications that rely on the identity store. In this case, it is necessary to obtain the full set of user information when adding new employees to the directory. There also needs to be a means to synchronize modifications across all stores and applications whenever details change.

For both attribute management and provisioning, strict policies should define who is authorized to request updates and whether or not any additional approvals are necessary. The rules may depend on the nature of the change and the type of information involved.

Lastly, there is a need for managerial oversight of the system. This can include periodic and ad-hoc reports as well as a dashboard that provides a view into the changes being made and that signals any irregular activity.

OpenStack Implementation

Note that from an OpenStack perspective, we need to look at Identity Management at two levels. At the higher level, we need to authenticate, authorize and record access to the OpenStack infrastructure itself. But, particularly for private clouds, we may also need to offer a standard identity management system for all the projects to use.

OpenStack Identity (Keystone) is a solution for the former. But any organization that needs both levels, should look at a common back-end that will cater to both needs.

OpenStack Identity (Keystone)

In this section we will look at OpenStack Identity, which offers a common means of authentication for all the other OpenStack services.

Every multi-user service needs some mechanism to manage who can access the application and which actions each person can perform. A private cloud is no exception and OpenStack has streamlined these functions into a separate project.

Keystone is the project name for OpenStack Identity, a service that provides token, policy and catalog functions via an OpenStack API. As is the case with other OpenStack services, Keystone represents an abstraction layer. It doesn't actually implement any user management functions. Instead it provides plug-in interfaces so that organizations can leverage their current authentication services or choose from a variety of identity management systems that are on the market.

Keystone integrates the OpenStack functions for authentication, policy management and catalog services. This includes registering all tenants and users, authenticating users and granting tokens for authorization, creating policies that span all users and services and managing a catalog of service endpoints.

The core object of an identity management system is the user. It is a digital representation of a person, system, or service using OpenStack services. Users are often assigned to containers called projects (formerly 'tenants'), which isolate resources and identity objects. A project can represent a customer, account, or any organizational unit.

Authentication is the process for establishing who a user is. Keystone confirms that any incoming functional call originates from the user who claims to be making the request. It performs this validation by testing a set of claims, which take the form of credentials. The distinguishing feature of credential data is that it should only be accessible (through knowledge, ownership or inherence) to the corresponding user.

Once OpenStack Identity has confirmed the user's identity, it will provide the user with a token that corroborates the identity and can be used for subsequent resource requests. Each token includes a scope that lists the resources to which it apples. The token is only valid for a finite duration and can be revoked if there is a need to remove a particular user's access.

Security policies are enforced with a rule-based authorization engine. Once a user is authenticated, the next step is to determine the level of authorization. Keystone encapsulates a set of rights and privileges with a notion called role. The tokens issued by the identity service include a list of roles that the authenticated user can assume. It is then up to the resource service to match the set of user roles with the requested set of resource operations and either grant or deny access.

One additional service of Keystone is the service catalog used for endpoint discovery. It provides a listing of available services along with their API endpoints. An endpoint is a network-accessible address, such as a URL, from which a user can consume a service. All of the OpenStack services, including OpenStack Compute (Nova) and OpenStack Object Storage (Swift), supply endpoints to Keystone through which users can request resources and perform operations.

Architecture

SECURE

Keystone processes all the API requests, providing Identity, Token, Catalog and Policy services. It is organized as a group of frontend services exposed via the API network.

- The *Identity* service validates authentication credentials and supplies any associated metadata.
- The *Token* service verifies and administers tokens used for authenticating requests once a user's credentials have been verified.
- The *Catalog* service provides a service registry that can be used for endpoint discovery.
- The *Policy* service exposes a rule-based authorization engine.

Each Keystone function supports backend plugins for integration into heterogeneous environments and to expose diverse functionality. Some of the more common back-ends include:

- Key Value Store (KVS) is an interface supporting primary key lookups, such as an in-memory dictionary.
- Memcached is a distributed memory caching system.
- SQL uses SQLAlchemy (a Python SQL toolkit and Object Relational Mapper) to store data persistently.
- PAM uses the local system's Pluggable Authentication Module (PAM) service to authenticate.
- LDAP connects via the Lightweight Directory Access Protocol (LDAP) to a backend directory, such as Microsoft Active Directory, to authenticate users and obtain role information.

Certificates

Many organizations are moving toward Public Key Infrastructure since it is a highly scalable standards-based technology. One of its benefits is that it allows delegated trust, which is vital for identity federation, and makes it possible to demonstrate authenticity through a tamper-proof link to a recognized and trusted certificate authority.

In practice this means that the public key must be signed with a certified X.509 certificate. For a purely internal implementation, it is possible to use keystone-manage to generate self-signed certificates. But in a federated environment, there may be the need for a certificate from an external Certificate Authority (CA).

Installing a certificate issued by an external CA involves:

- Requesting a signing certificate from an external CA
- Converting both the certificate and private key to PEM (Privacy Enhanced Email) format
- Installing the external signing certificate by copying the PEM files to the certificate directory

SECURE

Usage Scenario

Identity management is a supporting function that serves a less tangible purpose than most of the other OpenStack services. It should be seen as an enabler that simplifies service discovery and provides a unified means of enforcing security policies.

It is perhaps easiest to visualize its usage by dividing it into two parts. There are administrative functions in Keystone to define users and projects and assign the appropriate authorization. Once the environment is configured, then the projects and applications can interface with Keystone to perform queries and verify access controls.

Administration

We will start with the first, which is easier to follow since it is mapped to the Horizon dashboard. An administrator can create projects and users. The users can be assigned roles and aggregated into groups to simplify management.

The first step is typically to create at least one user. First you would need to log-in to the OpenStack Dashboard as an administrator. You would then click **Users** in the **Identity Panel** and press the **Create User** button (Figure 18-2).

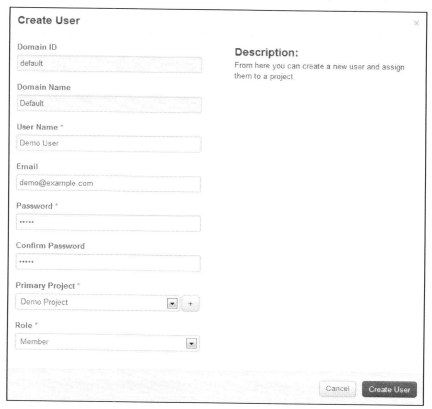

Figure 18-2: Create User

You may also want to create a new project. Click **Projects** in the **Identity Panel** menu and press the **Create Project** button (Figure 18-3).

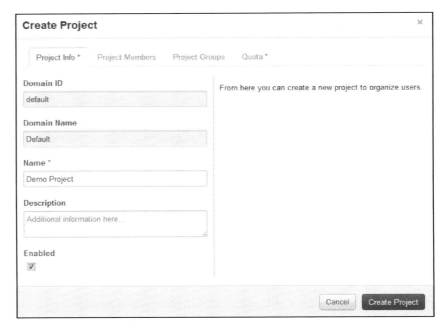

Figure 18-3: Create Project

You don't need anything other than the name and description at this point. Once you complete the form, you should see the new project in the list (Figure 18-4).

Figure 18-4: Projects

Next, you can edit the project (**Identity Panel / Projects / Edit Project**) to update the list of project members and change their roles (Figure 18-5).

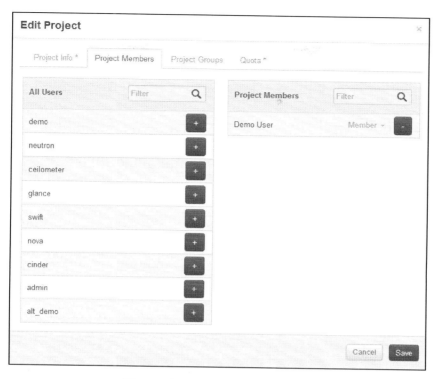

Figure 18-5: Project Members

You can also use the **Quota** tab to specify limits for the project (Figure 18-6). This is particularly useful in a multi-tenant environment to ensure that one project doesn't use excessive amounts of resources and starve other critical services running on the same infrastructure.

Figure 18-6: Project Quota

Catalogue

The second part of the scenario is the authentication of the services at execution time. Consider, for example, an application that will be using OpenStack Swift for object storage. It may, or may not, be running as part of an OpenStack Compute instance. Regardless, it needs to be able to authenticate, so it must have access to valid credentials.

The application first needs to connect to the authentication service, supplying its credentials. It will then receive an authentication token that it can pass to Open-Stack Object Storage for all container and object operations.

In some cases, the application may not be pre-configured with all the connection parameters. It can obtain these from Keystone, as well. For example, it can query Keystone to discover which projects it can access and request the URL of the service it requires.

Identity Federation

Identity management is still an evolving technology. There are several different standards and proprietary protocols in operation for identify federation. Unfortunately, many cloud providers haven't even begun to consider any of them. This can make life difficult for an application developer who wants to be able to offer universal Single Sign-On (SSO) connectivity but isn't prepared to implement a dozen different interfaces.

Amazon, Google, and Safesforce.com support the Security Assertion Markup Language (SAML). But they are the exception rather than the rule. Only a small fraction of the service providers in the cloud-computing market publicly support SAML and even fewer have committed to the other standards (Messmer, 2010).

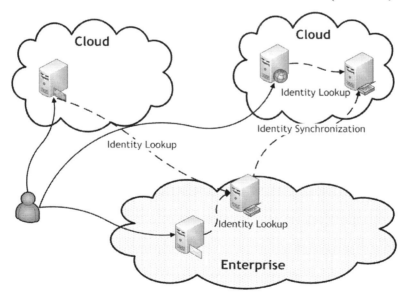

Figure 18-7: Identity Management

One alternative is to connect with trusted external parties that securely manage the identity of your users. Novell's Identity Manager works with Salesforce.com and Google Apps, as well as Microsoft SharePoint, and SAP applications to support a federated identity structure in the enterprise. Outsourcers, such as

IBM, offer hosted options for enterprise identity management. The external parties could also be IDaaS (Identity as a Service) providers (e.g. PingIdentity,
OneLogin, Symplified, SSOCircle, Janrain/myOpenID), or alternatively, identity
services of your partners (suppliers, customers or affiliated organizations).

Identity-as-a-Service providers, which are often cloud-based themselves, may
also be helpful in federating identity management (Figure 18-7). For example
they may help to abstract and manage complexity between versions (e.g. SAML
1.1. vs SAML 2.0) and frameworks. But, in including them in the solution, it
should be clear that they become critical cloud providers with all the drawbacks
of vendor lock-in, service level negotiation and single point of failure.

In a sense, OpenStack is itself a federated identity management system. Users
authenticate to Keystone. Keystone returns a token to the user. The user passes
this token to any authenticating service, such as Swift. And Swift can validate
the token by calling Keystone.

But it is also possible to extend the federation beyond OpenStack. Keystone
doesn't perform the actual authentication. Instead it calls an external identity
provider. It can use OAuth, SAML, OpenID, X.509 or any other federation protocol. To simplify authentication it can include all trusted Identity Providers in
the services catalogue along with details specifying how to call them.

While interoperability and standards are a critical part of the identity management challenge, there are other considerations as well, such as the supported authentication mechanisms, provisioning and precautions for identity theft. Where
security is a concern, it is vital that, in addition to robust password policies,
cloud providers support strong authentication either natively or via delegation
and support. Even strong passwords can be compromised and, in the case of a
breach, a hacker can automate attacks involving compromised credentials with
relative ease.

It is much more difficult to circumvent biometric and token-based authentication
or secure combinations of multiple factors. Identity solutions provide a variety
of authentication mechanisms such as SMS-delivered one-time-passwords,
browser certificates, smart cards, security questions, biometric scans and secure
tokens. An organization can combine these to achieve its preferred balance of
usability and strong security.

SECURE

Provisioning

Another consideration beyond single sign-on is provider support for provision-
ing/de-provisioning. Provisioning should be rapid to expedite the on-boarding of
new employees and changes in roles and responsibilities. De-provisioning is
even more critical. In cases of identity theft or contract termination there must be
a facility for immediate de-provisioning.

The primary standard for provisioning has the OASIS Service Provisioning Markup Language (SPML). Sadly, SPML was never widely implemented across cloud services. Even though many Identity Management vendors support the base protocol, they usually encapsulate it in a proprietary API that varies greatly between suppliers. At least in part, the reason for resisting the base API is that it requires implementation of the full SOAP stack, which imposes significant overhead and no longer enjoys great popularity.

The Internet Engineering Taskforce (IETF) has addressed some of these short-comings in an alternate specification called System for Cross-domain Identity Management (SCIM). It provides a lightweight REST API that describes Create, Read, Update, Delete (CRUD) operations for identity and access and is implemented by a variety of cloud providers including Salesforce, Google, Ping Identity, VMware and Cisco. It is not natively supported by OpenStack but there is no obstacle to introducing SCIM for the back-end of any Keystone authentication plugin.

Practical Recommendations

Identity Management is the key to your security strategy. It is the gate that controls access to your enterprise. In a simple environment, you may be satisfied with a basic authentication scheme like username/password stored in a local database. But as you scale or include access to sensitive data, you need to evolve in two directions.

Stronger authentication will validate user identity with greater certainty. This typically implies a second set of credentials, for example, a hardware token protected by a password.

OpenStack may also need to integrate with other systems to serve scalable and heterogeneous applications. To simplify user access and administration it may become necessary to federate the identity management systems.

Keystone's plugin architecture is a good foundation for handling both of these capabilities. But you still need to find the right providers and integrate them into the OpenStack environment.

SECURE

Chapter 19

Enforce the Rules

There is a tendency to relegate security to a set of technological tools and settings. This is very dangerous since it misses the fact that many breaches and other incidents are purely a product of human errors. A holistic security system needs to be much broader than the products and also include process, procedure, policy, proof and people controls.

Authorization is a core element of user access controls. There is a need not only to identify the users who interact with the system but also to restrict the scope of their activity. In the case of end users, this is relatively simple since they should only access the data that belongs to them. Increased sharing and collaboration make this more complicated. But as long as end users explicitly grant permissions, it is straightforward to determine who has access to which data.

The fundamental issue is that some users require access to data that doesn't belong to them in order to provide support, monitoring, troubleshooting and other administrative tasks. Allowing them access increases the risk of both intentional and unintentional abuse of the information.

Dishonest employees may access unauthorized information for their own purposes. If they are disgruntled, they can exact their revenge by deliberately vandalizing the information. Competitors involved in industrial espionage may also target individuals with access to sensitive data through extortion and bribery.

Not all information leaks are intentional. Other sources of compromised and lost data can be employee incompetence, lack of training or proper documentation. In many cases, the processes for oversight are simply insufficient to ensure that valuable data is not compromised.

Governance frameworks such as ITIL, COBIT, CMMI, Six Sigma and ISO 9001 can help standardize and formalize processes. They must be complemented with a risk assessment of the sensitive data, a suite of mitigation techniques and considerations including staffing, automation, staging, compartmentalization, segregation of duties and logging.

SECURE

Cloud Authorization

Staffing

Every data center requires at least some human supervision. There will be some personnel who have physical access to the equipment, but also some who have the credentials to access the most sensitive data. While it may be possible to implement some safeguards that mitigate the risks of abuse, the best starting point is to ensure that anyone with elevated rights is trustworthy.

Hiring

The first step is to carefully screen all prospective employees during the recruiting process. Security guards should submit to criminal background checks by third-party vendors, which are reviewed regularly, for example on a yearly basis. Others, such as cleaning personnel who require access to sensitive areas, may also need to undergo similar checks.

Obviously, the background check is only one part of the hiring criteria. The selection of the right people needs to include assessments of honesty, diligence and competence to not only prevent malicious activity but also minimize errors and omissions.

To ensure security is taken seriously, all users at the facility should sign Non-Disclosure Agreements (NDAs) as well as acceptance of the security policies in force.

Assignment

Anyone with sensitive duties should be enrolled in a structured and documented provisioning process. This includes a clearly defined job description explaining the role and enumerating the tasks. Since many of these responsibilities may be cross-departmental, it is helpful to present them as a responsibility assignment matrix (also called a linear responsibility chart).

SECURE

These matrices assign four different responsibility roles: Responsible, Accountable, Consulted, Informed (RACI).

Responsible: one or more who are expected to perform the task or ensure that it is performed

Accountable: individual who approves the completion of the task

Consulted: subject matter experts who provide counsel to those responsible and accountable

Informed: others peripheral to the project who have a dependency on the outcome of the task but no influence over it

Training

Hiring the right people and assigning them the right tasks and responsibilities are critical elements of secure administration. The only thing missing is to prepare them for their work. This can take the form of technical education as well as training on the processes and procedures in place. For example, administrators require instruction on the products they are using, guards must know to verify that everyone in the facility is wearing a badge, and all employees should be aware of the risks of social engineering.

There should also be some means of validating that employees have internalized the content of their training. Certification and other exams help to gauge the level of technical proficiency while internal programs covering policies and standards of business conduct provide an indication of the familiarity with company guidelines. At a minimum, they make it more difficult for dishonest employees to plead ignorance when they are discovered.

Off-boarding

All organizations have some turnover in personnel. Some leave on good terms, as a result of retirement or to take advantage of a better opportunity somewhere else. Others are disgruntled either by the way they were treated at work or the way that their employment was terminated. The need for careful off-boarding is obvious in the case of an unhappy separation, but it is also important when the circumstances appear amicable.

Employees working in the data center or utilizing the facility services should be de-provisioned immediately upon termination. This includes a block on physical admittance as well as user deactivation on all electronic systems, network databases, portals or any other applications that involve authenticated access.

Automation

A large proportion of security failures are attributable to human error. Good staffing and training procedures may help to reduce this error, but the safest course of action is to minimize human intervention from the beginning. One approach to achieve this goal is automation. Obviously even an automated system is designed by human beings and may contain flaws.

SECURE

However, it offers the benefits of being repeatable and verifiable. It is possible to reliably test the system before it is used and to review it after it runs. Along with minimizing the incidence of disruptive security events, it maximizes on-time and on-budget project delivery and accelerates the implementation of subsequent changes improving the agility of IT.

In practice this means a comprehensive configuration management database along with interfaces to external systems to enforce policies. The automation system defines and executes change management processes and objectives, monitors the environment for unauthorized or unexpected changes, and enforces consequences for deviations.

Provisioning

One of the quickest benefits of automation is the ability to accelerate provisioning across traditional, virtualized and cloud environments. Tools such as BMC Application Management Suite, capture and model current release processes, and provide planning, execution, and real-time tracking.

Automated provisioning can also facilitate the application release process. Quick deployment of new applications and features further relies on close collaboration of development and operations teams. Many organizations are using agile application development and continuous deployment as drivers for DevOps, which strives for an integration of these teams.

Orchestration

The next level beyond simple automation is orchestration. Automation is a set of disparate processes in place for repetitive tasks. Orchestration builds on this foundation additionally tying the processes together using workflows.

For example, to provision a new server will typically require network, storage, compute and possibly security provisioning. Rather than procuring each of these individually, an orchestration framework would present a portal where the administrator can supply the specifications for the required environment, including CPU speed, number of cores, RAM, hard disk space and network bandwidth. The system would then obtain and verify any necessary approvals and launch automated scripts to allocate and configure the necessary resources.

The orchestration engine would then remain connected to the change management system and the target applications to undertake and automatically adjust the infrastructure. It might scale the resources up or down depending on the system load or re-launch instances in the case of failure. It can also provide centralized management of the resource pool, including billing, metering, and chargeback for consumption.

SECURE

Monitoring

Automated monitoring can provide a level of consistency and thoroughness in addition to saving time and cost. Systematic collection of key metrics and performance indicators provides a current view of the people, processes and technologies that compose the IT environment. Dashboards offer drill-down visibility into key services through point-and-click analysis and advanced reporting.

These tools proactively alert administrators who find and fix issues before they impact users and business processes. Detailed diagnostics can facilitate root cause analysis and eliminate the need to reproduce problems. Automated repair mechanisms can trigger recovery actions immediately and without human intervention. In the long term, comprehensive tracking of service levels will drive continuous service improvement initiatives.

Policies

Another advantage of automation is consistency in the enforcement of policies – not just to ensure security and availability but also to meet regulatory obligations.

Policy enforcement across desktops, servers, mobile devices and networks control end-user devices, reducing downtime and user complaints. The system can address issues around poor performance, prevent malware infections and ensure proper configuration of security settings.

Enforcement systems also automate the management, control, and enforcement of middleware and application configuration changes. And they can compare device settings with regulatory compliance repositories for audits and meeting best-practice guidelines.

Self-service

Strictly speaking, self-service is not a form of automation. However, from the perspective of the IT department, it has a similar function in that it allows them to offload a significant amount of their activity and decreases errors due to miscommunication.

IT self-service empowers end users to solve their own IT problems. As such, support organizations can reduce costs due to a smaller request workload. Self-service can also improve customer satisfaction, provide incident trend analysis, identify training opportunities, and consolidate the knowledge that currently exists in silos across the support organization (Gartner, Inc., 2010).

However, it also is subject to several limitations. It only works well for specific incident types (e.g. how-to requests, FAQs and password resets). It also requires ongoing investment in staff resources and tools like knowledge management and password reset. Furthermore, the knowledge base needs continuous updating. Articles that do not fix the problem or that are difficult to understand make it more difficult for users to benefit from the system and present a poor image of IT.

Technical users and younger employees may be more willing to leverage self-service. But users with less computer skills may be reluctant to embrace an impersonal system and dig through unstructured documentation to find the answers to their questions.

Compartmentalization

Automation increases the potential impact of security incidents when they do take place. Two operational implications of this heightened vulnerability are that it is important to ensure only authorized users have access to sensitive systems and to minimize the power of those who are authorized.

Restricted access entails strong controls on storage and other physical resources. It also implies strong authentication as we saw in Chapter 18. But before these take hold, the organization needs to define who absolutely needs access to which resources. The more restrictive these policies are, the tighter the security will be. "Need to know" and "need to have" policies grant staff the least amount of access privilege required for them to perform their duties.

At a minimum, we should implement role-based security, also called role-based access control (RBAC), so that permissions to sensitive operations are not assigned directly to users but rather to the roles, representing various job functions in an organization. User rights management then involves assigning appropriate roles to the user's account. This simplifies common operations, such as adding a user, or changing a user's department. According to an analysis by the Research Triangle Institute, this leads to substantial financial benefits from reduced employee downtime, more efficient provisioning, and more efficient access control policy administration (O'Connor & Loomis, 2010).

We may also want to minimize data visibility by encryption of sensitive data with a key that is not accessible to system operators. The application should also enforce additional restrictions and potentially require workflow approvals for privileged actions.

Segregation of duties

An important aspect of compartmentalization is the segregation (also called separation) of duties, the requirement for multiple people to cooperate in completing a task. The underlying principle is that involving more than one individual in the execution of a task helps to prevent fraud and errors.

The idea is that a single person with overall authority has the potential to abuse this power. To minimize risk, it is necessary to identify multiple critical functions and divide them into separate steps that can be assigned to different persons.

Simple examples include the requirement for two signatures on a cheque or, more generally, two approvals for any action. However, the tasks may also be functionally and spatially distinct and could include a distinction between issuing and disbursing vouchers or operations such as authorization or review.

In electronic systems, we can require multiple users to perform sensitive actions. Split-key (M-of-N) authentication stifles unilateral actions by requiring multiple

(M) people possessing parts of a shared key (N) to participate in a successful authentication.

More generally, it is wise to separate duties around storage, networking, databases and system administration. And it is important to ensure that authorization, execution, recording and auditing functions are all kept distinct.

Privileged User Management

Privileged User Management (PUM) or Privileged Identity Management (PIM) is a sub-domain of identity management that focuses on governance over the user of privileged user accounts. This involves careful segregation of service accounts, minimizing the need for root access to perform user-level or administrative operations and tamper-proof logging of all privileged activity as we will see in the next section.

PUM solutions can help control administrator access to cloud infrastructures and are a critical cloud security control. They manage delegated administration through a centralized policy mechanism and accommodate the central definition of access control rules to allow or deny administrator activity based on a combination of username, typed command, hostname, and time.

By managing privileges this way, a PUM can control the commands administrators are authorized to run, along with the time and the location. PUMs also record all administrator actions, which is key for auditing, incident recovery and forensics.

Finally, PUMs typically include a switch user (su) functionality making it easier for operators and administrators to honor the principle of least privilege. Thanks to this, administrators can log on to the PUM using their normal day-to-day user credentials. The PUM will then automatically switch the user (if authorized to do so) to administrator account privileges for performing his actions against the back-end cloud infrastructure. A good example of a PUM solution is the Novell – NetIQ PUM.

For example, in order to access the PUM and to make the solution even more secure, you can also enforce a rule that operators only access the PUM from dedicated workstations that are located in a secured room within a secured facility and that also enforce 2-factor authentication for anyone connecting to the operator workstations.

Independently of all the technical components that you put in place to control administrator access to the cloud infrastructure, it is equally important to ensure these technical controls cannot be bypassed using non-technical means: For example, ensure that operators cannot modify firewall rules so they can bypass the PUM system, or ensure that security officers or auditors regularly perform physical audits to check whether operators comply with using operator workstations, from the operator room, while using 2-factor authentication.

At the time of writing there is no Commercial-Off-The-Shelf (COTS) solution available for PUM in an OpenStack-based cloud. But there are quite a few PUM functions that OpenStack can provide through its components. As such, you can create a Linux-based operator VM which is at the same time a VNC logger and proxy. OpenStack uses VNC to connect to VM consoles and sessions. Some other options to implement PUM include:

- VNC can be recorded and played back using a VNC proxy. TightVNC[1] is an example of such tool.
- You can enforce the use of logged ssh sessions using the "tee" command[2].
- OpenStack includes 2-factor authentication support in Keystone[3].
- The OpenStack Neutron firewall can enforce administrator access from a limited set of locations. For example, only from dedicated operator workstations.
- You can automate the deployment of a set of SSH authorized keys to a set of dedicated Linux PUM operator VMs.

Cloud Auditing

No matter what control mechanisms are in place to prevent unauthorized access and minimize the scope of abuse, there is still a need to allow some degree of human intervention and, lamentably, this permission can always be abused. As a last resort, it is critical to be able to reconstruct what has been done in order to mitigate the damages.

Automation tools have a side benefit of providing documentation and an audit trail, so the easiest way to be able to identify what has happened is to record activity both by system processes and user actions.

Auditing benefits

SECURE

Audit trails can help to accomplish several security-related objectives, including individual accountability, reconstruction of events (actions that happen on a computer system), intrusion detection, and problem analysis (NIST, 1996).

The most obvious benefit of an audit trail is the ability to reconstruct events after a problem has occurred. Authorized auditors can review log files to isolate how, when, and why an anomaly was introduced into the system. If a component fails

---

[1] http://www.tightvnc.com/rfbplayer.php
[2] https://www.jms1.net/ssh-record.shtml
[3] http://docs.openstack.org/security-guide/content/ch024_authentication.html

or the configuration changes, a root-cause analysis can reconstruct the series of steps taken by the system, the users, and the application.

A direct consequence of the ability to reconstruct changes in the system is individual accountability. When users are aware that they will be held accountable for their actions, and that these are logged, it helps to improve user behavior. They will exercise their responsibilities more diligently and are not as likely to abuse their permissions. Even if the users manage to evade a specific recording of their misuse, they will be aware that a forensic analysis based on extensive logging may be able to reveal patterns that point directly to them.

Another benefit of auditing is real-time monitoring. Audit trails combined with performance logs can help to identify performance and capacity problems as well as intrusion attempts and other security threats.

Auditing mechanisms

Fundamentally, there are two different approaches to auditing. It can be interface-oriented or state-oriented. In both cases it is important to capture as much contextual information as possible, such as the date and time, and the user who is logged in. Although it is more storage-intensive, a comprehensive audit would also include the actual content of any information that was changed.

An interface-oriented system would focus on the information that enters and leaves the system. Paths might include the network or peripheral interfaces to the system. Removable media also represent an interface as do the entire user interaction including keystrokes, mouse-clicks and screen displays.

A state-oriented system would monitor changes to the system itself. This could include configuration settings, database fields, or the content of unstructured files. At a minimum it would log the fact that this information was altered. But ideally, it would provide a complete transaction log with the specific changes so that the actual data could be recovered and the scenario replayed if needed at a later date.

SECURE

Clearly there is a tradeoff between the additional insight provided by comprehensive logging and the amount of storage it consumes. For highly volatile databases with low-value data, it would be impractical and economically prohibitive to record a complete timeline of data changes. On the other hand, providers of sensitive and largely static information services will be more likely to invest in a system that is easily traceable. Each organization will need to weigh the costs and benefits of logging and decide which information is the most valuable to them and how well it needs to be secured.

Protecting Audit Trail Data

Audit trails are only useful if they are complete. It is nice to have a PUM system in place that records all privileged activity but if users have a way to bypass it, then it is no longer authoritative and serves little purpose.

One final consideration with log data is that it, itself, needs to be carefully protected. There is no point in extensive logging if it is possible for someone to tamper with the logs and remove any trace of their actions. Mechanisms include the use of digital signatures or write-once devices such as optical media or even hard print-outs.

Again here, it is vital to implement a segregation of duties so that those who control the audit logs are separated from those who have the ability to access sensitive information or perform critical operations.

Unfortunately, OpenStack doesn't help us with most of these concerns. As described in Chapter 14, its current auditing scope is limited to debugging and monitoring, which is useful but not sufficient for a proper audit. It is therefore necessary to supplement it with additional tools and processes.

Cloud Server Control

Throughout these lifecycles there is a need to enforce secure access, tracking, monitoring and logging.

Sprawl

Virtual server sprawl is the uncontrolled growth of machines due to insufficient oversight. The source of the problem lies in the lack of defined ownership, with responsibilities shared ad hoc across multiple users in IT and the businesses. The issue is exacerbated by the ease with which users can create additional images and instances. It is trivial to try out a new product or a variant system configuration by copying a base image and only applying the necessary changes.

SECURE

However, each system will retain its own configuration and patch status and it is difficult to determine what it contains, who owns it and what risks it represents. The sheer volume of sprawl also wastes resources, increases the operational complexity and extends the exposure. After all, more systems imply a greater attack surface and unmonitored servers holding confidential data will extend the footprint of sensitive information.

In order to mitigate the risk, it is necessary to maintain accountability for the entire virtual environment. A drawn out procurement process with detailed requisitions may not be very popular but some degree of traceability is necessary. Extensive chargeback (or at least showback) reporting will also discourage unnecessary allocation as well a periodic review of the business need for every cloud resource (both for risk as well as cost management reasons).

Visibility and compliance

Guest machines are opaque to the outside observer. Their usage of compute cycles, storage, bandwidth and power is pooled and brokered through a physical server making it difficult for infrastructure managers to detect any abuse or other anomalies. Virtualization systems like VMware vSphere, Citrix XenServer, KVM or Microsoft Hyper-V include some amount of visibility and control. However, it is still important to document the configuration and security parameters of all internal workloads and to assess the information classification, business impact and vulnerability susceptibility.

Privilege misuse

Another control issue is the abuse of privileges. Whoever has administrative access to the virtualization management layer is no longer confined to a single system but can administer storage, networking, security, performance and even mobility.

Powerful APIs can further augment the security risk, particularly if they are not authenticated securely since expanded automation multiplies and accelerates the impact of user mistakes or malfeasance. To reduce these risks, the access and authentication process needs to be carefully examined and there should be a rigorous process for request management with a workflow that involves sign-off and approval of provisioning requests.

Adequate protection against privilege misuses calls for centralized authentication using LDAP, strong authentication mechanisms, secure remote access solutions, and a Role-based Access Control (RBAC) mechanism ensuring least privilege and Separation of Duties (SoD). Solutions such as NetIQ's Privileged User Manager's (PUM) can help control administrator access to Linux, UNIX, and Windows servers in a cloud environment. NetIQ PUM manages the delegated administration through a centralized policy mechanism. This allows the cloud platform owner to define rules for allowing or denying user activity based on a combination of user name, typed command, host name, and time (who, what, where and when). These facilities for managing privileges allow the cloud platform owner to control the commands users are authorized to run, along with the time and the location. PUM also logs all user activity.

Staging

Every change in the production system and its data presents a risk for the service. It may not be configured correctly. New algorithms may present a performance bottleneck. There could be new vulnerabilities.

Nonetheless, there is always a need for changes. They may be reactive, in response to problems or externally imposed requirements, such as legislative changes. Or they can be proactive, in the quest for improved efficiency and effectiveness, to enable new business initiatives, or from service improvement initiatives.

Change management imposes standardized methods and procedures that handle all changes in the IT infrastructure and its applications. A rigorous process minimizes the number and impact of any related incidents upon services and can balance the need for improvement against the potential for disruption.

One core component of change management is staging, which limits actions on the production systems until they have been carefully tested in a simulated scenario. It usually runs in an environment that closely reflects production. It not only deals with testing all the functionality, but also load testing and may be made accessible to customers to obtain their approval prior to final production release.

Unit and integration testing can be completed in a virtual environment. You should, however, conduct your performance testing in an environment with hardware and software that is identical to the production environment. The staging server should be a mirror copy of the production server. Its primary purpose is to test the completed application to ensure that the application doesn't break the existing production server applications. No actual code development should ever take place on a staging server—only minor tweaking of OS parameters or application settings.

When the application grows more complex, it often makes sense to introduce multiple levels of staging/testing. Some mission critical environments have as many as seven different environments along the path from development to production. Each one represents a step closer to what the production environment is like.

Cloud computing has the potential to dramatically accelerate this trend. Since you can fire up instances on demand, there is little cost associated with having a number of different variants to test multiple options in parallel. They can also be very useful if the need presents itself to rollback a live system to a previous version.

SECURE

Staging in the cloud includes running the application code in a production-like environment and going through all the production activities with a representative dataset. The actual technique for staging the application will depend very much on the platform used, but it is critical to keep the cloud testing environment as separate from production as practically feasible in order to minimize the risk of disruption.

Lifecycle Management

When looking at the lifecycle of guest machines, it is important to distinguish between the master images, which serve as templates for building new systems, and the instances that equate to running virtual machines. Theoretically, it would be possible to build the instances directly, similarly to the way in which physical systems used to be provisioned. The objective of introducing the notion of images is to standardize these instances and accelerate their deployment by reducing the amount of individual configuration.

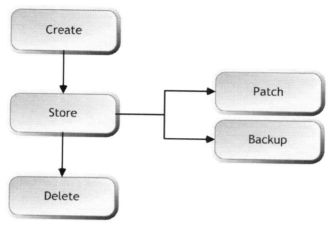

Figure 19-1: VM Image Lifecycle

The VM *image* lifecycle begins with creation when the operating system and applications are installed and configured (Figure 19-1). It is then stored securely in a location that can be accessed for provisioning instances. As new updates to the platform and layered software are released, they must be applied to the image, which must then be backed up for version and disaster recovery purposes. Finally, when the image is no longer needed, it must be securely deleted from storage.

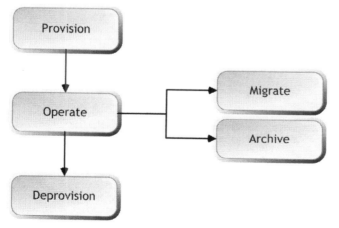

Figure 19-2: VM Instance Lifecycle

SECURE

The VM *instances* are spawned from the images in storage through a provisioning process (Figure 19-2). They will be used in operation where they must also continue to apply patching. For business continuity, there is a need to archive snapshots of the running images. There will also be cases where the image is migrated to a different host.

There are several critical areas across both of these lifecycles. It is vital to ensure that all VM guests (both the instances and the images from which they derive) are hardened to minimize any vulnerabilities. The images need to be stored and archived securely to reduce the risk of leakage. Similarly it is important to monitor their migration and deletion in order to prevent any unnecessary exposure.

Integrity Protection

In a cloud environment it is particularly important to provide integrity protection of the virtual components included in the platform. These include the virtual machine managers and the virtual machine instances. This integrity protection should cover the VM boot process as well as VM runtime protection.

To secure the VM boot process, any VM - including OpenStack compute, storage, network VMs – must be securely provisioned to the virtualization platform (Red Hat KVM, VMware ESXi). VM provisioning can use the Preboot eXecution Environment (PXE) protocol for the boot process on a separate and isolated management network. With the exception of the start of the PXE boot process (where DHCP and TFTP protocols are used), PXE downloads the VM provisioning information over SSL. New firmware projects are underway to also enable SSL during the early PXE boot process: for example, the iPXE project[1].

But also before a VM is provisioned, it is important to check that the underlying VMM and hardware are trustworthy. Today there are a variety of technologies available that can help you enable integrity protection of the early machine and VMM boot stages. Examples of such technologies are the Trusted Platform Module (TPM) and Intel's Trusted Execution Technology (TXT) that leverage the TPM-based root of trust for providing a "verified boot" mechanism. Another example is the Unified Extensible Firmware Interface (UEFI) firmware-based secure boot mechanism. The latter does not require a TPM, but a UEFI-compatible BIOS for anchoring the root of trust. Both the TPM and UEFI specifications have been defined by the Trusted Computing Group – an important industry consortium for developing and fostering trustworthy computing standards. TPMs are commonly included on enterprise laptops and desktops today, and are also becoming available in state-of-the-art servers. UEFI is supported in recent operating systems such as Microsoft's Windows 8.

For runtime integrity protection of VM instances, it is important to have an intrusion prevention system (IPS) solution that can cope with virtualized environments. The IPS solution should be able to scan both the inter-VM communica-

SECURE

---

[1] see http://ipxe.org/

tions (virtual network IPS) and the activity that occurs on the virtual host-level (virtual host IPS). For example, the HP TippingPoint IPS can provide a virtual network IPS through its Secure Virtualization Framework (SVF – that offloads the actual IPS to a hardware TippingPoint IPS appliance). And TrendMicro can provide a virtual host IPS using its Deep Packet Inspection (DPI) DeepSecurity solution.

Storage, Backup and Archival

VM image backups help to ensure that images will still be operational after a failure or a disaster. VM archiving, on the other hand, stores a copy of a VM image that is not in use. Both require access control mechanisms (to initiate backup/archiving and to authorize access) and secure storage using encryption and other integrity and privacy enforcement techniques, such as:

- It should not be possible for intruders to identify specific backup images even with access to the file system where the folder resides. If they obtain the entire folder, they should not be able to import the images to an alternate system without the corresponding credentials.
- Tape backups should enforce software and hardware encryption to reduce the risk if media are stolen.
- Security certificates should protect communications between clients and the storage server to prevent an intruder from masquerading as a client and requesting a restore of production data.

Migration

VM migration involves moving a guest machine from one physical system to another. The migration may be manual or automatic and might involve the same or different cloud platforms. Good examples of automated VM migration solutions are VMware's vMotion for vSphere and Microsoft's Live Migration for Hyper-V.

Although the flexibility of workload mobility entails many advantages in terms of infrastructure optimization, it also presents some additional security concerns such as snooping and tampering. As a result, the migration must be done over secure communication channels (isolated network paths or cryptographic overlays) and only executed after the person or service initiating the migration has been properly authenticated and authorized.

SECURE

Mobility implicitly makes it more difficult to track the physical location of any workload and should be accompanied with detailed monitoring and reporting capabilities. Furthermore the migration interfaces are not fully standardised and do not expose security requirements, which can make the movement between private and public clouds challenging.

Deletion

Once the image or instance is no longer needed, it should be deleted. This also applies to instances that have been migrated to other physical systems. In all cases, there should be reliable access control mechanisms to authorize deletion as well as verifiable deletion controls. This means that the process should not just rely on the operating system to de-link the file header but instead actually overwrite the file contents with zeroes or random data to ensure that no traces remain behind.

OpenStack Policy Enforcement

OpenStack does not have an elaborate policy framework, but Keystone does include the notion of roles which make it possible to build primitive role-based access controls (Figure 19-3).

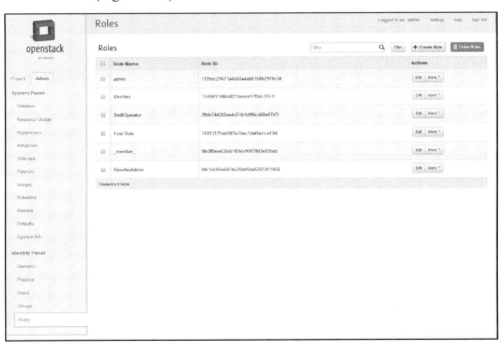

Figure 19-3: OpenStack Roles

The roles themselves don't have any permissions or other semantics associated with them. They are just a descriptive name (Figure 19-4).

Figure 19-4: Create Role

Users are assigned a role when they are created (Figure 19-5).

Figure 19-5: Create User

But the rights that go with the role are at the discretion of each service. Open-Stack services generally specify access rights with a policy file (policy.json) that is specific to them (Listing 19-1).

```
{
    "admin_required": "role:admin or is_admin:1",
    "service_role": "role:service",
    "service_or_admin":      "rule:admin_required     or
rule:service_role",
    "owner" : "user_id:%(user_id)s",
    "admin_or_owner":        "rule:admin_required     or
rule:owner",

    "default": "rule:admin_required",

    "identity:get_service": "rule:admin_required",
    "identity:list_services": "rule:admin_required",
    "identity:create_service": "rule:admin_required",
    "identity:update_service": "rule:admin_required",
    "identity:delete_service": "rule:admin_required",

    "identity:get_endpoint": "rule:admin_required",
    "identity:list_endpoints": "rule:admin_required",
    "identity:create_endpoint": "rule:admin_required",
    "identity:update_endpoint": "rule:admin_required",
    "identity:delete_endpoint": "rule:admin_required",


    . . .

}
```

Listing 19-1: Keystone policy.json

For example, Keystone stores its policy file in /etc/keystone. It uses the Oslo policy engine to parse the file and determine access rights to each of its API calls based on a set of rules that are derived from the user's role. Other OpenStack services operate similarly and external projects are also free to query the Keystone to determine the user's role and make access decisions based on the result.

SECURE

Enforcing policies on the OpenStack infrastructure is critical but it is only a part of the overall requirement in an enterprise environment. There is also a need to implement policies on the resources themselves. Microsoft Active Directory or Novell Identity Manager are solutions that can help to build a comprehensive framework.

FreeIPA is an open-source project (driven by Red Hat) that also facilitates centrally managed Identity, Policy and Audit (IPA). It relies on other open-source projects, including MIT Kerberos, '389 Directory Server' for LDAP, Dogtag Certificate Authority, Netscape certificate server, BIND DNS server (BIND) and a System Security Services Daemon (SSSD).

It is able to enforce host-based access control with SSSD and cross-domain trusts with Kerberos enabling it to operate as a more comprehensive identity management system for users, groups, hosts, hostgroups, services, certificates and DNS entries. As such it can unify the management of application users, VM administrators and OpenStack service administrators. It is possible to integrate FreeIPA into OpenStack to use Kerberos single sign-on (SS) for the physical layer and make FreeIPA the LDAP provider for Keystone.

Separately, there is also emerging work on a Policy-as-a-Service from Open-Stack using the codename Congress[1]. It aims to provide governance and compliance as well as integration with business-level policies. It can leverage Keystone as an input for these policies and also verify that any applications orchestrated by Heat are consistent with the business policies.

Finally, you should also take a look at the OpenStack Operations Guide, which contains guidelines for user management, logging, monitoring and back-up/restore[2].

Practical Recommendations

Securing OpenStack is not just a question of implementing a set of technology controls. It also requires rigorous processes and procedures. The people implementing these require comprehensive training. Policies should define exactly how to execute operations. And there is a need for traceable audits that prove the controls are effective and do not compromise sensitive resources or violate legal regulations.

OpenStack has some mechanisms, such as Keystone roles, that can form part of this effort by limiting access. Logging facilities may contribute to a comprehensive auditing process. The bulk of the non-technical controls are outside the scope of OpenStack, but they are still vital to a secure implementation.

SECURE

---

[1] https://wiki.openstack.org/wiki/Congress
[2] http://docs.openstack.org/trunk/openstack-ops/content/index.html

Empower

One intent of cloud computing is to create an environment that maximizes the benefits of economy of scale. At some point, it may reach a size where failures are inevitable. The most effective solutions will not attempt to prevent them at any cost but rather ensure that the infrastructure and applications are able to withstand these through their high level of redundancy and automated self-healing. A parallelized architecture also enables auto-scaling which reduces the human effort required when load changes. Finally, autonomous operation requires the reduction of dependencies on other vendors or technologies and products.

EMPOWER

Chapter 20

Ensure Resilience

Reliability of a service is one of its most important success criteria. Some systems are critical to the business. Even seconds of downtime would be devastating for a stock exchange and could be catastrophic for a nuclear power plant. But resilience is always important. Users expect their applications to behave predictably regardless of any external events or influences.

Before we look at what OpenStack has to offer, let's begin with a quick analysis of the challenges in a cloud environment and the general approaches we can use to maximize availability.

Cloud Reliability

Cloud computing introduces new topologies, architectures and infrastructural components that an organization needs to consider as it strives to ensure that its services will be able to continue reliably while accommodating the natural growth and evolution of the system. We will look at contingency planning for more serious problems in Chapter 22. This section focuses on resilience of systems in the face of minor faults, whether they are due to human error or mechanical failure.

The primary mechanism to achieve high availability is redundancy. This requires not only a duplicate instance of each vital component but also real-time replication and dynamic fail-over when needed. In the face of a partial outage, the system needs to respond automatically recovering any necessary data and configuration settings.

EMPOWER

Uptime

Availability measures the percentage of time a particular resource or service is in a usable state over a specified time interval. Ideally, all resources would be available 100% of the time. In practice, there is always some downtime due to technical problems or planned maintenance.

Before becoming too obsessed with a high level of availability, consider the price. The cost of each additional 'nine' increases exponentially. Yes, there is less than one hour per year difference between four 'nines' and ten 'nines', which is not significant for most services. It is important to match the consequential costs of downtime with the service costs of increasing uptime.

What constitutes a reasonable level of availability will also depend very much on the resource in question. Hardware resources have physical limitations that make them prone to failure over time. However, if sufficient redundancy and transparent failover is incorporated into the system, then these failures may not be noticeable by the service consumers.

In spite of potential fault tolerance at the virtualization layer, cloud implementations typically present a higher number of failures on virtual platforms than you might expect on a physical machine (Reese, 2009, pp. 54, 56). Furthermore, due to their non-persistent nature, all changes are lost when the VM is powered down.

However, standardized resources also have a significant benefit in that they are much easier and faster to repair. Rather than isolating and replacing a faulty component, it is sufficient to re-launch a virtual instance on another physical machine. Thus, you need to design redundancy into a solution at an application and management layer. If you are able to fail-over between virtual instances without data loss, and if your user transactions are stateless, then you may well be able to hide any downtime from your users.

For each connection and component, you should determine who is responsible and how critical it is. You can then assess the controls that are in place to establish whether there is any redundancy or if it represents a single-point-of failure.

There are several strategies to achieve high uptime. Traditionally the focus has been on ensuring high reliability of all components. Where this is not possible, or insufficient, there is an option of pursuing fault tolerance through redundancy and fast failover capability. At the same time, it is worth looking at the overall architecture to ensure that components are loosely coupled and complexity is kept to a minimum. A more recent approach is to accept occasional failures and instead concentrate on expediting the restoration of the service.

EMPOWER

Component Reliability

The first approach tries to select the highest grade parts for each component of the solution. In the past, disciplines such as Total Quality Management and Six Sigma have demonstrated that a lot can be achieved through diligence and a commitment to quality throughout the whole system.

There is much to be said for a focus on quality. However, it is not trivial to pursue this avenue in a cloud-oriented solution due to the complexity of the system and the lack of control over all the elements.

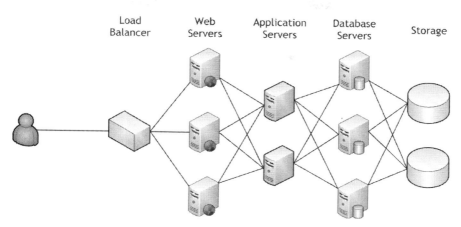

| Load Balancer | Web Servers | Application Servers | Database Servers | Storage |

Figure 20-1: Application Components

On the one hand, there are a number of components to consider (Figure 20-1). The applications may run over many different physical and virtual systems with data distributed even more widely. In addition to the three tiers of most web applications, you need to look at load balancers and the entire network infrastructure including the physical links, the routing tables and DNS.

Simply validating the hardware configuration will not be sufficient. The biggest threat to availability is typically software bugs, which are notoriously difficult to pinpoint. You need to ensure that all services perform as expected both in terms of functionality and performance. This guarantee doesn't automatically follow from a collection of error-free components. As the system scales, the number of linkages and dependencies tends to grow exponentially. A second problem is that many of the components are likely to be outsourced. Even in a pure private cloud implementation, there are network links and infrastructure that may be outside the control of the organization.

In addition to these technical obstacles, there are financial considerations. Adoption of premium components and systems runs counter to the principle of cloud computing to minimize costs by relying on standardized and commoditized parts. Even if systematic quality processes are achievable, they may not represent the most cost-effective avenue to reliability.

Fault Tolerance

In the world of Internet, services fail. Servers fail, networks fail, connections get stuck and responses are not sent back to requests in a timely manner. When dealing with massive volumes of compute capacity and complex network connections, it is a statistical fact that some elements will fail.

Given the challenges of ensuring that no part in the system fails, the next logical step is to accept that there may be local failures but strive for the system to be able to hide them. In other words: build the system assuming that things will fail, but ensure users never see outages and data is never lost.

You need to provide fault tolerance for all components at all layers of the architecture including: applications, file systems, CPU, I/O ports, network links, etc. In practice, tolerating faults involves making provisions for common failures or bottlenecks. A cloud-aware application must be able to cope with failures in services and infrastructure that lead to both planned and unplanned downtime.

Redundancy

Immunity to failures means never expecting the system to be stable. Instead, the application must assume nodes are continuously leaving, joining and failing. The most common technique in achieving fault tolerance is to provide some amount of redundancy along the same principles of Redundant Array of Interchangeable Disks (RAID), which has achieved great success in the area of storage.

By extending this concept to cloud components, we shift the burden from the individual elements to a means of effective synchronization, failover and election. The objective of high availability is to minimize downtime and data loss and it is achieved by eliminating Single Points of Failure (SPOFs).

The most common way to achieve high uptime is through redundancy of all critical resources, ranging from compute nodes, network equipment and storage devices to power and cooling. There are multiple configuration approaches you can use. The simplest is to replicate all components. This means that you have two or more of every system, storage device and network appliance. When one unit fails then you can designate the backup as the primary device. This may be a highly available solution, but it is not particularly efficient since you have idle hardware waiting only for a failure. An alternative is to configure one original system and replicate it into multiple zones but not start the system until it is needed. This may involve some switchover time but at least the standby costs are minimal.

Load Balancing

A third option is to implement load balancing. The simplest means of balancing loads is through DNS round robin. If multiple IP addresses for a given host name are registered in DNS, the DNS resolver will randomly assign clients to different resources in a defined pool. This is very easy to implement but also very limited. DNS Round Robin has no automatic server failure detection and is therefore not a failover solution.

Software load balancers, such as HAProxy, Zen, Apache and Squid, can easily run in almost any virtual environment and are able to monitor server health. For high-performance requirements, there is also the option to implement hardware load balancing, such as those offered by F5 networks, Cisco or Barracuda, for both local and global load balancing. Note that the latter is typically only feasible in a private data center or at least requires specific support from the provider.

As we look in more detail at load balancing, it is important to make the distinction between stateless and stateful services. Stateless services are implemented in such a way that there is no dependency between client requests. They often use REST to supply all state information as part of the HTTP request.

Stateful services usually involve multiple requests. They must therefore implement some form of stickiness or resource pool binding, for example using HTTP headers or HTTP cookies.

It is much easier to load balance redundant instances of stateless services. For stateful services it is necessary to implement a mechanism for all instances to have an identical state. So, for example, they must rely on the same back-end data store or else replicate all updates synchronously.

Fast Recovery

One final approach to cloud-related failures again assumes there will be problems, but deals with them by trying to minimize the impact through a fast recovery. In its extreme form, this means avoiding all troubleshooting (hence it is often called "lazy") and simply reinitializing the system when there is an incident.

The most important activity in this space is called "recovery-oriented computing". It focuses on synchronously redundant and heavily monitored data that is seamlessly partitioned. The underlying premise is that availability is not only determined by the mean-time-between-failures (MTBF) but also the mean-time-to-repair (MTTR). In a highly virtualized system it can be at least as effective to pursue MTTR which involves a focus on (Berkeley/Stanford, 2008):

- Isolation and redundancy
- System-wide undo support
- Integrated diagnostic support
- Online verification and recovery mechanisms
- Modularity, measurability and restartability

OpenStack High Availability

We need to look at high availability in OpenStack at two levels. The infrastructure itself must be resilient to any failures. Additionally, we may need to provide some support for applications that are running critical workloads. We will begin with the infrastructure and move on to the application support.

Infrastructure Resilience

As you look at infrastructure resilience, a good place to start is the OpenStack High Availability Guide[1]. Keep in mind that we need to deal both with stateless services (e.g. Nova API, Nova Scheduler) and stateful services (e.g. MySQL, RabbitMQ). As we mentioned above, balancing the load across stateful services is much more difficult because we must ensure that all state information is kept in sync.

In the case of OpenStack, this is particularly important for the databases of key services such as Cinder, Glance, Keystone, Nova and Neutron. There are multiple ways to implement these for high availability, but the most popular is with MySQL/Galera.

MySQL/Galera is a clustering technology that uses the MySQL database coupled with the InnoDB storage engine. It features synchronous replication in an active-active, multi-master topology. This means that it is possible to read or write to any cluster node without any lost transactions or slave lag, even in a highly scaled implementation. It also provides automatic membership control, so that nodes can join at any time and failed nodes will automatically drop from the cluster.

The second important stateful service is the message queue. One common approach is to configure RabbitMQ to use mirrored queues which are a built-in replication feature of RabbitMQ Cluster and will ensure its high availability across a cluster.

After clustering both MySQL/Galera and RabbitMQ, it would also be necessary to insert a load balancer that distributes incoming requests. One mechanism is HAProxy, which manages load balancing for HTTP and TCP-based applications. It can load balance the API services over multiple connections, forwarding and distributing all traffic to the designated endpoints.

However, this mechanism makes HAproxy itself become the single point of failure. To address this problem, we can use a health-check module, like Keepalived, which is based on the IP Virtual Server (IPVS) kernel module and provides transport layer Load Balancing. It implements a set of checkers to monitor service status and takes corrective action when needed. It leverages VRRP (Virtual Router Redundancy Protocol) to remap Virtual IPs (VIPs) in the event of a failure. This eliminates the single point of failure in a static default routed environment.

Distributing the load effectively is part of the solution. But we also need to keep track of any failures and restart the corresponding systems and services. Again there are multiple alternative approaches. Rackspace has documented their ap-

---

[1] http://docs.openstack.org/high-availability-guide/content/

proach using Pacemaker, Corosync and DRBD for high availability[1], so it is a good place to start.

Pacemaker is an open-source, high-availability cluster resource manager used for detection and recovery of machine and application-level failures. It achieves maximum availability for cluster services by detecting and recovering from node and resource-level failures through messaging and membership capabilities provided by cluster infrastructure.

Pacemaker can obtain the membership and quorum information it requires directly from Corosync. The Corosync Cluster Engine is a Group Communication System with support for high availability within applications. It includes a quorum system that notifies applications when quorum is achieved or lost. It can use UDP and InfiniBand based messaging to send quorum and cluster membership to Pacemaker.

DRBD (Distributed Replication Block Device) can be thought of as network-based mirrored storage. It is used to synchronize data of the block devices so that all cluster instances are using the same persistent information.

It's good to know that it is possible to configure OpenStack to be resilient. But if you are new to OpenStack, and generally to open-source, high-availability design, you may find the design and deployment overwhelming. If you want to implement high availability and don't feel up to the task of configuring all the components yet, you may want to check out Mirantis Fuel's HA deployment mode (Figure 20-2).

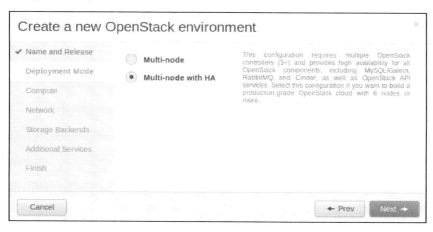

Figure 20-2: Mirantis Fuel Multi-node with HA

You need at least four systems, of which two will function as the controllers (Figure 20-3). In production, you would ideally have at least three controllers

---

[1] http://www.slideshare.net/kenhui65/openstack-ha

Chapter 20: Ensure Resilience

plus a set of multiple compute and storage nodes. But, if you just want to evaluate the concepts, then four will be sufficient.

Figure 20-3: Four-node Configuration

After deploying the environment, you can also run some HA-specific health checks to make sure that all the components are running as expected (Figure 20-4).

HA tests. Duration 30 sec - 8 min	Expected Duration	Actual Duration	Status
Check data replication over mysql	100 s.	31.2 s.	👍
Check amount of tables in databases is the same on each node	100 s.	44.1 s.	👍
Check galera environment state	60 s.	4.2 s.	👍
RabbitMQ availability	100 s.	4.0 s.	👍

Figure 20-4: HA Health Checks

Deployment Partitioning

Effective partitioning is important both for ensuring high availability of the infrastructure and also for the workloads. OpenStack offers several mechanisms to subdivide the deployment: regions, cells, availability zones (AZs) and host aggregates[1].

Regions are generally the highest level of compartmentalization. Each region has its own full OpenStack deployment, including its own API endpoints, networks and compute resources. However, different regions in the same organization may share one set of Keystone and Horizon instances for unified administration and access control. If multiple regions are in use, the login form will have a dropdown selector for authenticating to the appropriate region, and there will be a region switcher dropdown in the site header when logged in.

Within a region there may be multiple cells, which make it possible to organize groups of hosts as a directed graph (tree structure) for extremely large deployments. All of these hosts will use the same API server, but they will use their own message queue and database service.

Cells enable a second level of scheduling, beyond the nova-scheduler selection of compute hosts. As API requests come in to the central server, it will pass them on to the appropriate cells based on periodic broadcasts of capabilities and capacities.

Availability zones are another way of logically grouping compute hosts in a region. Typical criteria for defining availability zones are using a separate power supply or network equipment or to denote different classes of hardware. Administrators can only configure AZs at the command line, but they then become visible within the Horizon interface, too (Admin | System Info | Availability Zones: Figure 20-5).

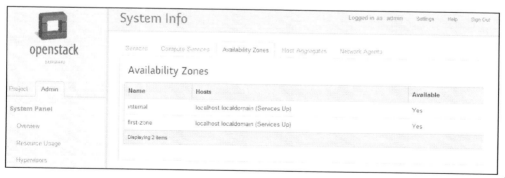

Figure 20-5: Nova Availability Zones

Once registered, the users can specify an AZ as they launch new instances (Project | Instances | Launch Instance: Figure 20-6).

---

[1] http://docs.openstack.org/trunk/openstack-ops/content/scaling.html

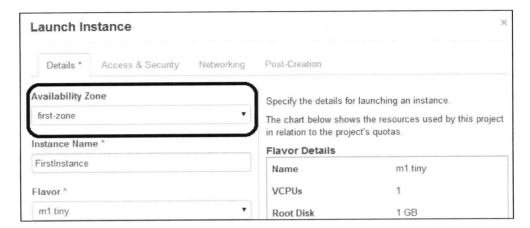

Figure 20-6: Launch Instance in Availability Zone

For example, they might spread their application resources across a dispersed set of machines to ensure resistance in the case of hardware failure.

One final level of segmentation is the host aggregate (Admin | System Info | Host Aggregates: Figure 20-7), which you can use to further partition an availability zone.

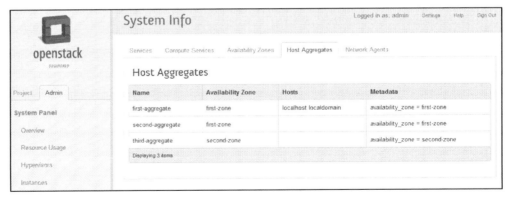

Figure 20-7: Host Aggregates

EMPOWER

The host aggregate is really just a set of metadata tags. For example, you can indicate nodes with special hardware features, such as SSDs, high-speed NICs or GPU cards.

The host aggregates are not directly visible to end users. Instead, the administrator can create customized flavors specifying the same metadata in key-value pairs known as "extra_specs". When booting an image, the Nova scheduler will try to assign the instance to a host with matching metadata.

OpenStack Load Balancing

LBaaS (Load-balancer-as-a-Service) is a Neutron extension that supports load balancing via multiple insertion mechanisms. Routed mode (where the load balancer also routes traffic between its public and private interfaces) is the most popular model for hardware appliances. The community reference implementation of OpenStack uses the simpler One-Arm mode (where the load balancer is plugged into a switch on the same network as the servers).

The key objects of a load balancer are: pools, members, health monitors and virtual IP addresses (VIPs) (Figure 20-8).

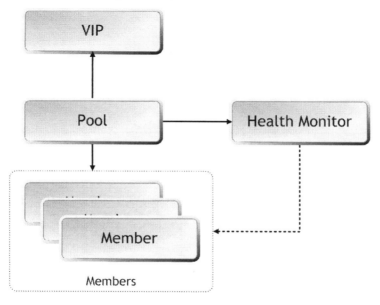

Figure 20-8: Load Balancer Objects

The core element is a pool, designating a collection of resources (instances) requiring a balanced load (Project | Manage Network | Load Balancers | Pools: Figure 20-9).

Chapter 20: Ensure Resilience

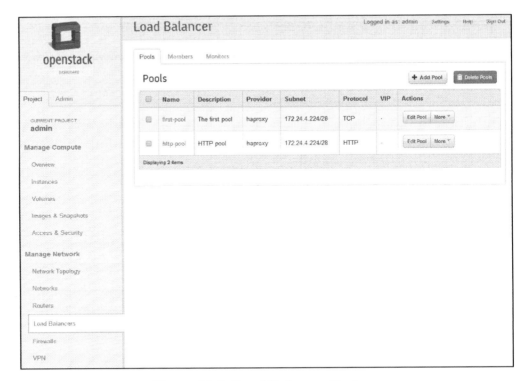

Figure 20-9: Load Balancer Pools

Each one of these instances is called a member (Project | Manage Network | Load Balancers | Members: Figure 20-10).

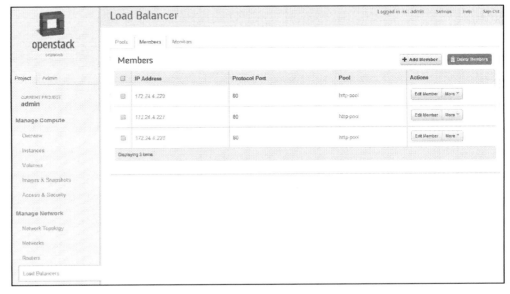

Figure 20-10: Load Balancer Members

An optional component associated with a pool is the monitor, which checks the health of each of the members (Project | Manage Network | Load Balancers | Monitors: Figure 20-11). It passes the latest status to the load balancer so that it can distribute traffic reliably.

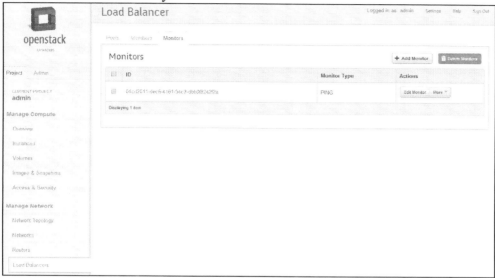

Figure 20-11: Load Balancer Monitors

As we shall see shortly, the pool will be reachable to end users via its VIP. In order to use the load balancer, we must do the following:

1. Create a pool
2. Add members to the pool
3. Add Virtual IP address to the pool
4. Optionally, create a health monitor and associate it with the pool

We begin by creating the pool (Load Balancers | Pools | Add Pool: Figure 20-12).

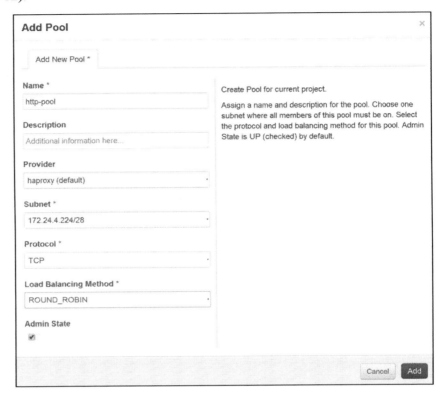

Figure 20-12: Create Load Balancer Pool

The reference implementation uses HAproxy as the Provider. However, it would also be possible to substitute a hardware load balancer such as F5 BIG-IP. TCP, HTTP and HTTPS are supported as protocols. And there are options for round robin, least connections and source IP address as load balancing methods.

Next we must add each instance as a member of the pool (Load Balancers | Members | Add Member: Figure 20-13).

EMPOWER

Figure 20-13: Add Load Balancer Member

We can distribute the load across each of the members equally or, if they represent different configurations, then we might want to choose weights that reflect the relative capabilities of each instance.

We must also add a virtual IP address to the pool so that the load balancer knows which incoming traffic belongs to the pool (Load Balancers | Pools | More | Add VIP: Figure 20-14).

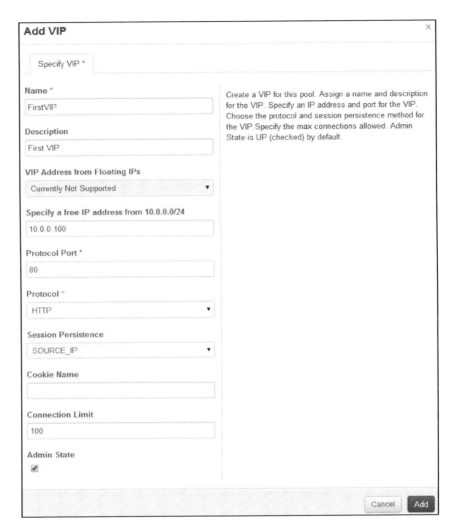

Figure 20-14: Add Load Balancer VIP

The protocol should match that of the pool (TCP, HTTP or HTTPS). We also need to indicate how to establish session persistence in the case of stateful connections. The supported options include Source IP, HTTP cookie and App cookie. We can also limit the number of simultaneous connections that the pool can support.

Lastly, we may want to add a health monitor (Load Balancers | Monitors | Add Monitor: Figure 20-15).

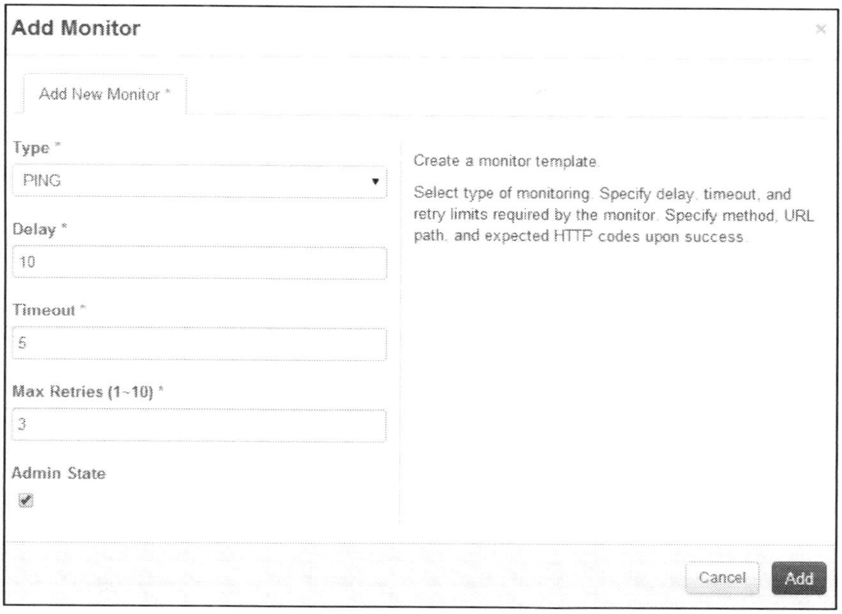

Figure 20-15: Add Load Balancer Monitor

There are several mechanisms the monitor can use (Ping, HTTP, HTTPS and TCP) to check whether the instance is alive. We can indicate the delay (interval between checks) and the maximum number of retries before changing the status to inactive.

Heat is able to manage most of the OpenStack resources, including load balancers. This is particularly interesting for auto-scaling as we will see in the next chapter. But just to give you an idea, below is the description of an elastic load balancer taken from one of the public Heat templates[1]:

```
ElasticLoadBalancer:
  Type: AWS::ElasticLoadBalancing::LoadBalancer
  Properties:
    AvailabilityZones: {'Fn::GetAZs': ''}
    Listeners:
    - {LoadBalancerPort: '80', InstancePort: '80',
      Protocol: HTTP}
    HealthCheck: {Target: 'HTTP:80/', HealthyThreshold: '3',
      UnhealthyThreshold: '5', Interval: '30', Timeout: '5'}
```

EMPOWER

---

[1] https://github.com/openstack/heat-templates/blob/master/cfn/F17/AutoScalingCeilometer.yaml

We can include some of the pool parameters above, such as protocol and port. And we can add configuration details for the health monitor. We'll look at the full template in more detail shortly.

Practical Recommendations

Multi-sourced services are difficult to operate reliably. Many of the conventional approaches to availability break down when they are delivered externally or involve significant geographical separation between components. As you work through the challenges, consider some suggestions:

- Begin with the physical infrastructure. Make sure you have a set of independent pools distributed across a wide geography, independent power sources and network providers.
- Map Availability Zones and Regions to the pools as cleanly as possible.
- Distribute critical workloads carefully across the AZs and regions to minimize any single points of failure.
- Consider load balancing to accommodate transient errors and enable fast recovery.

Chapter 21

Maximize Elasticity

Elasticity is another aspect of resilience. The previous chapter looked at how to maximize availability in the face of foreseeable and unforeseeable errors and events. We also saw how load balancing has the side-benefit of improving performance and providing seamless failover.

Nonetheless, the fastest network won't help if the servers are overloaded. Even if the capacity is available, it does not necessarily mean that its resources are being allocated and balanced efficiently. Elasticity is the art of allocating and utilizing resources whenever the system needs them so that it can cope with varying demand, both in the short and long term.

Cloud Scalability

The core problem when dealing with Internet applications is that they need to be able to scale in two dimensions. On the one hand, you may have a high volume of users who need to execute independent (but similar) transactions. In this case you have a single code base (which doesn't have to be very complex) that needs to execute in parallel for a large number of simultaneous users.

You may also have scenarios where you want to solve a big problem. It could be related to a large population, but differs from the first problem in that the process is inherently very complex and will not comfortably run on typical cloud-based-infrastructure services.

We will look at a few ways that you can address these problems including vertical scaling, application sharding and grid computing. Regardless of the technique you employ to permit high scalability, you also need to look at the resource allocation that will be necessary to achieve flexible and quick elasticity to cope with rapidly changing user demand and computational workload.

EMPOWER

Vertical scaling

From the perspective of the application, the simplest approach to adding capacity is through vertical scaling. By adding more powerful processors, additional memory and both network and peripheral interfaces, a demanding application can run unchanged for larger workloads. In the case of OpenStack, this would mean upgrading from a small instance to a large instance.

Vertical scaling bypasses the need to worry about partitioning data and application logic. This makes it far easier to achieve both high availability and high consistency, so the code needn't include special provisions for either. Until recently, it was possible to satisfy the increasing appetite of software applications for processing power, memory and storage through advances in transistor density and clock-frequencies, which improved single-threaded performance in an almost linear manner (Kaufmann & Gayliard, http://www.ddj.com/go-parallel/article/showArticle.jhtml?articleID=212900103, 2009). This approach has run into physical limits that prevent further advances without dramatically increasing power consumption and heat dissipation, and are therefore not cost effective or ecologically responsible.

By increasing the number of processor cores, it is possible to reduce per-socket power consumption. However, the job for the software developer becomes all the more difficult in exchange. An application cannot run faster than the aggregate of its sequential components. If an application does not parallelize effectively, then performance will not improve (and may degrade) with additional cores.

The main criteria in evaluating vertical scalability are the relative costs of different server instances and the degree to which they address the performance bottleneck. There may also be instances where a legacy application is not able to scale horizontally at all. In this case, vertical scaling is the only option.

Private installations of OpenStack have virtually no limits to the size of servers that could carry the infrastructure. Unfortunately, most public infrastructure service providers are specialized in low-end server instances and offer only limited high-performance virtual machines. However, given the existing need for high-end solutions, some providers have begun to offer high-end hardware configurations and high-availability clusters. By comparison, Amazon EC2 offers a High Memory Cluster Compute Eight Extra Large Instance with 88 EC2 Compute Units (2 Intel E5-2670 processors with 16 hyperthreaded cores each), 244 GB of memory, 2 120 GB SSDs of instance storage, optimal I/O Performance and 10 Gigabit Ethernet interfaces.

As the market matures, we can expect some Open Stack service providers to offer similar configurations. It may also be possible to arrange for specific high-end systems through the negotiation of special terms. In this case, the only obstacles to using the fastest computers in the industry are the flexibility of your provider and the price you are willing to pay.

An alternative to supercomputers is the consolidation of many low-end systems into virtual machines. ScaleMP, for example, offers a hypervisor that aggregates x86 nodes into larger systems of over 255 virtual processors. It relies on high-bandwidth, low-latency connections between the individual systems that may be challenging to guarantee in an opaque cloud but is worth considering in a private data center or a dedicated segment of a public cloud.

Sharding

Unfortunately, there are limits to the application workloads that vertical scaling can accommodate. Even before the system exhausts all the technical possibilities, the exponentially increasing costs of higher capacity make the approach unattractive.

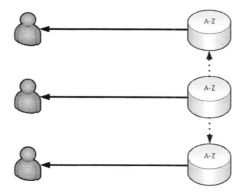

Figure 21-1: Replication

The most common strategy in cloud environments is to scale horizontally when additional capacity is needed. When the majority of transactions are read-only, the task is not difficult. You simply replicate, or cache, the information on multiple systems and ensure that user requests are balanced across all available systems. In effect, you create a content delivery network (Figure 21-1).

The picture changes when you need to accommodate a large number of write requests. You can still install the application in parallel on additional servers. However, you need to ensure that processing is completely independent on each system. We refer to this architecture as "Shared Nothing", which has given rise to the term "shard" or "sharding".

In its extreme form, sharding would imply that there is no common data at all. For example, you might have a set of web servers that are able to perform calculations based only on user input and local data. However, if you expand your interpretation slightly then you can also consider some amount of common static input data as well as external data feeds and repositories.

This is easiest to implement when the same operation is executed on every system, typically using different data. According to Michael Flynn's taxonomy (1972), this is a single-instruction multiple-data (SIMD) algorithm. It works particularly well where bulk data needs to be transformed or web transactions can be processed in isolation.

Sharding isn't applicable to every scenario but where it is feasible it provides a simple solution to scalability. The only technical challenges are to ensure that users are allocated equitably to the available servers and that any stateful information isn't lost between requests.

As we saw in the previous chapter, a load balancer is the simplest way to allocate users to servers. If any data is required, then it needs to be replicated in the background. Most commercial load balancers can also ensure that sessions are sticky, so that users will always be directed to the same server for each request. However, there may be reasons to partition according to a different dimension than the user.

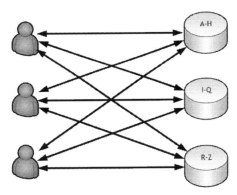

Figure 21-2: Sharding

For example, if requests rely on significant local data then you might want to split the index and shard according to a particular key. As shown in Figure 21-2, this approach means that each shard will only contain a fraction of the database. However, users may need to access several shards in the course of a transaction. To avoid potential contamination, it is advisable to ensure that all requests are stateless and that any intermediate data is maintained by the client.

EMPOWER

High Performance Computing

While application sharding tries to take a relatively simple problem and apply it to a large number of users or data streams, High Performance Computing (HPC) and Grid Computing attempt to solve very complex problems by decomposing them into smaller tasks that can be distributed on multiple systems.

At a high level, they distribute compute-intensive processing across a cluster of machines. APIs such as the Message Passing Interface (MPI) or OpenMP provide a framework to orchestrate task execution. The approach lends itself to compute-intensive jobs that do not need to transfer large amounts of data between systems. However, some amount of sharing is typically facilitated through the file system, running on a dedicated SAN.

Of the two dominant frameworks, OpenMP is generally considered easier to use. However it comes with several constraints, such as the need for a special compiler and a reliance on shared-memory. Its simpler use may also lead to less rigor, which contributes to application errors. As a result, MPI is more common for solutions with high reliability and scalability requirements.

MPI is the de facto standard for programming high-performance parallel computers. In addition to defining a protocol, it also specifies a set of language-independent APIs and describes an architecture including virtual topology, synchronization, and communication functionality. The software engineer has considerable flexibility, which makes it possible to design systems that scale almost indefinitely. However, the framework also requires explicit management of the entire process from defining and initiating data flow to checkpointing and restarting processes.

There are classes of problems that can only be solved through a complex architecture involving numerous compute-bound modules that collaborate to attain a solution. Although an MPI-based solution is not trivial to implement, it is certainly easier than redesigning an equivalent solution on your own. The challenge in implementing HPC in the cloud is that most providers do not offer infrastructure that is suitable for tight coupling. Without a guarantee of low latency between systems, the approach isn't technically viable. Furthermore, if intra-system bandwidth is expensive, then the costs become a problem.

We are now seeing some attempt to fill this need through private virtual clouds with strict service level agreements where the customer also has significantly more control over the hardware and physical placement of their systems. Unfortunately, there has been little published work around OpenStack and OpenMP or MPI. There is certainly no reason it cannot be done, but you would need to either be willing to invest significant resources or else wait until HPC deployments on OpenStack mature and additional guidance becomes available.

OpenStack Elasticity

The simplest way to accommodate larger workloads is through vertical scaling. In OpenStack, this would mean assigning increasingly large flavors to the instances as their resource requirements expand. OpenStack includes five standard flavors, which you can find under **Flavors** in the **System Panel** (Figure 21-3).

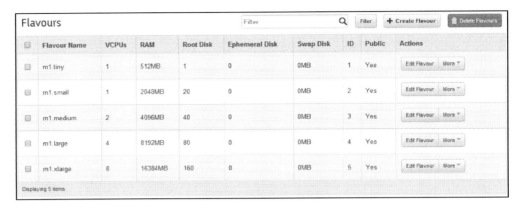

Figure 21-3: Default Flavors

You can also edit the flavors or add new ones if the existing set is inusfficient by pressing the **Create Flavor** button (Figure 21-4).

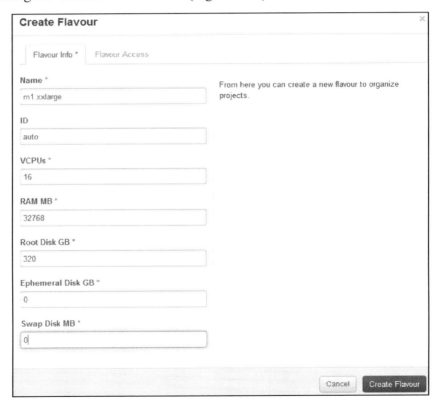

Figure 21-4: Create Flavor

Horizontal scaling requires a little more design effort. The easiest way to achieve it in OpenStack is through the orchestration functions. We already looked at

Heat in Chapter 12 and briefly touched on using it for load balancing in Chapter 20. Now, let's take a look at how we can use it to implement auto-scaling.

As shown in Figure 21-5, there are five essential auto-scaling components required by Heat. These are based on the AWS Template Reference[1].

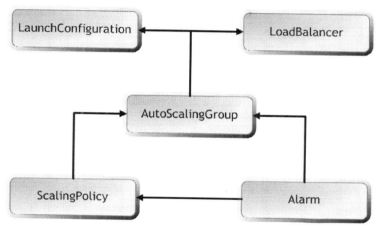

Figure 21-5: Heat Auto-scaling Components

The LaunchConfiguration defines the configuration of each autoscaled instance. The LoadBalancer distributes the incoming requests between all of the instances in this pool. The AutoScalingGroup forms the connection between the other elements. It specifies the LaunchConfigurations and corresponding LoadBalancers. The ScalingPolicy defines the action that Heat should take. And the Alarm is the trigger for any ongoing activity. It monitors the AutoScalingGroup and invokes the ScalingPolicy when specified conditions are met.

It's a little easier to understand the operation with a specific example. We will use one of the default Heat templates available on GitHub to create an auto-scaling WordPress application using Ceilometer[2].

It includes six parameters, which should be self-explanatory:

EMPOWER

---

[1] http://docs.aws.amazon.com/AWSCloudFormation/latest/UserGuide/template-reference.html
[2] https://github.com/openstack/heat-templates/blob/master/cfn/F17/AutoScalingCeilometer.yaml

```
Parameters:
  KeyName:
    Description: Name of an existing EC2 KeyPair to enable SSH access to
the instances
    Type: String
  InstanceType:
    Description: WebServer EC2 instance type
    Type: String
    Default: m1.small
    AllowedValues: [m1.tiny, m1.small, m1.medium, m1.large, m1.xlarge]
    ConstraintDescription: must be a valid EC2 instance type.
  ImageId:
    Description: the name or uuid of the image in glance
    Type: String
    Default: F17-x86_64-cfntools
  DBUsername: {Default: admin, NoEcho: 'true',
    Description: The WordPress database admin account username, Type:
String,
    MinLength: '1', MaxLength: '16', AllowedPattern: '[a-zA-Z][a-zA-Z0-
9]*',
    ConstraintDescription: must begin with a letter and contain only
      alphanumeric characters.}
  DBPassword: {Default: admin, NoEcho: 'true',
    Description: The WordPress database admin account password, Type:
String,
    MinLength: '1', MaxLength: '41', AllowedPattern: '[a-zA-Z0-9]*',
    ConstraintDescription: must contain only alphanumeric characters.}
  DBRootPassword: {Default: admin, NoEcho: 'true',
    Description: Root password for MySQL, Type: String,
    MinLength: '1', MaxLength: '41', AllowedPattern: '[a-zA-Z0-9]*',
    ConstraintDescription: must contain only alphanumeric characters.}
```

If you launch the template with Horizon, it would look like Figure 21-6.

EMPOWER

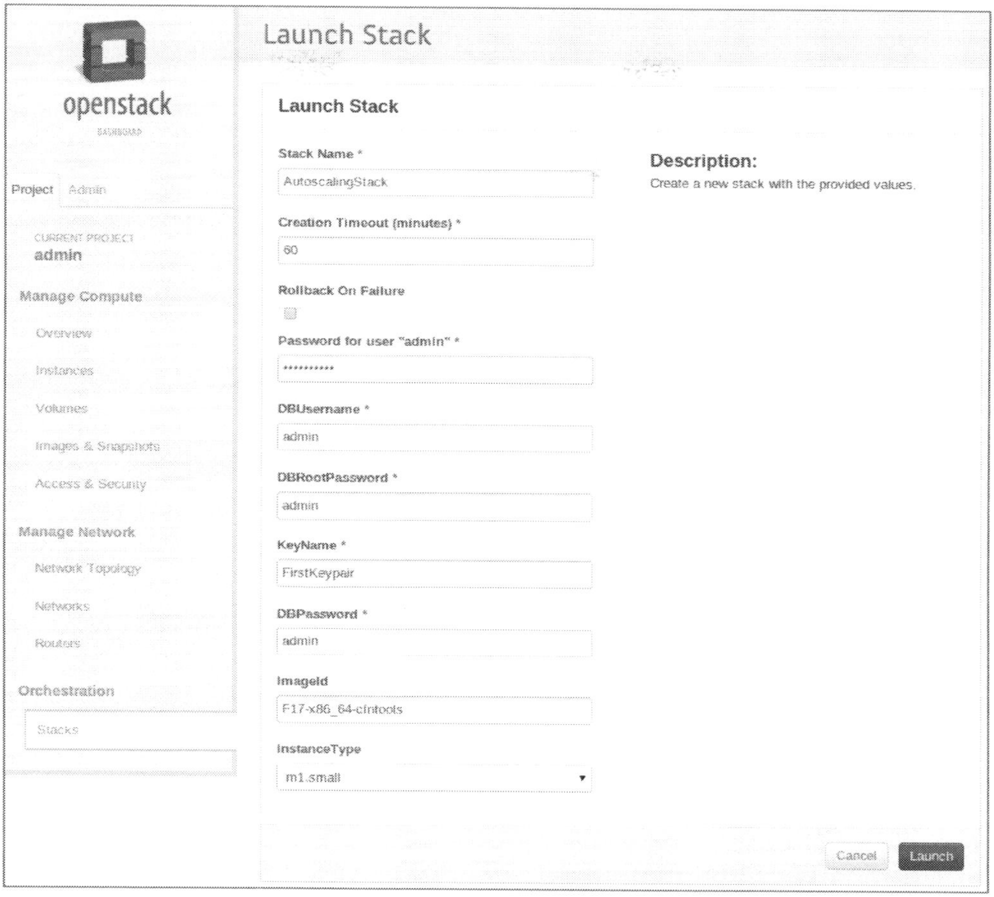

Figure 21-6: Heat Auto-scaling Template

We won't go through the whole template, which you can find in Appendix C, but just want to highlight some of the resources that you may not have seen yet.

The LaunchConfiguration specifies all information you would need to launch an instance. This includes the image identifier, its type (flavor) and keypairs. Additionally, you will find some basic configuration instructions in the Init Metadata and the UserData. These are used to create files, deploy packages and update the local database:

```
LaunchConfig:
    Type: AWS::AutoScaling::LaunchConfiguration
    Metadata:
        AWS::CloudFormation::Init:
            config:
                files:
                    /etc/cfn/cfn-credentials:
                        content:
                            'Fn::Replace':
                            - WebServerKeys: {Ref: WebServerKeys}
```

```
            WebSecretKey: {'Fn::GetAtt': [WebServerKeys, Secre-
tAccessKey]}
        - |
          AWSAccessKeyId=WebServerKeys
          AWSSecretKey=WebSecretKey
      mode: '000400'
      owner: root
      group: root
    /tmp/setup.mysql:
      content:
        'Fn::Replace':
        - DBPassword: {Ref: DBPassword}
          DBUsername: {Ref: DBUsername}
        - |
          CREATE DATABASE wordpress;
          GRANT ALL PRIVILEGES ON wordpress .* TO
'DBUsername'@'localhost' IDENTIFIED BY 'DBPassword';
          FLUSH PRIVILEGES;
          EXIT
      mode: '000644'
      owner: root
      group: root
  packages:
    yum:
      mysql: []
      mysql-server: []
      httpd: []
      wordpress: []
  services:
    systemd:
      mysqld: {enabled: 'true', ensureRunning: 'true'}
      httpd: {enabled: 'true', ensureRunning: 'true'}
Properties:
  ImageId: {Ref: ImageId}
  InstanceType: {Ref: InstanceType}
  KeyName: {Ref: KeyName}
  UserData:
    Fn::Base64:
      Fn::Replace:
      - 'AWS::StackName': {Ref: 'AWS::StackName'}
        'AWS::Region': {Ref: 'AWS::Region'}
        DBRootPassword: {Ref: DBRootPassword}
        DBPassword: {Ref: DBPassword}
        DBUsername: {Ref: DBUsername}
      - |
        #!/bin/bash -v
        /opt/aws/bin/cfn-init -s AWS::StackName -r LaunchConfig --
region AWS::Region
        # Setup MySQL root password and create a user
        mysqladmin -u root password DBRootPassword
        mysql -u root --password=DBRootPassword < /tmp/setup.mysql
        sed -i "/Deny from All/d" /etc/httpd/conf.d/wordpress.conf
        sed -i "/Deny from all/d" /etc/httpd/conf.d/wordpress.conf
        sed --in-place --e s/database_name_here/wordpress/ --e
s/username_here/DBUsername/ --e s/password_here/DBPassword/
/usr/share/wordpress/wp-config.php
        systemctl restart httpd.service
```

We already looked at the LoadBalancer in Chapter 20, so let's move on to the
AutoScalingGroup. As you can see, it does little more than point to the Load-

Balancer and LaunchConfiguration with an indication of the minimum and maximum number of instances.

```
WebServerGroup:
  Type: AWS::AutoScaling::AutoScalingGroup
  Properties:
    AvailabilityZones: {'Fn::GetAZs': ''}
    LaunchConfigurationName: {Ref: LaunchConfig}
    MinSize: '1'
    MaxSize: '3'
    LoadBalancerNames:
    - {Ref: ElasticLoadBalancer}
    Tags:
    - {Key: metering.server_group, Value: WebServerGroup}
```

Next we see that there are two ScalingPolicies. One is used to increment the number of instances and the other to decrement the number. There is a Cooldown period that specifies the number of seconds after a scaling activity completes before any subsequent scaling activities can start:

```
WebServerScaleUpPolicy:
  Type: AWS::AutoScaling::ScalingPolicy
  Properties:
    AdjustmentType: ChangeInCapacity
    AutoScalingGroupName: {Ref: WebServerGroup}
    Cooldown: '60'
    ScalingAdjustment: '1'
WebServerScaleDownPolicy:
  Type: AWS::AutoScaling::ScalingPolicy
  Properties:
    AdjustmentType: ChangeInCapacity
    AutoScalingGroupName: {Ref: WebServerGroup}
    Cooldown: '60'
    ScalingAdjustment: '-1'
```

Finally, we come to the corresponding Alarms. They indicate the Ceilometer parameters (meter name, type of statistic, evaluation timeframe and number of evaluation periods to consider. If the resulting value is over (or under, depending on the comparison operator) the specified threshold, then the alarm action will trigger the appropriate ScalingPolicy:

```
CPUAlarmHigh:
  Type: OS::Ceilometer::Alarm
  Properties:
    description: Scale-up if the average CPU > 50% for 1 minute
    meter_name: cpu_util
    statistic: avg
    period: '60'
    evaluation_periods: '1'
    threshold: '50'
    alarm_actions:
    - {"Fn::GetAtt": [WebServerScaleUpPolicy, AlarmUrl]}
    matching_metadata: {'metadata.user_metadata.groupname': {Ref: 'Web-
ServerGroup'}}
    comparison_operator: gt

CPUAlarmLow:
  Type: OS::Ceilometer::Alarm
```

```
Properties:
  description: Scale-down if the average CPU < 15% for 1 minute
  meter_name: cpu_util
  statistic: avg
  period: '60'
  evaluation_periods: '1'
  threshold: '15'
  alarm_actions:
  - {"Fn::GetAtt": [WebServerScaleDownPolicy, AlarmUrl]}
  matching_metadata: {'metadata.user_metadata.groupname': {Ref: 'Web-
ServerGroup'}}
  comparison_operator: lt
```

Resource Allocation

Designing the software so that it is scalable is only part of the answer. It is also necessary to make sure that the application has access to all the resources it needs – when it needs them. One of the great advantages of cloud computing is its elasticity. It can scale seamlessly up and down as resources are required. However, this doesn't automatically mean that no capacity planning is required. It is much easier and faster to change capacity, but you may still need to intervene to ensure your applications have the resources they need.

There are monitoring systems, such as RightScale, which observe load usage patterns and perform advanced analytics to project future resource requirements. Even if you do choose to use these tools, you should still have a good understanding of what your applications are using so that you can double-check the results and be aware of the costs you are incurring.

A solid capacity plan is based on extensive knowledge of current usage patterns. This includes a trend analysis and examination of any unanticipated spikes and drops to determine cause. Based on these, it is possible to project potential future bottlenecks, which could be along the dimensions of CPU, RAM, I/O Read or Writes, Disk Space and Network bandwidth. These metrics need to be investigated, not only for the application servers, but for the database servers, proxies, firewalls, load-balancers and any other nodes that may be part of the overall solution.

Note that an impending bottleneck doesn't necessarily mean that you need to increase capacity. It is important to perform a marginal analysis on the additional resources to determine your anticipated costs and revenue both in the case that you expand and the case that you don't. If the resources are required for mission-critical or customer-facing operations, then the equation is probably compelling. In other cases it may not be.

EMPOWER

Private Cloud Planning

The notions in the paragraphs above refer primarily to public cloud computing. The challenges are different for private cloud. Capacity planning is more critical given the hard barriers of fixed resources and the lead time in provisioning additional hardware. In some ways, the additional importance is offset by the fact that it is a known art – enterprises have been monitoring performance and using it to project future requirements for decades.

However, it should not be so easily dismissed. Increased virtualization and service orientation have the effect that the internal constitution of services running on hardware becomes opaque to the infrastructure managers. This can make it difficult to manually identify patterns and plan accordingly. It therefore increases the need for analytics that can mine aggregated performance information and correlate it to processes and activities.

Cloudbursting

As we saw already in Chapter 2, the most ambitious form of resource allocation exploits all available private assets, but combines these with the elasticity of public resources (Figure 21-7). When it is well designed and orchestrated, cloudbursting can minimize costs and maximize agility. However, while the approach sounds elegant in theory, it is difficult to achieve in practice.

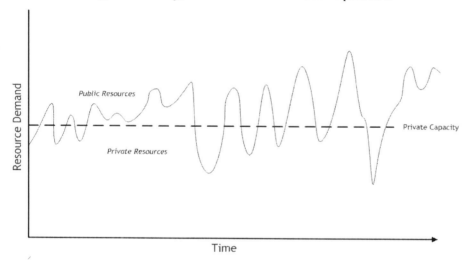

Figure 21-7: Cloudbursting

In order to shift load effectively, three prerequisites are needed: a trigger mechanism, capacity to launch public instances, and capacity to shift associated data.

The first requirement is for a defined means to detect that private resources are close to exhaustion and the launch of public services should be initiated. This implies effective instrumentation of internal utilization, for example using OpenStack Ceilometer Alarms. However, unless the inter-cloud launch can be executed instantaneously, measurement is not sufficient. You need to be able to project future utilization with sufficient lead time to make the transition. In other words, you must have a good grasp of your load patterns so that you can extrapolate based on current trends.

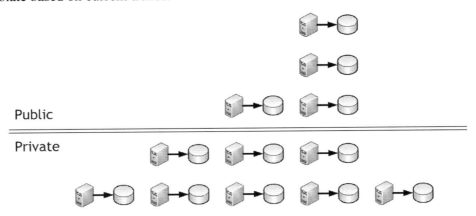

Figure 21-8: Instance Replication for Cloudbursting

The second item on the list is the ability to launch public compute instances (Figure 21-8). In cases, where you are using an OpenStack-based public cloud, it may be feasible to create an integrated hybrid deployment using partitioning elements, such as regions or availability zones.

Single-server tasks may start with a call to a public cloud management service. However, complex configurations with many different components should be planned in advance. All relevant parts of the internal infrastructure must be replicated in the cloud environment for the processing to transfer seamlessly. The interaction between any components running in different clouds need coordination, and after processing completes, the results require consolidation.

The last task is generally the most challenging. There is a need to pass all the associated data from the internal services to their external counterparts. In some cases this is not a problem: interactive applications usually involve very little data; other tasks may utilize predominantly static data sets that can be replicated to the public cloud in advance. However, there are many use cases that require large amounts of dynamic data. In these cases, cloudbursting could be difficult to achieve, especially with the speed required to be effective.

EMPOWER

Even if it is possible to address these three technical issues, it may not be financially attractive. The costs of a parallel infrastructure and shifting data between services need to be weighed against the additional benefits they provide. Nonetheless, it is wise to design any service with flexible sourcing options in mind. The economics may change in the future, but rebuilding agility after the fact is likely to remain an expensive proposition.

Practical Recommendations

Cloud computing automatically implies resource elasticity. However, it doesn't directly lead to application elasticity. As you design your service so that it will scale on demand, consider some suggestions:

- Most of your legacy applications will only scale vertically. You can monitor their load and choose bigger instances as needed.
- As you acquire and build new apps, make sure they scale horizontally. Try to decompose the business logic into parallel elements that can run autonomously. These services should allow you to implement auto-scaling which is the most effective form of elasticity.
- As you plan for cloudbursting options, look for opportunities to maximize data locality! Where possible adopt an associated data model by partitioning the workload and storage using the same scheme.

Chapter 22

Minimize Dependencies

We've covered building a resilient infrastructure that can scale elastically in the last two chapters. But we need to recognize that no architecture can sustain every possible adverse event. In order to ensure business continuity we need to minimize any dependencies and build a comprehensive set of contingency plans. These should cover every form of disaster or major disruption.

The most cloud-specific disruption is a separation from the cloud provider. The direst circumstances for changing vendors would be if the provider ceases business operations or closes services being used. A business dispute between customer and provider may also make it awkward to continue on with a service. More commonly, increases in renewal costs or a decrease in service quality may simply make the product unattractive. Likewise new competitive offerings may be able to beat existing services in price, functionality and quality.

The bottom line is that whether an outage is caused by a natural disaster, technical failure or commercial decision, we need to ensure business continuity. To address these problems we will explore three alternatives.

- Disaster recovery
- Interoperability
- Multi-sourcing

Disaster recovery is a catch-all solution that should be able to handle any unforeseen events. However, it implies a relatively long recovery time and is therefore not necessarily ideal for every circumstance.

EMPOWER

Interoperability between the operational and recovery environments is a more ambitious goal, but it will accelerate the recovery and is therefore preferable where it can be implemented.

The highest level of cloud computing optimization entails complete flexibility in sourcing services. This means the option to alternate between multiple private or public services in real time. Where it can be achieved, there is minimal dependency on any given provider or infrastructure.

Let's look at each of these in turn.

Disaster Recovery

Not all disasters are equal. They can have different degrees of impact from a minor outage to the complete destruction of both equipment and facilities. They may also vary according to their geographical scope from an incident in a local data center to a local, regional or even global catastrophe.

This doesn't mean that you need to accommodate full and immediate restoration for every disaster. However, it should be clear which scenarios you intend to address and what your objectives are in those cases. The most common goals are the RTO (Recovery Time Objective) and RPO (Recovery Point Objective). Some also refer to an RLO (Recovery Level Objective).

> *RTO* is the duration within which a business process must be restored after a disaster (or disruption). It includes time for fixing the problem, the recovery itself, tests and the communication to the users. In simple terms, how quickly after a catastrophic failure will you need to be back up and running?

> *RPO* refers to the last state prior to the disaster for which data must be recovered. In other words, how much application data can you afford to lose? Will the loss of a week's worth of streaming data lead to bankruptcy? Do you have to maintain copies of every transaction?

> *RLO* is a qualitative rather than quantitative measure. It specifies the scope of the system that needs to be restored immediately after a failure. Rather than attempting to recover the full system it allows IT to focus on the most mission-critical services and processes first.

A Business Continuity Plan (BCP) should be in place that describes the process to back up and recover the data. These may refer to a single RTO and RPO, or it may be necessary to specify a series of RTOs, RPOs and RLOs in order to cover all possible scenarios.

EMPOWER

The process can vary greatly depending on the requirements, applications and data. One way to achieve a very quick RTO would be to maintain a set of duplicate instances at another cloud provider's facility and simply redirect traffic to the new site. The main challenge in this scenario would be to continuously synchronize all the data with the alternate provider.

A slower, but significantly cheaper, approach would be to create application instances at a secondary location but to import the data manually (either through a network upload or a physical medium) in the event of a disaster. New transactions might be processed almost immediately, but any queries to historical data would be delayed until the information was uploaded into the new system.

One of the key questions to address is the level of geographical redundancy, which is clearly related to the scope of the disaster that needs to be survived. The ability of the application designer to specify locality will depend on the terms of the service providers. Infrastructure providers often let users decide where to position capacity. In OpenStack we can leverage the notion of regions to designate geographically distinct data centers. We may also want to include availability zones indicating physical rooms, aisles, power sources or network connections.

Ideally, the physical infrastructure should be replicated to a geographically removed location, so that it is unlikely to be affected by the same disaster. The more distant the two locations are, the better the chances that the second will survive a disaster of the first. A different continent is therefore ideal, but that level of precaution is probably not necessary in every case and may need to be weighed against compliance and performance demands.

An additional level of independence can be achieved if a backup is hosted by a second provider. In this case, an incident (e.g. large-scale intrusion or malware attack) cannot easily affect both the backup and the primary system. However, there are cost implications in distributing the applications, particularly when there is a need to synchronize them. Even within the same provider, there are often charges for data transfers between availability zones. If multiple providers are involved, there will invariably be significant network costs and there may also be an additional effort to integrate the data sources through differing interfaces.

Restorability/Reversibility/Rollback

Disasters are one of the main reasons for maintaining backups. However, they are not the only reason. It may be necessary to restore user information, system configuration, or application code for other reasons, too. Systems fail, users make mistakes and auditors may need to inspect historical data for legal or diagnostic purposes.

A prerequisite for a solid backup plan is a thorough inventory of both business and system data along with an indication of the lifetime and value of the information. You can then proceed to analyze patterns in information usage to identify options and derive a sensible plan.

Some questions to ask are: How valuable is the user data in your application? Can users delete something inside your service or your application? Do you back up user data only as a safeguard against infrastructure failures, or do you also allow users to recover data that they have deleted in error? Can you move user data into a holding area for a period of time, before deleting it?

EMPOWER

We will look at three different dimensions of safeguarding information for future use. Backup is the core activity that involves taking periodic snapshots of a wide range of information. Versioning is primarily intended to protect against user error, or at least a change of user intention. It provides a means to revert from the most recent release of a document, program or configuration setting to a prior state that presumably worked better. Archival is concerned with long-term retention of information to provide a basis for historical searches and queries.

Backups

Multiple levels of backups can help to achieve different RPOs. The most secure and reliable are off-site since they are not affected by regional outages and losses. These might be off-site tape backups, disk backups or simply off-site replication (to an auxiliary data center or service provider).

While off-site backups may be more reliable, there are obvious performance implications related to the additional physical distance and network latency. This may impact the cost and therefore the frequency with which backups are feasible. Given increasingly demanding business requirements for more frequent backups and faster restores, off-line backups may not be sufficient. In order to improve both the RPO and RTO, it makes sense to complement them with more frequent on-site tape or disk backups.

A common scheme would foresee weekly off-site backups in addition to daily on-site backups. It is possible to maintain much more current backups by clustering servers and storage, implementing continuous replication or by taking frequent snapshots and maintaining differential transaction logs.

Keep in mind that backup requirements are changing. Virtualization can help to automate disaster recovery by packaging images and making them easier to deploy. However, it also reduces scheduled downtime, which complicates the backup process. At the same time the demands on backup are becoming more aggressive with rapid growth in information volume and requirements for both encrypted media and long-term readability.

A complete backup/restore plan is likely to include a range of components, ranging from virtual tape libraries to disk appliances, and incorporate a variety of techniques such as disk-based data protection, continuous replications, snapshots and transaction logging. As mentioned above, the tradeoff between better, more accurate information and the higher cost of maintenance need to be evaluated to determine the best mix of backup for any given application and organization.

The OpenStack Operations Guide identifies some of the critical files in an OpenStack environment[1]. In particular, these include the configuration database

---

[1] http://docs.openstack.org/trunk/openstack-ops/content/backup_and_recovery.html

on the cloud controller as well as the Nova, Keystone, Glance, Cinder and Swift directories on their respective nodes. It is important to back these up regularly, ideally using an automated procedure.

Versioning

Some storage services, such as OpenStack Swift, provide facilities for versioning information. The advantage is primarily financial. In theory, it is always possible to implement your own versioning scheme simply by labeling the data with a version number. However, you would be multiplying your storage costs with each incremental version of the data. If you are able to access versioned storage, then you can reduce these charges.

If you are using flat storage and need to version information that is primarily static, you can also look at saving only the differential with each version. There will be some effort in comparing versions and reapplying changes when you need to revert, but it might be more cost effective.

In any case, for your application data as well as the application code and configuration you need to decide on the number of versions to maintain and develop a process for storing and retrieving them once needed.

Interoperability

A lack of interoperability (and also portability) locks the customer in to a particular cloud service provider, which restricts the ability to move to another cloud offering or to another vendor. At a minimum, data migration and conversion takes time and effort. Processing incompatibilities can often lead to a disruption of service. The costs increase even more when there is a need for application re-engineering, business process changes or retraining of personnel on new applications.

It is also important not to underestimate the security implications of lock in. A disruptive transition in service can easily lead to a loss of data or application security since different data protection, key management and operational policies may expose security gaps.

Interoperability and portability are related but not precisely identical (Cloud Security Alliance, 2011). Interoperability means that components use standard and open interfaces, allowing them to interoperate and exchange data with other non-proprietary systems. An implication of interoperability is that it should be possible to replace components with products of other providers without any need to reconfigure the rest of the system.

Portability describes the ability to move and reuse components within a heterogeneous environment. Using standard interfaces and formats is a very important factor as it is for interoperability. But the focus with portability is in ensuring that a product will be able to work on different platforms and operating systems and that it will integrate with the infrastructure wherever it runs.

These objectives facilitate flexibility and are relevant for all kinds of cloud computing. As selection criteria for cloud providers, they help to prevent vendor lock-in as well as facilitate disaster recovery and redundancy by allowing identical cloud deployments to occur in different cloud provider solutions. Interoperability and portability are always critical whether the delivery model is private, public or hybrid and whether the services consumed are infrastructure, platforms or software.

A key consideration for private cloud is the interoperability between hypervisors, such as VMware, Hyper-V, KVM and Xen. It also requires standard APIs for administrative functions, such as VM image management and storage management. In the public cloud, the question is whether the interfaces to cloud services are vendor specific or adhere to open specifications, such as the Open Cloud Computing Interface (OCCI). If they do not implement standard interfaces themselves, then at least the semantics should allow them to be abstracted with libraries such as Apache libcloud.

In addition to verifying the internal and external cloud providers individually, users of hybrid clouds need to minimize the number of different interfaces and APIs. They should also enable federation between cloud providers to simplify management points and maximize scalability.

Infrastructure as a Service

Infrastructure is generally modularized into standard architectural components. This makes it more suitable for interoperability than platforms and software. Still, the fact that it can be standardized doesn't mean that it necessarily is.

When physical systems have unique features and functions, there is the temptation to leverage the additional value to optimize the performance and usability of applications. However, the benefits need to be weighed against the disadvantages. These enhancements will invariably change over time and will not be supported by other providers. As such it is best to avoid direct hardware access where possible and instead create an abstraction layer for network and security devices that allows a standard API regardless of the physical implementation.

EMPOWER

Storage is an area of special attention. Starting at the highest layer, unstructured data should use an established portable format (PDF, Word, PowerPoint). Structured data is most portable if it is in a standard SQL database. However, there may be requirements for large data sets to be placed into NoSQL storage for scalability and speed of access. In this case, there is a need to assess and plan for any export and conversion of data in the event it is necessary to switch to a different platform.

Generally, virtualization is a step in the direction of interoperability since it abstracts most of the differences at the hardware level. However, given differences between common hypervisors (such as Hyper-V, Xen, VMware and others), there is a need for standardization at the virtualization level too. Open formats such as Distributed Management Task Force (DMTF) Open Virtualization format (OVF) help ensure interoperability.

Regardless of the technology, customers must identify any provider-specific extensions to the virtual machine environment and plan how to capture and port virtual images to other cloud providers that use different virtualization technologies.

Platform as a Service (PaaS)

PaaS delivers a platform on which developers can develop and deploy custom applications without infrastructure. This includes a runtime environment, a set of tools and an integrated application stack. Cloud platforms are highly diverse and show no signs of converging in the immediate future.

It is relatively difficult to create seamlessly portable PaaS applications. However, there are some environments that at least share components with each other. And the developers can often make choices that increase the ease with which applications can be migrated to another platform.

Ideally, the platform will expose APIs based on open standards (e.g. Open Cloud Computing Interface [OCCI]) and offer some tools for secure data transfer, backup, and restore. Common programming languages (e.g. Java, Ruby, Python) with standard syntax will make it easier to run the code on a different platform without modification.

Where there are provider-specific extensions, it will be helpful to abstract these in order to minimize proprietary components. Customers should also consider portability of administrative interfaces, such as monitoring, logging, and auditing.

Software as a Service (SaaS)

Interoperability and portability take on a different meaning in SaaS. The customer doesn't have access to the code or other internals, so it doesn't necessarily matter whether these are standards-based. However, there will be some interfaces into the application, and the service consumer will want to ensure that these can be easily replicated to other providers.

EMPOWER

The most obvious interface is the human user. If the user experience is intuitive and similar to that provided by other systems, there will be less need to change business processes and re-train users. It is also important to consider whether the service requires any plug-ins or client software on the user's device as these would need to be distributed, managed and eventually removed.

The biggest technical interface of a SaaS solution is usually the import and export of data. Particularly the latter is important to plan as part of an exit strategy. This will imply regular data extractions and backups of both primary data and metadata to a format that is internally readable.

Management

Regardless of the service, the customer must consider integration with its internal environment including management, monitoring, and reporting interfaces. If any custom tools are required, there should be a contingency plan to enable similar functionality to other vendors.

Defining standards for governance is not easy since SLAs will differ across providers and services. Customers will need to examine the differences and evaluate impact on business processes and internal service delivery. In particular, they will want to validate their access to system logs, traces and billing records.

Management frameworks should use standard APIs for interoperability and to facilitate migrating applications and data. At the very least, the APIs should be published. If they are not standard, the customer must analyze them and compare them to other competitive offerings both for syntax and functionality.

Last but not least, interoperable security for data and applications residing in the cloud will reduce the potential for exposure if there is a need to transition a service to a different provider. For example, standard authentication protocols (SAML or WS-Security) facilitate portability, assuming that internal IAM systems also support SAML assertions and accept SAML. Similarly, encryption mechanisms should be portable to different environments. This implies that the encryption keys and ideally the key management should be maintained locally. Furthermore log files should be regularly retrieved and converted to a standard format so that analysis tools can read the data even after the service is no longer in use.

OpenStack Interoperability

We need to consider interoperability of OpenStack at two levels. At the highest level, OpenStack has limited compatibility with other cloud platforms. It supports different hypervisors and image formats. It enables plugins for a number of other services. And it uses some of the same protocols and interfaces as other providers. For instance, OpenStack Orchestration is largely based on AWS CloudFormation and therefore partially interoperable with it.

However, we must be careful not to overstate these areas of overlap. They may decrease the friction of moving between providers but they certainly do not eliminate it. Migration is still a major undertaking and its effort will depend in no small part on the implementation choices (e.g. disk formats) of the OpenStack deployment.

At a lower level, we should also investigate interoperability between OpenStack implementations. If we use public OpenStack services, there can be significant differences in the services that are installed and the interfaces that are exposed. In a private environment, it is possible to contain the disparity, but only through careful planning and rigorous policies. Otherwise, differences in distributions, versions, configuration options and plugin choices can easily make the services diverge just as strongly as any two public cloud offerings.

Multi-source

Another option to reduce the dependency on a single vendor is to design solutions that span multiple providers. It is a sledgehammer approach with the potential to be very complex and costly to manage, but that isn't a reason to rule it out completely. It might be considered where dependency on a single provider is not a viable option.

There are several modes of multi-sourcing applications:

Double-active, replicated: The most efficient, but also most complicated, option is to run both providers in parallel and continuously replicate data between them. This assumes they can both provide the same functionality and there is a means of synchronizing their data.

Double-active, independent: A second option is to segment the application, for example by users or products, so that one provider takes care of one segment and another handles the other. There may be inconsistencies in the functionality but that doesn't need to be a problem. For example, certain user groups may need less functionality than others. In the case that one provider service terminates, there is still a ramp up on the other provider; but an existing agreement and limited experience make it easier than starting back at square one with a search for a new provider.

Active/passive: All services may be provided by a single provider with a second in stand-by position only. This means that the customer already has the agreements in place, and a contingency plan can be invoked to switch to the secondary provider if the case arises.

Multi-sourcing an OpenStack deployment is not trivial. In the short term, a double-active, independent or active/passive solution is the easiest way to get started and gain exposure to multiple installations or providers. Once these are operational, it may be feasible to look at a replicated scenario.

EMPOWER

For any of these approaches, it is likely that the administrative burden will be multiplied through selection of additional providers. To simplify the interface and ensure consistency across the deployment, it is worth looking at some of the heterogeneous cloud management platforms, such as RightScale or Dell Enstratius.

Contingency Planning

No matter what cloud service is being used, it is prudent to plan the exit path before commencing the service. In many cases, it will never be necessary to invoke the contingency plan, but before committing resources, services and business processes, it is good to have a fallback position.

At a minimum, this means identifying an alternate provider that could provide a similar service. There should also be a mechanism to export data from the primary provider and import it into the secondary. These mechanisms need to include all data including metadata, logs and reports. After the move, there should be a way to ensure that all sensitive data is deleted from the original system.

A close comparison of the offerings will probably also reveal some differences in functionality and implementation. It is important to identify any hardware/platform based dependencies and gauge their impact on later migration of the application/data.

Finally, it should be clear under what terms it is possible to withdraw from the service prematurely and what costs will be involved for moving data between cloud providers.

Note that even if it does come to an exit, there is no need to burn bridges with the original provider. It may also be that the secondary service fails to meet expectations. Instead, it is prudent to keep the relationship with the original provider on professional terms and potentially even negotiate a fallback option to extend the service or resume it at a later date.

EMPOWER

Practical Recommendations

Lock-in is an unfortunate byproduct of most emerging technologies. Innovation thrives when there are few restrictions on how vendors implement new features. As the market matures, there is a tendency to converge on best practices, which makes it possible to standardize at least a part of the core functionality.

Business Continuity should include three elements in its application to IT strategy:

There is a need for a systematic backup plan that can form the basis of a disaster recovery due to any unforeseeable circumstances.

Interoperability can help to reduce the impact of localized outages but only if the services and products adhere to standards. OpenStack is a good start in this direction but unfortunately it is still not fully interoperable.

Multi-sourcing can minimize disruption and dependency on single providers even more. But even if the other services are OpenStack-based there is still currently a need for a cloud broker to handle smooth interoperation and centralized management.

Extend

Getting the software deployed and working efficiently in production is not the end of the journey. Technology and markets are in constant evolution making it necessary to perpetually adapt. But beyond these externally imposed changes, it is always possible to improve business value by building and extending the infrastructure. Moving up the cloud stack into platforms will drive increased efficiencies for new workloads. Analytics allow IT to generate more business value. And any improvements in the underlying software will help to support new business initiatives and give additional impetus to the community that is building it.

EXTEND

Chapter 23

Build out the Platform

OpenStack is a comprehensive infrastructure offering that will run most applications. There are facilities to automatically deploy, launch, manage and scale these systems, which can make the life of an administrator a lot easier.

But it doesn't achieve all the benefits of cloud computing even in terms of maximizing resource efficiency. To attain this objective we need to re-architect the applications to share more than the base operating system. We need to leverage a common run-time environment and increase developer productivity. In other words, we need to build a cloud platform.

Cloud Platforms

What is a platform? Depending on the context, the word can carry very diverse meanings. For our purposes, it is the set of tools and resources that a programmer uses to develop an application. Every web-application is designed, built and deployed in some environment and is therefore based on a platform.

Some of the features of a platform might include an integrated development environment, a set of programming languages and compilers, a software development kit, run-time libraries and application programming interfaces. The developer may also make use of tools to test, debug and deploy the application. All of these help a programmer and therefore constitute his or her platform.

To illustrate the point, let's consider the other extreme. You could develop a web application that runs hand-coded machine instructions to process HTTP requests. In our experience, most readers will choose to pursue an easier path. We must emphasize that this doesn't automatically mean using a platform service. Platform as a Service (PaaS) is merely one approach to building cloud-based applications, but virtually everyone uses a platform since it is generally more effective and efficient to leverage existing tools and services than to reinvent the wheel.

EXTEND

Chapter 23: Build out the Platform

Components

Let's start with a closer analysis of what a platform entails. We can look at it as a set of tools that automate routine tasks and supply a generic infrastructure and reusable components, thereby freeing the developers from many repetitive tasks so that they can focus on designing added value. They become more productive.

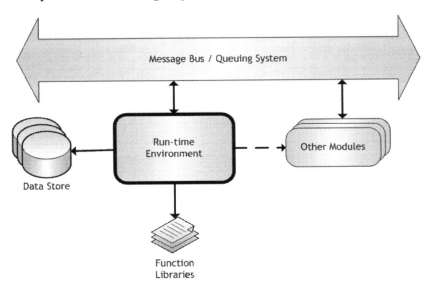

Figure 23-1: Platform Components

Many reusable components will be hosted separately (Figure 23-1). There could be storage facilities that offer highly available and scalable means to persist data and applications. Function libraries may offer computation and other services so that the applications can concentrate on their unique value and take advantage of capabilities that have already been optimized by others. There may also be queuing systems, and other integration infrastructure, that allows the application to easily scale out while working on common tasks in a coordinated fashion.

As mentioned in Chapter 1, platforms may also offer further functions to support the developers, for example:

Integrated Development Environment to develop, test, host and maintain applications

Integration services for marshalling, database integration, security, storage persistence and state management

Scalability services for concurrency management and failover

Instrumentation to track activity and value to the customer

Workflow facilities for application design, development, testing, deployment and hosting

User Interface support for HTML, JavaScript, Flex, Flash, AIR

Visualization tools that show patterns of end-user interactions

Collaboration services to support distributed development and facilitate developer community

Source code services for version control, dynamic multiple-user testing, rollback, auditing and change-tracking

Run-time Environment

One primary feature of the platform is the run-time environment. For a web-based application, this means a server that is on the public Internet and accepts requests, which it processes and passes on to the application. While a simple web site only needs to serve HTML over HTTP, it is very cumbersome to build complex and dynamic web sites that do not utilize some level of server-side business logic and information storage.

In order to facilitate the necessary functionality, a number of application frameworks have developed that alleviate the overhead of authentication, authorization, database access, page templating, server-side caching and session management.

These are often classified according the programming languages that they support:

Visual Basic, C#: ASP.NET is based on Microsoft's Active Server Pages (ASP) technology, revised to leverage the Common Language Runtime (CLR), which is compatible with all Microsoft .NET languages such as Visual Basic and C#. It leverages .NET pages, which consist of HTML as well as dynamic code that is pre-processed when the page is rendered. In addition to in-line mark-up, it is possible to separate the .NET code into a separate file that is only referenced in the .NET page.

While ASP.NET is a component of Microsoft Internet Information Server (IIS), and is closely connected with Microsoft Visual Studio, it is also possible to extend it with other frameworks, such as DotNetNuke, Castle Monorail or Spring.NET.

Ruby: Ruby on Rails is an open-source framework that supports Ruby, a dynamic and reflective object-oriented programming language that is based on Perl, Smalltalk, Eiffel, Ada and Lisp. Ruby on Rails received considerable attention as the original basis for Twitter. However, it suffered when Twitter switched to Scala for a significant portion of their infrastructure needs.

EXTEND

Java: Java requires little introduction as it is a de facto standard for open-source software. However, not all Java environments are identical. There are several Java application frameworks. The best-known include Apache Struts and Spring Framework.

Perl: Perl is a general-purpose programming language that was originally developed for manipulating text, but is now used for a variety of applications including system administration and web development. It is used in a variety of popular frameworks including Catalyst, Jifty and WebGUI.

PHP: PHP was originally developed for building dynamic web content, typically acting as a filter that processes input data and renders HTML. Application frameworks such as Drupal and Joomla have spawned popular ecosystems, which have delivered thousands of modules that enable developers to build extensive content management systems without any custom coding.

Python: Python is characterized by its support of multiple programming paradigms including object-oriented, structured, functional and aspect-oriented programming. One of its most popular application frameworks is Django, which is tailored toward complex, database-driven websites with multiple smaller applications forming the complete web experience. Django is very important in OpenStack since Horizon uses it as its application framework.

PaaS

Platform as a Service has evolved as a hybrid that combines the efficiency of web hosting with the pricing model of infrastructure services. It represents a design that tries to take the best of both while also addressing some of their respective limitations.

Infrastructure-as-a-Service offers many benefits to customers who wish to extend or shift their applications into a cloud-based environment. However, infrastructure services tend to run on platforms that were designed for desktops and traditional client-server environments. They may now be virtualized, but they have not been optimized for the cloud.

To better address the specific needs and advantages of cloud delivery models, some vendors have crafted new platforms that enable faster time-to-market, a common user experience, and an easier development environment. You might see them as an evolution of conventional integrated development environments to support on-line collaboration and a cloud target platform. Ideally, these platforms enable the creation of a new ecosystem that benefits both users and vendors.

EXTEND

Cloud platforms act as run-time environments, which support a set of (compiled or interpreted) programming languages. They may offer additional services such as reusable components and libraries that are available as objects and application programming interfaces. Ideally, the platform will offer plug-ins into common development environments, like Eclipse, to facilitate development, testing and deployment.

From the provider perspective, PaaS is a mechanism for vendors to apply a specific set of constraints to achieve goals that they feel represent the value proposition for their end-users (developers directly, but indirectly also the enterprise IT organization). Those goals tie to the core attributes of cloud computing as follows:

- Elasticity

- Multi-tenancy

- Rapid provisioning and deployment

- Leverage of web technologies and open source

- Integrated monitoring, management and billing facilities

To achieve the above goals the platform vendors usually must apply a set of constraints preventing functionality that might interfere with the required elasticity and security:

- Only specific languages and run-times are provided.

- Not all language/library features are enabled.

- Generic APIs typically replace some of the features or capabilities of traditional stacks.

- There may be size constraints on individual requests.

- Statelessness is encouraged to minimize the overhead of state management.

- Applications need to be written to support scalability following the PaaS vendors' specific requirements.

While these constraints are meant to allow the vendor to achieve the cloud computing goals, vendors usually also add additional value to sweeten the incentive of targeting applications to their platform:

- IDE plug-ins, SDKs and a local emulation environment

- Frameworks that provide the scaffolding and hooks to the platform

- Free developer accounts to accelerate or eliminate provisioning time

- APIs to ease the use of popular services and specifications (e.g. OpenID, Jabber IM)

EXTEND

In summary, the value proposition for PaaS is that it shows some benefits over traditional web platforms in terms of geographically distributed collaboration, facilitation of web service aggregation through centralization of code, reduced costs of infrastructure through the pay-as-you-go model and cost reduction through higher-level programming abstractions. At the same time, PaaS is also simpler to manage than IaaS, represents a smaller platform to distribute, and can leverage more functionality and services from the provider.

OpenStack Platform Services

OpenStack clearly focuses more on IaaS than PaaS, but this doesn't mean it has absolutely no platform capabilities. In fact, we can observe a general industry trend to blur the lines between the two so that it may not be meaningful to make a clear distinction between the two.

The OpenStack approach is similar to AWS, which started with IaaS and gradually added incremental applications-level capabilities. We can contrast that with Google App Engine and Windows Azure, which provided full platform capabilities from the beginning but only later added facilities to work with raw infrastructural resources like virtual machines.

OpenStack doesn't directly provide any run-time environment or client development tools, but it does offer some libraries and services that can also be useful for platforms. For instance, the Marconi queuing services help to support complex web-scale applications. These are critical to the asynchronous coordination of worker instances, which form the foundation of a horizontally scalable service.

Applications can also use Swift for automatically replicated storage. Or, if they have more advanced database needs they may take advantage of Trove (Database as a Service) or Savanna (Hadoop) as we shall see in Chapter 24.

Nonetheless, the fact remains that you need to fill in some additional components in order to launch a fully-fledged PaaS on OpenStack. We will take a look at two platform frameworks that have received a lot of press and have been successfully deployed on OpenStack: Cloud Foundry and OpenShift.

Cloud Foundry

Cloud Foundry is an open-source PaaS developed as part of the Pivotal initiative, a joint venture between VMware and EMC. It also serves as the base of a number of independent PaaS offerings including AppFog, Tier 3, Uhuru and ActiveState.

ActiveState Stackato, in particular, is often deployed in OpenStack environments. It also runs on other clouds such as EC2, VMware or a simple VirtualBox setup. In its simplest form, there are downloadable images for a "micro-cloud", which unites all the Stackato roles in a single instance that is functionally equivalent to a full Stackato cluster.

The platform implements multi-tenancy using Docker so that no tenant is aware of any other organization. It is possible for each customer to have multiple spaces (logical grouping of applications) for example for development, test and production and it is possible to assign different user access rights to each space.

A big benefit is auto-scaling, which is natively supported on OpenStack and CloudStack. It will launch instances whenever the available memory in a pool falls below a certain threshold.

Most of Stackato is available via a web-based GUI, which begins with a landing page (Figure 23-2).

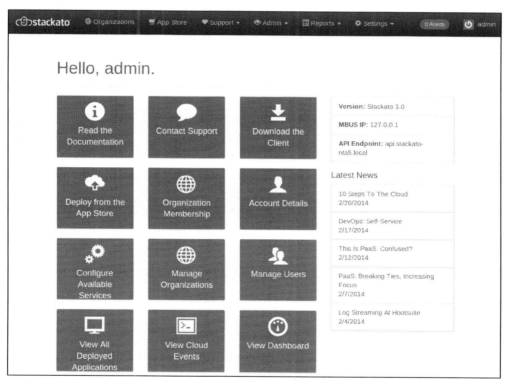

Figure 23-2: Stackato Landing Page

Typically you would begin by creating an organization and users and then assigning them space. You can configure the services available on each node within the cluster (Figure 23-3).

EXTEND

Figure 23-3: Stackato Cluster Node Configuration

The service types available include: filesystem, memcached, mongodb, mysql, postgresql, rabbit, redis, load_balancer, mdns and dea.

You can also look at the dashboard to get a status of the system including the number of requests and router statistics (Figure 23-4).

Figure 23-4: Stackato Router

And you can visualize the performance metrics on the primary node (Figure 23-5).

EXTEND

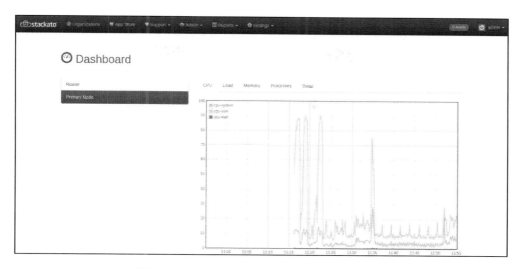

Figure 23-5: Stackato Primary Node

The actual PaaS functionality comes into play when you go into the App Store (Figure 23-6).

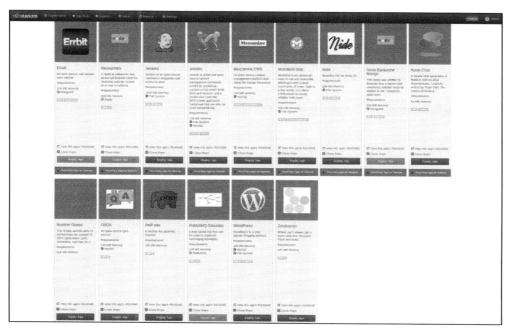

Figure 23-6: Stackato App Store

The App Store can access applications hosted on GitHub or in a local Git repository. They run in Linux containers and can use several runtime environments and languages (e.g. Java, Perl, PHP, Python, Ruby).

EXTEND

We can choose any application in the catalog and deploy an instance of it (Figure 23-7).

Figure 23-7: Stackato Deploy Application

And we can view all deployed applications at any time in the landing page (Figure 23-8).

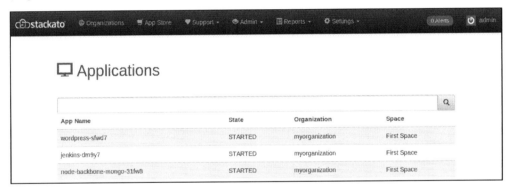

Figure 23-8: Stackato Applications

Those are the primary functions in the web interface. Any configuration of the actual application is done directly to the code. We can download a Stackato client from the landing page and receive the command-line interface that lets us download and update the code and configuration of the deployment. And we can use any tool we like (e.g. a simple text editor or an integrated development environment such as Eclipse) to modify the code.

Red Hat OpenShift

OpenShift is a second PaaS that runs well on OpenStack. It is developed by Red Hat and comes in three versions. The community open-source edition is called OpenShift Origin, which feeds the other two offerings. The commercially supported edition for a private cloud is OpenShift Enterprise. And there is also an online version called OpenShift Online, which is backed by Amazon EC2.

EXTEND

For your first exposure to OpenShift, you may want to try the online edition. It provides limited capabilities for free and doesn't involve any setup. Obviously, to test out OpenStack integration, you would then need to move on to one of the installed editions. You can even use Heat as the orchestration engine to get OpenShift up and running. There are some templates on GitHub[1] to help you out with a typical configuration.

The terminology of OpenShift is not always obvious, so you need to be careful you understand the components. A broker is the management host which orchestrates the nodes. A node is a compute host containing several gears. And a gear is an allocation of fixed memory, compute, and storage; resources for running applications.

Similar to Stackato there is an application catalog (Figure 23-9).

EXTEND

---

[1] https://github.com/openstack/heat-templates/tree/master/

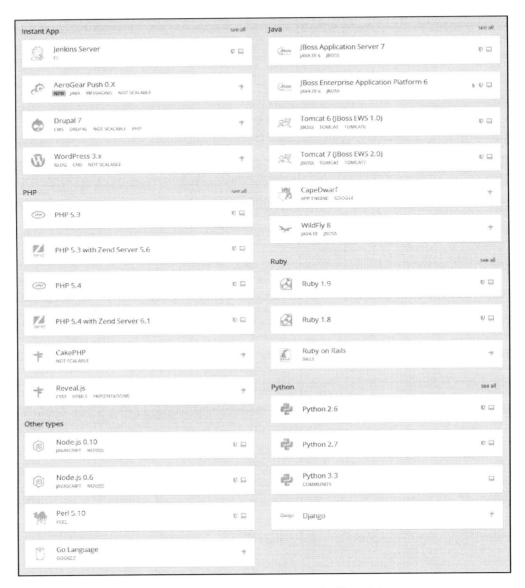

Figure 23-9: OpenShift Framework Cartridges

These applications are called cartridges. A framework cartridge is a technology stack (e.g. PHP, Perl, Java, Ruby, Python, MySQL or JBOSS) along with a procedure to deploy the applications.

EXTEND

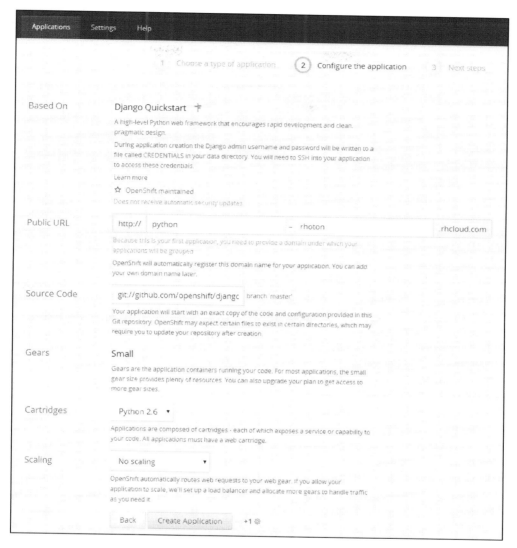

Figure 23-10: OpenShift Create Application

The user can choose any of these framework cartridges and configure an application based on it (Figure 23-10). Note that the term application refers to an instantiation of the cartridge and not to the end-user application. It is possible to specify the gear, scaling options and a Git URL.

The purpose for the latter is interesting. The server holds a Git repository and builds the application from the source. So the application developer does not use a separate client (like with Stackato) but instead just the regular Git interface. Or alternatively they can use an integrated development environment, like Eclipse, with an OpenShift plugin.

EXTEND

In addition to the framework cartridges that we just saw, there are also a set of embedded cartridges (Figure 23-11).

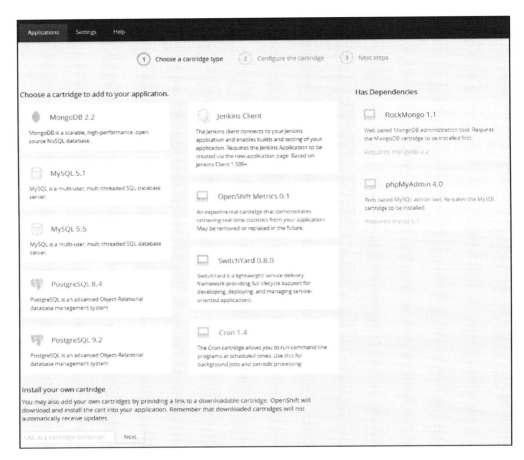

Figure 23-11: OpenShift Add Embedded Cartridge

There are embedded cartridges for Jenkins, Postgres, MySQL, MongoDB, which are only accessible to the corresponding framework cartridge and provide additional functionality to it.

EXTEND

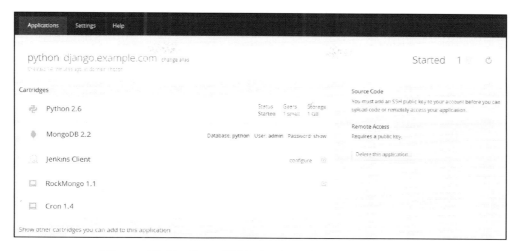

Figure 23-12: OpenShift Application Cartridges

An application can use multiple embedded cartridges which you can always see listed as part of its properties (Figure 23-12).

OpenStack Application Lifecycle Management (Solum)

Cloud Foundry and OpenShift are quite typical platform services for which there is no counterpart in the OpenStack core. However, there is one OpenStack-related project that some would consider to play in the same space.

OpenStack Application Lifecycle Management (Solum) is chartered with making it easy to start writing portable applications and taking them all the way to a production deployment. This sounds suspiciously like a platform service but the emphasis is a little different. In fact, both ActiveState and Red Hat are active proponents of Solum, which they see as complementary to their own offerings.

The focus of Solum is on taking source code, putting it through a continuous integration / continuous delivery process, giving developers the ability to build, review, test and gate the code.

It should automatically generate Heat templates and feed them into the deployment to monitor, scale and heal the application. In doing so, it would also leverage several of the other OpenStack programs including Keystone, Nova and Trove as well as other technologies such as Docker and popular run-time environments.

In any case, it is too early to make any real assessment of Solum. Coding didn't begin until late 2013 and the project was not even in official incubation in early 2014. There is no way to predict what will happen at this stage but it is an activity to monitor carefully.

EXTEND

Practical Recommendations

You'll probably have your hands full on your first deployment just setting up the infrastructure to run your existing software packages. But if you are already planning new development, you should consider how you can optimize it to leverage some of the benefits cloud has to offer.

While OpenStack has a few services that may be useful to applications, the richest environments for developing multi-tenant applications are platform services such as ActiveState Stackato or Red Hat OpenShift. There is some work on Application Lifecycle Management that certainly looks promising but isn't yet ready for production.

EXTEND

Chapter 24

Embrace Big Data

Big Data is usually defined using the three Vs: volume, velocity and variety. It involves large amounts of data being ingested rapidly from many sources. These include explicit human data collection and recording of business transactions but also data shared from partner companies, a vast set of public information from social networking sites, and even many machines, appliances and sensors that are now able to connect to the network. It lends itself well to cloud delivery because it involves highly resource-intensive workloads that typically run only periodically.

Start with Small Data

Before we dive into Big Data let's consider what we can do with 'small data'. One key differentiator between most Big Data systems and traditional databases it the absence of a relational model. Relational databases emerged in the 1970s. Until then data was stored in files in ad-hoc formats and accessing the data required a program that was able to navigate the internal structure. They include a collection of tables of data items, all of which is formally described and organized according to the relational model.

Relational databases are accessible via a Structured Query Language (SQL), both for interactive queries and for gathering data for reports. Over the last four decades, SQL databases have become pervasive as they are relatively easy to create, access and extend. And they provide a degree of interoperability between products and implementations.

The majority of today's applications run quite well on a SQL database and there is no reason you can't use them in an OpenStack deployment.

OpenStack Database as a Service (Trove)

Trove is Database as a Service for OpenStack. It isn't strictly a requirement to use Trove in order to include a SQL database in an OpenStack project. You could install the database yourself in a Nova instance and store the data on one

EXTEND

or more Cinder volumes. But Trove allows users to provision database instances on demand and leverage the features of a relational database without the burden of complex administration.

To provide scalable and reliable Cloud Database as a Service provisioning functionality for both relational and non-relational database engines, it uses three services: the Task Manager, Guest Agent and Conductor[1].

> The **Task Manager** manages the lifecycle of instances and executes tasks that it receives via the message queue, such as to create an instance or resize the database flavor.

> The **Guest Agent** runs within a guest instance and is responsible for managing and performing operations on the datastore itself. For example, it brings a datastore online and sends heartbeat messages to the API.

> **Conductor** is the counterpart of the Guest agent running on the host. It receives guest messages and processes them on the host.

As we mentioned above, Big Data is not only a question of the size of the data set. You can scale conventional databases to handle most application requirements. Big Data is about highly complex data processing often involving a whole ecosystem of complementary tools.

Hadoop and MapReduce

One specific technique for processing large sets of data in parallel is MapReduce. It is often associated with cloud computing since it lends itself well to cloud-scale problems and many cloud providers have created offerings that build on the MapReduce paradigm. The main principle behind it is not that difficult to understand, however an actual implementation can become quite complex.

It's beyond the scope of this book to explore the subject in great depth. We refer interested readers to one of the excellent books on Hadoop for more information, such as White (2012) or Holmes (2012). In this chapter, we will just look at the main concepts, which we approach through a series of basic questions:

- What is it?

- What is it good for?

- Why use it?

- What does it do?

- How does it work?

---

[1] https://wiki.openstack.org/wiki/TroveArchitecture

- How do you use it?

We will focus on Hadoop. Nonetheless, most of the principles would also apply to other implementations of MapReduce.

What is it?

Google was the first company to publicize MapReduce, inspired by the 'map' and 'reduce' functions from functional programming. They initially invented the technique to build production search indexes, but extended it into a general software framework. Its key attraction was its support of distributed computing on petascale data-sets using clusters of inexpensive computers.

MapReduce is also the core function included in Hadoop, an open-source project available from Apache. As we mentioned earlier, it was created by Doug Cutting, who used it for the Nutch search engine project. Since then, Hadoop has become the most popular open-source implementation of MapReduce, with a strong following in the grid and cloud computing communities, including developers at Google, Yahoo, Microsoft, and Facebook.

The Hadoop MapReduce framework requires a shared file system. It typically operates over the Hadoop Distributed File System (HDFS) but there is no absolute dependency for HDFS as long as a distributed file system plug-in is available to the framework.

The model receives its name from the two primary functions it executes:

Map is an initial ingestion step to process the raw data in parallel. The master node reads the input, segments it into smaller chunks, and distributes those to the processing nodes.

Reduce is an aggregation step which collects the output of all the Map functions and combines them to produce the result of the original problem.

There is some similarity to the concept of sharding, described in Chapter 21, in that there is an assumption of effective data partitioning making it possible for each of these two phases to implement a high degree of parallelism.

What is it good for?

MapReduce is ideally suited to processing very large data sets. It is useful in a wide range of tasks and applications including: batch processing, building search index engines, image analysis, distributed grep, distributed sort, graph traversal, web access log stats, inverted index construction, document clustering, machine learning algorithms and statistical machine translation. Some analytical frameworks, such as Hive and Pig, are also built on top of Hadoop. They facilitate extracting information from databases for Hadoop processing.

EXTEND

Hadoop includes a set of simple examples to illustrate how MapReduce works (Table 24-1), e.g. computing the maximum of a set of numbers, adding a set of numbers, and counting the occurrences of words in a large text or collection of texts (e.g. The Complete Works of William Shakespeare)[1].

AggregateWordCount	Counts the words in the input files.
AggregateWordHistogram	Computes a histogram of the words in the input files.
DBCountPageView	Uses DBInputFormat for reading the input data from a database, and DBOutputFormat for writing the data to the database.
Grep	Counts the matches of a regular expression in the input.
Join	Fragments and sorts the input values over sorted, equally partitioned datasets.
MultiFileWordCount	Demonstrates the usage of MultiFileInputFormat by counting words from several files.
PiEstimator	Estimate the value of Pi using quasi-Monte Carlo method.
RandomTextWriter	Run a distributed job without interaction between the tasks. Each task writes a large unsorted random sequence of words.
RandomWriter	Runs a distributed job without interaction between the tasks. Each task write a large unsorted random binary sequence file of BytesWritable.
SecondarySort	Sorts the data written by the random writer.
SleepJob	Sleeps at each map and reduce task.
Sort<K,V>	Uses the framework to fragment and sort the input values.
WordCount	Counts the words in a set of input files.

Table 24-1 : Hadoop Sample Classes

Although MapReduce can help to solve a wide range of problems, it is important to realize that not all use cases are suitable. In particular, interactive applications cannot leverage the framework synchronously as it is intended for bulk processing rather than real-time queries.

MapReduce is appropriate for write-once, read-many (WORM) applications with static data that may be analyzed repeatedly. As such it stands in contrast to

EXTEND

---

[1] As documented by Hadoop: http://hadoop.apache.org/docs/current/

relational databases that can handle data being continuously updated. The framework also shines when there is a need to process unstructured data, since it interprets the data at processing time rather than relying on intrinsic properties or schemas.

Why use it?

Just because MapReduce can handle a given problem doesn't meant that it is the best solution. You might even wonder why it is attractive at all since you could implement a distributed processing model yourself without the overhead and constraints of a framework. Where it fits, there are at least three clear benefits to using MapReduce:

Scale: Most importantly, the programming model scales transparently. The developer-written functions concentrate on mapping and reducing without taking the size of the dataset into account. It is the framework that orchestrates the workload, allocating it to the systems that are available.

Performance: MapReduce also offers good performance for processing petascale, data sets which are highly sensitive to latency and bandwidth constraints. Its first step is to co-locate the data with the compute node where possible so data access is local. An inefficient network topology can easily lead to saturated network links so MapReduce explicitly models the physical layout.

Fault tolerance: Fault tolerance is another benefit. The framework detects failed map or reduce tasks and reschedules replacements on machines that are healthy. The programmer can ignore the order of task execution and doesn't need to verify that they run successfully.

These three features are native to the framework. Unless you have very different requirements, it will usually be easier and faster to leverage a mature tool than to reinvent the functionality.

What does it do?

As mentioned above, the MapReduce model is based on two distinct steps for an application. The Map step processes individual records in parallel while the Reduce step aggregates and/or refines the output of many different Map systems. The framework is largely agnostic to the data structures involved, but requires them to be packaged as key-value pairs. The only constraint imposed is that the output of the map tasks must match the input of the reduce tasks.

EXTEND

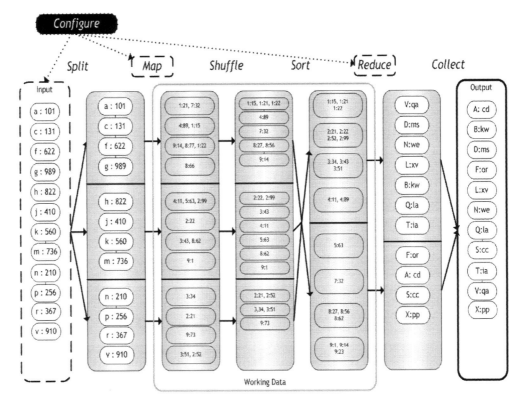

Figure 24-1: MapReduce Data Flow

As shown very simplistically in Figure 24-1, the key-value pairs have three possible data domains: the input data to the Map function; the output of the Map tasks, which also corresponds to the input format for the Reduce function; and the output of the Reduce tasks. In some cases, the input, intermediate and output data will be similar, while in other scenarios, they may be very different.

The steps involved in the MapReduce job include:

- *User*:   Configure
- *Framework*:   Split
- *User*:   Map
- *Framework*:   Shuffle
- *Framework*:   Sort
- *User*:   Reduce
- *Framework*:   Collect

EXTEND

Initially the user *Configures* the job by specifying the data locations for input and output and providing the Map and Reduce functions to the Framework.

The framework then aggregates the entire input (which may be spread across several files) and *Splits* it into equitable chunks. It then distributes the chunks to the Map processes that are running on the Hadoop cluster, passing the input in the form of key-value pairs.

The user-written *Map* function analyzes or transforms each data item from an input key-value pair into a set of output key-value pairs.

Each per-map output is then partitioned and sorted as part of the *Shuffle* stage. The output generated from each sorted partition is referred to as a spill. The framework will pull the spill from the output of each map task, and merge-sort these spills.

The entire output is then aggregated and repartitioned according to the number of Reduce processes available. A *Sort* function orders the key-value pairs before passing them on to the Reduce function.

The *Reduce* function again acts once on each input key and returns a set of key-value pairs for each call.

Finally the framework *Collects* all the Reduce outputs and returns them to the user.

How does it work?

To understand how Hadoop works, it is helpful to consider how it is structured and the responsibilities of each component. The master/slave architecture of HDFS is central to the way a Hadoop cluster functions. There are four required daemons in each Hadoop cluster:

NameNode: Manages the namespace, file system metadata, and access control.

JobTracker: Delegates tasks to the slave nodes (TaskTrackers).

DataNode: Implements the file system through its locally-attached storage. Each node stores a partial (or complete) copy of the blocks in the file system.

TaskTracker: Executes the map and reduce tasks.

There is exactly one NameNode and one JobTracker in each cluster. However, there can be more than one DataNode and TaskTracker. In fact, a replicated file system implies that you have more than one DataNode. Most clusters run the NameNode and JobTracker on dedicated systems for simplicity and performance reasons. On the other hand, in order to implement data proximity, it is most efficient for the other machines (called 'slaves') to run both DataNode and TaskTracker daemons.

EXTEND

In addition to the four components above, there is a Secondary NameNode that provides a degree of redundancy. It is critical since the NameNode represents a single point of failure in a Hadoop cluster – its absence could make the cluster and filesystem unavailable. The Secondary NameNode prevents permanent loss of state by performing periodic checkpoints of the namespace and putting size limits on the log files.

Hadoop comes with a web UI for viewing information about your jobs. It is useful for following a job's progress while it is running, as well as finding job statistics and logs after the job has completed. The web server on the NameNode reports the status of the DataNodes and capacity of the distributed filesystem. The administrator can also inspect the TaskTrackers and JobTracker.

How do you use it?

If you are expecting to run Hadoop in production, then you'll eventually need personnel with a strong knowledge of Linux and Java. However, you can easily experiment with it using prebuilt images and example programs if your intention is only to familiarize yourself with the technology.

To install Hadoop, you would first download and install all the required software[1]. Although Windows isn't recommended for production, you can run a proof of concept on the platform as long as you install and configure cygwin.

If you'd rather not install the software yourself there are VMware system images available on Google Code and Cloudera provides Debian and RPM installer files as well as pre-built Amazon Machine Images.

Hadoop supports three operating modes:

Standalone: The default Hadoop configuration is a single Java process. There is little value in running this mode for a production application but it is helpful for learning about Hadoop and debugging Hadoop applications.

Pseudo-distributed: In pseudo-distributed mode all the Hadoop daemons reside on a single system but each daemon (NameNode, DataNode, JobTracker, TaskTracker) runs in a separate Java process. A functioning NameNode/DataNode manages the HDFS, which is hosted in a separate namespace from the local file system and stored as block objects in a Hadoop-managed directory. It is possible to extend a pseudo-distributed instance into a fully distributed cluster by adding more machines as Task/DataNodes.

Fully-distributed: In fully distributed mode, Hadoop runs on multiple nodes with distributed NameNode, JobTracker, DataNodes, and TaskTrackers. The

EXTEND

---

[1] http://hadoop.apache.org/releases.html

simplest implementation involves two nodes, one running all four primary daemons, while the other node only hosts a DataNode and TaskTracker. Clusters of three or more machines typically use dedicated systems for the NameNode and JobTracker, and assign all other nodes as workers (running TaskTracker and DataNode).

As you may recall, the Hadoop MapReduce framework requires a shared file system. HDFS lends itself best since Hadoop is able to leverage its location-awareness in allocating tasks. However, MapReduce is not limited to HDFS. It can also use any distributed file system for which a plug-in is available. Hadoop Core supports the Cloud-Store (formerly Kosmos) file system and Amazon Simple Storage Service (S3) file system. Any distributed file system that is visible as a system-mounted file system, such as Network File System (NFS), Global File System (GFS), or Lustre can also be used with MapReduce.

Complex configurations involving multiple racks of machines can be optimized with HDFS but require special planning. If Hadoop knows which node hosts a physical copy of input data, it can schedule tasks on the same machine as the data. To minimize the possibility of data loss during rack failures, blocks should be replicated on multiple racks. A rack-aware placement policy can be enforced through a script or a Hadoop interface called DNSToSwitchMapping, with which Java code can map servers onto a rack topology.

The heart of a MapReduce system comprises the Map and Reduce functions. Hadoop can run MapReduce programs written in various languages; such as Java, Ruby, Python, and C++. The application developer needs to provide four items to the Hadoop framework:

- class that reads the input records and transforms them into one key/value pair per record
- map method
- reduce method
- class that transforms the key/value pairs from the reduce task into output records

To start off the process, the user provides the format and file-location of input and output data as well as a JAR file including the classes for the map and reduce functions.

Unfortunately, we can't go into much more detail on the actual programming in this book but instead refer you to aforementioned books on Hadoop as well as the copious online documentation.

EXTEND

OpenStack Data Processing (Savanna)

As described above, Apache Hadoop is an industry-standard, open-source MapReduce implementation. In theory, you could download the software or machine image as we described and create your own Heat templates to deploy a cluster based on these images.

Savanna simplifies this process by providing users with a pre-packaged means to provision Hadoop clusters only specifying some of the key parameters, such as Hadoop version, cluster topology and nodes hardware details. Savanna then deploys the cluster and facilitates the scaling of running clusters by adding/removing worker nodes on demand.

Savanna integrates tightly with the other OpenStack services (Figure 24-2). Horizon provides the user interface for administering the system while Keystone handles the authentication. Glance holds the images for all of the nodes that will run Hadoop jobs. These are then loaded into Nova as the clusters are provisioned. It is also possible to place all the Hadoop data into Swift objects, which the jobs can access and process.

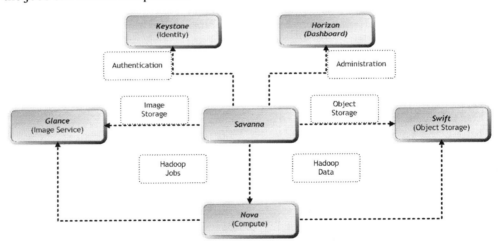

Figure 24-2: Savanna Integration into OpenStack

One of the first challenges to consider is how to get Savanna onto your OpenStack installation at all. It isn't a core project, so it's not bundled with most distributions. You should be able to find instructions for installing it with RDO on the OpenStack site[1], but the easiest way to try it out is to use Mirantis Fuel. You can enable Savanna by checking a box when creating your OpenStack Environment (Figure 24-3).

---

[1] http://docs.openstack.org/developer/savanna/userdoc/installation.guide.html

Figure 24-3: Fuel Savanna Environment

If Savanna is installed and has been added to Horizon, then you should see it appear as a third tab beside the Project and Admin tabs.

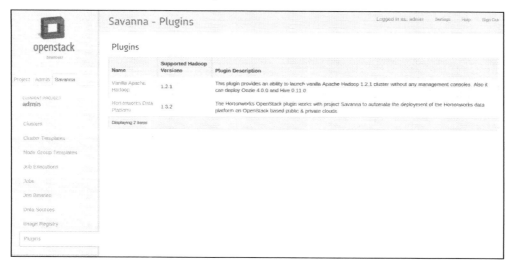

Figure 24-4: Savanna Plugins

One point to note is that there may be multiple plugins. For example, there may be a Hortonworks Data Platform plugin in addition to the Vanilla Apache Hadoop implementation (Figure 24-4).

EXTEND

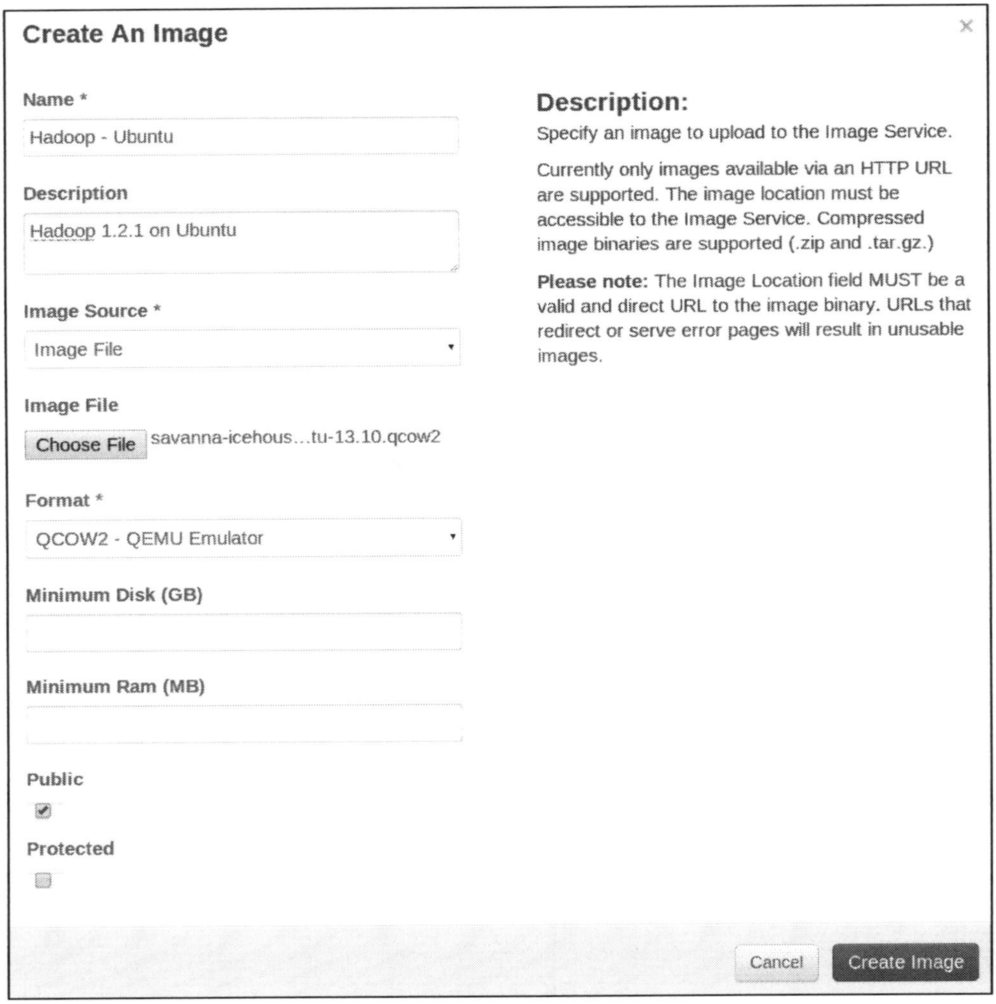

Create An Image

Name *

Hadoop - Ubuntu

Description

Hadoop 1.2.1 on Ubuntu

Image Source *

Image File

Image File

Choose File   savanna-icehous...tu-13.10.qcow2

Format *

QCOW2 - QEMU Emulator

Minimum Disk (GB)

Minimum Ram (MB)

Public
☑

Protected
☐

Description:

Specify an image to upload to the Image Service.

Currently only images available via an HTTP URL are supported. The image location must be accessible to the Image Service. Compressed image binaries are supported (.zip and .tar.gz.)

Please note: The Image Location field MUST be a valid and direct URL to the image binary. URLs that redirect or serve error pages will result in unusable images.

Cancel   Create Image

Figure 24-5: Upload Hadoop Image to Glance

Before you begin with the actual Savanna operations, you need to upload a Hadoop image to Glance (Figure 24-5). You should be able to find suitable images on the OpenStack documentation site[1].

EXTEND

[1] http://docs.openstack.org/developer/savanna/userdoc/installation.guide.html

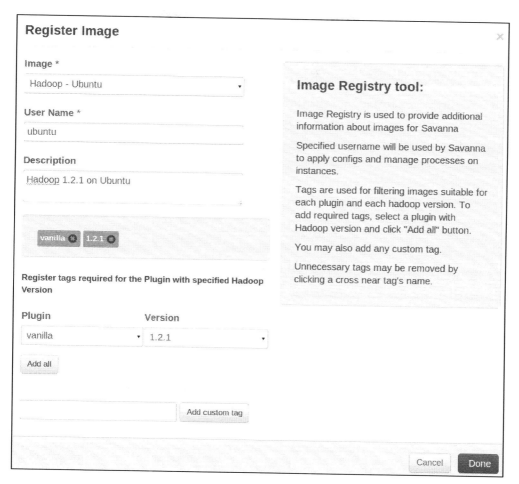

Figure 24-6: Register Image in Savanna

Next you register the image so that it is visible to Savanna (Figure 24-6).

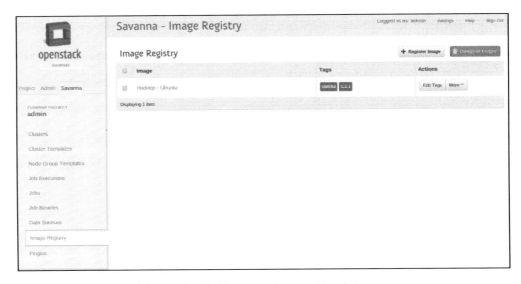

Figure 24-7: Savanna Image Registry

And it should appear in the registry (Figure 24-7).

The next steps assume you are familiar with some of the terminology introduced earlier in this chapter. It is possible to implement fully distributed Hadoop operation with multiple DataNodes and TaskTrackers in a single cluster. In order to segregate these resources into logical pools, it is also possible to define Node Groups. Each Node Group Template contains a list of Hadoop processes to launch on every instance within the group.

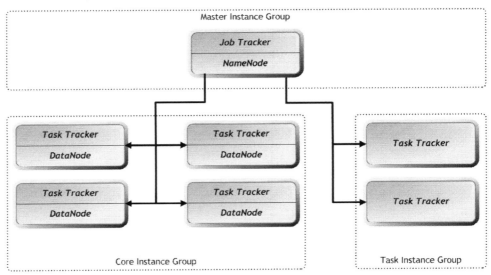

Figure 24-8: Sample Hadoop Cluster

EXTEND

For example, we might define a Hadoop cluster (Figure 24-8) with one group (Master Instance Group) holding only the JobTracker and NameNode and a second (Core Instance Group) containing the core instances, each consisting of a TaskTracker and DataNode. We may also have a third (Task Instance Group) that only has TaskTrackers.

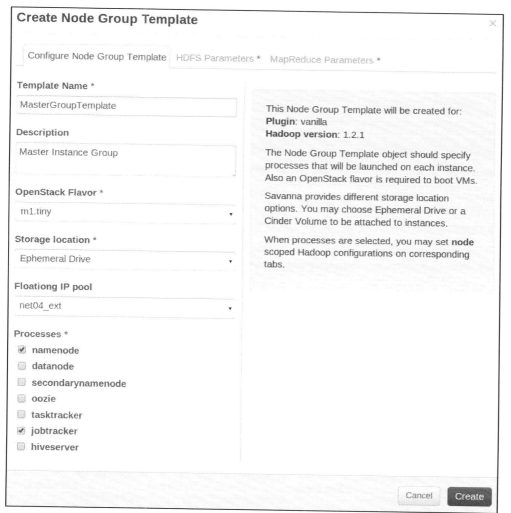

Figure 24-9: Create Savanna Node Group Template

We would begin by defining the Node Group Templates, which specify the OpenStack Flavor and the Hadoop processes that should run on these nodes (Figure 24-9).

Chapter 24: Embrace Big Data

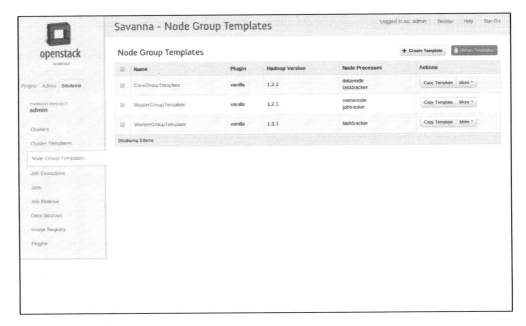

Figure 24-10: Savanna Node Group Template List

After creating all the required Node Group Templates (Figure 24-10), we can go on to create a Cluster Template that indicates which Node Groups comprise the cluster and how many instances to launch in each group (Figure 24-11). Here you can specify any anti-affinity settings to preclude processes being launched more than once on any physical host.

EXTEND

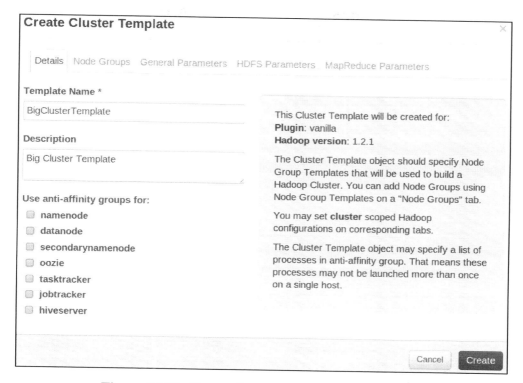

Figure 24-11: Create Savanna Cluster Template

You also need to identify which Node Groups belong to this cluster and indicate their instance count (Figure 24-12).

Chapter 24: Embrace Big Data

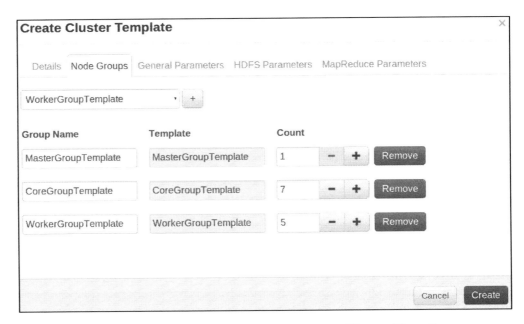

Figure 24-12: Add Node Group Templates to Cluster Template

You can repeat this step to create multiple different cluster configurations that you might need for different jobs (Figure 24-13).

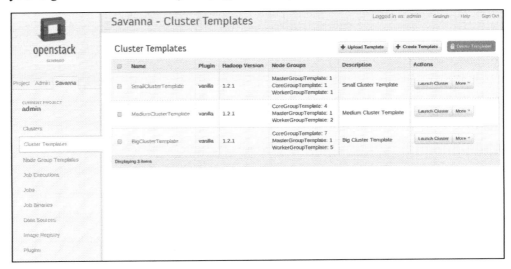

Figure 24-13: Savanna Cluster Template List

And finally you can launch the cluster (Figure 24-14).

EXTEND

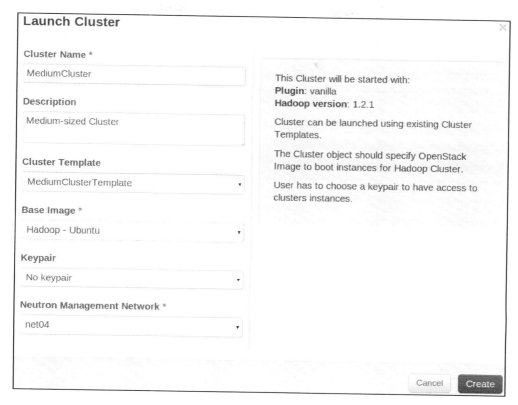

Figure 24-14: Launch Savanna Cluster

Obviously, there is a lot more to it if you want to perform any useful analysis. For example, you need to supply the MapReduce functions and import all the data. But that is beyond the scope of this chapter, which is just to expose you to the basic UI.

EXTEND

Practical Recommendations

Working with Big Data is a whole new ballgame. It isn't just a question of implementing the technology, but requires careful analysis of the business. You need an inventory of what data you have on hand or can easily obtain. And you need to determine what insight you require to serve your customers better, grow your market and improve your operating efficiency.

Then you have to figure out how to get those answers from the data available and write the functions to execute the business logic. When you have all this, you will need to set up the infrastructure to handle the load. This is where Savanna comes into the picture and it can do a great job of helping you deploy big and complex workloads.

However, if you haven't gone through all the requisite analysis yet, you may want to focus on traditional databases, for example using Trove, for your first deployments and legacy applications.

Chapter 25

Shape the Product

If you have had the patience to read the whole book up to this point, then you will realize that OpenStack has a great deal of capability covering a range of functions. But there are still quite a few gaps and areas for improvement and enhancement.

The momentum is impressive. The community is initiating, incubating and merging new projects on a regular basis. So if you need something that isn't available now, there is a good chance it may appear in the future. However, you may not have the luxury of waiting until then.

Since the software is open-source, you have the same opportunity as anyone else to extend the functionality yourself. You may need to invest to build the necessary competence, but there is no technical problem that you can't address on your own.

For those who choose to go down that path, an inevitable question is how to maintain and support the extended functionality. If you believe it gives you a strong competitive advantage, you may want to keep the extensions for yourself. However, this also means you need to update it with every release of the underlying technology and support it indefinitely. You won't be able to optimize it based on feedback from others or share best practices on how to implement it.

On the other hand, if you choose to share the new code with the community by committing it upstream, you obtain better quality control through the sheer number of expert reviewers. And you benefit from any of the innovation they can add to your extensions.

If you are planning on extending OpenStack at the code level, or just want to have a better idea of its internal workings, then you probably want to start by looking at the development process.

EXTEND

OpenStack Development Workflow

By definition, open-source development is open to contribution from anyone. Any project of size therefore needs to introduce a structure for coordinating modifications and extensions, so that updates don't overwrite each other or lead to an unstable system. In the case of OpenStack, development generally passes through a workflow that involves three main tools (Figure 25-1)[1].

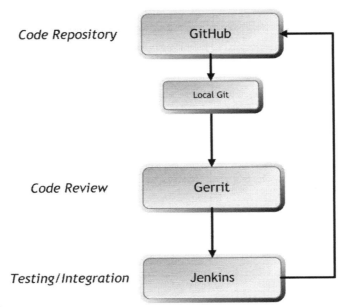

Figure 25-1: Code Review Process

The entire source is hosted on GitHub. Anyone who wants to make a fix would clone the relevant elements to a local system and apply any changes there.

The next step is to post the updates to Gerrit, where other interested parties can scrutinize the modifications and either reject or accept them.

If accepted, the last action is to run an automated tool that performs some functional tests to verify that the proposed change has not broken any other functionality. If these checks are successful, the update is applied to the central repository on GitHub.

Let's look at each of these three tools in more detail.

EXTEND

---

[1] https://wiki.openstack.org/wiki/GerritJenkinsGit

GitHub

GitHub is a popular cloud-based service for software development projects that use Git for revision control and source-code management.

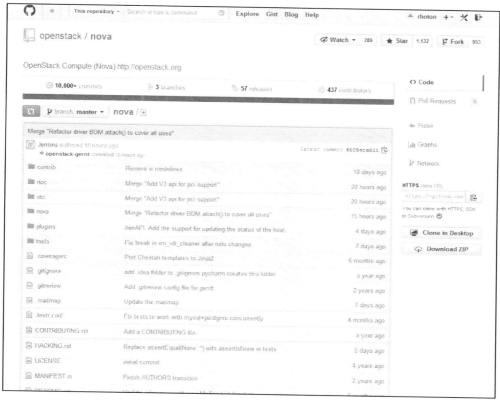

Figure 25-2: OpenStack Nova on GitHub

If you go to GitHub's OpenStack page[1], you will find links to Nova (Figure 25-2), Swift, Cinder and all the other main OpenStack programs. You can build an OpenStack deployment directly from source by cloning from GitHub (as we described in Chapter 6) or you can just browse through the repository to read the code and familiarize yourself with the software. The modules are well organized and largely self-documenting, so they should be readable for anyone with a development background and a basic understanding of OpenStack.

EXTEND

---

[1] https://github.com/openstack

Gerrit

Gerrit is a web-based, open-source code review system that is tightly integrated with Git. It adds visualization to the review process by showing changes in a side-by-side display and allows reviewers to add inline comments. It also permits authorized users to submit changes to the master Git repository rather than requiring a manual merge of approved changes.

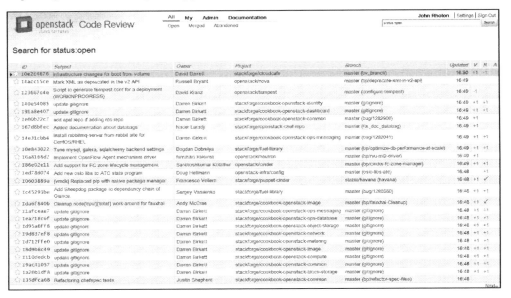

Figure 25-3: Gerrit Code Review Listing

On the Gerrit Code Review[1] page, you can find a listing of all proposed changes to OpenStack (Figure 25-3).

---

[1] https://review.openstack.org

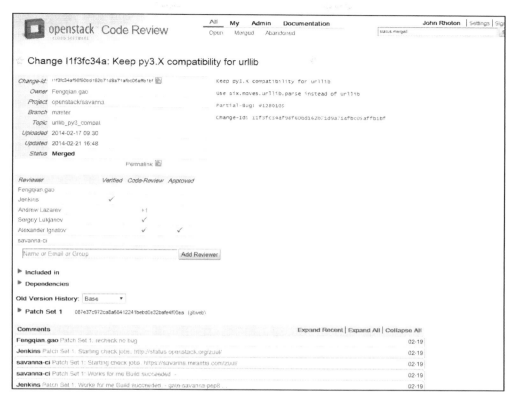

Figure 25-4: Gerrit Code Review Entry

You can drill down on any submission to see who has already reviewed it and what comments they have had (Figure 25-4).

Jenkins

Jenkins[1] is an open-source tool that was forked from Hudson. It provides continuous integration services for software development supporting Git as well as other Source Control Management tools such as CVS, Subversion and Mercurial.

Builds can be started by various means, including being triggered by commit in a version control system, scheduled via a cron-like mechanism, built when other builds have completed, or requested through a specific build URL. They can execute Apache Ant and Apache Maven based projects as well as arbitrary shell scripts and Windows batch commands.

EXTEND

---

[1] http://jenkins-ci.org/

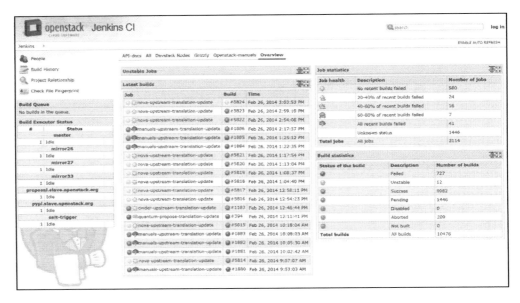

Figure 25-5: Jenkins Dashboard

OpenStack integration testing is performed by the devstack gate test framework, which runs a set of Jenkins Jobs and Tempest smoketests against a devstack installation. The latest build jobs are listed on the OpenStack Jenkins Dashboard (Figure 25-5)[1] along with an indication as to whether they were successful.

OpenStack Community

You can find most of the critical data on the OpenStack build process in the tools above. But there is also a wealth of out-of-band communication surrounding many of the proposed changes. Some of the OpenStack community collaboration tools are also a good place to look for background information or to ask for help when you run into difficulty.

Some popular tools include Launchpad, mailing lists and IRC channels.

Launchpad

Launchpad is a cloud service from Canonical that helps users develop and maintain software. OpenStack's Launchpad page[2] presents a consolidated view of the whole system, but you can drill down into the individual programs (Figure 25-6).

EXTEND

---

[1] https://jenkins.openstack.org/
[2] https://launchpad.net/openstack

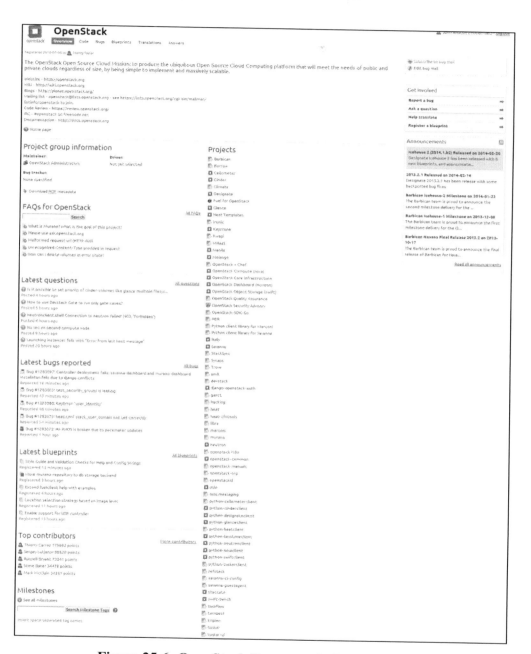

Figure 25-6: OpenStack Programs in Launchpad

You will then see a list of the bugs and blueprints for that project (e.g. you can see the page for Tempest in Figure 25-7).

EXTEND

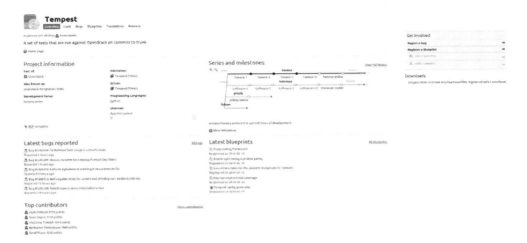

Figure 25-7: OpenStack Tempest in Launchpad

Blueprints are used for tracking specifications and new features from discussion through to review, approval and implementation. Bug tracking helps software teams collaborate on bug reports and fixes. Launchpad can track how a bug affects different projects and compute the estimated impact.

Launchpad also has facilities for source-code hosting, application localization, community support, mailing lists and code review. But these are not heavily used within OpenStack, which has selected other tools for these purposes.

Mailing Lists

E-mail may sound very old-school as a means of collaboration but mailings lists are still very effective for many-to-many communication and are used extensively within the OpenStack community.

EXTEND

lists.openstack.org Mailing Lists

Welcome!

Below is a listing of all the public mailing lists on lists.openstack.org. Click on a list name to get more information about the list, or to subscribe, unsubscribe, and change the preferences on your subscription. To visit the general information page for an unadvertised list, open a URL similar to this one, but with a '/' and the list name appended.

List administrators, you can visit the list admin overview page to find the management interface for your list.

If you are having trouble using the lists, please contact mailman@lists.openstack.org.

List	Description
Community	The OpenStack Community team is the main contact point for anybody running a local OpenStack Group.
Defcore-committee	OpenStack Board DefCore Committee
Elections-committee	[no description available]
FITs	Group to discuss the OpenStack Faithful Implementation Test (FITs)
Foundation	General discussion list for activities of the OpenStack Foundation
Foundation-board	OpenStack Foundation Board of Directors
legal-discuss	Discussions on legal matters related to the project
Marketing	The OpenStack Marketing list is the meant to facilitate discussion and best practice sharing among marketers and event organizers in the OpenStack community.
Openstack	The OpenStack General mailing list
OpenStack-announce	Announces about OpenStack new releases, stable releases and security advisories
OpenStack-dev	OpenStack Development Mailing List (not for usage questions)
Openstack-docs	OpenStack Documentation Mailing List
Openstack-es	Lista de correo acerca de OpenStack en español
OpenStack-fr	Liste de discussion génerale sur OpenStack en français
OpenStack-HPC	High-Performance Computing OpenStack List
Openstack-i18n	Internationalisation and Translation
OpenStack-Infra	Infrastructure support for the OpenStack project
Openstack-it	Discussioni su OpenStack in italiano
OpenStack-operators	Discussion list for operators of OpenStack
openstack-personas	Team focused on creating personas for OpenStack

Figure 25-8: OpenStack Mailing Lists

You will find that the OpenStack Mailing Lists[1] are divided into subtopics to keep the traffic isolated and focused (Figure 25-8).

---

[1] http://lists.openstack.org/

Figure 25-9: Mailing List Archives

And, if you don't expect to be a regular participant in the discussions, you may opt to look at the archives instead (Figure 25-9). In fact, even if you are a subscriber, you may find it easier to locate past discussion threads online than in your inbox.

Internet Relay Chat

One last collaboration medium that lends itself well when you need an urgent response is Internet Relay Chat (IRC). There are several channels for OpenStack, including "openstack" and "openstack-101", which are good resources for anyone getting started with OpenStack.

EXTEND

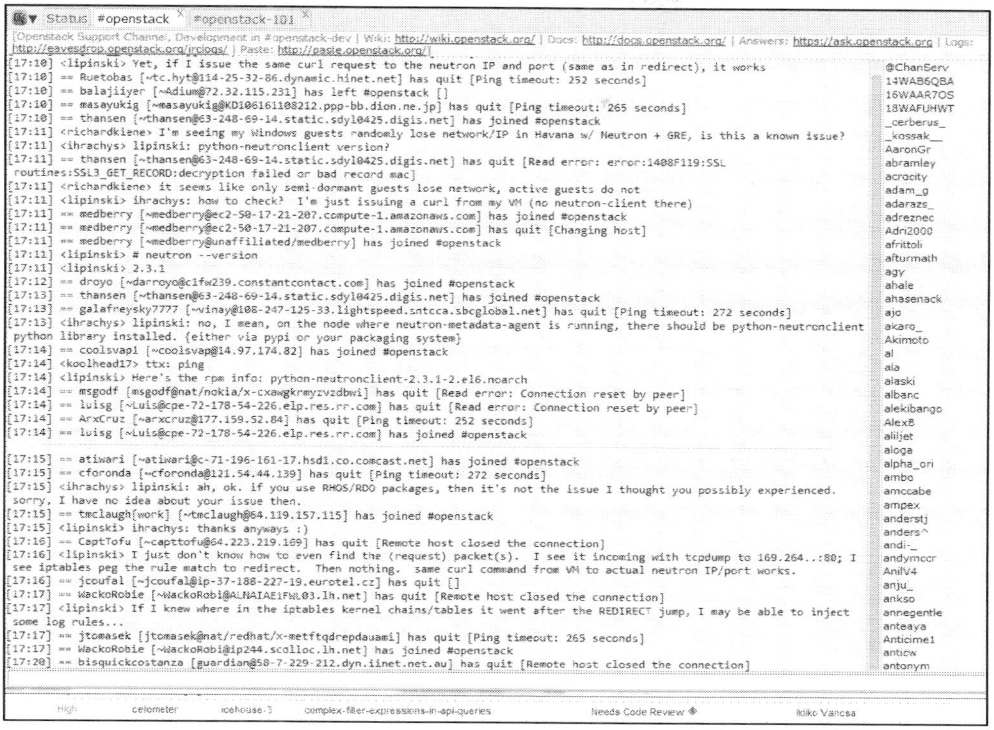

Figure 25-10: IRC Chat

To use IRC you can download and install a client. Or if you prefer, you can use the Webchat feature on freenode (Figure 25-10)[1].

IRC is the least formal medium, so the results may be hit-and-miss, but it has the benefit that it is interactive and you may receive a response in almost real-time.

Release Schedule

If you do decide to participate in the ongoing development of OpenStack, you probably want to start with the big picture of where the program is and what activities are ongoing. Your first point of orientation is to identify where you are in the current release cycle.

EXTEND

---

[1] http://webchat.freenode.net/?channels=openstack,openstack-101

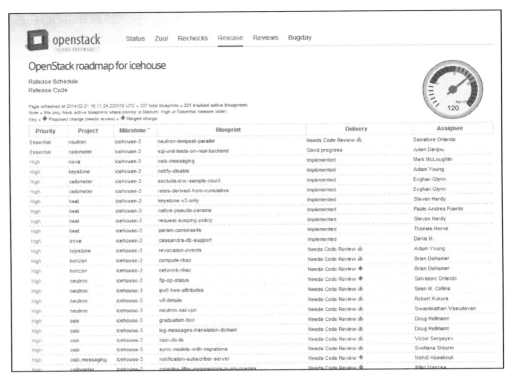

Figure 25-11: OpenStack Roadmap for Icehouse

You can find the roadmap for all the active blueprints on the OpenStack Release[1] page (Figure 25-11) along with a pointer to the Release Schedule (Figure 25-12).

EXTEND

---

[1] http://status.openstack.org/release/

Icehouse Release Schedule

- Status: Confirmed
- Integrated programs PTLs:
    - Russell Bryant (Nova)
    - Mark Washenberger (Glance)
    - John Dickinson (Swift)
    - David Lyle (Horizon)
    - Dolph Mathews (Keystone)
    - Mark McClain (Neutron)
    - John Griffith (Cinder)
    - Julien Danjou (Ceilometer)
    - Steve Baker (Heat)
    - Michael Basnight (Trove)
- Release Manager: Thierry Carrez (ttx) @

Important notes:

- Swift does not publish intermediary milestones (icehouse-X). They may release extra versions.
- New features must land in master branch by March 4, two days before icehouse-3 milestone delivery

Week (Thursday)		Common	Swift
2013	7th	Design Summit	
November	14th		
	21st		
	28th		
December	5th	icehouse-1	
	12th		1.11.0 (Dec 12)
	19th		
	26th		
2014	2nd	(End-of-year holidays)	
	9th		
January	16th		
	23rd	icehouse-2	1.12.0 (Jan 28)
	30th		
February	6th		
	13th		
	20th	FeatureProposalFreeze (Feb 18)	
	27nd		
March	6th	FeatureFreeze, StringFreeze (Mar 4) icehouse-3 (Mar 6)	
	13th		
	20th		
	27th		
April	3rd	Release candidates	
	10th		
	17th	Icehouse Release (2014.1)	
	24th		
May	1st	Recommended "Off" week	
	8th		
	15th	Design Summit	

Figure 25-12: Icehouse Release Schedule

Practical Recommendations

One of the greatest features of OpenStack is its momentum. You can expect significantly more functionality over the coming months and years. But that also means that you have to make an effort to keep current.

At a minimum keep your eye on what is happening. You can learn a lot about the direction the software is taking, why certain design decisions were made and what you need to do to implement it effectively.

This may complete your introduction to OpenStack, but as you can tell from the roadmaps and references to incubating projects you have seen throughout the book, OpenStack's journey has only really just begun.

EXTEND

Appendix A

OpenStack Programs

Below is a list of some of the main OpenStack programs currently in production and in development. This list is very dynamic. New programs spring up all the time. Some undergo several name changes. And occasionally a few are abandoned. Nonetheless, if you are new to OpenStack, you might find this overview helpful.

These programs have been integrated into the Havana (November 2013) release of OpenStack:

- Cinder: OpenStack Block Storage
- Glance: OpenStack Image Service
- Horizon: OpenStack Dashboard
- Keystone: OpenStack Identity
- Neutron: OpenStack Networking
- Nova: OpenStack Compute
- *(Quantum): Obsolete name for OpenStack Networking, now called Neutron*
- Swift: OpenStack Object Storage
- Ceilometer: OpenStack Metering
- Heat: OpenStack Orchestration

These programs are in various stages of development as of the Havana release:

- Barbican: OpenStack Key Management
- Designate: OpenStack DNS as a Service
- Ironic: OpenStack Bare Metal
- Kwapi: OpenStack Energy Metrics
- Manila: OpenStack File Storage

Appendix A: OpenStack Programs

- Marconi: OpenStack Queuing and Notification Service
- Murano: OpenStack Windows Application Catalog
- Oslo: OpenStack Common Libraries
- Savanna: OpenStack Data Processing (Hadoop)
- Solum: OpenStack Application Lifecycle Management
- Tempest: OpenStack Integration Test Suite
- TripleO: OpenStack on OpenStack
- Trove: OpenStack Database as a Service
- Tuskar: OpenStack Datacenter as a Service

Appendix B

Basic Heat Template

Below is the full template that was described in Chapter 12, written in JSON format. You can find the most recent source on GitHub[1].

```
{
  "AWSTemplateFormatVersion" : "2010-09-09",

  "Description" : "AWS CloudFormation Sample Template Word-
Press_Single_Instance: WordPress is web software you can use to create a
beautiful website or blog. This template installs a single-instance Word-
Press deployment using a local MySQL database to store the data.",

  "Parameters" : {

    "KeyName" : {
      "Description" : "Name of an existing EC2 KeyPair to enable SSH ac-
cess to the instances",
      "Type" : "String"
    },

    "InstanceType" : {
      "Description" : "WebServer EC2 instance type",
      "Type" : "String",
      "Default" : "m1.small",
      "AllowedValues" : [ "m1.tiny", "m1.small", "m1.medium", "m1.large",
"m1.xlarge" ],
      "ConstraintDescription" : "must be a valid EC2 instance type."
    },

    "DBName": {
      "Default": "wordpress",
      "Description" : "The WordPress database name",
      "Type": "String",
      "MinLength": "1",
      "MaxLength": "64",
      "AllowedPattern" : "[a-zA-Z][a-zA-Z0-9]*",
      "ConstraintDescription" : "must begin with a letter and contain only
alphanumeric characters."
```

---

[1] https://github.com/openstack/heat-
templates/blob/master/cfn/F18/WordPress_Single_Instance.template

```
      },

    "DBUsername": {
      "Default": "admin",
      "NoEcho": "true",
      "Description" : "The WordPress database admin account username",
      "Type": "String",
      "MinLength": "1",
      "MaxLength": "16",
      "AllowedPattern" : "[a-zA-Z][a-zA-Z0-9]*",
      "ConstraintDescription" : "must begin with a letter and contain only
alphanumeric characters."
    },

    "DBPassword": {
      "Default": "admin",
      "NoEcho": "true",
      "Description" : "The WordPress database admin account password",
      "Type": "String",
      "MinLength": "1",
      "MaxLength": "41",
      "AllowedPattern" : "[a-zA-Z0-9]*",
      "ConstraintDescription" : "must contain only alphanumeric charac-
ters."
    },

    "DBRootPassword": {
      "Default": "admin",
      "NoEcho": "true",
      "Description" : "Root password for MySQL",
      "Type": "String",
      "MinLength": "1",
      "MaxLength": "41",
      "AllowedPattern" : "[a-zA-Z0-9]*",
      "ConstraintDescription" : "must contain only alphanumeric charac-
ters."
    },
    "LinuxDistribution": {
      "Default": "F18",
      "Description" : "Distribution of choice",
      "Type": "String",
      "AllowedValues" : [ "F18" ]
    }
  },

  "Mappings" : {
    "AWSInstanceType2Arch" : {
      "m1.tiny"    : { "Arch" : "32" },
      "m1.small"   : { "Arch" : "64" },
      "m1.medium"  : { "Arch" : "64" },
      "m1.large"   : { "Arch" : "64" },
      "m1.xlarge"  : { "Arch" : "64" }
    },
    "DistroArch2AMI": {
      "F18"      : { "32" : "F18-i386-cfntools", "64" : "F18-x86_64-
cfntools" }
    }
  },

  "Resources" : {
    "WikiDatabase": {
```

```
        "Type": "AWS::EC2::Instance",
      "Metadata" : {
        "AWS::CloudFormation::Init" : {
          "config" : {
            "packages" : {
              "yum" : {
                "mysql"        : [],
                "mysql-server" : [],
                "httpd"        : [],
                "wordpress"    : []
              }
            },
            "services" : {
              "systemd" : {
                "mysqld"    : { "enabled" : "true", "ensureRunning" :
"true" },
                "httpd"     : { "enabled" : "true", "ensureRunning" :
"true" }
              }
            }
          }
        }
      },
      "Properties": {
        "ImageId" : { "Fn::FindInMap" : [ "DistroArch2AMI", { "Ref" :
"LinuxDistribution" },
                          { "Fn::FindInMap" : [ "AWSInstanceType2Arch", {
"Ref" : "InstanceType" }, "Arch" ] } ] },
        "InstanceType"  : { "Ref" : "InstanceType" },
        "KeyName"       : { "Ref" : "KeyName" },
        "UserData"      : { "Fn::Base64" : { "Fn::Join" : ["", [
          "#!/bin/bash -v\n",
          "/opt/aws/bin/cfn-init\n",
          "# Setup MySQL root password and create a user\n",
          "mysqladmin -u root password '", { "Ref" : "DBRootPassword" },
"'\n",
          "cat << EOF | mysql -u root --password='", { "Ref" :
"DBRootPassword" }, "'\n",
          "CREATE DATABASE ", { "Ref" : "DBName" }, ";\n",
          "GRANT ALL PRIVILEGES ON ", { "Ref" : "DBName" }, ".* TO \"", {
"Ref" : "DBUsername" }, "\"@\"localhost\"\n",
          "IDENTIFIED BY \"", { "Ref" : "DBPassword" }, "\";\n",
          "FLUSH PRIVILEGES;\n",
          "EXIT\n",
          "EOF\n",
          "sed -i \"/Deny from All/d\"
/etc/httpd/conf.d/wordpress.conf\n",
          "sed -i \"s/Require local/Require all granted/\"
/etc/httpd/conf.d/wordpress.conf\n",
          "sed --in-place --e s/database_name_here/", { "Ref" : "DBName"
}, "/ --e s/username_here/", { "Ref" : "DBUsername" }, "/ --e
s/password_here/", { "Ref" : "DBPassword" }, "/ /usr/share/wordpress/wp-
config.php\n",
          "systemctl restart httpd.service\n",
          "firewall-cmd --add-service=http\n",
          "firewall-cmd --permanent --add-service=http\n"
        ]]}}
      }
    }
  },
```

```
  "Outputs" : {
    "WebsiteURL" : {
      "Value" : { "Fn::Join" : ["", ["http://", { "Fn::GetAtt" : [ "Wiki-
Database", "PublicIp" ]}, "/wordpress"]] },
      "Description" : "URL for Wordpress wiki"
    }
  }
}
```

Appendix C

Auto-scaling Heat Template

Below is the full template that was described in Chapter 21. It uses a YAML format, which is slightly easier to read than JSON. You can find the most recent source on GitHub[1].

```
HeatTemplateFormatVersion: '2012-12-12'
Description: Creates an autoscaling wordpress application using Ceilome-
ter.
Parameters:
  KeyName:
    Description: Name of an existing EC2 KeyPair to enable SSH access to
the instances
    Type: String
  InstanceType:
    Description: WebServer EC2 instance type
    Type: String
    Default: m1.small
    AllowedValues: [m1.tiny, m1.small, m1.medium, m1.large, m1.xlarge]
    ConstraintDescription: must be a valid EC2 instance type.
  ImageId:
    Description: the name or uuid of the image in glance
    Type: String
    Default: F17-x86_64-cfntools
  DBUsername: {Default: admin, NoEcho: 'true',
    Description: The WordPress database admin account username, Type:
String,
    MinLength: '1', MaxLength: '16', AllowedPattern: '[a-zA-Z][a-zA-Z0-
9]*',
    ConstraintDescription: must begin with a letter and contain only
      alphanumeric characters.}
  DBPassword: {Default: admin, NoEcho: 'true',
    Description: The WordPress database admin account password, Type:
String,
```

[1] https://github.com/openstack/heat-
templates/blob/master/cfn/F17/AutoScalingCeilometer.yaml

```
      MinLength: '1', MaxLength: '41', AllowedPattern: '[a-zA-Z0-9]*',
      ConstraintDescription: must contain only alphanumeric characters.}
  DBRootPassword: {Default: admin, NoEcho: 'true',
    Description: Root password for MySQL, Type: String,
    MinLength: '1', MaxLength: '41', AllowedPattern: '[a-zA-Z0-9]*',
    ConstraintDescription: must contain only alphanumeric characters.}
Resources:
  CfnUser: {Type: 'AWS::IAM::User'}
  WebServerKeys:
    Type: AWS::IAM::AccessKey
    Properties:
      UserName: {Ref: CfnUser}
  WebServerGroup:
    Type: AWS::AutoScaling::AutoScalingGroup
    Properties:
      AvailabilityZones: {'Fn::GetAZs': ''}
      LaunchConfigurationName: {Ref: LaunchConfig}
      MinSize: '1'
      MaxSize: '3'
      LoadBalancerNames:
      - {Ref: ElasticLoadBalancer}
      Tags:
      - {Key: metering.server_group, Value: WebServerGroup}
  WebServerScaleUpPolicy:
    Type: AWS::AutoScaling::ScalingPolicy
    Properties:
      AdjustmentType: ChangeInCapacity
      AutoScalingGroupName: {Ref: WebServerGroup}
      Cooldown: '60'
      ScalingAdjustment: '1'
  WebServerScaleDownPolicy:
    Type: AWS::AutoScaling::ScalingPolicy
    Properties:
      AdjustmentType: ChangeInCapacity
      AutoScalingGroupName: {Ref: WebServerGroup}
      Cooldown: '60'
      ScalingAdjustment: '-1'
  CPUAlarmHigh:
    Type: OS::Ceilometer::Alarm
    Properties:
      description: Scale-up if the average CPU > 50% for 1 minute
      meter_name: cpu_util
      statistic: avg
      period: '60'
      evaluation_periods: '1'
      threshold: '50'
      alarm_actions:
      - {"Fn::GetAtt": [WebServerScaleUpPolicy, AlarmUrl]}
      matching_metadata: {'metadata.user_metadata.groupname': {Ref: 'Web-
ServerGroup'}}
      comparison_operator: gt
  CPUAlarmLow:
    Type: OS::Ceilometer::Alarm
    Properties:
      description: Scale-down if the average CPU < 15% for 1 minute
      meter_name: cpu_util
      statistic: avg
      period: '60'
      evaluation_periods: '1'
      threshold: '15'
      alarm_actions:
      - {"Fn::GetAtt": [WebServerScaleDownPolicy, AlarmUrl]}
```

```yaml
      matching_metadata: {'metadata.user_metadata.groupname': {Ref: 'Web-
ServerGroup'}}
      comparison_operator: lt
  ElasticLoadBalancer:
    Type: AWS::ElasticLoadBalancing::LoadBalancer
    Properties:
      AvailabilityZones: {'Fn::GetAZs': ''}
      Listeners:
      - {LoadBalancerPort: '80', InstancePort: '80',
        Protocol: HTTP}
      HealthCheck: {Target: 'HTTP:80/', HealthyThreshold: '3',
        UnhealthyThreshold: '5', Interval: '30', Timeout: '5'}
  LaunchConfig:
    Type: AWS::AutoScaling::LaunchConfiguration
    Metadata:
      AWS::CloudFormation::Init:
        config:
          files:
            /etc/cfn/cfn-credentials:
              content:
                'Fn::Replace':
                - WebServerKeys: {Ref: WebServerKeys}
                  WebSecretKey: {'Fn::GetAtt': [WebServerKeys, Secre-
tAccessKey]}
                - |
                  AWSAccessKeyId=WebServerKeys
                  AWSSecretKey=WebSecretKey
              mode: '000400'
              owner: root
              group: root
            /tmp/setup.mysql:
              content:
                'Fn::Replace':
                - DBPassword: {Ref: DBPassword}
                  DBUsername: {Ref: DBUsername}
                - |
                  CREATE DATABASE wordpress;
                  GRANT ALL PRIVILEGES ON wordpress .* TO
'DBUsername'@'localhost' IDENTIFIED BY 'DBPassword';
                  FLUSH PRIVILEGES;
                  EXIT
              mode: '000644'
              owner: root
              group: root
          packages:
            yum:
              mysql: []
              mysql-server: []
              httpd: []
              wordpress: []
          services:
            systemd:
              mysqld: {enabled: 'true', ensureRunning: 'true'}
              httpd: {enabled: 'true', ensureRunning: 'true'}
    Properties:
      ImageId: {Ref: ImageId}
      InstanceType: {Ref: InstanceType}
      KeyName: {Ref: KeyName}
      UserData:
        Fn::Base64:
          Fn::Replace:
          - 'AWS::StackName': {Ref: 'AWS::StackName'}
            'AWS::Region': {Ref: 'AWS::Region'}
```

```
            DBRootPassword: {Ref: DBRootPassword}
            DBPassword: {Ref: DBPassword}
            DBUsername: {Ref: DBUsername}
        - |
          #!/bin/bash -v
          /opt/aws/bin/cfn-init -s AWS::StackName -r LaunchConfig --
region AWS::Region
          # Setup MySQL root password and create a user
          mysqladmin -u root password DBRootPassword
          mysql -u root --password=DBRootPassword < /tmp/setup.mysql
          sed -i "/Deny from All/d" /etc/httpd/conf.d/wordpress.conf
          sed -i "/Deny from all/d" /etc/httpd/conf.d/wordpress.conf
          sed --in-place --e s/database_name_here/wordpress/ --e
s/username_here/DBUsername/ --e s/password_here/DBPassword/
/usr/share/wordpress/wp-config.php
          systemctl restart httpd.service
Outputs:
  URL:
    Description: The URL of the website
    Value:
      Fn::Replace:
      - IpAddress: {'Fn::GetAtt': [ElasticLoadBalancer, DNSName]}
      - http://IpAddress/wordpress
```

Acronyms

AAA	Authentication, Authorization and Accounting
ACL	Access Control List
AD	Active Directory
AMI	Amazon Machine Image
AMQP	Advanced Message Queuing Protocol
API	Application Programming Interface
ASIC	Application-Specific Integrated Circuit
ASP	Application service provider
AWS	Amazon Web Services
BCP	Business Continuity Plan
BIOS	Basic Input/Output System
BPEL	Business Process Execution Language
CA	Certificate Authority
CDN	Content Delivery Network
CIDR	Classless Inter-Domain Routing
CIFS	Common Internet File System
CLI	Command-Line Interface
CPU	Central Processing Unit
CRM	Customer Relationship Management
CSA	Cloud Security Alliance
DDoS	Distributed Denial of Service
DHCP	Dynamic Host Configuration Protocol
DNS	Domain Name System
DoS	Denial of Service
EBS	Amazon Elastic Block Store
EC2	Amazon Elastic Compute Cloud
EDI	Electronic Data Interchange
ERP	Enterprise Resource Planning
eSCM	eSourcing Capability Model
FAQ	Frequenty Asked Questions

FCoE	FibreChannel over Ethernet
FPS	Flexible Payments Service
GPU	Graphics Processing Unit
GRE	Generic Routing Encapsulation
GUI	Graphical User Interface
HDD	Hard Disk Drive
HDFS	Hadoop Distributed File System
HIPAA	Health Insurance Portability and Accountability Act
HPC	High Performance Computing
HTML	HyperText Markup Language
HTTP	HyperText Transfer Protocol
HTTPS	HyperText Transfer Protocol Secure
I2RS	Interface to the Routing System
IaaS	Infrastructure as a Service
IAM	Identity and Access Management
IETS	Internet Engineering Taskforce
IIS	Internet Information Services
IOPS	Input/Output Operations Per Second
IP	Internet Protocol
IPMI	Intelligent Platform Management Interface
IRC	Internet Relay Chat
iSCSI	Internet SCSI
ITIL	Information Technology Infrastructure Library
JSON	JavaScript Object Notation
KVM	Kernel-based Virtual Machine
LDAP	Lightweight Directory Access Protocol
LVM	Logical Volume Manager
LXC	Linux Container
MAC	Medium Access Control
MIB	Management Information Base
MPI	Message Passing Interface
MTBF	Mean Time Between Failures
MTTR	Mean Time To Repair
NAS	Network Attached Storage
NAT	Network Address Translation
NFS	Network File System
NFV	Network Function Virtualization
NIC	Network Interface Card
NRPE	Nagios Remote Plugin Executor
OASIS	Organization for the Advancement of Structured Information Standards
OLAP	On-Line Analytical Processing
OLTP	On-Line Transaction Processing
OSI	Open Systems Interconnection
PaaS	Platform as a Service

PAM	Pluggable Authentication Modules
PCEP	Path Computation Element Protocol
PCI	Payment Card Industry
PCI-DSS	Payment Card Industry Data Security Standard
PEM	Privacy Enhanced Mail
PHP	PHP: Hypertext Preprocessor
PUM	Privileged User Management
PXE	Preboot Execution Environment
QoS	Quality of Service
RAID	Redundant Array of Independent Disks
RAM	Random Access Memory
RBAC	Role-Based Access Control
REST	REpresentational State Transfer
RHEL	Red Hat Enterprise Linux
RPC	Remote Procedure Call
RPO	Recovery Point Objective
RTO	Recovery Time Objective
SaaS	Software as a Service
SAML	Security Assertion Markup Language
SAN	Storage Area Network
SATA	Serial Advanced Technology Attachment
SCM	Source Control Management
SCSI	Small Computer Systems Interface
SDC	Software-Defined Compute
SDDC	Software-Defined Data Center
SDN	Software-Defined Networking
SDS	Software-Defined Storage
SI	Système International d'unités)
SLA	Service Level Agreement
SMS	Short Message Service
SNMP	Simple Network Management Protocol
SOAP	Simple Object Access Protocol
SPML	Service Provisioning Markup Language
SPOF	Single Point of Failure
SQL	Structured Query Language
SSD	Solid-State Drive
SSH	Secure Shell
SSL	Secure Sockets Layer
SSSD	System Security Services Daemon
STP	Spanning Tree Protocol
TCP	Transmission Control Protocol
TLS	Transport Layer Security
TOSCA	Topology and Orchestration Specification for Cloud Applications
TPM	Trusted Platform Module
UDP	User Datagram Protocol

UEFI	Unified Extensible Firmware Interface
UUID	Universally Unique IDentifier
VHD	Virtual Hard Disk
VIP	Virtual IP address
VLAN	Virtual Local Area Network
VM	Virtual Machine
VPC	Virtual Private Cloud
VPN	Virtual Private Network
WAN	Wide Area Network
XML	Extensible Markup Language
YAML	YAML Ain't Markup Language

References

Amazon Web Serivces. (2010, December). Retrieved January 2013, from Amazon Web Serivces: aws.amazon.com/message/65348/

Anderson, J. C., Lehnardt, J., & Slater, N. (2010). *CouchDB: The Definitive Guide: Time to Relax.* O'Reilly Media.

AndroLib. (2011, March). *AndroLib Statistics.* Retrieved March 2011, from AndroLib: http://www.androlib.com/appstats.aspx

Armbrust, M., Fox, A., Griffith, R., Joseph, A. D., Katz, R. H., Konwinski, A., et al. (2009, February 10). *Above the Clouds: A Berkeley View of Cloud Computing.* Retrieved January 2013, from UC Berkeley - Electrical Engineering and Computer Sciences: www.eecs.berkeley.edu/Pubs/TechRpts/2009/EECS-2009-28.pdf

Barnes, J. A. (1954). Class and committees in a Norwegian island parish. *Human Relations*, 7:39-58.

Berkeley/Stanford. (2008, September). *The Berkeley/Stanford Recovery-Oriented Computing (ROC) Project.* Retrieved March 2011, from http://roc.cs.berkeley.edu/

Berkeley/Stanford. (2008, September). *The Berkeley/Stanford Recovery-Oriented Computing (ROC) Project.* Retrieved January 2013, from http://roc.cs.berkeley.edu/

Berners-Lee, T. (2006, July). *Linked Data.* Retrieved March 2011, from World Wide Web Consortium: http://www.w3.org/DesignIssues/LinkedData

Biggs, J. (2011, December). *A Dispute Over Who Owns a Twitter Account Goes to Court.* Retrieved November 2012, from The New York Times:

http://www.nytimes.com/2011/12/26/technology/lawsuit-may-determine-who-owns-a-twitter-account.html

BT Global Services. (2009, November). *The challenge for the CIO in 2010.* Retrieved January 2013, from BT Global Services: www.globalservices.bt.com/static/assets/pdf/Insights%20and%20Ideas/BTGS_Enterprise_Intelligence_Research_Report.pdf

Carr, N. (2009). *The Big Switch: Rewiring the World, from Edison to Google.* W.W. Norton & Co.

Carr, N. G. (2004). *Does IT Matter.* Harvard Business School Publishing Corporation.

Chang, F., Dean, J., Ghemawat, S., Hsieh, W. C., Wallach, D. A., Burrows, M., et al. (2006, November). *Bigtable: A Distributed Storage System for Structured Data.* Retrieved March 2011, from Google labs: http://labs.google.com/papers/bigtable-osdi06.pdf

Chauhan, S. (2012, February). *Virtualization Security: Hacking VMware with VASTO.* Retrieved July 2012, from Infosec Institute: http://resources.infosecinstitute.com/virtualization-security/

Cherry, S. (2010, October). *How Stuxnet Is Rewriting the Cyberterrorism Playbook.* Retrieved July 2012, from IEEE Spectrum: http://spectrum.ieee.org/podcast/telecom/security/how-stuxnet-is-rewriting-the-cyberterrorism-playbook

Chodorow, K., & Dirolf, M. (2010). *MongoDB: The Definitive Guide.* O'Reilly Media.

Ciurana, E. (2009). *Developing with Google App Engine.* Apress.

Cloud Security Alliance. (2010). *Top Threats to Cloud Computing V1.0.* Retrieved July 2012, from Cloud Security Alliance: cloudsecurityalliance.org/research/top-threats

Cloud Security Alliance. (2010). *Top Threats to Cloud Computing V1.0.* Retrieved January 2013, from Cloud Security Alliance: cloudsecurityalliance.org/research/top-threats

Cloud Security Alliance. (2011, November). *Security Guidance for Critical Areas of Focus.* Retrieved April 2012, from Cloud Security Alliance: http://cloudsecurityalliance.org/csaguide.pdf

Cloud Security Alliance. (2011, November). *Security Guidance for Critical Areas of Focus.* Retrieved January 2013, from Cloud Security Alliance: http://cloudsecurityalliance.org/csaguide.pdf

Compete, Inc. (2011). *Siteanalytics amazon.com*. Retrieved January 2013, from Compete: siteanalytics.compete.com/amazon.com/

DiNucci, D. (1999). *Fragmented Future*. Retrieved January 2013, from www.darcyd.com/fragmented_future.pdf

ENISA. (2009, November). *Cloud Computing Risk Assessment*. Retrieved April 2010, from European Network and Information Security Agency: http://www.enisa.europa.eu/act/rm/files/deliverables/cloud-computing-risk-assessment/

ENISA. (2009, November). *Cloud Computing Risk Assessment*. Retrieved January 2013, from European Network and Information Security Agency: http://www.enisa.europa.eu/activities/risk-management/files/deliverables/cloud-computing-risk-assessment

ENISA. (2009, March). *EFR Framework Handbook*. Retrieved April 2010, from European Network and Information Security Agency: http://www.enisa.europa.eu/act/rm/files/deliverables/efr-framework-handbook

ENISA. (2009, March). *EFR Framework Handbook*. Retrieved January 2013, from European Network and Information Security Agency: http://www.enisa.europa.eu/activities/risk-management/emerging-and-future-risk

EuroCloud #3. (2012, May). *Cloud Services - Lizenzen im Cloudvertrag*. Retrieved November 2012, from EuroCloud Austria: http://www.eurocloud.at/projekte/publikationen/leitfaeden.html

EuroCloud #5. (2012, September). *Cloud Computing: Steuerliche Aspekte in der DACH-Region*. Retrieved November 2012, from EuroCloud Austria: http://www.eurocloud.at/projekte/publikationen/leitfaeden.html

Friedman, T. L. (2007). *The World Is Flat 3.0: A Brief History of the Twenty-first Century*. Picador.

Gartner. (2012, September). *Gartner Says Worldwide Cloud Services Market to Surpass $109 Billion in 2012*. Retrieved December 2012, from Gartner, Inc: http://www.gartner.com/it/page.jsp?id=2163616

Gartner, I. (2010, January 13). *Key Predictions for IT Organizations and Users in 2010 and Beyond*. Retrieved March 2010, from Gartner: http://www.gartner.com/it/page.jsp?id=1278413

Gartner, Inc. (2008, December 8). *New Research: Predicts 2009: The Evolving Open-Source Software Model*. Retrieved October 2009, from Gartner Blog Network: http://blogs.gartner.com/mark_driver/2008/12/08/new-research-predicts-2009-the-evolving-open-source-software-model/

Gartner, Inc. (2010, August). *Gartner Highlights Four Myths Surrounding IT Self-Service.* Retrieved November 2012, from Gartner: http://www.gartner.com/it/page.jsp?id=1426813

Gorman, S. (2012, February). *Chinese Hackers Suspected In Long-Term Nortel Breach.* Retrieved October 2012, from Wall Street Journal: http://online.wsj.com/article/SB10001424052970203363504577187502 201577054.html

Greenberg, J. (n.d.). *JavaScript Optimization.* Retrieved March 2011, from http://home.earthlink.net/~kendrasg/info/js_opt/

Greenpeace. (2010, March). *Make IT Green - Cloud Computing and its Contribution to Climate Change.* Retrieved January 2013, from Greenpeace International: www.greenpeace.org/usa/press-center/reports4/make-it-green-cloud-computing

Henderson, C. (2006). *Building Scalable Web Sites: Building, Scaling, and Optimizing the Next Generation of Web Applications.* O'Reilly Media.

Hewitt, E. (2010). *Cassandra: The Definitive Guide.* O'Reilly Media.

Holmes, A. (2012). *Hadoop in Practice.* Manning Publications.

IDC. (2009). *Worldwide Messaging Security 2010-2014 Forecast and 2009 Vendor Shares: SaaS Is Here to Stay.*

ISACA. (2009, October). *Cloud Computing: Business Benefits With Security, Governance and Assurance Perspectives.* Retrieved April 2010, from ISACA: http://www.isaca.org/AMTemplate.cfm?Section=Deliverables&Template=/ContentManagement/ContentDisplay.cfm&ContentID=53044

ISACA. (2009, October). *Cloud Computing: Business Benefits With Security, Governance and Assurance Perspectives.* Retrieved January 2013, from ISACA: www.isaca.org/Knowledge-Center/Research/Documents/Cloud-Computing-28Oct09-Research.pdf

ITIL. (2007). *The Official Introduction to the ITIL Service Lifecycle.* London: UK Office of Government Commerce: TSO.

Jackson, K., & Bunch, C. (2013). *OpenStack Cloud Computing Cookbook* (2nd ed.). Packt Publishing.

James, C., & Stolz, M. (2009). *The True Cost of Latency.* Retrieved March 2011, from http://www.slideshare.net/gemstonesystems/true-cost-of-latency

James, C., & Stolz, M. (2009). *The True Cost of Latency.* Retrieved January 2013, from www.slideshare.net/gemstonesystems/true-cost-of-latency

Kamaraju, A. (2011, March). *The Many Colors of Cloud Encryption.* Retrieved November 2012, from TechNewsWorld: http://www.technewsworld.com/story/72173.html

Kaufmann, R., & Gayliard, B. (2009, January 13). *http://www.ddj.com/go-parallel/article/showArticle.jhtml?articleID=212900103.* Retrieved March 2011, from Dr. Dobb's: http://www.ddj.com/go-parallel/article/showArticle.jhtml?articleID=212900103

Kaufmann, R., & Gayliard, B. (2009, January 13). *http://www.ddj.com/go-parallel/article/showArticle.jhtml?articleID=212900103.* Retrieved January 2013, from Dr. Dobb's: www.ddj.com/go-parallel/article/showArticle.jhtml?articleID=212900103

Knowledge@Wharton. (2005, March). *Why Do So Many Mergers Fail.* Retrieved January 2013, from Knowledge@Wharton: knowledge.wharton.upenn.edu/article.cfm?articleid=1137

Konchady, M. (2008). *Building Search Applications: Lucene, LingPipe, and Gate.* Mustru Publishing.

Lam, C. (2010). *Hadoop in Action.* Manning Publications.

Lin, J., & Dyer, C. (2010). *Data-Intensive Text Processing with MapReduce.* Morgan and Claypool Publishers.

Linthicum, D. S. (2009). *Cloud Computing and SOA Convergence in Your Enterprise.* Addison Wesley.

Loeliger, J. (2009). *Version Control with Git: Powerful Tools and Techniques for Collaborative Software Development.* O'Reilly Media.

Logan, D., & Bace, J. (2008). *E-Discovery: Project Planning and Budgeting 2008-2011.* Gartner.

Mangino, M. J. (2008). *Developing Facebook Platform Applications with Rails.* Pragmatic Bookshelf.

Mather, T., Kumaraswamy, S., & Latif, S. (2009). *Cloud Security and Privacy.* Sebastopol: O'Reilly.

McCandless, M., Hatcher, E., & Gospodnetic, O. (2010). *Lucene in Action.* Manning Publications.

McCarthy, J. (2010, August). *Hadoop Day in Seattle: Hadoop, Cascading, Hive and Pig.* Retrieved March 2011, from Gumption: http://gumption.typepad.com/blog/2010/08/hadoop-day-in-seattle-hadoop-cascading-hive-and-pig.html

Meier, R. L. (2000). Integrating Enterprise-Wide Risk Management Concepts into Industrial Technology Curricula. *Journal of Industrial Technology, 16*(4).

Merriam-Webster. (2012). *Definition of Social Media.* Retrieved 2012, from Merriam-Webster: http://www.merriam-webster.com/dictionary/social%20media

Messmer, E. (2010, May 20). *Novell Identity Manager extended to cloud.* Retrieved March 2011, from Computerworld UK: http://www.computerworlduk.com/news/security/20357/novell-identity-manager-extended-to-cloud/

Mogull, R. (2011, September). *Data Security Lifecycle 2.0.* Retrieved November 2012, from Securoris: https://securosis.com/blog/data-security-lifecycle-2.0

Mogull, R. (2011, June). *How to Encrypt IaaS Volumes.* Retrieved November 2012, from Securosis: https://securosis.com/blog/comments/how-to-encrypt-iaas-volumes

Moon, B. (2009, October). *4 Emerging Trends of the Real-Time Web.* Retrieved March 2011, from Mashable: http://mashable.com/2009/10/29/real-time-web-trends/

Moore, G. A. (2002). *Crossing the Chasm.* Harper Paperbacks.

Murty, J. (2008). *Programming Amazon Web Services: S3, EC2, SQS, FPS, and SimpleDB.* O'Reilly Media.

Nickols, F. (2010, September). *Change Management 101.* Retrieved 2012, from Distance Consulting LLC: http://www.nickols.us/change.pdf

NIST. (1996, October). *Introduction to Computer Security: The NIST Handbook.* Retrieved October 2012, from National Institute of Standards and Technology (NIST): http://csrc.nist.gov/publications/nistpubs/800-12/800-12-html/

NIST. (2011, September). *The NIST Definition of Cloud Computing.* Retrieved December 2012, from National Institute of Standards and Technology: http://csrc.nist.gov/publications/nistpubs/800-145/SP800-145.pdf

NIST. (2011, September). *The NIST Definition of Cloud Computing.* Retrieved December 2012, from National Institute of Standards and Technology: csrc.nist.gov/publications/nistpubs/800-145/SP800-145.pdf

North, K. (2009, August). *Databases in the Cloud: Elysian Fields or Briar Patch?* Retrieved March 2011, from Dr. Dobb's: http://drdobbs.com/database/218900502

O'Connor, C., & Loomis, R. (2010, December). *Economic Analysis of Role-Based Access Control.* Retrieved November 2012, from NIST: http://csrc.nist.gov/groups/SNS/rbac/documents/20101219_RBAC2_Final_Report.pdf

O'Reilly, T. (2006, May). *Database War Stories #7: Google File System and BigTable.* Retrieved March 2011, from O'Reilly Radar: http://radar.oreilly.com/archives/2006/05/database-war-stories-7-google.html

O'Reilly, T., & Batelle, J. (2004). Opening Welcome. *Web 2.0 Conference.* San Francisco, CA.

Pepple, K. (2011). *Deploying OpenStack.* O'Reilly.

Perry, G. (2008, August). *Cloud Computing Terminology.* Retrieved March 2011, from Thinking Out Cloud: http://gevaperry.typepad.com/main/2008/08/new-cloud-compu.html

Pilgrim, M. (2010). *HTML5: Up and Running.* O'Reilly Media.

Ping Identity. (2009, September). *Digital Itentity Basics.* Retrieved March 2011, from Open Source Federated Identity Management: http://www.sourceid.org/content/primer.cfm

PingIdentity. (2009, September). *Open Source Federated Identity Management.* Retrieved Septemper 16, 2009, from http://www.sourceid.org/content/primer.cfm

Plugge, E., Hawkins, T., & Membrey, P. (2010). *The Definitive Guide to MongoDB: The NoSQL Database for Cloud and Desktop Computing.* Apress.

Porter, M. E. (1979). How competitive forces shape strategy. *Harvard business Review*, 137-156.

Porter, M. E. (1998). *Competitive Strategy: Techniques for Analyzing Industries and Competitors.* Free Press.

Porter, M. E. (1998). *The Competitive Advantage of Nations.* Free Press.

Raftery, T. (2012). *GreenMonk.* Retrieved 2012, from GreenMonk: http://greenmonk.net

Reed, A., & Bennet, S. G. (2011). *Silver Clouds, Dark Linings.* New York: Prentice Hall.

Reese, G. (2009). *Cloud Application Architectures: Building Applications and Infrastructure in the Cloud.* O'Reilly Media, Inc.

Reporter, V. (2008, April). *The Value of a Millisecond: Finding the Optimal Speed of a Trading Infrastructure.* Retrieved January 2013, from TABB Group: www.tabbgroup.com/PublicationDetail.aspx?PublicationID=346

Rhoton, J. (2011). *Cloud Computing Explained* (2nd ed.). Recursive Press.

Rhoton, J., & Haukioja, R. (2011). *Cloud Computing Architected: Solution Design Handbook.* Recursive Press.

Rhoton, J., De Clercq, J., & Graves, D. (2013). *Cloud Computing Protected.* Recursive Press.

Ricciuti, M. (2008, September 30). *Stallman: Cloud computing is 'stupidity'.* Retrieved January 2013, from cnet news: news.cnet.com/8301-1001_3-10054253-92.html

Rittinghouse, J. W., & Ransome, J. F. (2009). *Cloud Computing: Implementation, Management, and Security.* Boca Raton: CRC Press.

Roberts, A., & MacLennan, A. (2006). *Making Strategies Work.* Edinburgh: Heriot-Watt University.

Roberts, A., Wallace, W., & McClure, N. (2007). *Strategic Risk Management.* Edinburgh: Heriot-Watt University.

Roche, K., & Douglas, J. (2009). *Beginning Java Google App Engine.* Apress.

Romanski, P. (2009, October 4). *3Tera Adds IPv6 Support to AppLogic Cloud Computing Platform.* Retrieved January 2013, from Cloud Computing Journal: cloudcomputing.sys-con.com/node/1129095

Ross, J. W., Weill, P., & Robertson, D. C. (2006). *Enterprise Architecture as Strategy.* Harvard Business Press.

Ruth, G. (2009). *Cloud Storage: An Emerging Market.* Midvale, Utah: Burton Group.

Sanderson, D. (2009). *Programming Google App Engine.* O'Reilly Media.

SANS Institute. (2001, December). *Data Center Physical Security Checklist.* Retrieved July 2012, from SANS Information Security & Research: http://www.sans.org/reading_room/whitepapers/awareness/data-center-physical-security-checklist_416

Scalet, S. D. (2009). *19 Ways to Build Physical Security into a Data Center.* Retrieved July 2012, from CSO Data Protection: http://www.csoonline.com/article/220665/19-ways-to-build-physical-security-into-a-data-center

Simonds, J. (2009, Dec 21). *Analyst Predictions For 2010.* Retrieved January 2013, from Delusions of Adequacy:

johnsimonds.com/2009/12/31/analyst-predictions-for-2010-everyone-is-going-out-on-basically-the-same-limb/

Smiley, D., & Pugh, E. (2009). *Solr 1.4 Enterprise Search Server.* Packt Publishing.

Souders, S. (2007). *High Performance Web Sites: Essential Knowledge for Front-End Engineers.* O'Reilly Media.

Souders, S. (2009). *Even Faster Web Sites: Performance Best Practices for Web Developers* . O'Reilly Media.

Staimer, M. (2010, March). *Getting started with cloud archiving: Tips for smaller businesses.* Retrieved April 2010, from TechTarget: http://searchsmbstorage.techtarget.com/tip/0,289483,sid188_gci1381142,00.html

Staimer, M. (2010, March). *Getting started with cloud archiving: Tips for smaller businesses.* Retrieved January 2013, from TechTarget: searchsmbstorage.techtarget.com/tip/Getting-started-with-cloud-archiving-Tips-for-smaller-businesses

Symantec. (2011, April). *Internet Security Threat Report, Volume 16.* Retrieved November 2012, from Symantec: http://www.symantec.com/threatreport/

Symantec. (2012, May). *Internet Security Threat Report, Volume 17.* Retrieved November 2012, from Symantec: http://www.symantec.com/threatreport/

TABB Group. (2008, April). *The Value of a Millisecond: Finding the Optimatl Speed of a Trading Infrastructure.* Retrieved March 2011, from TABB Group: http://www.tabbgroup.com/PublicationDetail.aspx?PublicationID=346

Terremark. (2009, October). *Terremark Federal Government Facilities.* Retrieved October 2009, from http://www.terremark.com/industry-solutions/government/facilities.aspx

Turnbull, J. (2008). *Pulling Strings with Puppet: Configuration Management Made Easy.* Apress.

Urquhart, J. (2010, March). *Understanding the cloud and 'devops'.* Retrieved March 2011, from The Wisdom of Clouds: http://news.cnet.com/8301-19413_3-10470260-240.html

Vaquero, Rodero-Merino, Cáceres, & Lindner. (2009, January). *A Break in the Clouds: Towards a Cloud Definition.* Retrieved March 2011, from http://ccr.sigcomm.org/drupal/files/p50-v39n1l-vaqueroA.pdf

Vaquero, Rodero-Merino, Cáceres, & Lindner. (2009, January). *A Break in the Clouds: Towards a Cloud Definition*. Retrieved January 2013, from www.sigcomm.org/sites/default/files/ccr/papers/2009/January/1496091-1496100.pdf

Velte, A. T., Velte, T. J., & Elsenpeter, R. (2009). *Cloud Computing: A Practical Approach*. New York: McGraw Hill.

Venner, J. (2009). *Pro Hadoop*. Apress.

Vogelstein, F. (2009, July 20). *Why Is Obama's Top Antitrust Cop Gunning for Google?* Retrieved January 2013, from Wired Magazine: www.wired.com/techbiz/it/magazine/17-08/mf_googlopoly?currentPage=all

Wardley, S. (2009, July). *Cloud Computing - Why IT Matters*. Retrieved January 2013, from YouTube: www.youtube.com/watch?v=okqLxzWS5R4

Weinman, J., & Lapinski, J. (2009, April). *Why McKinsey's Cloud Report Missed the Mark*. Retrieved January 2013, from GigaOM: gigaom.com/2009/04/21/why-mckinseys-cloud-report-missed-the-mark/#comments

White, T. (2012). *Hadoop: The Definitive Guide*. Yahoo Press.

Wolf, C. (2012, May). *A Global Reality: Governmental Access to Data in the Cloud*. Retrieved November 2012, from Hogan Lovells: http://www.hoganlovells.com/hogan-lovells-revealing-study-about-governmental-access-to-data-in-the-cloud-detailed-in-white-paper-released-at-brussels-program-05-23-2012/

Index

About the Authors

John Rhoton is a Strategy Consultant who specializes in defining and driving the adoption of emerging technologies in international corporations. He provides workshops, training and consulting in business strategy and emerging technology around the world.

John has over 25 years of industry experience working for Digital Equipment Corporation, Compaq Computer Corporation, Hewlett-Packard and Symantec where he has led technical communities and driven the services strategies around a wide variety of initiatives including cloud computing, mobility, next-generation-networking and virtualization.

Feel free to follow him on Twitter (@johnrhoton), connect with him on LinkedIn (linkedin.com/in/rhoton) or find out more about his work (about.me/rhoton).

Jan De Clercq is a member of HP's Technology Services Consulting IT Assurance & Security Portfolio team where he develops new services and delivers consultancy to HP accounts worldwide.

He focuses on cloud security, software-defined security, networking security, mobility security, and identity and access management.

You can reach him at jan.declercq@hp.com.

Franz Novak is a Presales Consultant and Solution Architect in the HP Enterprise Group.

Franz has over 25 years of experience in the computing industry working for Silicon Graphics, Sun Microsystems and Hewlett-Packard. His areas of expertise include Enterprise Architecture, IT Transformation and SOA.

For the past five years he has worked in the area of cloud computing and solution design. He has an M.S. in Computer Science from the Technical University of Vienna.

Cloud Computing Explained
Enterprise Implementation Handbook
2013 Edition

Paperback: 472 pages
Publisher: Recursive Press
ISBN-10: 0956355609
ISBN-13: 978-0956355607
Product Dimensions: 24.6 x 18.8 x 2.5 cm

Cloud Computing Explained provides an overview of Cloud Computing in an enterprise environment. There is a tremendous amount of enthusiasm around cloud-based solutions and services as well as the cost-savings and flexibility that they can provide. It is imperative that all senior technologists have a solid understanding of the ramifications of cloud computing since its impact is likely to permeate the entire IT landscape. However, it is not trivial to introduce a fundamentally different service-delivery paradigm into an existing enterprise architecture.

This book describes the benefits and challenges of Cloud Computing and then leads the reader through the process of assessing the suitability of a cloud-based approach for a given situation, calculating and justifying the investment that is required to transform the process or application, and then developing a solid design that considers the implementation as well as the ongoing operations and governance required to maintain the solution in a partially outsourced delivery model.

Cloud Computing Architected
Solution Design Handbook
2013 Edition

Paperback: 384 pages
Publisher: Recursive Press
ISBN-10: 0956355617
ISBN-13: 978-0956355614
Product Dimensions: 24.6 x 18.9 x 2 cm

Cloud Computing Architected describes the essential components of a cloud-based application and presents the architectural options that are available to create large-scale, distributed applications spanning administrative domains.

The requirements of cloud computing have far-reaching implications for software engineering. Applications must be built to provide flexible and elastic services, and designed to consume functionality delivered remotely across of spectrum of reliable, and unreliable, sources. Architects need to consider the impact of scalability and multi-tenancy in terms of:

- New development tools
- Internet-based delivery and mobile devices
- Identity federation
- Fragmented services and providers
- Exploding information volume
- Availability and elasticity techniques
- New business models and monetization strategies
- Revised software development cycle
- Increased operational automation

This book looks at these and other areas where the advent of cloud computing has the opportunity to influence the architecture of software applications.

Cloud Computing Protected
Security Assessment Handbook
2013 Edition

Paperback: 412 pages
Publisher: Recursive Press
ISBN-10: 0956355625
ISBN-13: 978-0956355621
Product Dimensions: 24.6 x 18.9 x 2.1 cm

Cloud Computing Protected describes the most important security challenges that organizations face as they seek to adopt public cloud services and implement their own cloud-based infrastructure.

There is no question that these emerging technologies introduce new risks:

- Virtualization hinders monitoring and can lead to server sprawl.
- Multi-tenancy exposes risks of data leakage to co-tenants.
- Outsourcing reduces both control and visibility over services and data.
- Internet service delivery increases the exposure of valuable information assets.
- Ambiguity in jurisdiction and national regulations complicates regulatory compliance.
- Lack of standardization can lead to a lock-in binding customers to their providers.

Fortunately, there are also many security benefits that customers can enjoy as they implement cloud services:

- Highly specialized providers have the economy of scale to invest in best-in-class tools and expertise.
- Contractual terms can clearly define the function and scope of critical services.
- Public services receive unprecedented scrutiny from the collective worldwide community.
- It is possible to achieve unlimited levels of redundancy by subscribing to multiple providers.
- The global reach of the Internet and security specialists facilitates early alerts and drives consistent policy enforcement.

This book looks at these and other areas where the advent of cloud computing has the opportunity to influence security risks, safeguards and processes.

Made in the USA
Lexington, KY
05 November 2014